Black Cosmopolitanism

RETHINKING THE AMERICAS

Series Editors
Houston A. Baker, Jr.
Eric Cheyfitz
Joan Dayan
Farah Griffin

A complete list of books in the series is available from the publisher.

Black Cosmopolitanism

Racial Consciousness and Transnational Identity in the Nineteenth-Century Americas

Ifeoma Kiddoe Nwankwo

PENN

University of Pennsylvania Press
Philadelphia

10   9   8   7   6   5   4   3   2   1

Published by
University of Pennsylvania Press
Philadelphia, Pennsylvania 19104-4011

Library of Congress Cataloging-in-Publication Data

Nwankwo, Ifeoma Kiddoe.
   Black cosmopolitanism : racial consciousness and transnational identity
in the nineteenth-century Americas / Ifeoma Kiddoe Nwankwo.
      p.   cm.—(Rethinking the Americas)
   Includes bibliographical references (p.) and index.
   ISBN: 0-8122-3878-8 (acid-free paper)
   1. African Americans—Race identity. 2. Blacks—Race identity—West Indies.
3. Cosmopolitanism. 4. Transnationalism. 5. African Americans—Intellectual life. 6. Blacks—
West Indies—Intellectual life. 7.American literature—African American authors—History and
criticism. 8. West Indian literature—History and criticism. 9. Ethnicity in literature. 10. Race
awareness in literature. I. Title. II. Series.
E185.625 .N88   2005
05.896'07—dc22   2005042203

To Mr. Percival George Kiddoe,

aka Granpa,

aka Jamaica Railway Station Master Kiddoe,

who first taught me British

and

who first taught me the world

Contents

The time has fully come when we, as an oppressed people, should do something effectively . . . to meet the acual demands of the present and prospective necessities of the rising generation of our people in this country. To do this, we must occupy a position of entire *equality*, of *unrestricted* rights, composing in fact, an acknowledged and *necessary* part of the *ruling element* of society in which we live.

—Martin Robison Delany, *Report of the Niger Valley Exploring Party*, 1861

Introduction

The principles of creoleness regress toward negritudes, ideas of Frenchness, of Latinness, all generalizing concepts—more or less innocently. . . .
   Acknowledging differences does not compel one to be involved in the dialectics of their totality. One could get away with: "I can acknowledge your difference and continue to think it is harmful to you."
—*Edouard Glissant,* Poetics of Relation

Every ghetto, every city and suburban place I've been
Make me recall my days in the New Jerusalem.
. . .
Springfield Ave. had the best popsicles
Main street roots tonic with the dreds
A beef patty and some coco bread.
—*Lauryn Hill, "Every Ghetto, Every City"*

U-N-I-T-Y
Dat a unity
U-N-I-T-Y
—*Queen Latifah (Dana Owens), "U.N.I.T.Y"*

Origins

Musical artist Lauryn Hill uses lyrics and accents that evince both African American and West Indian flavors to reconstruct her life as a youth in Irvington, New Jersey. In particular, her reference to enjoying "a beef patty and some coco bread," a typical Jamaican lunch, and her location of the action on "Main Street, U .S. A." highlight the cultural meeting that characterized her youth.[1] Multimedia artist Queen Latifah employs a West Indian accented hook in a hip-hop song decrying sexism and misogyny in the Black community. The song subtly uses the idea that reggae is political to make a statement about sexism—a subject that classical reggae rarely treated. Coexisting along with the blending in the music of Hill and Latifah, however, are films such as *How Stella Got Her Groove Back* and *Cool Runnings*, which posit stereotypical images of West Indians, and *I Like It like That*, which represents negative attitudes toward Blackness in Latino communities.[2]

I, like Lauryn Hill, Queen Latifah, and so many others who grew up in the contact zones of the New York metropolitan area and the Caribbean, have always understood African American, West Indian, and Latin American cultures to be profoundly interwoven. I was born in Jamaica of a Jamaican mother and a Nigerian father who met in Madison, Wisconsin. I grew up simultaneously in Kingston and in Flemington, New Jersey, moving back and forth between the two throughout my first thirteen years. My formal education began at a virtually all White preschool in New Jersey, then moved on to an all Black primary school in Kingston. I spent my summers in New Jersey, enjoying summer camp, hanging out with my American friends, and improving my command of African American culture and language. During my school years in Kingston, I played "dandy shandy" (a version of dodgeball played with an old milk box filled with scrap paper) and Jamaican ring games, learning Anansi stories, folk songs, and other aspects of Jamaican culture from Miss Lou's television show, and perfecting my command of the English grammar book, *First Aid in English*. It told me that the feminine of "negro" is "negress" and the offspring is "picanniny." I also often heard about and/or corresponded with friends of the family in a range of sites including Panama and Belize. My grandfather, who was a railway stationmaster, always told me stories about all the different people, languages, and cultures he encountered during his years in that position. It made perfect sense to me that there were people who felt connected to both West Indian and Latin American or both African American and West Indian cultures.

Although life in primary school was not perfect (class tensions more than national or cultural tension), my migration to the United States in the mid-eighties forced me to confront the reality that some people did make significant and weighted distinctions between African American, West Indian, and Afro-Latin American people. Although I had always been traveling between Jamaica and America, at heart I had always seen myself as unquestionably Jamaican. At the same time, vacations in the U.S. had made me open to experiencing and learning American culture. I entered Piscataway High School in New Jersey along with several other immigrant girls from a range of countries. My closest friends, girls from Colombia and India, and I clung to each other as we learned our places in this new society. We sat together at lunch, in homeroom and classes (last names—Nwankwo, Osorio, and

Patel), hung out at each other's houses, went to the mall, and talked on the phone. That was our first year.

By the beginning of our sophomore year, everything had changed. We began to truly understand our places in U.S. society, and those places were clearly not overlapping. Suddenly, we were all in different and wholly separate social circles. I was no longer welcome at my Latin American friend's house. She and her mother had discovered their affinities with White Americans. My Indian friends only barely spoke to me. They were vacillating between sticking with each other and bonding with White Americans. I was slow to pick up on the rules, and continued to hang out with a range of people, including African Americans, White "metal heads," and White "hippies." I had fundamentally assimilated, however, into African American culture. It was during this year that a young woman I had known since my days at day care in Flemington chastised me for speaking African American vernacular, saying, "Why are you talking like that? You're not Black, you're Jamaican." Despite the fact that my stepfather was not particularly pleased with my newfound understanding and constantly admonished me for talking "that way" (African American vernacular) with my friends on the phone, I persisted. I was much like George Lamming's Trumper, who returns to the Caribbean from the U.S. with a new understanding of his "people" and his "race." My former friend's statement, my stepfather's disgust, and the other experiences of that year raised questions in my mind not just about the perceived differences between African Americans and West Indians, but also about the hierarchies often implicit in those perceptions. I became curious about where those perceptions came from, about who embraces and who rejects them, and about how they shaped the identificatory experiences and decisions of immigrants.

College raised more questions. As a result of the close and also sometimes tense relationship between the Paul Robeson special interest residence section, where I resided and held leadership positions, and the Latin Images special interest section, I began to ask about the meaning of "just like us" and "down with us" and more broadly about perceptions that "Blacks" and "Latinos" held of each other. Throughout my years there the sections continuously alternated between cooperating and emphasizing distinctions. The disparate visions of the significance of the African blood that flowed in the veins of the bulk of the members of both sections were a key but unspoken underpinning of both the sections' desire to collaborate and the drive to distinguish ourselves from each other. The sections were both profoundly linked and profoundly separate. We fought and made up like siblings. It did not always seem logical to everyone that we should collaborate on programs, proposals, and/or political statements. At the same time, it seemed to make sense to everyone that Blacks and Latinos would come together to form the "Minority Greek Council." Consequently, my time on "the floor" made me ponder not just the perceived differences between "Blacks" and "Latinos," but also the rationales behind the highlighting and/or downplaying of those differences in particular situations.

As I moved through my college years, I learned about the U.S. careers of Marcus Garvey and Claude McKay, two individuals who figured prominently in my education in Jamaica. (Marcus Garvey is, in fact, a Jamaican national hero.) I was struck by the fact that their Jamaican careers were never mentioned in my U.S. classes, and that their U.S. careers had never been mentioned in my Jamaican classes. Such facts forced me to consider the impact of silences (particularly, in the creation of histories and intellectual and political genealogies) on African American-West Indian relations.[3] In addition, I was amazed that the curricula of two academic worlds in which I lived on campus, the English and Spanish departments, functioned as wholly separate, unrelated, and irreconcilable units. I would often be studying literary movements that occurred at the same time in the Hispanophone and Anglophone worlds, but no one, it seemed, ever spoke of the two together. That separation was truly strange to me. I had grown up during the Michael Manley era in Jamaica, an era in which positive conceptions of Cuba abounded. I had heard much about Jamaican immigrants and people of Jamaican descent in Cuba. Cuba was part of my world. Afro-Latin Americans had been part of my epistemological world as a child but not of my formal educational experience. To me, the Anglophone and Hispanophone worlds, while different in many ways, were not just deeply connected; they were incomprehensible without each other. This division structured my educational experience in college, feeding my desire to investigate and interrogate it. In fact, in my graduate school applications, written in my senior year, I spoke of undertaking comparative work on Gwendolyn Brooks and the Spanish writer Azorín (José Martínez Ruíz).

The questions that developed as a result of my life between and among American cultures (in both the continental and the national sense) continue to drive me. This project, in particular, has been undergirded by the following questions: First, what are the perceived differences between African Americans, West Indians, and Afro-Latin Americans? Second, when and how did those perceptions develop? Third, what hierarchies are implicit in those perceptions? Fourth, who holds and/or articulates those perceptions and why? Fifth, how do those perceptions shape relations between the groups? Sixth, when and how are affinities/bonds between the groups highlighted and/or downplayed? When I began research on these questions, the contemporary issues were clearer to me. In addition to my personal experiences in cultural contact, there were the "ten job" image of West Indians on the television show *In Living Color*, grand dame of African American letters Margaret Walker's passing mention of her Jamaican father in a speech at the University of Alabama, and the paucity of discussion of the impact of African American rhythm and blues on the music of Bob Marley, which highlighted the issues of interracial tension and stereotyping, cultural blending, and genealogical silences respectively. I was curious about the history of these modes of relating, so I began to move backward in time. I did research on the Harlem Renaissance era, among others, and found similar modes of relating—potentially problematic forms of othering coexisting with profound engagement and bonding. The friendship of Nicolás Guillén and Langston Hughes as well as the Caribbean anthropology of Zora Neale Hurston illustrate the persistence of these issues.

I was still not satisfied that I understood why and how these modes of engagement developed, so I went farther back to the eighteenth and nineteenth centuries. The texts from that era, I thought, might provide hints about how the ideas of separateness and/or sameness developed. To my surprise, I found no views or even mention of people of African descent from other sites in nineteenth-century American (broadly defined) narratives of slavery. I assumed that this absence had to be an aberration, and continued examining as many narratives as I could get my hands on. The plain fact was, however, that while the eighteenth-century slave narratives, such as that by Olaudah Equiano and Venture Smith, made reference to people of African descent in a range of sites, the nineteenth-century narratives did not. My research suggested that something cataclysmic had clearly happened to make the nineteenth-century texts so different from the eighteenth-century ones in their approaches to the world of people of African descent. The nineteenth-century narrators, primarily creoles by that point, generally do not refer to people of African descent in other locations. This is the case despite the frequent appearance of people of African descent from other sites in the writings of free Blacks, both pro- and antislavery Whites, and other writings by the (ex)slave narrators themselves. I decided to focus on this moment, one that seemed to be clearly a marker of identificatory transition—a pivotal period in people of African descent's self-definition as "Black" (as in citizen of a Black world) and/or as a citizen of a particular nation. *Black Cosmopolitanism* is, therefore, an integrative reading of disparities, similarities, and interactions between the varied approaches to identity in general and Blackness in particular articulated by people of African descent in Cuba, the United States, and the British West Indies during the nineteenth century.[4] It lays bare the mechanics of identificatory positioning implicit in contemporaneous texts by and about six individuals of African descent, and ultimately suggests that the desire for modernity, per se, was not, in fact, at the root of choices they (and their descendants) made (and make) about identity. Their goal was to be perceived as equals, and exhibiting and/or proving their modernity was a means to that end.

The "Shout of Battle" Heard Around the World

As numerous contemporary and nineteenth-century thinkers have noted, the Haitian Revolution (1791–1804) was a crucial turning point for Americans of African descent. Martinican thinker Aimé Césaire quite rightly identifies the revolution as the moment "where negritude rose for the first time."[5] The revolution prompted African American leaders like James T. Holly not only to see the revolution as a potent symbol for all Black people, but also to advocate for and enact emigration to Haiti. Holly celebrates the revolution as "one of the noblest, grandest, and most justifiable outbursts against tyrannical oppression that is recorded on the pages of the world's history," during which "a race of almost dehumanized men—made so by an oppressive slavery of three centuries—arose from their slumber of the ages, and redressed their own unparalleled wrongs with a terrible hand in the name of God and humanity."[6] He lauds the overthrow as "A Vindication of the Capacity of the Negro Race for Self-Government and Civilized Progress as Demonstrated by Historical Events of the Haytian Revolution; and the Subsequent Acts of That People Since Their National Independence." In light of this event so laden with symbolism for African Americans, Holly encourages African Americans to emigrate to Haiti, by saying

It may well be a question with us, whether it is not our duty, to go and identify our destiny with our heroic brethren in that independent isle of the Caribbean Sea . . . in order to add to Haytian advancement; rather than to indolently remain here, asking for political rights, which, if granted, a social proscription stronger than conventional legislation will ever render nugatory and of no avail for the manly elevation and general well-being of the race.[7]

The revolution also stoked the fires of anger that are so palpable in David Walker's famous *Appeal to the Coloured Citizens of the World* (1829), in which he describes Haiti as "the glory of Blacks and terror of tyrants."[8] William Wells Brown sought to secure the place of the revolution in the annals of world history with the publication of another rhetorical aftershock of the revolution—his speech "St. Domingo: Its Revolutions and Its Patriots" (1855), in which he details the roots and results of this "shout of battle" (his phrase).[9]

This moment, however, was not only a turning point because of the symbolic value of the revolution for Black radicals. *Black Cosmopolitanism* contends that Whites' fear of the revolution and its presumably contagious nature forced people of African descent throughout the Americas, particularly those in the public and published eye, to name a relationship to the Haitian Revolution, in particular, and to a transnational idea of Black community, in general. The revolution made a fear of uprising and, by extension, of transnationally oriented notions of Black community, into a continent-wide obsession. The fear was not just of people of African descent in a particular location rising up and rebelling against the power structure in that location, but rather of people of African descent from and in a variety of locations connecting with each other and fomenting a massive revolution that might overturn the whole Atlantic slave system. In the wake of the uprising, people of African descent had to decide whether to define themselves as citizens of the world, specifically of the Black world that included the revolutionaries. Public published figures responded to this challenge by developing approaches to self-definition and community delineation that negotiated global and local affinities and exigencies. Many, like William Wells Brown (in his slave narrative), chose to negate or not mention people of African descent in other countries—an implicit articulation of a relationship, albeit one of distance. Others, like the aforementioned David Walker, chose to embrace the revolution and use it as a threat. People of African descent had to decide where to position themselves, particularly in print, and decide whether and how to embrace both national/local and transnational/global affinities. Within this context of White fear and potential recriminations, of which they were profoundly aware, they had to decide whether and how to express their connection both to their country of residence and to the world of people of African descent beyond that country. The uprising was significant, therefore, not only because it brought into being the first Black republic in the Americas, but, more importantly, because it encouraged new visions of the interrelatedness of people of African descent in disparate locations as well as of their place in the world. Those approaches established new models for public and published interactions between the people of the African Diaspora in the Americas.

Public published individuals posited newly refined and reconfigured definitions of "Blackness," including delineations of who was to be included in that identity and why. *Black Cosmopolitanism* argues, through a range of texts by both freeborn and formerly enslaved people of African descent, that individuals' decisions about how and whether to include people of African descent from other parts of the Americas constitute philosophies of Black and American identity. Those texts include Martin Robison Delany's novel *Blake; Or, the Huts of America* (1851–1862) in which he dramatizes the making of a hemispheric Black Revolution, in significant part through representations of Cubans of color. The poetry (1830–1844) of Plácido, the Cuban poet of color based on whom Delany created his Cuban main character, while not explicitly articulating racially based notions of community, uses romantic tropes and both nationally and internationally oriented themes in order to construct subjectivity. Also under study here are Frederick Douglass's autobiographies and speeches (1845–1895)—texts that reveal the profound relationship between his decisions about how to represent African American community, and his engaging the Black world beyond the U.S. in general and Haiti in particular. The spatial and ethnographic language of West Indian ex-slave Mary Prince's narrative (1831) locates her not only within a Black world but also in the world at large. The autobiography of Cuban ex-slave Juan Francisco Manzano (1840) forces us to confront the issue of racial disidentification directly.

These nineteenth-century texts illustrate modes of conceptualizing the relationships between people of African descent in the Americas and throughout the Atlantic World that are pivotal to a theoretical/conceptual genealogy of which the twentieth-century texts (such as W. E. B. Du Bois's *Souls of Black Folk* and Claude McKay's *Banjo*) that feature so prominently in recent scholarship on the transnational engagements of Black Diasporan subjects are a part. The nineteenth-century texts ponder the complex meanings and methods of being both "Negro" and "American," broadly defined, and reveal the struggle to define self and community between multiple local and global affinities, as the later texts do. Unlike the twentieth-century ones, though, these earlier texts do so while also confronting the realities of slavery in the nineteenth century, including both Whites' fear of continent-wide rebellion and the official view of a man of African descent as three-fifths of a man.[10]

My goal here is not to posit these as the ur-texts of the African Diaspora in the Americas, to present these individuals as the ultimate representatives of the development and articulation of identity during this period, or to hold up the U.S., Cuba, and the British West Indies as the only sites in which these negotiations of identity took place. I aim to present them as case studies that, while born of specific local conditions, index trends in approaches to conceiving and articulating relationships to the Black world, in particular, and to the world at large, that recur in any number of texts from this period, whether we are reading the documents on the Black sailors discussed by Julius Scott, Jeffrey Bolster, and Marcus Rediker and Peter Linebaugh, the rebellious slaves on ships explored by Maggie Montesinos Sale, the Black women travelers studied by Cheryl Fish, or the slaves who tell their stories in the autobiographies analyzed by William Andrews.[11]

Modernity, Cosmopolitanism, and the Black Subject

Implicit in the Atlantic power structures' fear of violent uprising and designation of people of African descent as less than a whole (hu)man was the notion that they were primitive savages, that is to say, premodern barbarians. The perception of people of African descent as less than human and not worthy of being seen as equal to those of European descent operated in tandem with the construction of people of African descent as an antithesis of the modern. People of African descent's desire to be seen as equal was always already bound up with their desire to be seen as modern, so statements made in the public sphere were grasped firmly as opportunities to prove the individual's or the community's modernity.

Cosmopolitanism, the definition of oneself through the world beyond one's own origins, was a crucial element of modernity (and the Enlightenment). Imperialism and Orientalism were in fact forms of European cosmopolitanism, and more specifically of the ways Europeans constructed their definitions of self and community in relation to and through their relationship to the broader world.[12] Orientalism, as Edward Said explicated it, "*is* . . . a certain *will* or *intention* to understand, in some cases to control, manipulate, even to incorporate, what is a manifestly different (or alternative and novel) world."[13] It should come as no surprise, then, that responses and resistance to these totalizing and hegemonic cosmopolitanisms also often employ cosmopolitanism as a conceptual frame. Immanuel Kant, for example, had a vision "of cosmopolitical culture as the promise of humanity's freedom from, or control over" "the finitude of human existence."[14] Karl Marx also posited a utopian cosmopolitanism, through which the proletariat would cast off loyalty to the nation and its economy in favor of the creation of "a universal class transcending boundaries."[15] As part of this historical and ideological context, people of African descent in the nineteenth century evaluated the usefulness of cosmopolitanism for their struggle to be recognized as human and equal.

People of African descent's approaches to public self-representation were born, in significant part, of the Atlantic power structure's attempts to deny them access to cosmopolitan subjectivity. The White fear that arose in the wake of the Haitian Revolution was not only a fear of violence, but also a fear of people of African descent's embrace of cosmopolitanism—of their defining themselves through a Black world that included the Haitians. This denial of access for people of African descent to cosmopolitan subjectivity coexisted with a denial of access for that same population to both national subjectivity and human subjectivity, and, perhaps most significantly, with an emphasis (from above) on their race, effectively determining the possible parameters of identity for people of African descent. The result was a uniquely tenuous situation. Race, nation, and humanity were three major referents through which individuals defined themselves and others in their world (the Atlantic world), but only one of the three referents was allowed people of African descent—race. Consequently, this population essentially had to prioritize, and choose which of the parameters denied them they most wished to challenge, and by extension which referent they most wanted to have the right to claim.

The modes of self-definition I describe collectively as "Black cosmopolitanism" were, consequently, born in this period.[16] The term is not meant to indicate that people who were already "Black" became cosmopolitan, or that cosmopolitanism was a corrective alternative to Blackness, but rather that Blackness and cosmopolitanism became two pivotal axes of identity in relation to which public people of African descent defined themselves.

The Blackness of Black cosmopolitanism inheres not in the race of the individuals who express it (as illustrated by the fact that analyses of Cuban government documents and White abolitionist writings are key subjects in this study),[17] but rather in the ways individuals and entities seek to define people of African descent and articulate the relationship among them and between them and the world at large. Faced with dehumanization and the Atlantic power structures' obsession with preventing the blossoming of their cosmopolitanism, people of African descent decided to stake their claim to personhood by defining themselves in relation to the new notions of "Black community" and ubiquitous manifestations of cosmopolitanism that the Revolution produced. The fear created by the Haitian Revolution forced these individuals to take a position on both Blackness and cosmopolitanism whether or not they wished to do so. At the same time, they were forced to work through and with the three aforementioned referents—race, nation, and humanity.

In both its emphasis on engagements with an Enlightenment approach to self-definition (cosmopolitanism) and its allowing for the possibility of racial disidentification, this notion differs significantly from Pan-Africanism. Central to Pan-Africanism as understood by Pan-Africanist leaders and scholars then and now is political action that seeks to ameliorate the lives of all people of African descent everywhere.[18] Consequently, I do not use the term to describe the writing or ideology of most of the writers I engage. I call attention instead to the complexity of their perceptions of and relationships with people of African descent from other places. Instead of taking pan-Africanism as a given or as a broad spectrum term that can be applied to all texts that treat the experiences of people of African descent in different locations, I choose to move more methodically by analyzing the method, ideology, and implications of those treatments.

The term transnationalism is also inadequate for indexing the complicated approaches to defining self, community, and other I uncover here. Although useful for referring to general physical or ideological movements across national boundaries its usefulness for describing how and why such movements drive or constitute arguments with dominant nineteenth-century discourses about civilization versus barbarism (and, in particular, people of African descent's barbarism) as well as about appropriate bases for identity is limited.[19] In addition, it foregrounds geographical-national boundaries and presumes them to be salient, which is not a viewpoint put forth by a number of the individuals and ideologies engaged in this study. The term cosmopolitanism allows for attentiveness to a range of modes of defining oneself and one's community in relation to the world.

Cosmopolitanism is not posited here, however, as a race-less panacea that serves as a counterpoint to an essential or essentializing notion of Blackness, but rather as one of the master's tools (Blackness being another) that people of African descent tested for its possible usefulness in attempting to at least get into the master's house, if not to destroy it.[20] The goal is to explicate the stance toward cosmopolitanism and Blackness taken by individuals occupying a range of geographical and identificatory positions, rather than to attach a particular value judgment to any of them. Because of the Haitian Revolution, the constitution and articulation of "Blackness" at this moment was always already bound up with a decision about whether or not to espouse cosmopolitanism. In investigating the ways in which a range of thinkers of African descent negotiated between the two and came to vastly different conclusions about how to best locate themselves, this study simultaneously interrogates the notion that cosmopolitanism was an unproblematic and always desirable alternative and reveals the mechanisms by which Black identity and community were imagined.

Black cosmopolitanism therefore does not simply complicate, but also often undercuts traditional understandings of cosmopolitanism. The cosmopolite is typically understood as a "citizen of the world," whose relationship to a specific nation is distant if it exists at all. In Mihai Grunfeld's discussion of cosmopolitanism, for example, he describes the cosmopolite as "un ciudadano universal, una persona que considera el universo como patria suya"[21] ("a citizen of the universe, a person who considers the universe as his nation"). Grunfeld presents cosmopolitanism in opposition to national identification—a conceptualization frequently replicated throughout the scholarly discourse on cosmopolitanism.[22] This binary is insufficient for interpreting the relationship between cosmopolitan subjectivity and national affinity for people of African descent in the nineteenth century. It cannot take into account the power dynamics that produce or prevent the production of the cosmopolite, and more specifically the ways in which the Atlantic power structures' denial of humanity, cosmopolitanism, and national citizenship to people of African descent, their obsessive fear of their cosmopolitanism, and their obsessive focus on defining them racially, and people of African descent's own desire to be recognized as equal interacted to produce distinctively configured approaches to engaging the world and representing the self.

The person of African descent's citizenship in his or her specific nation of residence has been denied, negated, and generally troubled. Positing national identity and cosmopolitan subjectivity as polar opposites presumes that national identity is available to all individuals. Our understanding of cosmopolitanism must consider that, for some (people of African descent in this case) national identity may be desired but inaccessible, and consequently that cosmopolitanism, while not necessarily the object of desire, may be conceptualized as a means to the end of gaining access to national identity (as it is for Frederick Douglass) and/or as the basis of a substitute national identity in itself (as it is for Martin Delany). In addition, that substitute national identity may include people in places they have never visited, and with whom they have never had contact, because the connection they imagine is based on the common experiences of slavery and discrimination and African heritage, rather than shared terrain or face to face encounters.

As a result, the questions whether the person of African descent in the Americas conceptualizes him- or herself as a citizen of a specific nation or of the Black world, or how she or he claims citizenship in both, demand answers that go beyond positing cosmopolitanism and national affinity as two sides of a neat binary. The dynamic interaction between the two, and the push/pull forces that have pushed the person away from cosmopolitanism, national identity, and humanity and toward race have produced his or her approach to self-representation. Black cosmopolitanism is born of the interstices and intersections between two mutually constitutive cosmopolitanisms—a hegemonic cosmopolitanism, exemplified by the material and psychological violence of imperialism and slavery (including dehumanization), and a cosmopolitanism that is rooted in a common knowledge and memory of that violence. The violence may remain unacknowledged, but is nevertheless the basis of the desire exhibited by public figures of African descent to imagine or reject a connection with people of African descent in other sites or with the world at large. The desire to be recognized as an agent is interwoven with the desire to be a citizen, and both desires determine both individual identity and textual and ideological engagements with people of African descent in other sites.

Contemporary and historical definitions of the cosmopolite characterize (and gender) him or her as one who loves to travel. As scholars such as Melvin Dixon have pointed out, Black people's relationship to travel and movement is inherently fraught because of the way in which they were brought to the Americas. People of African descent did not "travel" to the Americas, inasmuch as travel implies leisure and volition. They were forcibly brought as commodities. Given this history, one of the pivotal questions of this study is whether a slave can "travel," define himself/herself through the places to which s/he travels, and by extension be considered cosmopolitan. Slavery sought to control the movements of people of African descent (both free and slave). This effort was quite often in vain. People of African descent found ways to move between physical and/or geographical sites. They also, as is evident in the texts interpreted here, moved conceptually between sites as they constructed their ideologies and identities. Those conceptual movements, whether manifested through an explicit bonding with people of African descent in other sites as in Martin Delany's *Blake; Or, the Huts of America* (1861–62) or through the dedication of a Romantic poem to Poland as in Plácido's poem "A Polonia" took place in the service of eking out a space for subjectivity—a space wherein an individual or a community could be recognized as human and as equal to those at the top of the Atlantic world.

Traditional understandings of the cosmopolite assume that the person has the means to travel, reflecting the inherently classed nature of cosmopolitanism as most often articulated. Inderpal Grewal has hinted at this issue in her discussion of the classed nature of the terms immigrant and exile. Those with education and means are exiles. Everyone else is denigrated and designated an immigrant. Similarly cosmopolitan is reserved for those at the top, and everyone else is viewed as comfortably provincial. *Black Cosmopolitanism* traces the dialectics of a cosmopolitanism from below.[23] It is one that came of age at the same time that the forces of hegemonic cosmopolitanism in the Atlantic world (cosmopolitanism from above) were forced to reconfigure themselves to deal with the new threats posed by the uprising in Haiti.[24]

It is worth noting, however, that the drive to be acknowledged as equal ensures that not all those who display Black cosmopolitanism have a desire to travel, whether materially or conceptually, in terms of the definition of self or community. In fact, even the individuals who seem to travel the most simultaneously exhibit a certain resistance to doing so. This irony inheres both in hegemonic forms of cosmopolitanism (as Said's aforementioned comment on Orientalism suggests) and in "cosmopolitanism from below" because the latter, although resistant, is fundamentally concerned with proving a group or individual an equal member of the societies that produced the hegemonic forms. In fact, in people of African descent's published demands for citizenship, cosmopolitanism is often viewed both as an obstacle to the achievement of that goal and as the quality that proves that the individual or group is worthy of citizenship. The case of ex-slave Frederick Douglass who became U.S. consul to Haiti shows this conundrum especially clearly. Douglass and other U.S. Black writers are one part of a continent-wide discourse inspired by the revolution in Haiti on the question of how people of African descent should locate their own subjectivities in relation to each other and the broader Atlantic world.

My close readings of the texts by Douglass and the aforementioned others highlight the mechanics of self-definition and approaches to representing, engaging, or defining people in other sites. I pay particular attention to the methods individuals developed to negotiate ever present tensions between local and global affinities during this period. Those methods include creation of a transnational notion of Blackness and "Black" history; intense focus on claiming the nation of residence; manipulation, reconfiguration, and redeployment of the tropes and conventions of Romantic poetry and the slave narrative; employment of nation as a metaphor for race; binaristic Blackness—the idea that in order for one group of people of African descent to be protected, elevated, or humanized, the other must be made vulnerable, debased, or dehumanized; cosmopolitan cartography—mapping the world at large through language; cosmopolitan consciousness—a simultaneous embrace of Black consciousness and cosmopolitanism; community autoethnography—the ethnographic representation of a community that is foreign (geographically or linguistically) in order to create, reveal, or emphasize kinship; the highlighting of one's own individual intellect and achievement or that of others one wishes to mark as a member of one's own community; and disidentification with the Black race. As they formulate these modes of self-definition and self-articulation, these public figures' approaches to shaping their texts are framed by several expected or imposed understandings of identity—the White power structure's fear of their cosmopolitanism (and by extension the attempts to control their textual and physical movements), the presumption that everyone must define himself/ herself through the referents race, nation, and humanity (and by extension the denial of the latter two to people of African descent), and the traditional geographical and identificatory boundaries of particular genres.

Beyond the Boundaries: Locating Black Discourses

In historical scholarship comparative and transnational work have long had a strong presence.[25] Several of the most touted historical analyses of slavery and early Black life on the continent are transnational in scope.[26] Melville Herskovits writes in his classic *The Myth of the Negro Past* (1941) that "the approach in the ensuing pages, though oriented toward the study of the Negro in the United States, takes into full account the West African, South American, and West Indian data, lacking which, I am convinced, true perspective on the values of Negro life in this country cannot be had."[27] The notion that African American culture refers to the cultures of Blacks in the Americas is a significant aspect of the highly controversial work *The Birth of African American Culture* by Sidney Mintz and Richard Price.[28] The concept of the Atlantic world conveyed to literary studies through Paul Gilroy's *The Black Atlantic: Modernity and Double Consciousness* has long been a structuring unit in historical scholarship.[29] The work of Richard Price, Herbert S. Klein, Alfred Hunt, David Barry Gaspar and Darlene Clark Hine, and John Thornton among many others bears this truth out.[30]

Toni Morrison's *Playing in the Dark*, Eric Sundquist's *To Wake the Nations*, and Dana Nelson's *The Word in Black and White*, begin to engage the related question of otherness within, in terms of the engagements between White American literature and the figure of the Black.[31] This issue of the "other within" has undergirded British cultural studies works such as Iain Chambers' *Migrancy, Culture, Identity* and Stuart Hall's many essays.[32] Literary scholars such as Houston Baker in *Modernism and the Harlem Renaissance* have formidably taken up the issue of the biculturalism within the constitution of African American identities and literary traditions.[33]

African American literary criticism has begun to reevaluate itself as a result of an increasing number of calls for an inclusion of other Black/ American literatures in the scope of what is called African American literature and calls for the development and application of a cross-national critical methodology. Examples include pioneering work by Hortense Spillers on reconceptualizing/recutting the border between U.S. and Nuestra American literature, by Vévé Clark on the importance of going beyond the binary of Black Us and White Them in Black American literary criticism and theory, and by José David Saldivar in his inclusion of Ntozake Shange in *The Dialectics of Our America*.[34] The burgeoning discourse on the impact of Intra-American migration on Black American identities exemplified by Carol Boyce Davies's *Black Women, Writing, and Identity* and Farah Jasmine Griffin's *Who Set You Flowin'?* amplify this call and initiate the articulation of a response.[35] At the same time, recent years have seen the growth of scholarship on the Black (literary) transatlantic, exemplified by Paul Gilroy in his work on the European ideological encounters of seminal African American figures Richard Wright and W. E. B. Du Bois.[36] Brent Edwards's analysis of the parallel, distinctive, and intersecting worlds of Black expressive culture in the United States and the francophone world in the 1920s and 1930s builds on the foundation established by Gilroy and earlier by James DeJongh (*Vicious Modernism*, 1990).[37] The comparative method of George Handley's study of the "family ties" between U.S. and Cuban literatures of the twentieth century, particularly in the area of race, bridges the transnational impetus in recent African Diaspora discourse with its increasing attentiveness to the place and function of race in the formation and representation of U.S. and Cuban subjectivity.[38]

In addition, recent years have seen an explosion in critical and theoretical scholarship calling attention to the multiplicity within the Black community in terms of gender, class, and color. From J. Martin Favor's analysis of the problematic implications of the "perceived necessity" to identify "authentic Blackness" during the Harlem Renaissance era, to Hazel Carby's interrogation and ultimate rejection of the concept of the "race man," scholars have revealed the continually moving and always already tenuous ground on which assumptions about the meaning of "Black community" rest.[39] Work by Stuart Hall on identificatory hybridity, Carole Boyce Davies on "migratory subjectivities," and Myriam Chancy on women in exile has similarly revealed the range of ways individuals relate to and define Caribbeanness.[40] At the same time, publication of literature and scholarship by and about Afro-Latin Americans has increased markedly. Historical work on slavery in Latin America such as Franklin Knight's work on slave society in Cuba has been supplemented by pioneering work by Richard Jackson on historical images of Blacks in Latin American literature, Marvin Lewis on Afro-Argentinean literature, Carol Mills-Young on Afro-Uruguayan life and literature, and Laurence Prescott on Afro-Colombian literature.[41] These important explosions have largely occupied separate spheres within academia, in large part because literature departments and the study of literature are generally organized according to language and/or nation. *Black Cosmopolitanism* links the interrogation and expansion of notions of Blackness represented by the new directions in these fields, and posits a theoretical framework for comprehending and analyzing the historical and contemporary relations between African American, West Indian, Latin American and Latino (including Afro-Latin American) discourses and groups.

Black Cosmopolitanism is a conversation with these scholars and a call in itself for a rethinking of the very terms and grounds of the discourse. We need to rethink what we mean when we say "African American" so that we include the other Black Americas there (in "Nuestra América"), as well as here (in the United States). I focus on the points where here and there meet, and where the lines between the two not only cross but become blurred. Reading the identificatory and ideological border crossings of people of African descent produces a reconceptualization of these literatures as arising out of intra-Diasporic dialogues. Going beyond the nationally bounded and the comparative brings us closer to the hemispherist and integrative critical approach that, as this book will illustrate, is so often begged by the texts themselves and the lives of the people who produce them.

W. E. B. Du Bois famously prophesied that the greatest problem of the twentieth century would be the color line. In fact, debates over lines demarcating differences on the "Black" side of the line, both explicit and unspoken, have long been concomitant with the color line. Treatments of ethnic and national difference on this side of the Black-White color line lay bare both the conceptual underpinnings of the color line itself and of people of African descent's methods of engaging that line that are not as apparent when the focus is on interactions with Whites. Edouard Glissant identifies negritude as a generalizing concept that is powerful precisely because it enables the minimizing of differences between people from disparate sites. He goes on to identify, in his discussion of Western European thought, the limitations of acknowledgments of difference. A key question, then, for this study in particular and for work that explicates the multiplicities within the African Diaspora, is whether attentiveness to difference and/or cultural mixture can exist within or coexist with the "generalizing concept" of Blackness. Glissant suggests "acknowledging differences does not compel one to be involved in the dialectics of their totality. One could get away with: 'I can acknowledge your difference and continue to think it is harmful to you.'"[42] Brent Edwards argues that "*décalage* is proper to the structure of a diasporic 'racial' formation, and its return in the form of disarticulation—the points of misunderstanding, bad faith, unhappy translation—must be considered a necessary haunting."[43] Disjointedness and difference are as constitutive of African Diaspora culture and history as are manifestations and evidence of contemporary and historical bonds.

Analyses of the treatment of or engagement with intraracial difference have focused almost exclusively on twentieth-century texts and expressive culture. Implicit in this focus is the notion that such engagements began in the twentieth century, in the wake of World War I. The result of this orientation has been an emphasis on moments of physical contact between thinkers of African descent in disparate sites and on the ways in which they consciously linked their political or artistic movements. Through the focus on the nineteenth century here, the equal importance of ideas held about each other in the absence of such direct contact becomes clear. The twentieth-century focus has allowed us to miss the pivotal importance of nineteenth-century texts in the development and public articulation not just of Black or African Diasporan identity, but also of ideas about the significance of transnational engagement for those identities. The result has been that the discourse on the identity constitution undertaken in slave narratives (including the work of Houston Baker, William Andrews, and Frances Smith Foster) has come to be understood as separate from the discourses on Black transnationalism and pan-Africanism. Slave narratives are representative not only of individual identity and the individual's struggle to be recognized as human, but also of a worldview (quite literally, a view of the world). In fact, the bulk of the phenomena identified by scholars of twentieth-century Black transnationalism have evident roots in the nineteenth-century texts in general, and often slave narratives in particular.

The rise of Black modernity, for example, has been a central concern in the discussions of twentieth-century texts. It stands to reason, though, that this would be an even greater concern in texts produced at the very moment in which the people of African descent in the Americas were seeking to be freed from the bonds of slavery. They also sought to free themselves from the concomitant understanding of them as uncivilized beings, and to prove themselves part of the civilized (aka modern) world.[44] Why else would James Holly feel the need to characterize the Haitian Revolution as "A Vindication of the Capacity of the Negro Race for Self-Government and Civilized Progress as Demonstrated by Historical Events of the Haytian Revolution"? Why would Frederick Douglass make a point of representing Haiti at the 1893 Columbian Exposition, noting that "I have, since my return to the United States, been pressed on all sides to foretell what will be the future of Haiti— whether she will fall away into anarchy, chaos, and barbarism, or rise to the dignity and happiness of a highly civilized nation and be a credit to the colored race? I am free to say that I believe she will fulfill the latter condition and destiny."[45] Both his evident pride in Haiti's growth as a republic and his subtle ambivalence about Haiti's distance from barbarism (clearest in the fact that he spends most of the speech either explaining why Haiti is not primitive or explaining away the aspects of Haitian culture that might be perceived as primitive) reveal the relationship between the transnational desires to be seen as modern, that is to say, to be seen as civilized, human —and equal—and transnational engagement. For both Holly and Douglass the fate of African American modernity (civilization, humanity, and equality) is tied to the fate of Haiti and the Haitian people.

These statements illustrate that during the ninety-six years after the success of the Haitian Revolution (that is, the wake of the Revolution) people of African descent sought to determine the specific configurations of their paths to freedom and equality (aka modernity). One of the crucial decisions facing them was whether racial community or national affinity was the more effective means to their desired end. As Kathleen Wilson's book on "the island race" of England as well as Dana D. Nelson's oeuvre and Eric Hobsbawm's (subsequently controversial) *Nations and Nationalism Since 1780* (1990) have shown, both race and nation were frequently understood as anchors of identity and as evidence of ontological subjectivity.[46] Public figures of African descent understood and employed the language and conceptual frameworks of their period. The structure of *Black Cosmopolitanism*, therefore, is based on the ways in which these two referents were used in tandem, separately, and dialogically by a range of individuals of African descent in order to prove their status as equal, human, and modern.

Black Cosmopolitanism begins by illuminating the ways Blacks and Blackness were created during the ninety-six years of the nineteenth century that followed the creation of the Haitian Republic, spotlighting the tensions around made Blackness and the self-concepts of those who were made Black.

Part One, "The Making of a Race (Man)," lends insight into the multiple agents of racial identification during this period by considering Plácido (aka Gabriel de la Concepción Valdés), the Cuban poet who was executed by the Spanish government in Cuba for allegedly leading the largest antislavery conspiracy in Cuban history to that point. He was constructed as a "race man" by the Cuban colonial government as well as by white European, American, and African American abolitionists. This section uses the language and ideological nuances of these three groups' texts to index implicit tensions and surprising similarities in the racial identity and ideology they ascribe to Plácido. All groups construct their desired image of Plácido by way of the three referents I argue were pivotal for people of African descent during this period—race, nation, and humanity—emphasizing certain referents and downplaying or negating others.

Part Two, "Both (Race) and (Nation)?" begins by discussing racial identity and national affinity in Plácido's verse, including his political and pastoral poems, revealing a methodology for conceptualizing and articulating racial identity that is not based on divorcing it from national identity. It continues with an exploration of the ways Frederick Douglass's "twice-doubled" consciousness, evident in his writings on Haiti, was foreshadowed in his *Narrative*. As U.S. consul to Haiti, Douglass found himself in the awkward position of feeling a kinship with the Haitian people while charged with overseeing the U.S. imperial enterprise of obtaining a part of Haiti for a military base. He had to balance being U.S. American and U.S. Negro, and also being U.S. American and racial brother of the Haitian people—a "twice-doubled" or "complicated" consciousness.

Part Three, "Negating Nation, Rejecting Race," considers attempts by public, published figures to find identity, and by extension humanity and equality, beyond the referents of race or nation. Significantly, they are unable to let go of both simultaneously, reinforcing the pivotal role of these referents in the search for the recognition of humanity and equality and in the conceptualization of identities and relationships between disparate groups within the African Diaspora.

Mary Prince posits a notion of Black identity that includes Blacks from a variety of geographical sites, but does not express connection to a particular nation. Her conceptualization thus cannot accurately be described as transnational; it can, however, be described as cosmopolitan. The autobiography of Cuban slave poet Juan Francisco Manzano serves as the medium for exploring disidentification with a Black community in terms of the identity formation of people of African descent in the Americas. Manzano repeatedly marks the difference between himself and the Blacks in his autobiography. As I illustrate, this distancing is more than simply "selling out."

I thus explore the implications of the fundamental question of what drives tensions between people of African descent from disparate sites for both historical and contemporary relations. Specifically, *Black Cosmopolitanism* asks us to take a moment to reconsider our assumptions about the bases on which we construct African Diaspora canons in general and nineteenth-century African American canons in particular.

PART ONE

The Making of a Race (Man)

By black I mean men of African descent who claim an identity with the race.

—*Martin R. Delany,* Report of the Niger Valley Exploring Party

P art One explicates the making of a race man in the middle of the nineteenth century. The man is Plácido, free Cuban poet of color. In deciding to highlight or downplay Plácido's racial and national identities (as well as, less explicitly, his gentlemanly or uncivilized carriage) the Cuban government, white abolitionists, and Black abolitionists construct not only an individual but also a racial community. The making of the race man is also the making of a race. The actual Plácido, a.k.a. Gabriel de la Concepción Valdés, was executed in 1844 by the Cuban government for leading what the government perceived as one of the largest conspiracies of slaves and free people of color against Cuban whites. The conspiracy was called the Conspiración de la Escalera (the Ladder Conspiracy) after the torture tool for which the Cuban government was infamous.[1] In death, Plácido became a symbol for both pro- and antislavery forces inside and outside Cuba. From the perspective of these forces, his symbolic value resided in large part in his racial identity. Their representations not only ascribe a racial identity to him, but also link him to or detach him from the Cuban nation, in the service of achieving the authors' pro- or antislavery goals. I contend, in fact, that making this individual into a race man by three disparate and often competing groups—the colonial government in Cuba, white U.S. and British abolitionists, and Black abolitionists—highlights the extent to which multiple agents shaped the constitution of "Black" identity in the Americas and therefore marks a signal moment in the development not only of notions of "Black" community, but also of the relevance and appropriate treatment of differences within that community. At the same time, the making of Plácido into a race man by groups from inside and outside Cuba illustrates the pivotal importance of cosmopolitanism to the battle over the definition and representation of people of African descent. They variously celebrate, decry, and deny his status as a citizen of the world who matters to people beyond Cuba or a citizen of a Black world that extends well beyond the island.

In 1861 African American activist Martin Delany suggested that the term "Black" indexed a specific group of men connected by common origin and claimed identity. The term "Black" has never been as simple or as self-evident as this statement and so much of the discourse by and about people of African descent have implied. Notions of a Black community did not arise organically out of the experience of slavery. They were created and constructed by multiple agents, including people of African descent themselves. These conceptualizations imagined a community into being, while also implicitly delineating the appropriate treatment of difference (whether geographical, identificatory, linguistic, or national) within that community. The articulation of community always already carries within it a vision of the ultimate exemplar, as well as, by extension, an implicit ignoring, subsuming, or negation of those who are not the ideal. As Hazel Carby has noted, it is still too widely believed that detailed analyses of the meanings of "black folk" in W. E. B. Du Bois's discourse are superfluous. In particular, she critiques Cornel West's assertion that Du Bois's "patriarchal sensibilities speak for themselves." She argues that, along with similar statements by a number of other Black male scholars, West obscures the ways in which "gendered structures of thought and feeling permeate our lives and our intellectual work, including *The Souls of Black Folk* and other texts which have been regarded as *founding* texts written by the *founding* fathers of black American history and culture."[2] I contend that the persistent ideas that the term Black applies to everyone of African descent and that we therefore "know" who Black people are (or that we can easily point out who are Black people) obscure the subtle and overt ways in which people in a range of sites who may not define themselves primarily or at all through their race are still imagined into "the Black community." Definitions of Blackness, such as that put forward by Delany, have within them an always already totalizing vision that proscribes an attitude towards difference. Rather than cast off these totalizing notions of racial community as fascist (Gilroy, Mostern) or as appropriately nationalist (Moses) but fundamentally self-evident and transparent in terms of the racial identity of the community members, I delve into the grounds of Black community articulated by a colonial government, white abolitionists, and black abolitionists and explicate the mechanisms by which an individual can be made Black.

Although the term "race man" is most often used to describe twentieth-century figures, scholarship on race leaders of the period (such as Frederick Douglass) illustrates that "race men" certainly did exist then.[3] I purposely employ the term in an anachronistic fashion to emphasize the extent to which the idea predated the development of the term—a concept Carby indicates is underpinned by "concern about the continuity about intellectual generations," and more specifically Black male intellectual generations.[4] The making of the Cuban Plácido into a heroic representative of Black manhood by Black abolitionists reveals that the vision of Black leadership (that later came to be termed "race man") was a tool used in the nineteenth century by people of African descent to construct cosmopolitan intellectual and historical genealogies and, by extension, to prove their level of civilization. Importantly, both the dominant forces in the slave societies under study here and white abolitionists also put this conception to use, albeit in the service of ends that variously undercut or mirror those pursued by people of African descent themselves.

Inasmuch as the term is applicable to Douglass and Delany, it is also especially appropriate as a description of the Plácido created by these representations. I use the term to reflect the position of leadership ascribed to Plácido by both pro- and antislavery forces, and to spotlight both the racial and gender dimensions of the term. He is constructed as the representative and leader of a race, a race that while made up of men and women, can only be led by a man.[5] The making of a race man, then, was at once the conceptualization of a race and the creation of a notion of (savage or heroic) Black manhood. The battle over the humanity of people of African descent was fought, therefore, through dueling representations of Plácido as a savage leader of an inhuman population or as a noble hero of an embattled collective.

Journalist and commentator Charlayne Hunter-Gault defines a race man as "very conscious of the image of black men, especially in America and especially in the South . . . [and] determined to prove that black men were as good as any men, and that they were not inferior."[6] Carby's definition of a race man echoes that of Hunter-Gault, although she quite rightly criticizes the gendered assumptions implicit in the common understanding of a race man as a man who is somehow understood to be representative of his race. The chapters that constitute this section resonate with her analyses of Du Bois and Robeson in their focus on the relationship between individual, own group, and dominant group constructions of an individual as a race man. Zora Neale Hurston also launched a critique of "race men," suggesting not only that their rhetoric was empty, their "claim to greatness being the ability to mount any platform at short notice and rattle the bones of Crispus Attucks," but also that they were the puppets of the power structure.[7] The definition of a "race man" in Hurston's critique also recalls Hunter-Gault's. Hurston criticizes the race men for only feigning commitment to the community, and for pretending to value Black people's revolutionary history. Inherent in the criticism, as she constructs it, is the idea of what they should be, of what a race man should be—one who is actually committed and who does value and celebrate Blacks' history of revolution, in addition to emphasizing their claim to Americanness. Plácido was made into this type of individual by the colonial government, white abolitionists, and Black abolitionists. The race-ing of this one individual is a case study in the complex geneses of notions of racial connectedness and consciousness, of the role of national affinities and transnational engagements therein, and more generally of the ways the identities of people of African descent were both the roots and results of Black cosmopolitanism.

The View from Above: Plácido Through the Eyes of the Cuban Colonial Government and White Abolitionists

The Haitian Revolution (1791–1804) and the fear its success prompted caused profound changes not only in Haitian society but in slave societies across the hemisphere. It sent a shiver up the collective spine of the slaveholders (and abolitionists) because it forced the realization that Black uprisings could actually be successful. A Virginia newspaper carried what must have seemed to its White readers to be horrific news from the revolution: "between five and six hundred White persons fell under the bloody hatchet of the Haitians, and the warm stream of blood which ran from them, quenched the thirst of their murderers, who went to their knees to receive it."[1] On one level, then, the fear was a fear of actual violence. On another it was a fear of the unification of people of African descent across class, color, and geographical lines.

The fear of connections between people of African descent across the Americas provoked by the Haitian Revolution shows up particularly clearly in discourse on Cuba. With the precipitous drop in Haitian sugar production caused by the revolution, Cuba began to fill that void and consequently experienced an economic boom. Needless to say, that boom demanded and was largely fueled by an exponential increase in the population of African slaves in Cuba. Although the African slave trade was officially illegal at this point, Cuba was able to grow its labor pool through the booming illegal trade.[2] There existed among both White Cubans and White Americans a deep and abiding fear of the Africanization of Cuba, and more specifically of Cuba becoming another Haiti. As contemporary commentator J. G. Wurdemann put it, "The most prominent obstacle to the permanent tranquility of the island is the African slave-trade. The annual intermingling of several thousand wild savages . . . with the partially-trained laborers . . . tends to keep up a constant . . . insubordination."[3] There was a belief that the Blacks of Cuba, Haiti, and the United States perceived themselves as bound to each other, whether politically, ideologically, or otherwise, and that the result would be the demise of Whites in both locations. For example, in 1854 a U.S. State Department agent expressed his fear that without U.S. intervention Cuba would become another "'Black Empire' like Haiti, 'whose example they would be proud to imitate' in destroying the wealth of the island and launching 'a disastrous bloody war of the races.'"[4]

This chapter analyzes the ascription of particularly configured understanding of racial consciousness and national identity to people of color in Cuba, in general, and to Plácido, free poet of color, in particular. Through readings of the treatment of the visions of Plácido and other Cubans of color and of the significance of racial and national identity, both in the sentence pronounced by the Cuban government against Plácido and the other alleged conspirators (hereafter the *Sentencia*) and in celebrations of Plácido by British and U.S. abolitionists, I illuminate the nuances of dominant visions of the bases and configurations of people of African descent's approaches to identity. These are the visions within, against, and beyond which Plácido, other Cubans of African descent, and people of African descent in the Americas more generally sought to define themselves. In order to understand people of African descent's own representations of themselves and of others of African descent (the focus of the bulk of this study), we must first grasp the mechanics of the conceptual frameworks with which they were in dialogue.

Background: Slavery in Cuba

Slavery in Cuba did not officially end until 1886.[5] The tardiness of abolition, relative to the British and French Americas, was a consequence of the deep-seated fear of Black uprisings and/or takeovers on the part of Whites on all sides of the battle over Cuba. Throughout the battle for Cuba, Spanish officials, Creole *independentistas*, and U.S. officials were all generally tentative about or downright hostile to immediate and complete emancipation. In fact, the sugar industry in Cuba, and by extension the slave trade, began to experience a boom just when the industry and trade were in decline in the British and French colonies in the Americas. Slavery was abolished in the British colonies in 1833. The Haitians took their freedom in 1804. Both events were actually boons to the Cuban economy because they allowed Cuba to fill the supply gaps created by the reduced or nullified sugar production of these colonies. Cuba took San Domingue's place as the preeminent sugar-exporting colony. The decline in the British West Indian sugar industry (along with the "American" Revolution) left one of the largest consumers of sugar in the world—the United States—without a stable supply. Louis Pérez tracks the unbelievable increase in trade with the United States subsequent to these key events. According to the documents he uncovered, the number of North American ships arriving at Cuba increased from 150 in 1796 to 2088 in 1851–56, while the U.S. share of Cuban trade went from 39 percent in 1850 to 82 percent in 1877.[6]

Cuba, like most of the colonies in the Americas at this time, was fraught with tensions between the three levels of colonial society—the Spanish crown, the White Creoles, and the people of color (free and slave).[7] In the case of Cuba, and the other Spanish and Portuguese colonies, the church could be thought of as a fourth level, albeit one that was virtually conjoined to the crown.[8] Contemporary Bostonian observer J. G. F. Wurdemann documents the crown's mistrust of White Creoles, noting that "every movement of the Creole is watched."[9] Particularly during Cuba's post-revolution boom, the crown was determined to continue to reap the lion's share of the benefits of the growing economy, and did so by imposing and manipulating prices, tariffs, and other trade laws. The members of the Creole elite were therefore fighting to free themselves from the Spanish yoke and to claim the profits of the boom for themselves. In their drive to escape Spain, they even went so far as to call for annexation to the U.S.

One especially noteworthy fact is that concomitant with this economic boom was a phenomenal increase in the number of Africans being brought to the island as slaves. The number of slaves increased by 149,553 between 1827 and 1841.[10] A table on slave importation reproduced by historian Franklin Knight also shows a boom in the importation of slaves between 1835 and 1840.[11] Needless to say, there were continuing "tensions," to put it mildly, between the African-descended population and those in power, whether the Creole elite or the Spanish crown. Uprisings were continuous and therefore continually feared.

Government Constructions of Black Community

Both pro- and antislavery forces writing from or about Cuba embraced a conception of a fundamental connection between people of African descent in order to further their goals. Proslavery forces invoked the notion to dredge up fresh memories of the Haitian Revolution and incite fears of its recurrence elsewhere. The discourse of the Cuban colonial government in the wake of the revolution is rife with references to this threat. Throughout the nineteenth century the Cuban government was obsessed with keeping "foreign" Blacks off the island so that they would not taint Cuban Blacks. Countless extant documents ranging from 1790s to the 1870s reveal the Cuban ruling class's intense fear of the "hostile designs of Blacks and mulattos in the French part of Santo Domingo,"[12] as they described them. Government offices kept track of the travels of known foreign troublemakers, such as a "conspiring negro" who had been expelled from Charleston, and a negro who had participated in an insurrection in Jamaica who was said to be coming to Cuba.[13]

Needless to say, French Blacks appear most often as the greatest threat. In 1826 proceedings were brought against Salvador Lafrontaigne described as a "negro francés" (French Black) for sedition.[14] In 1802, the government blocked the disembarkation of an insurrectionary Black from Guadaloupe.[15] Jamaican or English Blacks, however, are not far behind in terms of numbers of references. Even in 1750, well before the boom in Cuban slavery as a result of the Haitian Revolution, the Cuban government expressed concern about the presence of three slaves who fled from Jamaica to Santiago de Cuba.[16] Males were not the only troublemakers. A "morena inglesa" (Black British woman) is repeatedly referenced in the government's discussion of the Aponte uprising of 1812, the largest uprising in Cuba before the Ladder Conspiracy.[17] The aforementioned French Black, Salvador Lafrontaigne, was accused along with "otras negras esclavas" (other Black female slaves).[18] The officials kept track of uprisings on the neighboring islands. Doing so for Jamaica was particularly important given the proximity of the island to Cuba. In the midst of Cuba's economic boom, the antislavery movement in England and the British colonies saw its most significant success—the abolition of slavery in the British colonies. After abolition took place in the British colonies in 1833, the Cuban government's task of preventing transnational movement and/or interaction was especially difficult because then it also had to block greater numbers of Cuban Blacks from fleeing to Jamaica. Recognizing the new challenge, one official proposed in 1841 that the Cuban government return all foreign Blacks. The inability of the Cuban government to control the transnational movements of all Blacks is clear. In 1842 the government complained about one José Inocencio Rizo, who was given a passport to Jamaica but used it to go to Haiti instead.[19] In 1844 one expelled Black formed a revolutionary junta in New York.[20] Frequent discussions began to take place in the Cuban government about the potential spread of freedom.[21]

In addition to controlling the movements of other Caribbean Blacks, the government had to deal with troublesome U.S. Blacks, particularly those from Charleston and Florida.[22]

Foreign Blacks were not, of course, the only troublemakers who concerned the Cuban government. The government also found it difficult to prevent people of color on their own soil from uniting with subversive aims. Along with Cuba's economic boom came a boom in uprisings against slavery, several of which were known to have included Whites and free people of color as well as slaves. Revolts in Matanzas in 1825 and 1843 were among these broadly supported uprisings.[23] Rebellions were often stirred up by Afro-Cuban mutual aid societies called *cabildos*, New World manifestations of organizations formed by Africans on the continent and in Spain. These societies often served (and serve) economic, religious, and cultural functions in their communities. One of the best-known rebellions carried out by one of these groups was the abovementioned Aponte rebellion in 1812, named after the director of the troublemaking *cabildo*, José Antonio Aponte, leader of the Cabildo Shango Tedum. Aponte and the other members of his society enacted their plan by bringing together a range of Cubans of color from different *cabildos*, regions, and classes as well as enlisting the support of "white abolitionists and a small group of free men of color and slaves in the United States, Santo Domingo, Haiti, and Brazil."[24] Historian Philip Howard notes, "To Aponte and his followers, Africans were one people because they shared similar conditions of oppressions."[25] The rebellion did meet with some success before it was discovered and destroyed by the colonial government. The rebels attacked several military installations and decimated a major sugar mill and estate. Although the rebels, including Aponte, were put to death by the Cuban government, their example continued to inspire other societies and served as a model for the planning and enacting of rebellions (29).

Maroons and runaways were also a major problem for the Cuban government, as illustrated by the information provided to Miguel Barnet by Cuban maroon Esteban Montejo as well as the repeated discussions of *cimarrones* and *apalencados* (maroons and runaways) in the government archives of that period. Montejo, through Barnet, spotlights this obsessive focus by pointing out that

Since the Cimarron was a slave who had escaped, the masters sent a posse of *rancheadores* [ranchers] after them. Mean *guajiros* [white peasants] with hunting dogs so they could drag you out of the woods in their jaws . . . they were trained to catch Blacks. If a dog saw a Black man, he ran after him.[26]

Government officials lived in fear, apparently reading virtually every movement of the *cabildos*, maroon groups, and free people of color as an indication of a potential insurrection.[27] María de la Luz Sanchez was one of the government's objects of scrutiny because it believed that she was involved in a "commoción de los negros" (disturbance among the Blacks) in Guanabo.[28] The Cuban government went so far as to keep track of meetings of "negros apalencados."[29] Clearly, keeping people of color from striking out for freedom, whether for themselves as individuals or for those who they perceived as their kin, was almost impossible.

The Cuban government's perception of and response to these national and transnational movements would seem to suggest an acknowledgment of the fact that national, geographical, and linguistic boundaries seemed to matter but a mite to people of African descent. Interestingly enough, however, that acknowledgment is at once implied and negated in the government's notions of Black community. An analysis of the Cuban government's envisioning of the "Black" community reveals the prevalence of that contradiction in official representations of the ties that bind and differentiate that community. In addition, though, it illustrates that the official discourses born of the fear that the revolution would be replicated also implicitly included specific notions of the cosmopolitanism, racial consciousness, and national identity of people of African descent. In particular, it reveals the dialectical, dynamic, and dialogical relationship between views of people of African descent's identities from above and from below. People of African descent acted together to foment uprisings, leading to official discourse about them as a collective. At the same time, the official perception of people of African descent as an undifferentiated (inhuman) mass instigated the uprisings and the notion of connectedness that produced them. Proslavery discourse on the "Black" community is therefore both an index and an impetus for people of African descent's processes of self-identification, ergo the position of this chapter as the first in this study of Black cosmopolitanism.

The *Sentencia*, the official document that prescribed the sentence to be imposed by the Cuban government upon Plácido and the other alleged conspirators of the "Ladder Conspiracy" simultaneously showcases the profound contradictions implicit in proslavery ideas about the place of difference in the identificatory and political choices made by people of African descent.[30] The racial classification system, as understood by the proslavery government forces that produced this document, was one that had different terms for individuals based on their appearance or proportion of African blood. The first population census of colonial Cuba, for instance, classifies people of color first as either *libres* (free people) or *esclavos* (slaves), then divides each of these categories into *mulatos/as* (mulattos) and *negros/as* (Blacks). So, the categories for people of color are *mulatos libres, negros libres, mulatos esclavos, negros esclavos, mulatas libres, negras libres, mulatas esclavas,* and *negras esclavas* (free mulattos, free Black men, mulatto slaves, Black male slaves, free mulattas, free Black women, mulatta slaves, Black female slaves).[31]

The *Sentencia*, written to be read by those who could (primarily Whites) and to be heard about by those who could not (primarily people of color) displays a convoluted racial logic that simultaneously subsumes all people of African ancestry into one group—which wants to unite and make Cuba into another Haiti—and differentiates between them according to this multipartite classification system. Ultimately, it plainly shows the binary underpinnings of the racial classification system that on the surface appears to be multipartite.[32]

The narrative of the conspiracy is completely racialized. The movement was headed, as the officials repeat frequently, by Plácido, a free *pardo* (mixed race person).[33] The Cuban government in the sentence against Plácido and his alleged fellow conspirators describes the uprising repeatedly as " la conspiración proyectada por la gente de color . . . para el esterminio de la . . . población blanca." The officials *believed* that the conspiracy was fomented by people of color with the express purpose of exterminating Whites. Among their list of conspirators they specifically name "pardos libres," "morenos libres," "negros esclavos," "las negradas," thereby implicating and linking all racial groups with any named or claimed African ancestry—free mixed race people, free Blacks, Black slaves, and the Black masses.[34] The conception of the connection between all the people of color of all classes is emphasized throughout the *Sentencia*. This description of the insurrection, repeated throughout the *Sentencia*, reinforces the broad notion of Black community indexed in the fear of the reproduction of the Haitian Revolution. The repetition of this phrasing highlights for the White Cuban elite that the danger of this uprising lies, not simply in its existence, but more importantly in the coming together of people of color across various boundaries. It announces that the boundaries that are supposed to keep these people separated are crumbling, and that Haiti is beginning to happen here. As if to reiterate this point the document includes a detailing of how these different groups that are supposed to be separate came to unite.

At the same time, the narrative is clearly gendered male, constructing women of color as followers. This battle between people of color and Whites is represented in the *Sentencia* as a battle between the government's and the

Creole's civilized manhood of the government, the *pardos'* and *mulatos'* willingness to give up their potential access to noble manhood, and the Blacks and slaves' barbarism of the Blacks. (I will return to the issue of the perceived place of women of color in these constructions of racial and national community later in this chapter in my discussion of the Cuban government's use of stereotypes, and in the next two chapters in my readings of Black abolitionists' constructions of Plácido and Plácido's own poetry.)

In attributing disparate motivating factors to each group, the government reveals a tension between the desire to negate differences between people of color, subsuming them into one group, and the drive to accord symbolic and social value to class and color differences. According to the government author, the *pardos* joined the conspiracy with the object of gaining, through the movement, concessions that would improve their social condition. The *morenos* (free Blacks) were reluctant to enlist because they were free and realized that they would not benefit from the plan. The document doesn't venture a guess about why the Black slaves agreed to participate, though it does mention their superior strength. The government's narrative is that

Individuos pardos seducían a morenos, y estos a los pardos, luego es evidente que los partidos de las distintas razas se amalgaron posteriormente y formaron uno solo, ecsaltado y decidido por el esterminio y estinción de todo blanco, haciéndose de este modo duenos de la Isla, conservandola por si, y con la ayuda y protección de fuerzos estrangeras.

(Mixed race people seduced the free Blacks, who seduced the mixed race people, then it is evident that the parties from the different races came together afterwards and formed a single group, fired up to exterminate and make extinct all Whites, making themselves in this way the owners of the island, keeping it for themselves, and with the support and protection of foreign forces.)

In the government's view, the *pardos* seduced the *morenos*, the *morenos* seduced the *pardos*, and then these races united and formed one, with the goal of the extermination and extinction of all Whites, making themselves the owners of the island. The document is, in effect, outlining the creation of a new racial collective within which class and color differences are of minimal relevance.

Significantly, the slaves are not mentioned in this narrative of agency. Orlando Patterson, in his seminal text *Slavery and Social Death* (1982), identifies slavery as fundamentally a "relation of domination" based ideologically on the belief in the master's "total power" and the slave's "total powerlessness."[35] The denial of slave agency, and in Patterson's terms the imagining of the slave as "a socially dead person," were crucial to the maintenance of slavery.[36] The erasure of slave agency in the conspiracy serves several purposes, including stirring up Whites' fear of *pardos* and *morenos*. The free movement of free people of color had been proving a challenge to the Cuban government, as previously mentioned cases illustrate. Controlling this movement and reducing the transmission of revolutionary ideas by these roving troublemakers was a priority for the government. The specific punishments meted out to the alleged conspirators reflect the government focus on immobilizing *pardos* and *morenos* and keeping them away from the pure, servile slaves. The overwhelming majority of the *pardos* and *morenos* accused of participation were sentenced to death or to exile in overseas jails. The latter were banned from returning to Cuba or going to Puerto Rico under penalty of death. The repetition of the race and class status of accused individuals in the pronouncement of their sentence underlines the government's purgative purpose. For instance the sentence reads

La pena de muerte fusilado por la espalda . . . *al pardo libre* Jorge Lopez acusado por catorce individuos sobre . . . *al de la misma clase* Santiago Pimienta . . . a la referida pena. . . a Manuel Quiñones . . . *reclutador de la clase de morenos*, a la misma pena. (my emphasis)

(The penalty of death by being shot in the back . . . *to the free mixed race man* Jorge Lopez accused by forty individuals . . . *to another of the same class* Santiago Pimienta . . . the same penalty . . . to Manuel Quinones . . . *recruiter of the free Blacks*, the same penalty.)

The class and race of all *pardos* and *morenos* accused of participating in the conspiracy are mentioned alongside the specific roles witnesses testified that they played, as they are sentenced to death by being shot in the back. The juxtaposition of their social and racial status with their alleged misdeeds makes unclear which of their crimes—the crime of conspiring or the crime of being a *pardo* or *moreno*, resulted in their death sentence.

Implicit in this focus on the *pardos* and *morenos* and the apparent denial of slave agency, however, is recognition of that agency. It stands to reason that if the slaves were as vapid and servile as the *Sentencia* narrative suggests, they would not have the intellectual wherewithal to comprehend the plan for the insurrection. Perhaps recognizing this slippage, the official states that

Habiéndose decidido a adaptar tal temperamento el partido moderado de la clase de pardos, sin duda por haber meditado no podian contrarestar al furioso y ecsaltado de los negros en razon a ser este muy superior en fuerzas.

(Having decided to adapt that posture the moderate group within the class of mixed raced people, without a doubt after having thought carefully could not counteract the fury and hot-headedness of the Blacks because the Blacks were so superior in strength.)

Moderate *pardos*, he says, adopted this plan because they deduced that they could not counteract the strength of the Blacks. He notes slave agency in the conspiracy but immediately tries to undercut that recognition by marking their strength as purely physical. The *pardos* were the thinking agents. They "decided" to adopt a particular stance,"meditated" on this issue, understood their position, reasoned that they were outmanned, and adopted the plan. The slaves simply had superior forces.

The simultaneous denial and recognition of slave agency is especially instructive when it appears in the specific sentences given to slaves accused of participating in the conspiracy. Two slaves were sentenced to death—one for shooting his owner and the other for being a leader in the conspiracy. The other accused slaves, few in number when compared to the number of accused and convicted *pardos* and *morenos*, were sentenced to eight or ten years in jail on the island or on their master's plantation, where they were to be shackled and treated as prisoners.

Replicated in the government narrative are stereotypes of each of these groups that are evident in Cuban literature in the nineteenth century— among them the *pardo* who will do anything to become like a White man or hates the White man with a special passion, the *moreno* who is either complacent or unwilling to distance himself from the slaves, and the slave who is either vapid or always ready for violence. (Although this point will not be discussed here, it is important to point out that these figures also permeated literature about Blacks in the United States during this period.) One of the texts that most clearly illustrate a number of these stereotypes is the novel by Cirilo Villaverde entitled *Cecilia Valdés*, first published in 1839.[37] The novel gives a complex and useful representation of the racial politics of nineteenth-century Havana, following a young *mulata* through life and love.[38] Claudette Williams identifies it as the nineteenth-century Cuban novel in which "the Cuban fascination with the *mulata*" is most conspicuous.[39] Cecilia is stereotypically represented through exaggerated Romantic terminology as a model of female beauty. She also exemplifies the stereotype of the mixed race individual who rejects her own heritage in pursuit of whiteness on multiple levels. She rejects her free mulatto boyfriend, Pimienta, in favor of her White half-brother Leonardo. Similarly, another character, Tirso, born of a slave woman, casts off his mother because of her skin color and the status it represents. Cecilia's mulatto boyfriend, however, refuses to detach himself from the community of people of color. Humberto López Cruz puts it bluntly: "en ningún momento aspira a usurpar el puesto del blanco" (at no moment did he aspire to usurp the position of the white)" and emphasizes the contrast between the two men's relationships with their mother —Tirso (child of a slave) hated his mother while Pimienta (free mulatto) loved his.[40] Significantly, her mulatto boyfriend eventually kills her White brother-boyfriend, illustrating the figure of the free individual of color who both stubbornly maintains his ties to the community, and is prone to exhibiting the violence associated with those beneath him.

By replicating these stereotypes in the *Sentencia* against the accused conspirators of La Escalera, the government author makes the logic of his narrative seem indubitable to proslavery advocates, particularly because it shows people of color behaving in accordance with advocates' preconceived notions.[41] The reproduction of these types also negates the agency of the individuals of color, suggesting that their actions are a result of their race, rather than of their own decision-making. Racial marking functions as a way of denying agency, even when drastic and/or violent actions are the focus of the discussion. At the same time, the downplaying of slave participation in the sentence also negates slave agency by determining the contours of racial or political community. Patterson argues usefully that a fundamental aspect of slavery was "natal alienation": "the alienation of the slave from all formal, legally enforceable ties of 'blood,' and from any attachment to groups or localities other than those chosen for him by the master, that gave the relation of slavery its peculiar value to the master."[42] This statement helps to spotlight the contradiction in the discourse of slave agency in the *Sentencia*. The question who has the right to determine the grounds of community undergirds the racialized discourse of the sentencing. The Cuban government is attempting to actuate their vision of the formation of this racial/political community through the sentence. That vision is, not surprisingly, in line with what "gave . . . slavery its peculiar value to the master."[43] Through the denial of slave agency, the concomitant attribution of agency to mixed race individuals, and the claiming of the ultimate agency in determining the structure of relations within this community, the government officials endeavor to impose their idea that racial identity is determined from above rather than below.

In this way, racial identifications in the *Sentencia* speak volumes about the link between the Cuban government's conception of people of African descent's identities, and their denial and attribution of agency. The attribution to the English consul of the ultimate agency for the uniting of these racial groups in particular, and conspiracy in general, further indexes this connection. It also reinforces my earlier point about the colonial government's fear of people of color's potential international engagements. Slavery depended on the cosmopolitanism of those in power and on the denial of cosmopolitanism to those subject to this power. According to the government, the idea for the conspiracy came from David Turnbull, a troublesome abolitionist English consul to Cuba. He supposedly inculcated the people of color with the idea of liberty and seduced them with a future that featured improved jobs and social standing. Turnbull wanted nothing more, the government said, than to make ruins of this jewel in Castile's crown. He called the first meeting of the men he thought would be appropriate as generals. It was his emissary who supposedly smoothed out the differences between the groups and ensured the cooperation and uniting of the people of color. These statements construct the conspiracy as a battle between England and Spain, and the people of color as pawns in this European game. As such, the statements most clearly highlight the contradictions of the Cuban government's views of people of color, and their connections to each other. On the one hand, the government fears and obsesses about the uniting of these groups. On the other, it must tell itself that these African-descended people could not be the catalysts for or the agents of this uniting. A logical deduction to be made based on this convoluted vision is that connections between disparate groups of people of African descent are determined by White Europeans. People of color are not really agents in the decision to revolt; they are not agents in deciding who they will consider their community. They do not have the wherewithal to unite on their own, or to use the Europeans against each other. Of course, the entire undertaking attracts so much government attention precisely because of its fear of the agency, intelligence, and strength of the people of color, and because it is clear to the officials that the people of color, Cuban and non-Cuban alike, refuse to respect their boundaries.

The Cuban government is forced, however, at least to attempt to represent people of color's own agency in creating a racial community. Although in much of the *Sentencia* people of color are represented as coming together either at someone else's behest—out of selfish consideration for their own subgroup or simply their deep desire to exterminate the Whites—it proves especially difficult for the government to deny Plácido's agency completely, and further to represent him as anything other than a "race man." The government begins by presenting him as one of the individuals present at the first meetings of conspirators from different regions of the island. In that first presentation it represents Plácido and the others as blank slates upon whom Turnbull wrote, stating that as a result of these meetings these individuals became full-fledged adherents to the ideas of consul Turnbull. That representation is undercut by the fact that these men journeyed of their own accord from all over the country to meet and discuss the uprising, as well as by everything else the document goes on to say about Plácido. He was, the government itself says, a key member of the principal junta, and the first one elected president by the group. He willingly swore "horrible oaths" to carry out the plan of the extermination of all Whites upon penalty of death. Not surprisingly, in the government's narrative, Plácido is reportedly named by the most witnesses—thirty-two. Of all the sentences, his is the most detailed, signaling that he was clearly a special target for the Cuban government. As the government tells the story, he did more work for the conspiracy than any of the others, serving as president of the principal junta, recruiter, instigator, one of the first agents of the conspiracy, elected official, and first director of it. He is the only individual named in the caption of the document. (That he was a poet is also repeatedly noted in the *Sentencia*.) All these aspects of the government's approach to representing Plácido implicitly project on him a profound commitment to this united racial community. As the alleged president of the conspiracy, and by extension as a leader of this new racial collective, he is therefore the greatest threat to the government. In aiming to represent this figure as the ultimate threat, the government ends up revealing its own fear. The government's representation of Plácido illustrates and that proslavery forces and texts in Cuba did play a noteworthy role in the development and dispersion of ideas of racial community during slavery highlights the contradictory nature of this proslavery racialization process.

Significantly, proslavery discourse also played an important role in the dissemination of ideas about the potential relationship between people of color and the outside world. Implicit in the fear that slaves in Cuba, the West Indies, or North America would repeat the Haitian Revolution was the idea that slaves were aware of the happenings beyond their own plantation, town, or country. Governments' attempts to track and control the movements of free people of color index an acknowledgment of the fact that slaves and free people of color were able to communicate with, connect to, and potentially have a direct impact on communities of color in other locations. As the accusation of the English consul illustrates, though, the Cuban government was worried not only about the people of color's potential to communicate with other communities of color. Equally dangerous, if not more so, in the government's estimation, was the potential for people of color to create links with their enemies in general, and with their abolitionist enemies in particular.

White Abolitionists, Black Martyr

Plácido posed a major threat to the Cuban government even after his death because his story and poetry traveled. London resident British West Indian abolitionist Joseph Soul, in an 1845 letter to the editor of the *Jamaica Guardian and Patriot* calls for the erection of a monument in Jamaica to honor Plácido:

> Why should it not be done, and done without delay?—The idea is a good, and to my mind a very proper one. It will perhaps be the first Monument erected to the memory of an African poet—it will most certainly be the first erected to the memory of one so nearly related to slavery as he was.[44]

Plácido clearly had an impact on members of the English abolitionist community. Noteworthy here is Soul's valuation of Plácido as a poet and his emphasis on Plácido's close relationship to slavery. The circulation of his poetry, as reflected here, illustrates just why the Cuban government placed so much emphasis on his status as a poet in their sentencing. Soul's letter to the editor suggests specifically that Plácido's poems had already appeared in the abolitionist newspaper the *Anti-Slavery Reporter*, further indexing Plácido's importance to English abolitionists. Soul begins the letter by saying,

> I dare say that you, and all your readers have been made acquainted with the painful circumstances attending the execution of the justly celebrated "Plácido". . . They have been recently detailed by the public press in Spain, England, and throughout the whole civilized world, especially in connexion with a very beautiful Poem . . . [that] appeared in the *Anti-Slavery Reporter* already. (81)

He goes on to say that "It is well know [sic] that in some affecting poems, written by Plácido he had said it would be useless to kill him by shooting him in the body, they must strike his heart to make it cease its throbbings" (82).

As Soul's narrative structure and language show, Plácido's story had become a grand melodrama that bared the horrors of slavery and tyranny. Soul emphasizes the injustice of the execution of Plácido as well as qualities such as his "fortitude" and "noble bearing," noting too that he is "justly celebrated" (81). Soul's recreation of Plácido's execution even includes musical accompaniment, referencing priests chanting "in sepulchral voices" (82). Plácido, he says,

carried a crucifix in his hand and recited in a loud plaintive yet firm voice a beautiful prayer in verse . . . which thrilled on the hearts of the attentive masses of people who lined the road as he passed along. (82).

He said solemnly "Adiós Mundo" and sat to face his fate, "wearing an expression of superhuman courage." He gives the command to fire at his heart and "he died a victim to slavery." Soul's article is the coming to life of a nightmare that had to have been among the Cuban government's worst. No confusion, then, about why the Spanish consul would see the need to send this article as quickly as he did to the Cuban Captain-General. Plácido alive was a nightmare as a committed free *pardo* who could incite Cubans to revolt, but Plácido martyred was even more terrifying because he could even further incite foreign abolitionists to bring about the demise of Cuban slave society. Soul and other abolitionists were certainly inflamed. The letter even goes so far as to threaten retaliation against the Cuban government after explicitly condemning its treatment of Plácido: "Yes! 'he died a victim to slavery,' in that foulest of all slave spots—Cuba. Butchered by that bloodthirsty monster, O'Donnell. Depend upon it his day of reckoning is at hand" (82–83).[45] The threat lends a measure of validity to the government's fears of the danger posed by links between Cuban people of color and the outside world, while also indexing the ways in which the Cuban government's own actions increased both the Cubans' and outsiders' desire for such connections.

Soul's letter, in addition to illustrating the danger inherent in interactions between Cubans of color and the outside world, also reveals Soul's racialization of Plácido by making this Cuban of color into an international abolitionist symbol. Earlier in this chapter I delineated proslavery approaches to race and racial community in Cuba. Here I wish to take a moment to explicate how this White abolitionist's approach resonates with and differs from the proslavery accounts in noteworthy ways. Like the governmental authors of the *Sentencia*, Soul also makes Plácido into a type of "race man." He identifies Plácido unequivocally with "the African Race" throughout the letter. The term used in the letter, "African," would seem to mark this racialization as different from that of the *Sentencia*, which focuses on designations based on proportion of African blood, such as *pardo*, *moreno*, and *negro*. The positive valuation of "African" in Soul's letter and the negative

presentation of *pardos*, *morenos*, and *negros* in the sentence also differentiate these usages of racial markers. Soul explicitly says that the story of Plácido, this African poet, will "prove that those who traduce and despise the
African Race, know nothing about them, and that all their slanderous asser-
tions tending to degrade them . . . will one day recoil on their own heads"
(82). His positive view of "the African race" comes across clearly here, as
clearly as did the Cuban officials' negative view of *pardos* and *morenos* who
organize insurrections. These proslavery and abolitionist documents are
clearly at odds in terms of both the descriptive terms for and opinions of
people of color.

Tellingly, divergent narratives of Plácido's social status appear in the
sentence and the letter. The Cuban government focuses on his status as a
free *pardo*, and as discussed previously, pay him especially negative attention because he does not sit quietly and appreciate his lucky birth. Rather,
he decides to become politically active and imagines himself as connected to
the Black slaves beneath him. Soul, on the other hand, replicates an error
made repeatedly by Plácido's biographers—the error of thinking that he
was a slave.[46] Plácido was actually born free. This error reflects the confusion about Plácido's life that permeated the discourses about him outside
of Cuba during this period. Soul, in particular, notes that Plácido was a
slave whose freedom was bought by "the most respectable young men of the
Havana" (83). This error actually strengthens the abolitionist narrative, more
specifically the narrative about the horror of slavery in Cuba. It is, no doubt,
one of the reasons that so many biographers accepted this misinformation
so easily. The construction of Plácido as a slave serves the purposes of the
abolitionists well. His execution allows them to criticize the "bloodthirsty
monster, O'Donnell," the Cuban governor they describe as butchering Plácido. From the abolitionist perspective, the story of a slave who became a
leader and was executed by this horrible government is much more compelling and useful than that of a free man. (Similarly, for the Cuban government, the story of a free *pardo* who listened to the English and became
an instigator, recruiter, president, and junta leader in an uprising aimed at
exterminating all the Whites is much more poignant than the story of a
noble man who saw the injustice of slavery and decided to right it.) The difference between Plácido's social status in these two documents highlights
even further how crucial a battleground the symbol of Plácido was for both
the Cuban government and non-Cuban abolitionists. The control of the
representation of this individual was perceived as tremendously vital for
those who wanted to uphold Cuban slavery as well as those who wanted to

destroy it. Both social status and racial terminology were seen by the groups as pivotal elements of that representation.

In addition to racial descriptors and social status, the battle over this race man in the making was also fought on the terrain of national identity. All three areas of symbolic combat—racial descriptors, social status, and national identity—were invoked extensively and repeatedly by the participants in this battle. In the cases of the two documents under discussion here, national identity is spotlighted through the inclusion or exclusion of references to his Cubanness, specifically as encapsulated in the adjective "Cuban."

In the text of the *Sentencia*, the government never refers to Plácido or any of the other accused conspirators as Cuban or even as subjects of the Spanish crown (Cuba was still under the crown of Castile). They live on the island of Cuba but have neither any right nor any true connection to it. Only the government officials have a bond with Cuba: "Capitanía general de la siempre fiel Isla de Cuba" (Captain General of the always loyal island of Cuba). They have the right to indignantly decry the English consul's betrayal and abuse of confidence, especially since England was "our ally and friend." Since Plácido and the other conspirators are not Cuban, their case could not possibly illustrate the English consul's demonstration of loyalty to Cuba and Cubans, albeit to Cubans of color. They are not accused of treason because they are neither citizens nor full subjects, even though some of them may be freemen. To the Cuban government Plácido is a free *pardo* (social status and race) who has taken on a politics they view as negative, rather than a treasonous Cuban (national identity).

Foreign abolitionists like Soul, however, actually insist on referencing Plácido's connection to Cuba.[47] The title of Soul's letter is "Monument to Plácido, the Cuban Poet," and he emphasizes in the body of the letter that Plácido is even better known as "the Cuban Poet." The writings of U.S. abolitionist William Hurlbert of Boston echo all Soul's approaches to representing Plácido, but go a step farther in terms of engagement with his poetry. In an 1849 issue of *North American Review*, Hurlbert locates Plácido in the canon of Cuban poetry.[48] (The sketch's inclusion in the larger article on "The Poetry of Spanish America" featuring sketches, poems, and literary critical readings of works by poets from across the region speaks to the authors' estimation of Plácido's status as a literary figure as well.) Hurlbert quotes the praises that have been heaped, even by a Spaniard, upon Plácido's poetry: "I know no American poet . . . who approaches him in genius, in inspiration, in courtesy, and in dignity" (149). He calls Plácido one of "the three great names of Cuban poetry," and actually deems some of Plácido's poems too Cuban, and decides that "it is only on those of his poems which appeal to universal feelings that a foreign judgement of Plácido's poems can be fairly founded."[49]

In order to strengthen Plácido's power as a martyr, both Hurlbert and Soul highlight the deep connection that other Cubans seemed to feel to him. Such an approach implicitly indexes his Cubanness as seen through the eyes of his countrymen. The biographical sketch of Plácido included in Soul's letter describes in detail Plácido's procession to the place of execution, "saluting with graceful ease his numerous acquaintance" (82). As the reference to his "numerous acquaintance" reiterates, the Cuban people's love of Plácido also seems to be important to the writer of this sketch as well as to Soul. The repeated references to the people's love of Plácido and the assembling of a "great crowd" along the route to his execution further highlight this valuation. Hurlbert repeatedly mentions Plácido's "numerous friends [and]visitors whom . . . admiration attracted to his cell" and predicts that "by the inhabitants of Cuba the memory of this true son of the people will always be gratefully cherished."[50] Both abolitionists represent Plácido as a martyr who is beloved by all his people, thereby making the Cuban/Spanish officials' treatment of him appear even more horrific and aberrant. Significantly, in their emphasis on Plácido's Cubanness these abolitionists also implicitly construct Cuba as a nation of color, contradicting and negating the vision of people of color as interlopers who seek to destroy the real (White) Cuba evident in the *Sentencia*.

There is, however, a hidden dynamic at work in these abolitionists' representations of Plácido's link to Cuba. In a sense, the foregoing discussion of the disparities between pro- and antislavery discourses could have been anticipated. One would expect differences between abolitionist and proslavery discourses. As important, and perhaps even more significant for this discussion of nineteenth-century notions of Black community in the Americas, though, is the fundamental similarity. Both discourses rest on a valuation of racial identity and social status and a devaluation of national identity. The relationship between racial identification and national identity in these abolitionists' texts illustrates their prioritization of Plácido's racial identity (as they understand it) over his identity as a son of Cuba (or a subject of the Queen). Soul repeatedly refers to Plácido as a member of the African Race, clearly naming his valuation of Plácido's racial identity. For Soul, Plácido's Cubanness is useful for identifying him (the Cuban Poet), and for illustrating O'Donnell's tyranny, but it does not undercut his place as a powerful exemplar of the African Race. It is significant that when both Soul and R. R. Madden, whom Soul quotes in his letter, are being most emphatic in their call for the erection of the monument, they invoke Plácido's African-ness rather than his Cubanness. Madden, for instance, says "I think there ought to be a monument erected in JAMAICA to his memory, as a man of the AFRICAN RACE, who was an honor to it, and a victim to the tyranny of its oppressors."[51] Cuba is the place where Plácido was born, and experienced the tyranny of the oppressors of the African Race, but he is fundamentally and primarily a member of the African Race. Soul's presumption that all members of the African Race, regardless of national location, would contribute to the erection of the monument (a monument to a Cuban in Jamaica) speaks to this race-first perception: "I can easily imagine that every . . . enlightened African will contribute his mite towards the object." Although the abolitionists' goal is clearly the opposite of the Cuban government's, emphasis on specific elements of Plácido's identity is analogous. The terminology (African versus *pardo*) is different, indexing different systems of racial classification, but the basic object of focus—race—is the same. Significantly, though, the interest is not simply in naming him or identifying his racial category, but more specifically in making him part of a racial group that is connected despite differences in color or location. The White abolitionists and Cuban colonial government, in their discourse, were constructing a broad racial community, based, in part, on the same presumption of the preeminence of race as an identificatory category on which contemporary writers of African descent based their own sense of connection, later called pan-Africanism. The questions begged by this similarity are whether and how these writers' approaches to conceptualizing and representing Cubans of color diverge from those of the White abolitionists and proslavery forces. Answering this question will provide significant insight into the nuances of the construction and representation of the identities of people of African descent in the Americas in the age of slavery. The next chapter does just that.

Chapter 2

The View from Next Door: Plácido Through the Eyes of U.S. Black Abolitionists

Tales of the life and death of Plácido, Cuban poet of color, spread widely after his execution in 1844 for allegedly leading one of the largest uprisings in Cuban history. Inherent in the discourse on Plácido (then and now) is a tension between the view of him as an exemplar of the particularities of the Cuban context and the perception of him as a representative of the elements of the broader experience of people of the African Diaspora in particular, and of humans more broadly.[1] Cosmopolitanism is, therefore, implicated in representations of Plácido in two ways. First, his story itself travels and becomes part of the discourse of the Atlantic world. Second, those who represent him seek to achieve their goals by either highlighting or negating his connection to the world beyond Cuba.

Among those who found the stories particularly compelling and useful were Black abolitionists in the United States. The stories provided a clear way for the Black abolitionists to link the struggles of people of African descent in the United States and Cuba through the story of one well-known individual figure, rather than through statistical information or general reports of insurrections or mutinies. This chapter explicates the nuances of Black abolitionists' representations of Plácido, illuminating the ways in which they construct the Black race and argue for the appropriateness of particular approaches to difference within the race—the ways they make a race (a community) as they make a race man (an individual). These abolitionists, unlike either the Cuban colonial government or the White abolitionists, consciously aim to create a Black community.

As illustrated in the previous chapter, although the colonial government in Cuba and White U.S. and British abolitionists differ in the specific terminology they employ in their representations of Plácido, with the colonial government characterizing him repeatedly as a *pardo* (mixed race person) and the White abolitionists describing him as a member of the African race, both locate his value for their project in his race. The colonial government's goal was to vilify him, and to make an example of him in a way that would discourage other *pardos* from debasing themselves by claiming and enacting connections to *morenos* and *negros*—that is to say, those classified as Black. The White abolitionists' intention was to push for abolition in Cuba by representing him as a noble gentleman who was debased by the barbarism of the colonial government on the island.

The two parties diverge, however, in their treatment of his national identity, (gentle)manhood, and social status, even though all three are vital aspects of the Plácido they construct. The government refuses to identify him as a son of Cuba; the White abolitionists emphasize his Cubanness. The government stresses his decision to lead this decidedly un-gentlemanly uprising; the White abolitionists highlight his gentlemanly dignity. The government emphasizes his status as a free person; the White abolitionists (incorrectly) identify him as a slave.

For the White abolitionists he is heroic because he is (gentle)manly. The symbolic battle between the parties is over men of African descent's access to gentle-manhood in addition to being about people of African descent's humanity—that is to say, their capacity for civilization. Women of African descent do not seem to figure in either the colonial government's or the White abolitionists' goal-oriented discourse. From the government's and the White abolitionists' perspectives the debasement or elevation of individual men of African descent is the key to both their conceptualization of the race and their decisions about their treatment of the race.

In a connected move, the government does not emphasize his status as a poet. The White abolitionists, in contrast, repeatedly index his mastery of this gentlemanly art. At the same time, the government also calls attention to Plácido's class (free), decrying his willingness to cross class lines. The White abolitionists, interestingly enough, represent him as a former slave— an error often made by other Plácido biographers, bolstering these abolitionists' concept of him as a true civilized gentleman who was dehumanized by the barbaric slave system. Significantly, however, neither the colonial government in Cuba nor the White abolitionists imagined themselves as part of Plácido's community or Plácido as part of theirs. Black abolitionists in the United States certainly did. While Black abolitionists' representations of Plácido differ in their specific content from those of the government and the White abolitionists because of that sense of connection to him, they are based on the same referents as the texts of the government and the White

abolitionists—race, nation, (gentle)manhood (in both the sense of an
emphasis on one gender and the opposition between civilization and barbarism), and social status. They do, however, focus more explicitly on the
referent that underpins the focus on the aforementioned ones—the humanity of people of African descent.

William Wells Brown, for example, includes Plácido in his book *The
Black Man, His Antecedents, His Genius, and His Achievements* (1863), thereby racially marking Plácido as Black. Plácido, from Brown's perspective,
advances his stated goals for the book—to "show that he [the Black man]
is endowed with those intellectual and amiable qualities which adorn and
dignify human nature."[2] Brown wants to talk back to those who believe in
the "natural inferiority of the Blacks, and claim that we were destined only
for a servile condition," and he believes that his racial brother Plácido helps
him to do just that (5). Understanding Brown's definition of Black—that is,
just what Brown is identifying Plácido with when he marks him as a Black
man—opens the door to identifying distinctions along a range of notions of
Black identity during the nineteenth century (several of which are addressed
in this book). At the same time, Brown reinforces the aforementioned idea,
evident in the White abolitionists' discourse, that uplifting the Black race is
best accomplished through the elevation of the Black man. Brown's statements suggest that the most desirable way to encourage the recognition of
people of African descent's humanity is to emphasize the way in which the
Black man is human and gentlemanly.

One of the key pillars of Brown's notion of Black community is common African origin. In this he reflects the Ethiopianism that was prevalent
in African American discourse during the eighteenth and nineteenth centuries. The proponents of this tradition often quoted the passage from
Psalm 68:31 that states, "Princes shall come out of Egypt; Ethiopia shall soon
stretch out her hands unto God," understanding this passage as the proph-
esying of the coming triumph of Africa and its descendants.[3] Brown details
the accomplishments of the Black man's antecedents in Ethiopia and Egypt,
and notes how many historians, ethnologists, and mythologists have re-
marked on the distinguished history of Africa and Africans, saying

In the earliest periods of history, the Ethiopians had attained a high degree of civilization. . . and that to the learning and science derived from them we must ascribe
those wonderful monuments which still exist to attest to the power and skill of the
ancient Egyptians. . . . These are the antecedents of the enslaved Blacks on this continent. (32, 35)[4]

For Brown, ancestry is what both connects "Blacks on this continent" and distinguishes them from their oppressors. Prominent pan-Africanist Edward Wilmot Blyden's echoing of Brown's focus on ancestry in his 1880 speech, significantly entitled "Ethiopia stretching out her hands unto God or, Africa's Service to the World," shows that this valuation of common ancestry remained central to Black activists' notions of Black community. Blyden states clearly that "the exiled Negro, then, has a home in Africa. Africa is his, if he will. He may ignore it. He may consider that he is divested of any right to that country . . . but . . . he is entitled to a whole continent by his constitution and antecedents."[5]

Implicit in Brown's discussion of the Black man is the extent to which negative views of "the negro" have shaped his idea of Black community. He designates as Black all who have African origin and are included in the group of those assumed by the oppressors to be naturally inferior. For example, he takes issue with newspapers for the racism implicit in their "misrepresenting the effect which emancipation in the West Indies had upon the welfare of those islands" and further for their suggestion that "general ruin followed the Black man's liberation" (37). He uses the improvement in the "moral and intellectual condition of both Blacks and Whites" in Jamaica that resulted from the abolition of slavery to prove that the U.S. could also benefit from the liberation of Blacks, and more specifically that Blacks in the U.S. were fit for freedom (40). This understanding of Black community—that Blacks in the U.S. and the Caribbean are linked by their origin and oppression—is another reason that Plácido, for Brown, is unquestionably Black.

Brown deems Plácido such an important exemplar of the Black man, his antecedents, and his genius as to profile him fifth, ahead of Frederick Douglass, Denmark Vesey, Toussaint L'Ouverture, Alexander Crummel, and forty-three others. It is especially interesting that, given this valuation, Brown actually confuses Plácido, who was born free, with Juan Francisco Manzano, who was born into slavery. The first half of Brown's profile of Plácido is actually the story of the first half of Manzano's life, from birth to his early love of poetry, to the distribution of his poems by a White Englishman, to the "number of young whites" who bought his freedom. Although it is impossible to tell whether Brown's error is purposeful or accidental, it does speak to the greater value placed on the story of a writer or intellectual who had actually experienced slavery. It is no coincidence that Brown decides to profile all those who had a direct experience of or familial connection to enslavement, save Frederick Douglass, ahead of the free Black activists. Plácido is claimed as Black by Brown, in part, because of his presumed proximity to slavery.

Combined, the first half of Manzano's life and the last half of Plácido's do constitute an abolitionist's dream story: the experience of slavery, then freedom, followed by activism and martyrdom. The dramatic tone of Brown's description of Plácido's march to his execution recalls Soul's, and highlights his interest in showing the (enslaved) Black man's dignity: "The fatal day came; he walked to the place of execution with as much calmness as if it had been to an ordinary resort of pleasure. His manly and heroic bearing excited the sympathy and admiration of all who saw him" (89). Brown goes on to reproduce the Plácido poem that seems to have been the one most often reproduced by Anglophone abolitionists, including Soul, Brown, and Hurlbert, entitled "Plegaria a Dios" (A Prayer to God). The poem is said by these individuals and other biographers to have been written by Plácido in his cell the night before his execution. Brown's narrative of Plácido's death recalls both Soul's and Hurlbert's in tone, content, and to a great extent racial identification, with one key addition. The White abolitionists made a point of linking Plácido to his people and emphasizing how much the Cubans loved him. Brown goes a step farther by explicitly spotlighting Plácido's role as an inspiration and instigator for slaves, even in death. Brown notes that "his songs are still sung in the bondman's hut, and his name is a household word to all" (90). As such, Plácido is valuable to Brown as an exemplary Black man because of his activism and his power to inflame the hearts of the enslaved even after death. He is the ultimate race man.

Brown's deftly veiled threat of violence is further revealed when he links the future Cuban uprising that will take place in the name of Plácido to the French and Haitian revolutions, writing,

As the Marseillaise was sung by the revolutionists of France, and inspired the people with a hatred to oppressors, so will the slaves of Cuba, at a future day, sing the songs of their poet-martyr, and their cry will be, "Plácido and Liberty." (90–91)

This approach differs greatly from that of the White abolitionists discussed above in its direct reference to violence. The goal for the book that Brown states at the outset, "vindicating the Negro's character," showing "that he is endowed with those intellectual and amiable qualities which adorn and dignify human nature," is definitely in line with those of the White abolitionists. (Recall Soul's statement that Plácido's life and the monument are a rejoinder to those who "traduce and despise the African Race."[6]) His mention of the French Revolution and his only slightly shaded reference to the

Haitian Revolution, however, invoke slave violence against the oppressors in ways that previously discussed abolitionist authors did not. Brown goes beyond demarcating or referencing Black community to naming its power. Because of his experience of slavery, his poetic ability, and his "manly and heroic bearing" (ie. dignity) Plácido exemplifies the counter to the discourse of natural inferiority that Brown needs to achieve the stated goal of his book. His leadership of the insurrection makes him an impetus for righteous violence, a force that Brown needs to communicate the unstated threat contained within his book.

Evident in this chapter so far, through the foregoing readings of the representations of Plácido, are three views of the meaning and significance of Black community that concur with and contradict each other in noteworthy ways. These perspectives diverge most clearly in their attitudes toward the enslavement of people so named, and in their perception of the level of agency possessed or exhibited by those individuals, and converge most perceptibly in their valuation of race as the preeminent source or ingredient of identity, and their relative devaluation of national identity. In particular, for the authors of the Escalera sentence, such a community must be constructed by outside powers and exists only to bring about their destruction or to satisfy the social ambitions of a small group. From the perspectives of Soul and Hurlbert, there is a connection between particular people based on blood and geographical origin that makes them part of the African Race. For Brown, those he names as Blacks are linked by African origin and common oppression and degradation, in particular the presumption of natural inferiority.

Clearly, choosing to identify a person as Black or as a member of a Black or of color community was about more than a simply phenotypical reference, a naming of origins, or a marking of individuals of "African descent who claim an identity with the race."[7] Doing so was also a political action aimed at advancing specific goals, rather than the naming of an always already obvious identity. This point is fundamental to this project that excavates the intricate mechanics of the imagining, representation, enactment, and articulation of Black community, across national, linguistic, and identificatory boundaries in the age of slavery. People of African descent were identified and identified themselves in a range of ways, based on a variety of factors. This study recovers several of these disparate and varied modes of identification in order to promote a more nuanced understanding of the worlds that the slaves, slaveholders, and free people of color made.

Cuba and Cubans in Martin Delany's *Blake; Or, The Huts of America*

The most complexly nuanced literary vision discovered to date of a meeting between these varied identifications to be produced during this period was a novel by U.S.-born Black activist Martin Robison Delany. Between 1859 and 1862 Delany published a series of stories in the two most prominent African American newspapers (the *Anglo African Magazine* and the *Weekly Anglo African*) about the planning of a hemispheric Black rebellion. The stories were collectively entitled *Blake; or, the Huts of America.*[8] The rebel leader and protagonist of the novel is Henry/Henrico Blacus, an African American/Cuban slave who travels throughout the U.S. South and to Cuba fomenting a transnational uprising. Included among the many Cuban characters in the novel is Plácido. From Delany's perspective, Plácido was a Cuban version of Henry, a vision reiterated through his representation of Plácido as Henry's cousin.

Why Delany decided to include Plácido as a character, and by extension to set the second half of the novel in Cuba, is crucial to understanding the symbolic value of Plácido for U.S. Black abolitionists like Delany. Eric Sundquist suggests that Delany chose to include Plácido in order to highlight his "belief in the political function of literature" and to allow for a plausible representation of the "degree of cooperation across class and color lines" that he imagined.[9] It is not clear, though, why a representation of this kind of line crossing in Cuba, by a figure like Plácido, would be any more plausible than a representation of the same crossing in the U.S. One could argue productively that that kind of crossing was even less plausible in Cuba because of the institutionalization of color and class separations. As the sentence meted out by the Cuban government shows, the groups (*pardos libres*, *morenos*, and *negros esclavos*) were conceptualized as separate, with differences between the expectations for behavior for each group and the group's level of access to freedom and status. The level of surprise expressed by the authorities at the groups' uniting suggests an expectation of separateness on the authorities' part.

More plausible is the idea that Delany chose Plácido and Cuba, at least in part, because the fact that those class and color boundaries were so institutionalized in Cuba would make their transgression, as represented in the text, even more dramatic. (The anger toward the free *pardos* who chose to connect themselves with free *morenos* and enslaved Blacks displayed by the colonial government in Cuba in the *Sentencia* illustrates this point.) This interpretation tends to support Sundquist's point about Delany's valuation of literature as a political tool. *Blake* is clearly meant as a threat to those in power, emphasized in its dramatization of a pan-American version of the Haitian Revolution. As I have discussed above, fear of a repeat of the Haitian Revolution permeated proslavery discourse during this period.

Also raging was the debate over the annexation of Cuba to the U.S. Cuban Creole elite support for annexation was strong, for economic as well as political reasons. These Cuban-born White elites had already begun to increase their trade with the U.S. in the wake of the Haitian Revolution, and saw great economic advantages to strengthening that relationship. In addition, they believed that becoming part of the U.S. union would save them from the tyranny of Spain, which included what they saw as unbearable commercial taxes. One key member of the Creole elite courted U.S. support for annexation with the words

We admire your institutions, your laws, and your form of government; we see that they procure your prosperity and happiness. Now such being the circumstances of our situation there is naturally but one course for us to take, which is to solicit union with you. . . . It appears to me that such a measure must be equally interesting to both parties. . . . [It] would besides making us rich and happy, add incalculably to your national wealth and political importance.[10]

He calls particular attention to the economic benefits that would accrue to both parties upon annexation. Thomas Jefferson expressed his support for annexation, saying "I candidly confess that I have ever looked on Cuba as the most interesting addition which could ever be made to our system of States."[11]

Pivotal to the annexation debate was the idea that Cuba was undergoing a process of Africanization because of the large numbers of African slaves being brought to the island to keep the sugar mills running. The threat of a mass uprising of those Africans struck fear in the hearts of many U.S. and Cuban government officials and members of the elite. That threat, some said, could be minimized by U.S. annexation, and the concomitant preservation of the system of slavery. Others, however, believed that should the U.S. decide to annex Cuba, it would be annexing a country with a very high probability of a Haitian Revolution-like uprising within its gates. Martin Van Buren spoke out against any attempt in Cuba to "throw off the yoke" of Spain because of the threat such a move would pose to the U.S., saying,

Other considerations connected with a certain class of our population, make it in the interest of the southern section of the Union that no attempt should be made in that island to throw off the yoke of Spanish independence, the first effect of which would be the sudden emancipation of a numerous slave population, the result of which would not be very sensibly felt upon the adjacent shores of the United States.[12]

Van Buren's fundamental concern is the potential spread of the desire for freedom from Cuba to the United States, should slaves in Cuba get any glimpse of freedom. Cognizant of circulation of the latter idea, the Spanish crown directly threatened the Creole elites with the emancipation of the slaves, should they continue to push for annexation to the U.S.[13] Delany craftily interweaves these discourses and debates to make his threat even more powerful, using Cuba and Plácido to unsettle the nerves of proslavery advocates everywhere.

Delany posits a particular vision of the relationship between U.S. Blacks and Cubans of color in particular, and between people of African descent in different American sites more broadly. His representation of Plácido is, in effect, an argument for a particular understanding of racial identity and community. By choosing to represent a non-U.S. person of African descent in such a detailed fashion, Delany is attempting to represent, enact through fiction, and argue with the nature, nuances, and impact of the ideas of national and transnational Black community that were circulating at the time. An analysis of Delany's version of Plácido yields great insight into both Delany's notion of Black community and the place of national, geographical, or linguistic difference within that conception.

Plácido's Vision of Community in Blake

Racial Identity and Ideology

Delany's Plácido is racially ambiguous in appearance. In his first appearance in the novel, Plácido is described as having an "orange-peel complexion, Black hair hanging lively quite to the shoulders, heavy deep brow and full moustache, with great expressive Black piercing eyes" (*Blake*, 192–93). This ambiguity stands in sharp contrast to the emphasis throughout the text on Henry's obvious "Blackness" and purity of (African) blood: "Henry was a Black—a pure Negro—handsome, manly, and intelligent" (16). Plácido, in comparison to Henry, is less Black. In addition, as is concomitant with Delany's (and Brown's, and the White abolitionists', and the Cuban government's) construction of true Blackness as essentially male, Plácido is less masculine, described as being "of slender form" and "sinewy."[14]

The effect of the racially ambiguous representation of Plácido is to emphasize Henry's position as the real man, the real (Black) man, the real race man. As his statement quoted earlier also iterates, Delany equates Blackness with Black manhood. The representation of Plácido reflects that the equation remains the same even when the limitations of national boundaries are being overcome. The expansion of the territorial boundaries of Blackness does not lead to an expansion of the gender boundaries of Blackness or of the definition of a true race leader. Delany's own racialist beliefs in the supreme importance of purity of blood are detailed in his text, *The Origin of Races and Color* (1879).[15] In this fascinating and scientifically oriented text, Delany explicates his belief that there are only three pure races—yellow, Black, and White—and that "A general intermarriage of any two distinct races would eventually result simply in the destruction . . . of the less numerous of the two." His point is that continual mixing between the races will eventually result in the predominance of one of the races in the descendants. Although the offspring of an intermarriage "becomes a mixed race," "that mixed race is an abnormal race," and will eventually, with continued crossings, once again become one of the pure races" (92–93). Given these views, his initial representation of Plácido as racially ambiguous makes it difficult to tell whether that representation is meant to be positive, and, perhaps more important, whether we are supposed to read Plácido as Black.

Delany endeavors to clear up this confusion quickly, though. Despite Plácido's racially ambiguous appearance, Delany makes his Plácido one who embraces a broad notion of Black community that crosses boundaries of color, class, and nation. Delany displays some flexibility here with respect to the physicality that is defined as Black, surely forced, at least in part, by the descriptions of the apparently very fair Plácido circulating in the North American media, but absolutely no flexibility with respect to politics. Although Plácido does not share Henry's phenotypical Blackness, he does share his ideological and political identity. Although he does not specifically address this opposition between politics and phenotype, Gilroy rightly notes that "the version of Black solidarity Blake advances . . . makes Blackness a matter of politics rather than a common cultural condition."[16] Very early in the Cuba section of the novel, Henry and Plácido express their common commitment to (what Delany represents as) their race and begin to exchange information about what they have done and will do to remove the yoke of oppression that binds their race. Plácido says

"Give me your hand, Henry"—both clasping hands—"now by the instincts of our nature, and mutual sympathy in the common cause of our race, pledge to me on the hazard of our political destiny what you intend to do. . . . Heaven certainly designed it, and directed you here at this auspicious moment, that the oppressed of Cuba also may 'declare the glory of God!'" (195)

To emphasize their connectedness, Delany includes several images and phrases that call attention to their bond—"clasping hands," "our nature," "mutual sympathy," "common cause," "our race." Through these images Delany ascribes to Plácido a definition of Blackness that includes common blood, an activist political stance, and a more profound spiritual connection (invoked by the image of clasped hands and the idea that Heaven "designed it" and directed Henry there "at this auspicious moment"). He believes whole-heartedly in the "common cause" and hopes only that "the oppressed of Cuba" should be partakers of it. This statement is the first of many such statements Delany puts in the mouth of his Plácido that speak to a broad conception of racial community.

During the process of creating the constitutional basis for the nation-state, Delany's Plácido presents a powerful poem that highlights the grounds of racial identity in the texts and expresses the fundamental beliefs and goals of the revolutionaries. The poem is an impassioned one that invokes God and calls on God to free "Africa's sons and daughters" from "the white oppressor," to loose the "Blackman's chains," and allow "Ethiopia's sons to rejoice" (259–60). Delany constructs his Plácido as an individual who embraces a fundamentally binary racial logic, one that sees the world in Black and White above all. Given the inherent tension between this binary logic and the multipartite racial classification system of Cuba, the poem precipitates a discussion about the meaning of "Ethiopia's sons," and specifically whether the individuals of mixed blood in the group are left out by Plácido's use of that terminology. Plácido agrees, "we are not" all Ethiopians but we are all "necessarily implied in the term and cannot exist without it" (260). He goes on to explain to the questioner, a wealthy mixed Cuban woman, his belief that "colored persons, whatever the complexion, can only obtain an equality with Whites by the descendants of Africa of unmixed blood" (260). His point is that because African blood is so despised no person with any African blood can truly be accepted as equal until African blood is recognized as equal to White blood. This is one of the few cross-gender political discussions in the Cuba section of the novel. Here the woman is constructed as the listener-learner, paralleling the relationship between Plácido and Henry (in which Plácido is often the listener-learner). Significantly, the wealthy mixed

Cuban woman questions what she views as the displacement of mixed race people in Plácido and Henry's political vision, but not the silence on and of women in that vision. In portraying her in this way, Delany naturalizes the race man—the man who speaks (for) the race.

It is no coincidence, then, that Delany's Plácido demonstrates a profound connection to and knowledge of Africa. He enlightens his countrywoman about the distinction between the negative perceptions of Africa and Africans, including the notion that they are "savage, lazy, and idle" and the positive realities including the fact that "in Africa . . . they are among the most industrious people in the world" (261). Plácido predicts that Africa will "rise to the first magnitude of importance in the estimation of the greatest nations on earth" (261–62). He spends substantial time educating his countrypeople about Africa's history and future, including information about everything from the invalidity of the negative conceptions of Africans, to the population density of the continent, to the production of art and fabrics. Delany's Plácido has extensive knowledge of Africa and believes strongly that New World Blacks must recognize, value, and support Africa and their African roots. That Plácido gives this lecture and not Blake illustrates Delany's desire to represent the existence of indigenous Black Cuban racial activism. In this reading, I differ from Robert Levine, who reads Plácido's celebration of Africa as simply "echoing" Delany's 'civilizationist' stance."[17]

Delany did not have to put these words in Plácido's mouth. He could have just as easily had his hero Henry say all of them. I submit that Plácido's comments, although certainly reflective of Delany's own viewpoints, construct a specifically configured image of Cubans of color in particular, and of the meaning of and possibilities for transnational Black community more broadly. Despite the fact that Delany's views do dominate the text, he seems to be confronting issues that a Cuban race man may have to deal with that he, Delany, or an African American race man might not have to engage. This exchange between Plácido and the mixed Cuban woman and his subsequent lecture illustrate Delany's attempt to engage those differences. More specifically, the exchange makes the points that there are Cubans who already have a Black racial consciousness and that others do not yet have it but are open to it (as the questioner here shows herself to be). It indicates that an understanding of the meaning of "our race" or "the Black race," and the connection between differently located "children of Africa," is not an always already, particularly in Cuba.

Importantly, the mixed woman chooses to be involved in the movement even before she becomes aware of all the background information that

Plácido gives her about the functioning of racism in the Americas and about Africa. This fact suggests that Delany does not wish to present Plácido's broad knowledge and his high level of racial and political consciousness as a necessary prerequisite for becoming involved in racially based political action. One need only understand the implications of her African blood and want to strive for the political uplift of others with the same heritage, regardless of whether one considers herself "Ethiopian." Delany makes this point through this woman and the other Cuban characters who are not as knowledgeable about the world or racial ideologies as Plácido's. This point is vital for Delany to make in a novel that articulates a vision of transnational Black collectivism, because it provides a key element of a possible methodology for the imagining and enacting of transnational Black interaction. Delany's implicit suggestion here that cultural and identificatory differences within "the Black community" must be acknowledged and engaged in some way in order for that notion of community to be enacted is the most important contribution that *Blake* makes to African Diasporan discourse. He notes wisely that the movement is undercut rather than bolstered by the application of a particular standard of racial consciousness as a litmus test for determining who can or cannot be legitimately involved in the movement.[18] (At the same time, he posits a clear vision of the appropriate position(s) of women in the movement—listener-learner and helper.)

Religion is also crucial to Delany's conceptualization of what makes these disparate groups and individuals a racial community. At one point all the revolutionaries meet to create the governmental and constitutional infrastructure of their planned Black Cuban nation state. Plácido is appointed Director of Civil Government. They decide to embrace "no religion but that which brings us liberty," and to cast off their particular sects and denominations in favor of sharing a common belief in "one God, who is and must be our acknowledged common Father" and "a faith in a common Savior as an intercessor for our sins" (258). Victor Ullman reads this passage as primarily illustrative of Delany's point that "organized religion (as a church, not a faith) . . . is still another deception practiced upon the slave to keep him docile."[19] Embedded in this reading is the idea that a commentary on religion itself is the primary object of Delany's representation of religion. I submit that religion functions here as both means and metaphor for the expression of the revolutionaries' shared political commitment. Their willingness to cast off their religious differences, the statement implies, should parallel their willingness to cast off their color and class differences. In this way, Delany interweaves religion, politics, and race in his delineation of the grounds of this community. He does not advocate in his novel for the complete casting off of Christianity, but rather for living a Christianity that is based on the best interests of the race.

Delany's Plácido is part of the conversation almost every time that the issue of the link between religion, politics, and race is raised in the novel. The theme of religion, and specifically the question of whether religion encourages Blacks' submissiveness or serves as a powerful basis for rebellion (that is, the relationship between religion and politics) is the subject of much debate within Delany's novel. The revolutionaries frequently invoke the name of God and offer up prayers and hymns pleading for strength and liberty. At one point, Plácido is asked "why so many more of our people than the whites attend church," and he replies, "because . . . we are really more religiously inclined than they." The person attempts to take the conversation farther by following the initial question with the statement "I have also often wondered why it was that we are so much more submissive than they" (282).

The ambiguous attitude toward religion expressed by the character Plácido reflects the debate about religion occurring in Black abolitionist circles during this period. Many Black abolitionist leaders were Christian ministers, including transnationally oriented leaders such as James T. Holly.[20] There were other leaders, however, like Frederick Douglass, who viewed Christianity as a millstone placed around the neck of the Black, and White Christians as the very personification of hypocrisy.[21] Delany's Plácido is unwilling to completely negate Christianity or religion. The impromptu poems and hymns that Delany puts in the mouth of his Plácido all evince a strong faith in the God that will help them fight their oppressors and gain their freedom. One of those poems reads

On God and our own strength rely,
And dare be faithful though we die;
But trusting in the aid of Heaven,
    And willing with unfaltering arm,
The utmost power which God had given—
Conscious that the Almighty power
    Will nerve the faithful soul with might,
Whatever storms around may lower,
Who boldly strikes for the true and right. (289, ll. 1–9)

The poem imagines God as the ultimate supporter and protector of the revolutionaries. They are in the right and God is with them. The repetition of the concept of God using three different words (God, Heaven, Almighty) in this poem of only nine lines reinforces the sense that for this Plácido faith in God is and must be a core value of the revolution. Henry, however, seems to be more wary of its potentially deleterious effects and the vile ways in which it has been used by those who oppressed him and his race. Plácido avows that "we would what God wills" (285), but hesitates to fully address the link between submissiveness and religion hinted at by his questioner. Through the theme of religion, and specifically through setting up the contrast between Plácido and Henry on this issue, Delany brings Plácido into the broader Black abolitionist discourse. He implicitly dramatizes a conversation between Plácido and one of those (Douglass or Blyden, for example) who questioned Blacks' naïve embrace of Christianity. Blyden argues that Christianity, because it was introduced to Blacks while they were already "a subject race in a foreign land," has done nothing but make Blacks dependent and submissive: "There is no Christian community of Negroes anywhere which is self-reliant and independent."²² Significantly, Delany has Plácido occupy a position closer to Delany's own than to that of Douglass or even Blyden, further indicating that both Blake and Plácido are his representatives within the pages of the novel.²³

Transnational Vision

Delany spotlights Plácido's awareness of the world beyond Cuba throughout the Cuba section of the novel, emphasizing the scope of his identificatory world, the world of those Plácido considers to be his people. Delany's Plácido is very aware of the political happenings in the rest of the Americas. One of his fellow revolutionaries asks him whether they can hope for help from the Blacks on Cuba's Caribbean "sister islands." Plácido, demonstrating a keen insight into the functioning of power and oppression, points out that those in the British Caribbean, although free, cannot help because their current goals are different from that of the Cubans: "What they most desire is freedom and equality politically, practically carried out, having no objection to being an elementary part of the British body politic" (288). He explains that they are "free and equal under the law" and as such are "a constituent part of the body politic" and therefore "subject alike to the British government and laws which forbid any interference in foreign affairs by any of her Majesty's subjects." His point is that the Blacks in the British Caribbean have become members of the society on paper and are pushing for the practical carrying out of the promise implied in that declaration. He contrasts that situation to the Cuban one, in which "here in Cuba we are the political and social inferiors of the whites existing as freemen only by suffrance, and subject to enslavement at any time." His point is that so long as slavery exists in Cuba, none of the people of color in Cuba can truly be free. In the British Caribbean, by contrast, the people "have all been fully enfranchised." In addition, he points out that in Cuba there is a two-headed proslavery Hydra (Spain and Cuban Creole elites) that they must fight to gain their freedom.

Plácido's compatriot then asks about the probability of help from Haiti. Plácido notes that Haiti is a "noble self-emancipated nation," but that it is not able to help except to offer shelter to those who decide to go there. He does not provide a specific reason or go into any detail as to how he knows that Haiti cannot help. Liberia cannot help either, in Plácido's estimation because its people are "too weak, and too far off," even though they are making "praiseworthy efforts to develop their own nationality, and the stale products of their native Africa" (289). This representation of Plácido as having a broad knowledge of the economic and psychological state of countries and people of African descent across the Atlantic world effectively brings to life the worst fears of proslavery forces. These fears of Blacks who both were aware of the world beyond their own and had a commitment to changing it were exemplified in the sentence against the Escalera conspirators and the official obsession with tracking the migrations of freemen. Through his Plácido Delany plays on these fears.

Delany, Plácido, and Intraracial Difference

Based on the definition of Blackness as a political and ideological position, as well as an identity based on having some African blood, as evident in this section of the text, Delany represents the diversity within the community of people of color in Cuba as a boon to the revolution Blake is fomenting. He repeatedly emphasizes the involvement of people of color from all points on the shade spectrum: "There were still others of the fairest complexion among the quadroons, who were classed as White, that faithfully adhered to the interests of the African race, and were ready at any moment to join them" (247). The fairer revolutionaries are able to act as double agents. In his mind's eye, at least for the purpose of this novel, all the people of color are committed to the goal of freeing "their race" from the yoke of the oppressors. There are many moments throughout the text that reiterate this image. Cubans of color from a variety of levels show themselves to be actively involved in the movement and willing to engage in whatever political action is necessary. For instance, one of the group's acts of defiance is a flouting of the Black curfew ordinance, which stated that "at nine o'clock in the evening, every Negro and mulatto was compelled to be within doors, or if caught out fifteen minutes after to be imprisoned in the calaboose until the sitting of the police court . . . subjected to a fine or whipping" (274).

Delany's narrator tells us that "subsequently to the demonstrations of the Grand Negro Councils, these ordinances were violated and set at defiance by Negroes and mulattoes of all grades and classes, with impunity, passing at all times and places" (274). This section illustrates Delany's image of a broad-based notion of collectivism among people of African descent in Cuba regardless of color or level of mixture. One of these is a servant in the royal palace who proves his mettle by beating up two policemen who try to arrest Blake and Plácido. It is virtually impossible to determine whether these moments represent Delany's actual vision of life in Cuba or his consciously fictionalized utopian hope for Cuba. The point is that, in the Cuba Delany presents in much of the Cuba section of *Blake*, collectivism among many people of African descent, including in the mind of Plácido as the Cuban coleader of the movement, is a given.

There is a tension in the text, however, between Delany's desire to impose that broad conception on all the characters and his recognition of the differences that exist in reality between such individuals and communities. That tension is clearly evident in his decision to make the "orange-peel"-complexioned Plácido the cousin and second-in-command of the unmistakably Black Henry, despite his own professed views of the abnormality and inferiority of mixed race people. Although, as I illustrate in the next chapter, Delany has taken great poetic license in many aspects of his representation of Plácido, he does not make Plácido as phenotypically Black as Henry. Although physical descriptions and representations of Plácido vary in terms of his size, they share the characterization of his skin tone as definitely not dark.[24] Delany, like William Wells Brown, wants to claim Plácido as an exemplary Black man (and race man), but must do something with the reality of Plácido's difference in order to do so. Whereas Brown makes Plácido fit his definition of a Black man (and race man) by (knowingly or unknowingly) representing him as an African-born slave, Delany chooses to make him politically, if not phenotypically, Black.

It is no coincidence, then, that shortly after this physical description of a racially ambiguous Plácido, this same Plácido expresses radical antislavery politics. Delany's Plácido reads to his cousin Henry the poem he has written for a meeting of revolutionaries, in which he not only decries slavery, but also presents slaves' anger and violence against their enslavers as righteous.

The poem is an explicitly political one in which the speaker dreams of killing those who oppress and enslave him. It recalls Brown's depiction of Plácido in its use of violence. It reads, in part,

> Were I a slave I would be free!
>   I would not live to live a slave;
> But rise and strike for liberty
>   For Freedom, or a martyr's grave!
>
> One look upon the tyrant's chains
>   Would draw my sabre from its sheath
> And drive the hot blood through my veins
>   To rush for liberty or death.
> . . .
> Arm'd with the vindicating brand,
>   For one the tyrant's heart should feel;
> No milk-sop plea should stay my hand,
>   The slave's great wrong would drive the steel
>
> Away the unavailing plea!
>   Of peace, the tyrant's blood to spare;
> If you would set the captive free,
>   Teach him for freedom bold to dare. (195–96, ll. 1–4, 9–12, 17–21)

Rather than live in slavery, the speaker vows that he would risk his life in a struggle for freedom. The shades of the Haitian Revolution are clearly present here, as they are throughout the novel, and as they were in Brown's presentation of Plácido. The Plácido who writes the poem, Delany's Plácido, is one who believes in using violence to gain freedom if necessary. In addition, the poem is devoid of specific geographical references and thereby emphasizes the belief of Delany's Plácido that the enslaved and oppressed everywhere share a common condition that binds them regardless of specific national or geographical location.

Significantly, though, the poem does not include any specific racial references, standing in sharp contrast to the repeated emphasis on and explicit naming of "our race" at other moments in the text (discussed above). The primary opposition here is between slavery and freedom, oppression and liberty, and the primary focus is the speaker's claiming of his own humanity. He refers explicitly to his humanity by saying,

> One look upon the bloody scourge
>   Would rouse my soul to brave the fight

And all that's human in me urge
    To battle for my innate right! (195, ll. 5–8)

Inflamed by looking at his chains and his "tortured wife," he would butcher the oppressor and take his freedom. The mention of his wife in a later stanza further emphasizes the humanity focus of the poem:

One look upon my tortured wife
    Shrieking beneath the driver's blows
Would nerve me on to desp'rate strife
    Nor would I spare her dastard foes! (195–96, ll. 13–16)

The vivid image of his wife "shrieking" as she is being beaten emphasizes the speaker's humanity while also highlighting the justifiability of his anger. The racial consciousness of Delany's Plácido as put forth in this poem is an implied one. The greater focus on humanity, and on the overthrow of all tyranny suggests Delany's Plácido as believing that the struggle against slavery is one that is not only, or even primarily, about race as such. The apparent contradiction between this vision and the almost overwhelming focus on his commitment to the uplift of his (and Henry's) own racial community throughout the text reveals Delany's uneasiness with intraracial difference, especially as to whether it can be acknowledged while still claiming race as the grounds for revolutionary action. Robert Levine suggests that Delany intended Plácido's speeches and poems to serve as further validation of Blake's positions, going so far as to say that Delany makes Plácido "into a kind of ventriloquist's dummy."[25] While that is certainly true when Delany has Plácido express the rigid racial beliefs noted above, its veracity becomes more questionable in moments such as this one, where Delany actually grapples in some way with ideological differences within "our race." Although Delany's presentation of Henry as the ultimate race man is unmistakable, he does, at points, put up for debate the centrality of race to identity and political action.

Such moments when they do appear, however, seem to be repeatedly undermined by returns to the reification of race. Immediately after reading the poem to his cousin, Henry, the protagonist of the novel, Plácido speaks in specifically racial terms, albeit about Whites: "though you consider us here free—those I mean who are not the slaves of the white man—I do assure you that my soul as much pants for a draft from the fountain of liberty!" (196). Although, at first glance, this statement seems to be purely in racial terms, it also invokes the language of condition (or status). Here he defines "us" based on condition and "them" based on race. In the poem above, the speaker's battle is for the liberty to which he has an "innate right" (195). Delany's Plácido shifts between a commitment to the betterment of "our race," specifically, and a focus on liberty for all throughout the text. In representing Plácido as having a commitment to both liberty for "our race" and liberty more broadly, Delany acknowledges the complexity of calls for liberty in the Cuban context—a context within which the White Cuban Creoles were demanding freedom from the tyranny of the Spanish Crown at the same time as Cuban slaves were demanding freedom from the White Creoles. He employs that Cuba-specific knowledge in his representation of Plácido, calling attention to differences between those indexed in his use of the term "our race," and more specifically to the particularities of the context within which his Cuban characters of color resided.

The poem was not written by the actual Plácido, but perhaps, as surmised by Floyd Miller, the first editor of the compiled stories known as the novel *Blake* (1970), by Delany himself.[26] (Although this poem is not listed among them, Sundquist notes that Delany also borrowed several poems he ascribes to Plácido in the novel from African American poet James Whitfield.[27]) Although this fact seems to support Levine's statement about Delany's making Plácido into a ventriloquist's dummy, a statement actually made in relation to this particular poem, it does not negate the effect of Delany's choice of the poem (one without explicitly racial terminology) on our understanding of the political ideology of Delany's Plácido and of Delany's Cubans of color. This important moment brings to the fore the tension running throughout the text between sameness and difference within "our race."

Delany actually spends substantial time in the novel parsing the differences between Cuban and U.S. racial infrastructure. Although the novel is based on a presumption of connection between these revolutionaries, a connection that is at least in part a racial one, Delany takes great pains to note differences in ideology and history among those who would participate in Henry's revolution. At one point he has his narrator call attention to differences in the ways people of African descent are identified in Cuba and the U.S. As one part of the plan is beginning to be enacted, the narrator remarks that

among the first few who appeared on the quay was a mulatto gentleman. There was nothing very remarkable about this, because were Cubans classified according to their complexion or race, three out of five of the inhabitants called white would decidedly be claimed by the colored people, though there is a larger number much fairer than those classified and known in the register as colored. To this class belonged the gentleman in question. (238)

Here he states explicitly that many individuals classified as White in Cuba would be "claimed by the colored people" in the United States. Henry has been working as a sailor on board a slave ship that has just returned from Africa with a shipment of slaves, and Plácido, the mulatto who appears on the quay, is secretly helping him delay the auction and organize a mutiny. One of Plácido's major tasks is to spread "news" of the mutinous nature of the captives to discourage speculators from buying them. In addition, he hires fair-skinned people of color as agents for their political cause. They are to pretend to be slave buyers, purchase slaves, and take them to safety. Delany emphasizes these agents' color: "These agents were among the fairest of the quadroons, high in the esteem and confidence of their people, the entire cargo of captives through them going directly into Black families or their friends" (238). By acknowledging differences between racial infrastructures while simultaneously emphasizing common political action, Delany situates Plácido as part of a transnational Black freedom network that cuts across racial infrastructures. He implies here that it is irrelevant whether Plácido and the others are fair, mulatto, classified as White, or classified as colored. What matters is that he and they are part of the push toward the common goal of freedom. Blackness is more about politics than about purity of blood.

Delany's racial logic here recalls, in curious ways, that of the Cuban government's sentence against the Escalera conspirators, and dramatizes the racial nightmare they imagined. Like the officials who wrote the sentence, Delany suggests that differences in color and classification are irrelevant when revolution is the issue. In his novel, as in the *Sentencia*, the *pardos*, *morenos*, and *negros* unite to plan this revolution. Delany's Black Cuban world reflects the diversity and complexity of nineteenth-century Cuba. It is populated by individuals of a wide variety of skin tones, occupations, classes, and origins, from slaves like Henry and his wife Lotty/Maggie who came from the U.S. South, to Cuban Creole slaves like Dominico, to newly captured Africans like Mendi and Abyssa, to "educated, wealthy ladies" like Madame Cordora and her daughter, to the surgeon Pino Golias. All these individuals unite despite their differences in the service of the freedom of all who have African blood. Delany's approach to portraying the character Gofer Gondolier, the palace caterer who can easily be thought of as the most violent figure in the novel given his "Cuban carver," a knife meant not for carving meat but for "carving of a different kind," makes this point powerfully (255). In fact, it is Gondolier who speaks the last and most threatening words of the novel: "Woe be unto those devils of whites, I say" (213). The point that Delany makes through his painting of Cuba is a powerful and clear one—

people of African descent, regardless of their status, color, or national location, should have a common interest in the freedom of all members of the collective.

Despite the novel's predominant leaning toward this vision of Black unity, though, it is still plagued by a tension between unity above all and the representation/recognition of differences similar to that which appeared in the sentence meted out by Cuban officials against the Escalera conspirators. Delany, through his narrator, does acknowledge that these revolutionaries represent a portion of the population, and that in the larger social structure divisions between classes of people of color are made and adhered to:

> The four great divisions of society were white, Black, free and slave; and these were again subdivided into many other classes, as rich, poor, and such like. The free and slaves among the Blacks did not associate, nor the high and low among the free of the same race. And there was among them even another general division—Black and colored—which met with little favor from the intelligent. (276)

Through Plácido and the other Cubans of color, Delany engages the differences between modes of identification, but is always sure to balance that attention with an emphasis on both the African blood that runs through all their veins and the common goal of freedom.

What Is Cuba to Delany and His Plácido?

So far, I have noted the ways Delany has attempted to confront and represent the differences between Cubans of color and African Americans, while also constructing a community based on political and ancestral commonality. Delany's treatment of Plácido's Cubanness illustrates his attitude toward the place of nonracial national identity and difference in his idea of racial community, and more specifically in his conception of a race man. As previously mentioned, Plácido and Henry are represented as cousins. In fact, Henry is, as he puts it, "the lost boy of Cuba" (193). Both Henry and Plácido are Cuban, but they differ in their relationships to their Cubanness. Plácido is tied to Cuba geographically and culturally, whereas Henry simply has his origins there. As if to emphasize the irrelevance of national roots for a real race man, however, Delany strives to make the reader unsure about Henry's Cuban roots. Even though he identifies himself as "the lost boy of Cuba," at another point he describes himself as "African born and Spanish bred" (200). During the section of the text that takes place in the United States, Henry is distinguishable from (what seem to be) his fellow African Americans only by his speech.[28] Henry has no nation but the Black racial nation. As if to reiterate this point, Delany has his wife describe him as "that strange man that came with the Americans" before she speaks with him and recognizes who he is (168). It is the Americans who are described in terms of geographical origin and national identity, not Henry.

In general, Delany constructs nonracial national affinities as irrelevant, and further as hindrances to the enactment of transnational Black community. This point is illustrated on the very first page of the Cuba section, when the first Cuban of color we see is referred to by the narrator as "a *Black* driver" (163; my emphasis). Regardless of whether he is Cuban, from Delany's perspective he is Black in terms of both phenotype and status, and Delany is sure to make that clear. Plácido is Cuban for Delany insofar as he was born, raised, and lives in Cuba and is wholly familiar with the political, social, and cultural dynamics of the Cuban context. From Delany's point of view, though, that Cubanness makes little difference in Delany's representation of what his vision of race might be.

Although we can read the broader Cuban struggle against the Spanish crown into the absence of specific racial terminology from the poems and statements such as these, Delany does not use any words that speak specifically to the link between the fight for abolition and the struggle for Cuban independence. As historian Ada Ferrer notes, the two struggles were interwoven in the minds of many of the *mambises* (fighters) of color who fought and died during the wars for Cuban independence.[29] Delany does, however, have Plácido display nonchalance about the Spanish crown and what the Whites in power consider to be Cuban culture or national events. At one point Plácido informs Henry that the next day will be "the celebration of the nativity of the Infanta Isabella," "a grand national fete" (240). Plácido exhibits no interest in actually celebrating with his countrymen, and instead (along with Henry) sees this day as a prime opportunity to actuate the revolution.

Dana D. Nelson's theorization of the strategic value of being identified with a general class or by one's own particularities is particularly useful for thinking about Delany's treatment of Plácido's Cubanness. Nelson tells the story of White American political leader Benjamin Rush, who has a dream in which he enters a grove filled with African Americans engaged in a religious celebration who are "cheerful and happy," until they see him, that is.[30] He asks them the reason for their great change from happiness to "general perturbation," and they tell him, "we perceive you are a white man." For them, as they go on to explain, his Whiteness, "which is the emblem of innocence in every other creature of God, is to us a sign of guilt in a man." They remind him of the atrocities the Black race has suffered at the hands of his group. As Rush begins to explain himself as a friend and advocate, one of the people recognizes him and calls him by his name and rushes up to embrace him. For Nelson, this dream exemplifies "white manhood's privilege, the liberal franchise of individual exceptionality" (180). She points out that whereas he is "named, particularized, and recognized," we only learn the name of one of the Blacks.

Delany simultaneously particularizes and generalizes Plácido. On one hand, through his construction of Plácido as an individual, exceptional figure, Delany claims this privilege for Cubans of color as well as other members of the African Diaspora. On the other, he does not choose to represent the Cuban particularities that might have resulted in a figure like Plácido having a different view of racial identity from that of Delany (or a figure like Henry), or actually feeling an affinity for La Infanta Isabella. (This possible affinity is discussed in further detail in the next chapter.)

The emphasis on individual exceptionality highlighted in both Rush's dream and Delany's portrayal of Plácido is fundamentally gendered (male). As I noted earlier, the construction, celebration, and/or denigration of a race man—of an individual Black male leader or hero—was a crucial means by which a range of individuals and groups sought to determine the future of the Black race. The exceptional individual is always already male. Nelson's reading of Rush suggests that this ascription of import to a male gendered individual exceptionality is not limited to those seeking to construct a Black community, but is rather a foundational element of the very way in which U.S. individual and national subjectivity have been articulated and enacted. The distinctive point I am making is that, whereas Rush's individual exceptionality is built on the denial of particularity to Blacks, the individual exceptionality of Delany's Blake and Plácido are actuated by way of the alternating negation and recognition of Plácido's Cuban particularities. The fact that Delany's text was created in the service of achieving a stronger and more unified African Diasporan community does not prevent it from replicating approaches to the Other prevalent in other parts of U.S. discourse.

Rush and Delany converge in their gendering of the exceptional individual, in part because Delany is imagining a (Black) nation. As the work of Nelson, Carby, and others has illuminated, the idea that nations are founded by founding fathers—also known as great men—has structured visions of the U.S. nation as well as the Black community. Delany seeks to elevate the Black nation by proving Blake's and Plácido's manhood and greatness—their individual exceptionality. Delany's employment of the trope of the exceptional man reveals the extent to which his pan-Africanist vison is inherently also a battle against White Americans' denial of particularity to Blacks. Delany, like Brown, is seeking to prove Black people's humanity and distinctiveness by illustrating the individual exceptionality of Black men. Although Rush and Delany may seem to diverge in their defining of the masses because Rush's is so clearly racial (White individual and Black masses) and Delany's is so evidently not (Black race men and Black masses), I would argue that they are actually strikingly similar. That similarity resides not only in their common focus on men, but also in their implicit reliance on class in their drawing of the line between the exceptional individual and the masses. Class in Delany's text is understood not simply in terms of status (slave or free), but in terms of manliness—meaning both gentle-manliness/gentility and physically powerful masculinity. Blake and Plácido are the exceptional individuals (the race men) because they are physically and intellectually powerful and politically engaged and genteel, respectively. From Delany's perspective, they are also exceptional men because they are both cosmopolitan and locally grounded.

In the novel, then, cosmopolitanism and the ability to be a citizen of both the world and a specific place are at once valued and gendered. It is not a coincidence that Blake, Delany's protagonist and the most "manly" figure in the novel, is also the most cosmopolitan character. He is, however, a cosmopolite who is also a local. Nothing exemplifies this quality more than his equal comfort in both the U.S. South and in Cuba—part one and part two of the novel respectively. Delany represents Blake as a son of both the U.S. South and Cuba, and as one who is welcomed as such by his brothers and sisters in both sites. He speaks as easily with Mammy Judy, a character in the first half, as he does with the mixed race Cuban woman in the second half. (Significantly, both women are presented as listener-learners who do not quite understand all the dimensions of Black community or the revolution Blake is planning.) Delany's exceptional individuals, then, seek not only to claim the access to individual exceptionality that Nelson argues has been "white manhood's privilege," but also to illustrate the ways in which that individual exceptionality can benefit and lead to the uplift of the entire Black community. Whether Delany's democratizing gesture effectively forces White readers not only to look at the individual and deem him human, but also to look at the broader group remains to be seen.

One of the reasons the potential effectiveness of the gesture is difficult to gauge is that Delany's Cubans function for him in much the same way that the Blacks do for Rush in his dream. Rush's dream functions, Nelson argues, to reinforce the fraternity of White manhood, and "repurify" White manhood. The Blacks are simply the means by which this end is ensured. She contends more specifically that through "altero-referentiality" the community of White men is reinforced: "the recognizing, diagnosing, and managing of 'difference' promised white men a unifying standpoint for national identity."[31] Although the purification aspect of Nelson's argument is not relevant to my discussion of Delany, her point about the use of the other as a means for strengthening community certainly is more so. This theory inspires caution in the lauding of Delany's abovementioned engagements with differences within his "Black community," particularly because his implicit and persistent argument is still that despite those differences they are, in fact, members of one community. Nelson's argument raises the possibility of reading Delany's construction of Plácido as Delany's using the different other to validate his (envisioned) Black community. The particularities of Plácido are relevant to Delany only insofar as they help to advance his vision of racial identity. In order to be a race man from Delany's point of view, Plácido could not have too much of an affinity for Cuba. Nelson makes another point that resonates with what Delany appears to do here. She suggests, in her reading of Herman Melville's *Benito Cereno* (1855), that Delano "achieves 'brotherhood' . . . only by emptying another person and mythologizing her as his (their) other" (17). Delany seems to achieve his vision of Black community by emptying Plácido of his Cubanness and mythologizing him as Henry's mirror image.

Save for one American vernacular and Spanish three-word phrase uttered once ("dis si his'n"), none of the Cubans in *Blake* speak Spanish (175). We are told of Henry's facility with Castilian, but the text contains no Castilian words. At another point the narrator notes that one of the Black men with whom Henry is having a conversation answers him in Creole. There are no such notes about Spanish. The absence of Spanish, particularly when considered alongside the prevalence of African American dialect throughout the text, also provides an interpretive lens through which Delany's treatment of difference can be viewed. No evidence has yet been uncovered by Delany's biographers that indicates definitively that Delany knew Spanish, despite the fact that he championed emigration to Central America.[32] Although this absence is in part attributable to Delany's own linguistic knowledge, the fact that he makes the decision not even to try to represent the linguistic difference between Cuban and U.S. Blacks hints at a willingness to downplay differences in order to maintain the image of the racial whole. Such facts demand a measure of hesitation before celebrating the "truly pan-African diaspora sensibility" of *Blake*, as Gilroy does when he writes, "the version of Black solidarity *Blake* advances is explicitly anti-ethnic and opposes narrow African American exceptionalism in the name of a truly pan-African diaspora sensibility."[33]

The Role of Cuban Particularities in Delany's Revolution

The representation of racial politics and identifications in *Blake* bolsters Delany's threat against those who would oppress people of African blood. A key goal of the radically racialist ideology of Delany's Cuban revolutionaries is to evoke or heighten White (American, Cuban, and Spanish) fears of Cubans of color in particular and people of African descent in the Western Hemisphere in general. The Cuban revolutionaries in *Blake* believe that they have a historical claim to the Western Hemisphere because "the western world had been originally peopled and possessed by the Indians—a colored race—and a part of the continent in Central America by a pure Black race." They inherited this earth "by birth, paid for the soil by toil, irrigated it with their sweat, enriched it with their blood" and therefore have the right to claim it. They decry the occupation of their terrain by Whites who are "there by intrusion, idle consumers subsisting by imposition" (287). Their fight is for their land as well as for their freedom. Delany's representation of Black Cuban revolutionary ideology in this fashion indicates a desire to reiterate that people of African descent everywhere can and will rise up against their oppressors, regardless of their racial classification (mulatto, Black, *pardo*), regardless of status (free or slave), regardless of language or colonial power. His representation seeks to shatter the idea that Blacks in particular places are more or less content than Blacks in other places. This point is significant because Delany's novel was directed at a White audience, as well as a Black one. The extensive, tremendously detailed forays into the minds, conversations, homes, and other private spaces of Whites in this novel illustrate his approach to engaging his anticipated White audience. Delany's goal seems to be to let those who would oppress people of African descent know that he knows what they are thinking and what goes on when they think they are alone. He uses historical detail and historical methodology to achieve this aim. For example, he includes substantial information on American merchants' involvement in the illegal slave trade out of the ports of Havana and New Orleans:

American slave dealers in the Negro brokerages of the Southern states, a number of whom may always be found in Cuba watching the foreign slave trade for the purpose of purchasing souls to drive on their plantations. It is confidently believed upon good authority that the American steamers plying between Havana and New Orleans, as a profitable part of their enterprise, are actively engaged in the slave trade between the two places. These facts, though seen and known by all employees and passengers of such vessels, are supposed to be a legal traffic of masters removing their slaves. (295)

He blurs the line between his novel and a history book in his construction of a fictional account of the arrest of the British Consul in Cuba (294). As discussed earlier in this chapter, those in power in Cuba during that period did feel, express, and act upon the great animosity, even hatred that they felt for the British consul. As the sentence illustrated, they had no fear of accusing him of fomenting rebellion and generally working to bring about the end of slavery in Cuba. He was among those named in the witch-hunt (for antislavery activists) that resulted in the execution of Plácido among many others.

Blake reads as an extended threat to the Whites who oppress Blacks everywhere on the globe. Delany purposely blurs the line between historical and fictional writing in order to inspire fear in an anticipated White audience. He writes, for example, a scene in which someone comes to tell the ruling Cuban Count about the discovery of a possible insurrection in Matanzas. Using an innovative literary technique for blending historical facts with creative license, Delany has the insurrection take place in the dream of a planter's wife. The planter's wife has had a recurring dream in which she is captured and attacked by the rebels. In her dream they take the form of Black serpents, revealing another innovation in this novel—Delany's blending of Afro-Cuban spirituality with Cuban political reality. The snake is a powerful figure in Afro-American religions, as exemplified by the loa Damballah or Danbala in vodou.[34] This scene takes place a few days before the large scale revolution being planned by Blake and his fellow abolitionists is scheduled to take place. Delany's inclusion of this scene speaks to actual historical facts. Specifically, it mirrors the actual Cuban authorities' attribution of sinister motives to the trips taken to Matanzas by the actual Plácido in the days leading up to the day that Cuban authorities marked as the day that the Conspiración de la Escalera was supposed to culminate in large-scale national rebellion. They assumed that he was coordinating plans for the rebellion with people in that city.[35]

Ironically, in Delany's text the Count completely discounts the woman's dream and the threat of potential insurrection contained within it because he saw "no good reasons for detailing at the bedside of a crazy woman a corps of military" and insisted that "it is neither the desire nor the duty of the executive of this colony to carry the national troops in battle array to divert the phantoms of a prostrated maniac" (297). Since the readers of the novel know that Blake and the others are planning a large scale rebellion, they can see that the Count is gravely mistaken in his decision. Delany's imagined White audience would have identified with the Count up until this point. Through this scene he warns them that if they make the same mistake, they will experience the brunt of all the righteous and violent anger Blake, Plácido, and the others have expressed. Delany's evident research and use of historiographical methodology in the creation of this moment in particular, and of his Cuba in general, reinforce the idea that he wanted to write a work of fiction that would be read by his White audience as a documentation of fact.

The historical details, along with the expansive geographical scope of the novel, which includes ports, nations, seas, and peoples from a variety of sites in both hemispheres, are meant to ensure that the global White audience understands that they too are at risk. Delany wants them to know that their Blacks could also be planning this revolution. He wants them to think about the fact that Black sailors like Henry are crossing the seas on merchant vessels, and are not only working for the White captains and slave traders even though they may seem to be. They are also working for their people, carrying information and fomenting multilocational rebellions. Mulattoes like Plácido, who may appear to be happy to have a little of the privilege of being White, may actually be the ones who strike the ultimate death blow. Delany is saying to his audience, you may want to believe that the only radical Blacks are those "voodoo ones" in Haiti, but if you do not want to die, I strongly encourage you to rethink that position.

So, on one level, Delany is employing the Cubans as a synecdoche for all people of African descent everywhere. The fact of their Cubanness is simultaneously pivotal and irrelevant to their symbolic value for Delany. It is crucial because it allows Delany to talk back to the popular White view of Cubans of African descent as at low risk for large scale rebellion because they were divided by a multipartite system of racial classification, and as people who were not as violent as their Haitian neighbors to the east, who had taken their freedom with such violence, or as their Jamaican neighbors to the south, who had used violence to force the British to emancipate them. Their Cubanness is also important because it allows Delany to play on the fears of the Africanization of Cuba that were rampant throughout the nineteenth century. In addition, during this period the U.S. was debating annexation of Cuba, and the Cuban elites were all too willing to acquiesce because the Spanish appeared to be succumbing to British pressure to end slavery on the island. This text speaks specifically to the Cuban situation, warning the U.S. officials to make sure that they really understand the fight that they would be getting into. But in another sense what is important to Delany is that they are a group of people of African descent in this hemisphere who are willing to unite and take their people's freedom by violence. He could just as easily have set the second half of the novel in Brazil during that period, or in any other part of the Americas before emancipation. That novel, however, would certainly not have had the same potential to inspire fear as this one because of the emphasis in contemporary discourse on Cuba in particular, and more generally on the volatility of that Western Caribbean triangle—Cuba the slave society, with free Black Haiti on its right and emancipated Jamaica to its south.

Like the authors of the *Sentencia*, Delany links conflict between Whites to the insurrection of people of color. He does so, however, in a distinctly different fashion and with a markedly different goal. His invocation of intraracial conflict between Whites is meant to point out that such conflict can leave those in power more vulnerable to being unseated. Delany provides keen insight into the politics within the White world, including into the class tensions within the White communities in the U.S. and Cuba. In one chapter Delany reveals the burning anger beneath the uneasy alliance between American planters, Creole elites, U.S. merchants, U.S. governmental forces, and peninsular powers in Cuba. He delves deep into the capitalist, imperialist, and annexationist avarice that underpins the profound hatred between them. We are told of the palpable tension between

the Count [who] was a proud and haughty Castilian, and the planters near Matanzas generally being Americans, a restless dissatisfied class, [who were] ever plotting schemes to keep up excitement in the island, thereby having continual cause for complaint; he hated them as only a member of the Cortez Council could do a colonial "patriot," as the American party termed themselves. (298)

The American planters in the Matanzas region of Cuba continuously filed complaints against the Spanish Count because they believed that as a representative of Spain, a foreign country in their eyes, he had no right to rule them. The Spanish officials, Delany's narrator tells us, ignored them because they believed that these statements were really from U.S. merchants who were eager to annex the Cuban market. The Spanish Captain General and his loyalists bore the American and Creole planters' insolence but were "becoming impatient" and "maturing a decisive course toward them" (298). This statement highlights his focus on not just a White audience, but specifically a White planter audience. He advises them that the same type of revolutionary, rebellious fire and energy that was driving them to rebel against those they perceived as tyrants was also driving those below them. In essence, he shows that the American and Creole planters were in grave danger of attack from both above and below. Through his inclusion of these discussions of the tensions between groups of Whites, and the increasing impatience of those above the planters, alongside a detailed dramatization of the plotting of a rebellion from below, Delany uses a literary text to create a powerful not-so-veiled threat. He uses his novel to warn White planters that if they are not careful they will be crushed to death by forces from both above and below.

Delany goes so far as to represent the workings of violent racism in Cuba, and the ways in which both Cuban elites and American merchants maintain and enforce it. In one instance, a Black man is shot and jailed by officials during the African festival. The next day in court when he is about to testify on his own behalf, the White Americans object to "the testimony of a Negro being taken before White men's" (303). They are permitted to testify first, effectively nullifying whatever testimony he would give and sealing his fate because the law stated that "a slave could not rebut the evidence of a freeman whatever his color." His Plácido experiences it first hand when he is beaten by an American shopkeeper. Before and during the beating the American shopkeeper repeatedly addresses Plácido using the word "Black," calling him a "Black villain," and a "Black rascal." The shopkeeper's unequivocal racial marking of Plácido reiterates Delany's point that, regardless of color, official racial classification, or status all people of African descent are equally subject to the vicissitudes of ruling individuals and groups in a fundamentally racist social structure. Delany further highlights this point by including a footnote mentioning that "a similar circumstance really transpired in Wheeling, Va., between a White man called a "gentleman" and a Black man" (307). In a further illustration of Cuban racism during this period, Delany has "a respectably dressed White man" run to Plácido's aid but decide to leave him to bleed to death "on observing him to be colored" (308).

The ambiguity concerning the value of religion surfaces again when the same man, upon hearing Plácido praying, thinks that Plácido is a preacher and admonishes himself for treating this preacher so badly. He says that he knew several Black preachers in Baltimore and that they were "good religious Black men," "clever Black fellows," and "[knew] their place." Here Delany is commenting on the hypocrisy of the Whites. Ultimately it is that attack on Plácido that incites the revolutionaries to begin their rebellion in earnest. This act committed against one of their most important figures purely because of the color of his skin unites the group in anger and transforms even the "house slave" into the rebel leader who sounds the battle cry of "woe be unto those devils of Whites, I say" (313).

Symbol Versus Subject: Delany's Plácido as Representative Race Man?

At this, the end of the novel, Delany positions Plácido as an object rather than a subject. Plácido becomes the medium through which all come to see the need for revolution, rather than the agent who issues the call to arms. Delany intensifies the threat he issues to Whites throughout the novel by having an attack on Plácido be the impetus for the revolution. The attack on Plácido in the novel mirrors the actual execution of Plácido by officials in Cuba for supposedly heading the Conspiración de la Escalera. The ominous and abrupt ending "woe be unto those devils of whites" suggests that Delany wanted his imagined White audience to live in fear of those who would avenge the death of Plácido and who would strike for their own freedom. This decision on Delany's part and his extrication of Plácido (and Blake, the protagonist) from the culmination of all the planning that they have been engaged in is also significant, because it advises Delany's imagined White audience against believing that there is truly only one leader of a revolution, and by extension that they can extinguish the revolutionary fire by killing one person. He warns that killing one person will probably actually fan the fire. That Delany's Plácido goes from subject/agent to object also speaks to Delany's valuation of Plácido as a symbol for Black revolution not just in Cuba, but more importantly from his perspective throughout the hemisphere. The question, though, is where Plácido the man fits in the symbolic universe Delany has created for the Plácido of his imagination and research. There seems to be little room in these representations of Plácido's racial and political ideology for his agency, and more specifically for his own determination of his racial and political affinities. He was constructed by all these disparate individuals and forces, but all in the service of the particular ideological and/or political aims of the writers. These constructions provide profound insight into the minds of the representers, and more generally into the multiple agents of the construction of racial identity in the nineteenth century, but little into the mind of Plácido, the author. The next chapter addresses just that.

PART TWO

Both (Race) and (Nation)?

The Cuban Negro does not aspire to true freedom, to the culture and happiness of men, to happy working conditions in an atmosphere of political justice, to the independence of man in the independence of the country, to the growth of human freedom in that independence—the Cuban Negro. . . does not aspire to all these things as a Negro, but as a Cuban!

—*Jose Martí,* Patria

He could not understand my conduct as proceeding from other or better motives than that of over-affection for the Haitians. In his eyes I was, from that time, more a Haitian than an American, and I soon saw myself so characterized in American journals.

—*Frederick Douglass,* The Life and Times of Frederick Douglass

A s Part One has shown, the ascription or denial of racial consciousness and national identity constituted a crucial and prevalent element of public representations of people of African descent in the Americas in the wake of the Haitian Revolution. Part Two centers on the attempts by two public figures of African descent to formulate and publicly articulate a definition of self and community while juggling their racial and national affinities. The first figure is Plácido, the individual who was the subject of Part One and who was represented as a race man by the colonial government in Cuba, white U.S. and British abolitionists, and African American abolitionists. The second is Frederick Douglass, an individual often thought of as a "founding father" of African American intellectual and political thought. (See Chapter Four for a more in-depth discussion of the celebration and questioning of the positioning of Douglass at the head of this genealogy.)

Neither individual was free to articulate and define himself publicly as he wished. The context, meaning both the broader context framed by white fear of a repeat of the Haitian Revolution and the specific national context(s) within which they lived, determined not only the referents they could use, but also the relative weight they could accord to each. The epigraphs above begin to provide insight into the expectations that characterized the contexts of Plácido's and Frederick Douglass's decisions about the most appropriate way to index their identities and their affinities without evoking an anger that would put their lives at risk (see Chapter 3 for a more detailed discussion of the timing and context of Martí's statements). The specificities of the Cuban and U.S. contexts shape the bases from which Plácido and Douglass sought to position themselves in relation to racial consciousness and national identity—Plácido by way of Romantic tropes and Douglass by way of American and individual exceptionalism.

Particularly noteworthy, though, is that both the statements construct racial affinity and national identity as opposites or incommensurate with each other. So, despite the fact that they wrote in disparate national arenas, both had to be sure not to risk their (and their people's) access to national citizenship by allowing racial affinities to dominate their discourse. Both, I argue, seek to escape, or at the very least minimize, the impact of that conundrum by representing themselves as profoundly connected to and invested in the local, as well as by engaging the international in ways that reveal their cosmopolitanism but still speak to and from the Cuban or U.S. context. Both men seek to claim national citizenship for themselves and for their racial communities. As these representative epigraphs suggest by positing racial and national affinities as being in conflict, Plácido and Douglass would need to downplay their link to racial community in order to strengthen their case for national identity. The citizenship they seek, however, is always already tenuous because of the dominant (negative) perceptions of their racial communities, and the concomitant negation of those communities' humanity and suitability for membership in the national community. In addition, potential access to that citizenship would be further jeopardized if they tended too much toward an embrace of racial community.

In order to understand their relative weighting of race and nation, we need to examine the particularities of the Cuban and U.S. national contexts. As suggested by the *Sentencia* pronounced by the colonial government in Cuba against Plácido and the other alleged conspirators in the Ladder Conspiracy (discussed in the first chapter), Plácido, as a free person of color, endangered his access to being seen as a fellow gentleman (i.e., as human), and therefore as one who might come to be seen as a Cuban, by choosing to enact community with Blacks. Frederick Douglass sought to make the case for his own and other U.S. Blacks' claim to U.S. citizenship by emphasizing the ways in which he and they shared (and often exemplified) the values of other Americans. His case runs into difficulty, however, when he begins to be viewed by U.S. government officials and media as enacting racially based bonds with non-Americans, in this case Haitians. Plácido and Douglass both resort to cosmopolitanism at points in order to bolster their case for citizenship. At the same time, their relationship to the nation in which they seek to have citizenship is both strengthened and undercut by the world's engagement with them (the representations of Plácido after his death, for example) and their engagement with the world (Douglass's position in Haiti, for instance). The three chapters that follow delve into the contexts, nuances, and implications of Plácido's and Douglass's balancing acts.

On Being Black and Cuban: Race, Nation, and Romanticism in the Poetry of Plácido

As the previous chapters illustrate, in the two decades following his 1844 execution, Plácido, Cuban poet of color and political activist, was held up by disparate forces inside and outside Cuba as the ultimate example of a race man. Officials of the colonial government in Cuba, white European and American abolitionists, and Black abolitionists attributed to Plácido a belief in the predominance of racial consciousness over national identity. This minimizing of national affinity stands in stark contrast to subsequent representations of him. (Even the 1959 revolutionaries claimed him as a consummate Cuban martyr.[1]) This disparity is a result of two distinct but related phenomena—first, a contrast throughout the nineteenth century between people of color in Cuba's relationship to Cubanness and perceptions by others (including the colonial government and non-Cuban White and Black abolitionists)of that relationship, and second, the racial and racist underpinnings of battles over the meaning of Cubanness. As I noted earlier, a fundamental driver of the disparities between approaches to representing Plácido used by the colonial government and by the White abolitionists was a difference in notions of the racial identity of Cuba. The colonial government denied Plácido and the other alleged Ladder conspiracy accused any access to Cubanness, constructing Cuba as ostensibly White, whereas White abolitionist Joseph Soul portrayed Plácido as a beloved son of Cuba who was loved by all Cubans, defining Cuba as a country of color.

Activist, poet, and intellectual José Martí is often revered by forces both within and outside Cuba as a key founding father of the Cuban nation because of his pro-independence writings during the final push for Cuban independence. As Jeffrey Belnap and Raúl Fernández point out, he is actually viewed as "the martyred 'apostle' of the Cuban nation" by both Fidel Castro and the anti-Castro proponents of "Radio Martí" in Florida.[2] In particular, he is inextricably linked to the notion that "a Cuban is more than mulatto, black, or white" and further that any focus on racial particularities under-cuts the strength of the Cuban nation.[3] As the uses of Martí indicate, this idea has continued to undergird discourse on the Cuban nation. This grasp of this presumption on discourses about identity in Cuba, although circu-lating earlier, became stronger during the battles for Cuban independence from Spain between 1868 and 1898.[4] The first war of Cuban independence (1868–1878) began with an armed uprising of Black and White Cubans known as the Grito de Yara. The movement was led by a White Creole sugar planter and slaveholder, Carlos Manuel de Céspedes, who as part of his movement not only freed his slaves, but went so far as to address them as "citizens" and call them to "help 'conquer liberty and independence' for Cuba."[5] Martí's statements were made during the second war, the Little War (1879–1880), just before the third and final War of Independence (1895–1898), while he was leader of the Cuban Revolutionary Party he founded in 1892. His words here are a call to embrace and defend the nascent Cuban nation.

Cubans of primarily African descent were both participants and lead-ers in the wars of independence, making them an integral part not only of the birthing of the Cuban republic, but also, as Cuban historian Fernando Martínez Heredia explicates, of the ideological and philosophical nature of the Cuban nation. To this day leaders such as Antonio Maceo and Juan Gualberto Gómez are held up as fathers of the Cuban nation. Martí himself describes Cuba as the "island where Negroes and white men in almost equal numbers are building a country for whose freedom they have been fighting together for so long against a common tyrant."[6] Martínez speaks to the rhet-orical power of the call put forward by revolutionaries like Martí, noting that "revolutionary policies strongly and effectively summoned the masses of the country to join a general insurrection, creating a truly racially plural move-ment and army . . . [and promoting] the adoption and mass exaltation of nationality."[7] The elevation of nationality above racial identity pronounced by Martí and the other *independentistas* (independence advocates) became a foundational element of subsequent Cuban approaches to self-definition.

Also part of the context in which these approaches were born was rac-ism. Racism was a persistent presence in Cuban society, even during the wars of Cuban independence when individuals like Martí were lauding the irrelevance of race to Cubans.[8] Ferrer notes, for example, the rumors that mulatto *independentista* general Antonio Maceo was fighting not for a mul-tiracial Cuban nation, but for the establishment of a black republic like Haiti.[9] Organizations of people of color were seen by the government as a threat to the island's security, and as a result were frequently the object of repression and monitoring.[10] Céspedes himself backtracked on his initial call for freedom and citizenship for slaves in an attempt to appease other White Creole *independentistas* who feared that Blacks would take over the movement, and by extension Cuba.[11] Both White Creole *independentistas* and Spanish authorities espoused the racist belief that Blacks, should they be freed, would make Cuba into another Haiti.[12] Both also sought to use Blacks' strength to their advantage when necessary, alternately courting and repudiating Blacks in general, and their demand for abolition in particular.[13]

Cubans of African descent therefore had to conceptualize and articulate their identities in a context that included both the presumption that nationality is a more important aspect of identity than race, and the harsh reality of racism. During the wars of independence, insurgents of color cleverly responded to this racist discourse (that constructed any demand for Black rights as an obstacle to the Cuban cause) by constructing White racism and fear of Blacks as the real danger to the Cuban nation.[14] As a result of the complex and multiple discursive and material battles over the character of the nascent Cuban nation that took place during the revolutionary period (1868–98), much of today's scholarly discourse on race and Cuban national identity has focused on the revolutionary period and beyond. Significantly less has been written about the half-century leading up to the revolutionary period. This chapter centers on that period, driven by the belief that the foundations for the conceptualizations of self and nation articulated and enacted in the revolutionary period were laid much earlier through published literary self-articulations. A complex relationship between affinities for what they understood to be their race, for Cuba, and, at times, for the Spanish crown was being negotiated by writers of primarily African descent well before the Grito de Yara.[15] Although the notion of the raceless Cuban nation had not yet fully taken hold, as literary scholars such as William Luis have shown in the early texts, such as White Creole Cirilo Villaverde's *Cecilia Valdés* (1839), in which the authors attempt to work through questions about the relationship between race and Cuban national identity.[16]

Placing Plácido

The penalty of death by shooting in the back: To Gabriel de la Concepción Valdés alias Plácido, named by thirty-two individuals as President of the principal junta, recruiter, instigator, and one of the head agents of the conspiracy. (*Sentence pronounced by the military commission established in the city of Matanzas to investigate the cause of the conspiracy of the people of color*)[17]

These words from the sentence handed down in 1844 by Cuban officials to those who allegedly participated in the Conspiración de la Escalera
pronounce the violent ending to the life of Cuban *poeta de color* Plácido.
The presumed crime here is the crime of trying to end slavery, trying to take
freedom. Hundreds were executed for supposedly plotting to commit this
theft. Plácido was indicted, convicted, and executed for being a leader of this
uprising, one that was spoken of by Cuban officials as being so large in scope
that it included free and enslaved people of color throughout Cuba, as well
as David Turnbull, the former English consul to Cuba, and other English
abolitionists. To this day, many questions surround the supposed conspiracy
and Plácido's role in it. Plácido's travels in the period just before the "discovery" of the conspiracy suggest that he was involved in the insurrection in
some way. Most of the biographies of him note increased travel throughout
Western Cuba, between Havana and Matanzas in particular, during 1843 and
1844, but are hesitant to present those movements as definitive proof of his
involvement. Many scholars, including Frederick Stimson, author of the foremost English language biography of the poet, and Franklin Knight, author of
the seminal text *Slave Society in Cuba During the Nineteenth Century* (1970),
point to questions about whether the conspiracy existed at all, whether it was
the result of the colonial Cuban government's fears of a rebellion like the one
that took place in the neighboring San Domingue (Haiti), or whether it was
all that the government feared that it was. Others, such as Robert Paquette,
state just as unequivocally that the conspiracy did exist.[18]

I argue that it is possible to reconstruct an image of Plácido's relationship to the visions of racial consciousness and national identity evident in
textual representations of him through an analysis of his poetry. My point
is not that the poems are transparent texts that amount to unfettered testimony, but that they suggest an ideology and a particular approach to nego-
tiating political concerns, racial issues, and audience that lend insight into
the history of discourse on the racial character of "Cubanidad." Scholars have
studied the writings of José Martí and other well-known fathers of the
Cuban nation in order to illuminate and comprehend the ideologies upon
which the Cuban nation created by the wars of independence was founded.[19]
I submit that an interdisciplinary critical reading of the poetry of Plácido is
as crucial to understanding Cuban identity and nationalism.

Despite the paucity of direct evidence of his leadership in this insurrection, Plácido has since his execution become, in the eyes of many Cubans
and non-Cubans, then and today, a Cuban symbol of the struggle against

slavery and colonial monarchy. As illuminated in the first chapter, the editors of an 1845 Jamaican newspaper, prominent White abolitionists in Boston, and African American antislavery activists, among others, all referred to the poet as exemplifying the very essence of struggle of people of color in Cuba. What is not clear, however, is the extent of the similarity between the man and the symbol, between his own ideas and negotiations of the gaze of those in power and what others imagine his ideas to be. The striking differences between the romantic airiness of many of his poems and the activist life attributed to him by the Cuban inquisitors and his biographers, as well as between those poems and his widely reproduced angrier "prison poems," I submit, not only raises questions about the value of the symbol of Plácido for different groups, but also spotlights Plácido's own agency in the construction of his public self. This chapter analyzes this issue through an analysis of the conceptualization of Black racial identity and Cuban identity in Plácido's poetry. I explicate the nuances of what Plácido seemed to want people to think about his relationship to other people of African descent and Cubans, and by extension, how he went about creating that perception.

Ideas of Blackness in Cuba

The material conditions in Cuba during the nineteenth century have been documented and detailed by a multitude of scholars and observers from J. G. F. Wurdemann (*Notes on Cuba*, 1844), to Pedro Deschamps Chapeaux (*El negro en la economia habanera del siglo XIX—The Black in the Economy of Nineteenth Century Havana*, 1971), and Herbert S. Klein (*Slavery in the Americas*, 1967). The process of the construction of identity (racial and national in particular) undertaken by the Africans who were brought to Cuba before and during this boom and their Creole cousins, however, is of primary concern here. The approaches to identity born out of those material conditions warrant at least as much scholarly attention as the material conditions themselves.

As the previous two chapters illustrated, people of African descent in Cuba were described as a group by government officials in Cuba, by White English and U.S. abolitionists, and by African American abolitionists using the terms Black, of color, and African. All three entities/groups presumed racial identity to be the primary basis of connection between the group members. The Black identity ascribed to them, and to Plácido in particular, by African American abolitionists is of particular interest here because it simultaneously constructs and presumes a connection between the racial identities of African Americans and people of African descent in Cuba, assuming, in particular, that people of African descent in Cuba share African Americans' relationship to the concept of Black identity.[20]

Blackness, as I am using it here, has two elements. The first is the embrace of a fundamental connection between people of African descent, based on that descent. The second is the belief that the destinies of all people of African descent are linked, both because of their origin and because of their common experience of racist oppression. This definition comes out of the presumptions of unity and connectedness that have long permeated discourses on people of African descent. In the previous chapters, I explicated the conceptualizations of Black community that were ascribed to Plácido by the government in Cuba, by English abolitionists, and by African American abolitionists. The fundamental elements that these conceptualizations had in common was the valuing of race as the primary mode of defining self and community and the belief in a transnational linkage between people of African descent. Contemporary scholars continue to attribute similarly sweeping notions of Blackness to people of African descent across the globe during the nineteenth century, including those in Cuba.[21] However, I wish to urge caution in the ascription of such approaches to racial identity to prerevolutionary Cubans of African descent.

Doubtless Cuba had (and has) a significant African-descended population. That fact, however, does not necessarily mean that the grounds of community were defined in racial terms by all or even most people of African descent. Their common continental origin did not automatically lead them to consider themselves part of the same community. Former slave Esteban Montejo, for example, distinguishes definitively between Lucumí, Congo, Mandingo, and Carabalí people (in terms of appearance, culture, and behavior) and points out the way those distinctions were maintained in the slave community. He is sure to emphasize the peculiarities of each group: "In the plantations there were blacks from different nations. Each one had its own traits. . . . The Mandingos were slightly reddish-colored. Tall and very strong. . . . I swear on my mother's grave they were crooks and a bad bunch. They always went their own way."[22] From their arrival in Cuba in the sixteenth century, Africans in Cuba formed powerful organizations (similar to Masonic organizations) called *cabildos*, whose beliefs, rituals, and mode of operation clearly reflected the members' particular cultural and ethnic origin. For example, according to historian Philip Howard, one of the best-known organizations, the Cabildos Secretas de Abakua, has continued the reverence of the leopard held by its foreparents, the Ekoi people.[23]

New forms of community were also developed and enacted by people of African descent on the island, particularly by Creole (or Cuban-born) people of African descent. One new form was a notion of community based on valuing shared continental origin, skin color, or common oppression. An illustration is the founding of racially based mutual aid organizations that did not have connections to a specific African ethnic group. These organizations, which Howard describes as "Pan-Afro-Cuban," were primarily formed during the revolutionary period (1868–98), as the government of Cuba began to increase restrictions on *cabildos*, including prohibiting Creole blacks from joining (151). The government initially supported the development of these organizations because it saw them as a safe alternative to the too politically active *cabildos* (151).

The place of the idea of racially based community in the discourse of people of African descent in the six decades preceding the revolutionary period is not so clearly evident. As a result of the government's fear of uprisings, and by extension of any politically oriented organization that linked those it dominated, documentary evidence of the existence of "Pan-Afro-Cuban" organizations in those decades is rare. Evidence of many antislavery rebellions and insurrections, however, lends insight into the interaction between understandings of community. For example, the Aponte uprising in 1812, one of the broadest antislavery conspiracies ever discovered by the government on the island, was organized and led by Aponte, a respected member of a powerful African-centered secret society who united diverse groups of *cabildos* from all over the island in pursuit of the common goal of rebellion (75). The conspiracy illustrates the presence of notions of community founded both on particular African ethnic origin and on common oppression based on race.

The coexistence (due to the continued importation of Africans onto the island) of Africans and Creole people of African descent well into the nineteenth century makes the issue of racial identity and community in Cuba, perhaps more than any other American country during this period, a complex one that demands the avoidance of simplistic assumptions about the meaning of terms such as "Black," "of color," "African," "Afro-Cuban," and "community" to people of African descent. The rebellions suggest that there was a sense of connectedness present among people of African descent in Cuba, but one cannot assume that they all shared the same conception of the terms of their connectedness.

The specific terms that were used by those in power to describe people of color were *pardo, moreno/mulato,* and *bozal,* each indicating a proportion of African to Spanish blood, and by extension a certain level of civilization. Of the three, the *bozal* had the most African blood (100 percent) and the *pardo* the least (and the most visible Spanish blood). Creoles and people who had just been brought from Africa, called *bozales,* were variously seen by those in power as part of one undesirable group and as separate groups, made up of those who are "more civilized, like us" and "barbaric savages." As discussed in the previous chapter, the sentence pronounced against the Escalera conspirators decries the "uniting of the mixed-bloods and the Blacks to exterminate the whites" while also distinguishing between the groups in the attribution of motivations.[24] Wurdemann, for instance, expresses a belief that the free people of color, because they have become educated and have elevated themselves to a higher level of intelligence and industriousness than the others of African descent would "join the whites in any insurrection among the slaves."[25] He describes the *bozales* as so completely lawless and uncivilized that they have to be muzzled, clearly setting them apart from the more civilized free people of color (249). Tellingly, he points to the *bozales'* willingness to turn on each other as evidence of their barbarism: "They bring with them from Africa all their original animosity against each other" (257). This statement belies his earlier, seemingly positive remarks on the civilized free people of color. They have, in fact, not progressed and continue to share the same barbaric trait as the *bozales.* He actually speaks of the free people of color's presumed willingness to join with the Whites as born of and illustrative of "the little sympathy that the African races show for each other" (250).

Implicit in Wurdmann's simultaneous decrying and lauding of the traitorous tendencies of both the free people of color and the *bozales* is an assumption that they should be loyal to each other, and that they should feel connected to each other because of their common racial heritage. (If he is correct in his identification of this trait, it is clear that neither the *bozales* nor the free people of color shared his belief.) We cannot assume, because of the prevalence of the dominant discourses' terminology and racial reasoning, that people of African descent completely embraced these approaches to defining themselves and their community. In making this point, I am calling attention to the distinction between the ways in which people are identified by others, the ways in which they identify themselves, and the terms they use to communicate that identification or identity.

Certainly, the numerically dominant presence of people of African descent as compared to Whites produced a population and a culture with significant Africannesses in appearance as well as culture.[26] So pervasive was African-based culture that Whites even joined the African religious organizations created and run by Blacks.[27] It is also important that these Africannesses were often claimed and embraced by Creoles. The point here is that practice of an African-based culture does not necessarily equal an embrace of Blackness per se. Africanness is not the same as Blackness. From the early period into today there have existed in Cuba a wide variety of organizations and societies, religious and less explicitly so, that have been tremendously active in maintaining African-originated cultural practices and pushing for the rights of Cubans of African descent. As mentioned above, there have also been and continue to be organizations, primarily formed during the 1880s, that self-identify as Black organizations.[28] Olivia Hevia Lanier identifies 140 such organizations in her *El directorio central de las sociedades negras.*[29]

Thus, to say simply that Cubans of African descent were Black, and to leave the discourse there, misses the complexity of the racial identity in general, and of the historical relationship to the sign of Blackness in particular, in Cuba. This statement is especially true of the articulation and representation of racial identity in general and Blackness in particular in literary texts. Teasing out that relationship in nineteenth-century texts is especially challenging because of the multiple powers (e.g., colonial government, anti-slavery White Creoles) that the writers had to please, not just to be published, but also to avoid the very real possibility of physical harm. An ex-slave writer like Juan Francisco Manzano, another poet of color with whom Plácido was frequently confused and who is the subject of the final chapter of this volume, had to please Domingo del Monte, the Cuban patron who encouraged him to write his autobiography, the English abolitionist Richard Madden, who brought his poems and life to the world beyond Cuba, as well as his fellow people of color, some of whom (Plácido in particular) perceived him as a "sell-out."[30] He also had to satisfy his own wishes as an artist to have his artistry recognized. His Arabesque play, *Zafira*, points to an attempt to escape being locked into being read based on slavery-related content rather than artistry.[31] The play also illustrates the familiarity with and in some cases connection to Spanish culture and history that Black intellectuals in Cuba during this period often had. Plácido's poetry reflects the use of this Spanish "colonial library." Manzano's writing evinces an ambivalent and ambiguous relationship to Blackness. As will be discussed later, in the autobiography he separates himself from "los negros," whereas in his poetry he expresses a sense of connection to his people, the oppressed Blacks. Even though Plácido was born free, his literary representation of race and of his relationship to the sign of Blackness are no less complicated.

Plácido's Life

There is consensus among Plácido biographers and nineteenth-century Cuban observers on key points: (1) the slave population in Cuba was increasing exponentially as more slaves were being brought in to feed the boom in the Cuban sugar-based economy; (2) the colonial government was cognizant and deathly afraid of the real possibility of rebellions like the one on the neighboring island in San Domingue, given the population ratio; and (3) the abolition of slavery in the British colonies in 1833 increased the colonial government's fear while also creating pressure on Spain to move toward abolishing slavery. (Spain actually signed a treaty with England promising that it would cease its African slave trade by 1820.) A logical conclusion, embraced by several scholars, is that the colonial government latched on to what may have been an isolated rebellion and used it as an opportunity to spread its anti-abolitionist net as widely as possible. Regardless of the details of the conspiracy, though, the fact is that Plácido was executed by firing squad on June 28, 1844. Although before that point Plácido was an important figure on the Cuban literary and political scene, on that date he became more powerful and dangerous than he could have ever been alive.

There is debate about many of the details of Plácido's life. The absence of certitude in terms of the Conspiración de la Escalera itself ironically mirrors the fact that many questions remain unanswered, and perhaps unanswerable, about Plácido's life, about the veracity of the stories told by those who have written about him, and about the authorship of his most widely read and reproduced poems, his "prison poems," said to have been written while he awaited execution. Although several biographies of him have been written there is disagreement between the authors in several areas, particularly between the nineteenth-century biographers.[32] These disparities are in several cases the result of the confusion of Plácido with Juan Francisco Manzano, as discussed in Chapter 2. There is significantly less disagreement among mid- to late twentieth-century biographies.[33] The most recent full-length biography is Jorge Castellanos's 1984 study; recent articles on Plácido's poetry by Vera Kutzinski and Enildo García also include substantial biographical data.[34] The most detailed information comes from the 1984 edition of the *Diccionario de la literatura cubana* (1059–62).

Plácido was born free in Havana in 1809 of the "amores clandestinos" or "secret love" between a White ballerina, Concepción Vazquéz, and a mulatto barber/hairdresser, Diego Ferrer Matoso. To hide their relationship, he was left by his mother on the doorstep of the House of Benificence and

Motherhood within a few days of his birth.[35] His father, however, rescued him from the house a few months later. He wrote his first poems at the age of twelve, despite only a few sporadic periods of official schooling. Like Benjamin Franklin and Marcus Garvey, interestingly enough, he became an apprentice to a printer, and through this position he made many connections with the members of Cuba's literary circles. As one might expect of an apprenticeship, the job did not pay well, so Plácido decided to use his artistic ability in a more lucrative fashion, making tortoise-shell hair combs.[36] He became quite successful and moved to Matanzas, where he began to study literature more seriously with the support of the contacts he had made while at the printer.[37] While in Matanzas he fell in love with the woman who would remain the great love of his life, a Black woman named Rafaela. He mourned her death through his poems, including the well-known "La Siempreviva" (the everlasting flower).[38] As more of his poetry was published, he began to be invited to special events sponsored by Cuba's literati and became a regular contributor to key literary magazines, including *La Aurora* and *El Pasatiempo*.[39] His increased connections with the literati, many of whom were anticolonialists and antislavery activists, led to increased surveillance by the Spanish colonial authorities. It was perhaps this greater visibility that led to his being arrested for presumed participation in the Conspiración de la Escalera.[40]

While it is clear that slaves in Cuba during this period were planning and enacting rebellions, as slaves throughout the Americas had since the inception of New World slavery, the evidence linking the Cuban rebellions in 1844 to each other is sparse. Given this fact, scholars, including Itzhak Bar-Lewaw, author of one of several Spanish language Plácido biographies, have tended to focus less on trying to prove the actuality or scope of the conspiracy than on speaking to the function that the presumption of such a broad movement, and the concomitant leeway to arrest and execute antislavery activists, served for the colonial government in Cuba.

Plácido and Race

As illustrated in Chapters 1 and 2, disparate nineteenth-century texts ascribe to Plácido a broad understanding and embrace of racial solidarity. Given these representations, it is significant that race and the idea of Blackness appear rarely, if at all, in his poetry. Consequently, looking for Plácido's conception of race and the idea of race-based solidarity that would have led him to organize a conspiracy like the Escalera is a daunting task, to put it mildly. But it must be undertaken, I am convinced, if we are to continue the work of finding his voice in the sea of discourse about his participation.

The difficulty inherent in the process of recovering his voice on this issue is illustrated by the disparities concerning the first word of one of his prison poems, "La Fatalidad" (Destiny or Ill-Fortune).[41] The opening words are variously represented in collections and biographical studies as "Ciega Deidad" (Blind Divinity) and "Negra Deidad" (Black Divinity).[42] While this difference likely arose from an illegibility in the original text, it exemplifies the search for Blackness per se in Plácido's poetry. Very few modern day editors of Plácido collections note the difference, and none of the editors or writers who do note it comment on its significance or indicate how the difference may have arisen. The difference between "blind" and "black" in this poem I contend is of great import. The meanings of the two beginnings are essentially opposites. One suggests that Plácido believed in a Black God/god/ divinity/deity and immediately bolsters the notion that he was Black-centered, as those I have discussed above represented him. The other suggests a belief in or desire for a color-blind God/god/divinity/deity.

An argument could be made as to why either one is in keeping with the image of Plácido in the sentence, but only one, "negra deidad," is in keeping with the African and Black race-centeredness suggested by the letter to the editor of the Jamaican newspaper and the texts of Brown and Delany. Significantly, one of the collections in which this version appears also has international origins—a collection of the complete poems of Plácido published in Paris in 1862. The other collections/biographies in which "negra deidad" appears are Antonio López Prieto's *Parnaso cubano*, a critical anthology of poems by a range of Cuban poets published in 1881, Bar-Lewaw's *Plácido: vida y obra*, published in 1960, and Cintio Vitier's 1962 edited collection *Los poetas romanticos cubanos*.[43] The chronological disparity in all these texts negates any interpretation of the appearance of "negra deidad" as related to the exigencies of a specific historical moment. The phrase seems to be simply a consequence of the particular source used by the creators of the collection of poetry (a source not identified by them) rather than of any desire to represent Plácido's racial or political ideology in a specific way. The idea that such choices are devoid of politics, however, is implausible particularly within the context of long tug-of-war between scholars and observers in and outside Cuba over Plácido's image, ideology, and identity.

There is a tension between the fiercely racialist leader presented in the *Sentencia* and the abolitionists' writing and the peaceful, color-blind racial poet who is said to have written "ciega deidad." Two logical interpretations of this tension are that Plácido himself chose to racialize this poem and the editors chose to deracialize it, or that Plácido did not racialize the poem and the editors decided to racialize him. Both are plausible because, as I have mentioned, many of the texts written about Plácido ascribe a sense of racial solidarity to him, but most of his poems do not explicitly mention race, suggesting that he may have made a conscious decision to downplay this aspect of his identity. A deracialized Plácido, particularly during the revolutionary periods of 1868–198 and 1959, would have been a valuable symbol of national identity and sacrifice. Within the context of the ideal of a color-blind nation popularized by José Martí among others, a deracialized Plácido would make a perfect symbol of martyrdom for the broader Cuban fight against Spanish domination. In the later revolutionary period a deracialized Plácido would similarly emblematize the strength of the raceless Cuban nation.

The import of decisions about how to print this line, and by extension the fact that Plácido was and is a battleground upon which battles over racial identity in Cuba continue to be fought, becomes even clearer upon analysis of the content of the poem. The deity in Plácido's poem is merciless, surrounds him with painful thorns at birth, seeks to prevent him from rising to greater heights, and resides in hell. The content does raise several significant issues. Certainly, the attribution of such negative characteristics and behavior (whether by Plácido or the editors) to a black divinity is congruent with the ideas about the link between evil and blackness that had long been circulating in the West. In that context, the ascription of those negative traits to a blind divinity would be the more antinomian approach. If we believe that Plácido took that approach, as most of those who have written on him or edited collections of his poems do, it reinforces the idea of him as a radical who sought to subvert the racist discourse that dominated Cuban society. As such, Plácido foreshadowed Martí's idea of a Cuban nation in which race was irrelevant, expressing that idea several decades before Martí did, and before even the shout that began the 1868 Cuban war of independence. Unfortunately, though, because of the disparities in the reproduction of these lines we do not know for sure which of the phrasings Plácido wrote. That most of the texts on Plácido print "blind" strongly suggests that "ciega deidad" was his phrasing, but the existence of the other phrasing demands caution. An analysis of the place of race in his broader oeuvre promises to be a source of a nuanced vision of his perception of his own racial place and his negotiation of the racial discourse of his time.[44]

The Love Poems

Plácido does mention race, or at least color, in several of his love poems, particularly those that use the Cuban landscape as metaphor.[45] In the poem in which he casts off his White lover, Celia, Plácido describes her beauty as "como la nieve, deslumbrante y fría" (like the snow, dazzling and cold). He bemoans the fact that he does not find in her "la extrema simpatía / que mi alma ardiente contemplar procura/ni entre las sombras de la noche oscura / ni a la esplendida faz del claro día" (the profound sympathy/ that [his] passionate/burning heart muses over finding / [but does] not between the shadows of the dark night / nor in the resplendent beginning of the clear day). He ends the poem by saying that he wants to kiss "una deidad de llamas" (a goddess of flames) and to embrace "una mujer de fuego" (a woman of fire).[46] The racial undertones in his use of day and night and hot and cold are even clearer when the poem is read in light of the fact that his greatest love was a Black woman (Rafaela) whom he mourned until his death.

In the poem "La flor de la caña" (Cane Flower), Plácido uses the distinctively Caribbean metaphor of the cane flower to praise the beauty of a Cuban woman of color working in a sugar cane field. Claudette Williams rightly identifies this poem as a sign of the birth of a "Caribbeanized discourse" that resulted from the reformulation of the "Romantic ideal" in Caribbean terms.[47] Plácido speaks of the woman as a "trigueña tostada" (a toasted/tanned/wheat colored/brown woman)

que el sol evidioso	who the sun, envious
de sus lindas gracias,	of her beautiful graces
o quiza bajando	or perhaps coming down
de su esfera sacra,	from its sacred sphere
prendado de ella	out of being taken with her
le quemó la cara.[48]	burned her face.

The poem is certainly reminiscent of contemporaneous Western European modes of idealizing female beauty. The infusion of Cuban terminology and elements into the poem, the hot sun and the term *trigueña*, distinguishes it from European and North American forms. The poem is also distinguished by its class orientation, more specifically its focus on a woman who works in the fields. Her complexion is clearly not alabaster, and could not possibly be, both because she works in the fields and, the poem suggests implicitly, because she is of Cuba, a land of the sun that burns people brown (that is, a racial mixture). The poem represents the transformation of the White

European and North American poetic ideal (the alabaster woman) by virtue of being in the Cuban sun, by being racially mixed, and by being at the bottom of the Cuban sugar economy.

This reading reflects a partial disagreement with Vera Kutzinski's interpretation of this *trigueña* as an index of "the fact that legal practice in nineteenth-century Cuba tended to 'darken' white women desirous of interracial alliances," essentially reading her as a slightly darkened image of the alabaster ideal. Although Kutzinski also notes, rightly, that the poem seeks to question Cuban racialist ideology by highlighting the "messy historical foundations" of Cuban culture, she surmises that his use of the word *trigueña* (light brown woman) "does not definitively establish the woman's identity as nonwhite," but leaves it "undetermined."[49] Plácido's emphasis on her color and the marked disparity between the alabaster ideal and his *trigueña* do identify her as nonwhite. The alabaster ideal does not exist in this poem, replaced by this light-brown-skinned laborer, this sugar cane flower who works Cuba's tobacco. Through her, Plácido illustrates that the alabaster ideal is not and cannot logically be a child of Cuba, represented here by the sun, the tobacco, and her class status. Plácido's cognizance of race, or at least of color, is evident here. He clearly presents a positive view of brown skin, and believes it to be worthy of the sun's envy and/or adulation. He clearly sees color, and seeks to recuperate the woman of color and subvert the more dominant negative discourse about her. That approach suggests an understanding, on Plácido's part, of the way in which racial identification and racist discourse converge in the Cuban context. He perceives himself as being involved in political and ideological battle over understandings of the value of (people of) color.[50] What is not made clear in the poem, however, is whether that consciousness translates into an embrace of Black racial solidarity as such.

In another poem, entitled "Flor de café" (Coffee flower), the poet refers to his own color as well as to the color of his beloved. By most accounts, Plácido was very light skinned and could almost pass for White.[51] He says:

Quiéreme, trigueña mía   Love me, my brown
y hasta el postrimero día   and until the last day
no dudes que fiel seré   don't doubt that I will be true:
tu serés mi poesia   you will be my poetry
y yo tu flor de café.[52]   and I your coffee flower.

His use of the coffee flower, a white flower that comes from and later produces dark fruit, as a metaphor to describe himself is especially fascinating because through that reference he speaks simultaneously to his white appearance and his dark heritage. Here we have a naming of his own position on the color spectrum, and by extension an indication of the fact that he was not colorblind or "ciega" like the deity in "La Fatalidad." It is significant also that he identifies himself as a coffee flower, while identifying the *trigueña* in the previous poem as a tobacco picker.[53] William Luis's analysis of the social values and history implicit in tobacco, coffee, and sugar, an analysis that takes place in dialogue with Fernando Ortiz's *Cuban Counterpoint: Tobacco and Sugar*, is particularly helpful here. Both texts suggest that the crops discussed were more than just crops, but also important reflectors of social relations in Cuba and key means through which social issues and identities were worked out. These analytical frameworks allow for deeper study of Plácido's linking of himself and his personas to particular crops.

Luis argues that tobacco and coffee sought to unseat sugar as the core of the Cuban economy in the nineteenth century. The insurgent crops were produced by gentler means than sugar and created different social relations: "Sugar promotes total control and latifundism, but coffee supports tolerance, and tobacco independence and liberty."[54] Ortiz viewed tobacco as "a symbol of sovereignty, and the island's contribution to the world's economy."[55] Read in that sense, Plácido, the coffee flower, and his tobacco picking *trigueña* are connected by their links to insurgency.[56] This insurgency, this struggle for different social relations in Cuba, binds them more profoundly to each other, as Plácido represents them, than does race as such.

It is telling, though, that Plácido does not mention the race of the love of his life, Fela, in any of the many poems about her. Frederick Stimson, one of the most careful Plácido biographers, describes Fela, based on his research, as the child of a slave and Black/*negra*.[57] He also refers to a nineteenth-century characterization of her as the "Ethiopian Venus."[58] In addition, none of Plácido's poems celebrate a *negra* (a black Black woman, as opposed to a *trigueña* (a brown Black woman). This omission suggests that he was willing to make racial references when talking about women who were not as important to him as his Fela. In the Fela poems he continues to use the Cuban landscape but without the explicit references to color. In "Egloga Cubana" (Cuban eclogue) he writes

Cuando Fela con ceno mira airada,	When Fela frowns in anger
turbado bate el mar la arena muda,	the perturbed sea beats the mute sand
la pradera de flores salpicada	the meadow of flowers is spattered
el bravo cierzo con furor desnuda	the fierce cold northerly wind denudes in fury

y el sol tras numbe densa y dilatada	and the sun behind it dense and dilated
su carro esconde y su camino duda;	its carriage hides and its pathway doubts;
pero si luego rie, en el momento	but if then she laughs, in the same moment
brilla el sol, calma el mar, serena	the sun shines, the sea becomes calm, the
el viento.[59]	wind becomes serene.

Seeking answers to the question of the significance of his choice here with respect to naming race or color could well shed light on Plácido's conception of race. One possible reason for the choice is that he loved Fela so much that he did not see her race or color as he saw the race or color of the other women. This recalls the color-blind "ciega deidad" referred to earlier. It would be difficult to say that his nonmentioning of race in his Fela poems is a pure reflection of his recalcitrance about mentioning race in general. After all, he does mention it in the poems about the other women. This choice is better read as evidence of Plácido's connection with romanticism, both European and Cuban, and particularly the use of nature as a way to speak to the universal elements of human existence and emotions.[60] By focusing on nature and linking her so clearly to its movements and vicissitudes, Plácido makes Fela into the ultimate romantic heroine: "the idealized woman is pure idea—a flat character who appears in plots or poems because of her symbolic force, not because of any value that might be attributed to her individual psychology."[61] Spanish Romantic poet José de Espronceda's "A Matilde" ("To Matilda") exemplifies this approach: "Tal, Matilde, brilla pura / tu hermosura celestial; / y es más cándida tu risa / que la brisa matinal" (Matilde, brightly does your celestial beauty shine, and your laugh more true than the morning breeze).[62] John Rosenberg notes that in the writing of Espronceda's fellow romantic Gustavo Adolfo Becquer, "the feminine . . . is a reduction and distillation of woman that has little to do with the corporeal or psychological reality of women he might have known."[63] Although the Fela of the poem is clearly modeled after Placido's love Rafaela, distinguishing his treatment of her from the Becquerian approach, the language he uses to describe her elevates her above and beyond the earthly realm. Plácido's Fela is almost supernatural, like William Blake's "Evening Star," who "washes the dusk with silver" and protects the sheep with her "sacred dew."[64] Race is part of the earthly realm, and therefore of the world from which he detaches her in order to celebrate her to the fullest possible extent.

Blake's "The Little Black Boy," Emerson's writings on slavery, and contemporary scholarship by Debbie Lee and Helen Thomas illustrate that race had a significant presence in U.S. and British Romantic thought.[65] As Lee points out, though, British Romantic engagements with the racial other reveal an inherent conflict between self-interest and self-sacrifice, between the self that is "distanced from its own ego" and exists "for the other," and the "confident, expanding" British self.[66] As a result, alterity was a fundamental element of the Romantic imagination. Cuban writing was similar in terms of its focus on personal freedom and its engagement of alterity. In the Cuban case, however, the other of Romantic poetry was often the indigenous people of the Americas.[67]

Explicit references to color difference and Blackness as they existed or functioned in the Cuba of the day, however, are absent from the poetry of Plácido's Cuban mentor and friend, fellow *siboneista* José María Heredia.[68] A more typical way of representing women in love poems is exemplified by Heredia's poem "A mi esposa" (To My Wife), a poem replete with images of fires, storms, and other natural elements. He speaks of dedicating the burning fires of youth in his veins and songs and "the tempestuous eagerness of his passions" to his wife, of love "inflaming our pure hearts," of his being "lost in the turbulent seas."[69] Even when Heredia blends his passion for the woman and his passion for Cuba, as he does in "A Emília" (To Emilia), he uses natural phenomena and elements rather than race or color to represent Cuba.

As Vera Kutzinski and Frederick Stimson have emphasized, Plácido is a Romantic poet and must be read as such. His sporadic use of explicit racial terms is a function, then, of the meeting between Cuban racial infrastructure detailed earlier in this chapter and his material and/or stylistic connections to other Romantic poets, including both his use of nature, his evocation of an idealized feminine ideal—particularly in his ethereal representation of Fela, and the ambiguous approach to race exemplified by the blind-Black divinity debate. His status as a Romantic poet, and by extension his affinity for the conventions of European, American, and Cuban Romantics with respect to race, however, does not negate the possibility of his also articulating a racial politics or being committed to racial solidarity. Kutzinski, in her comparative article on African American writer Jean Toomer and Plácido, argues convincingly that both writers, despite their complicated relationships to "Blackness" as such, comment "subtly but incisively on the sentimental commodification of 'blackness' in the literary and nonliterary discourse of their respective societies."[70] Toomer's *Cane*, a collection of short stories on the South and on migration north, includes some of the most beautiful and vivid ever written.[71] His desire not to be limited or read only in racial terms does not make them any less so or make him any less worthy of or interested in inclusion in *The New Negro*, the inaugural literary collection of the Harlem Renaissance. It is simply that his desire must be factored into readings of his work. Similarly, Plácido's romanticism is a key factor to consider in the process of trying to uncover his views about race because it determines the poetic codes through which he writes. A cognizance of his literary school reminds us to look behind the metaphors of love, native, and nation.[72]

Nation Poems

The valuation of national identity in Plácido's poetry also provides some insight into his views about race, and about Black racial solidarity in particular. W. E. B. Du Bois's concept of double consciousness speaks to the challenge of balancing race and nation confronted by Blacks in the West. That concept is based on the presumption of an imposition of or a belief in a divorcing of racial and national affinities. The extent to which that was (or is) true in Cuba, and for Plácido in particular remains to be seen. On one hand, Plácido loved Cuba and sincerely wanted the best for his nascent nation.[73] Castellanos avows Plácido's nationalism and ties it to the European and American Romantic tradition of "nacionalismo intenso" (intense nationalism), "patriotismo profundamente sentido y vigorosamente expresado" (a profoundly felt and vigorously expressed patriotism).[74] He writes, "Plácido amaba a Cuba con hondísima pasión" (Plácido loved Cuba with a tremendously profound passion). This affinity for his home is evident in the numerous poems about a range of aspects of Cuban culture, history, flora, and fauna.[75] "Los dos gallos" (The Two Roosters), for example, is an improvised poem about a cockfight, a favorite pastime of nineteenth-century Cubans in general and of Plácido in particular, written in the voice of the victorious rooster.[76] The poem "Al Yumurí" is a celebration and prayer for the Yumurí River in western Cuba. He praises it for its "fina y brillante arena" (fine and bright sand) and imagines its history, thinking that perhaps at one time "un joven indio / del continciñio en la hora / te atraveso recitando / amantes y dulces trovas" (a young indigenous boy / in the dead of night / crossed you reciting / loving and sweet verses).[77] His poem "Al pan de Matanzas" (To the pan of Matanzas) uses the classical figure to celebrate his hometown, Matanzas, and his beloved country, Cuba. These poems certainly illustrate the profound, intense passion noted by Castellanos.

On the other hand, though, Plácido also uses the nation as a reverse synecdoche for people of color. As mentioned earlier, Cuban elites were fighting for liberation from Spain at the same time that Cubans of color were battling those same members of the elite for their own freedom. Plácido employs the rhetoric of the elites' fight against Spain to implicitly call for liberty for all Cubans. He does this in poems dedicated to the monarchs as well as poems directed to his fellow Cubans. The poem "Habaneros libertad!" exemplifies the latter. Plácido writes:

¿O somos libres o no?
Pues nos burla el orbe entero,
Si soís salvajes, no quiero
Morar con vosotros yo,
Ya el tiempo feudal pasó
De opresión y obscuridad.
Oíd en la inmensidad,
Do el regio planeta habita,
Que una voz grita:
—¡Habaneros, libertad!⁷⁸

Are we free or not?
The whole world mocks us
If you are savages, I don't
Want to live with you,
The feudal era of oppression
And gloom is long over
Hear in the vast space
Where the regal planet resides
That a voice shouts:
—People of Havana, liberty!

This is a radical poem, even without an explicitly racial element because it simultaneously decries Spain's oppression of Cubans and Cuban slavery advocates' denial of freedom to people of color. As it stands, the poem is one of the most powerful and explicitly political poems of Plácido's oeuvre. The reference to the feudal era connects the poem to Europe, and more specifically to Old Spain. Here Plácido invokes the Cuban (Creole elite's) battle against Spain. The use of the word "salvajes" (savages) along with the vosotros (you plural) conjugation of to be, marking the object of the discourse as individuals other than the speaker, inverts the colonial racialist discourse of (White/European) civilization versus (of color/African) barbarism. In that inversion, he offers a stern rejoinder to the ideology of the civilized European and the barbaric African that permeates the racial discourse of the period, including, most notoriously, Argentinian colonial official Domingo Faustino Sarmiento's essay.[79] Through that inversion, his reference to savages, as well as his use of the term "we," and his call to the "people of Havana," he reminds the Creole elites themselves that they have also tried to recreate the feudal era. Through "we" he emphasizes that "we" are all Cubans and "we" are all entitled to liberty. By using "people of Havana" he utters a battle call that seems to transcend race, color, and class, but that also almost uncovers the palimpsest of racial rebellion implicit in his battle cry.

It is significant that this poem speaks to and of the people of Havana, because urban slavery was much more crucial and present in Cuba, in Havana in particular, than in other sites in the Americas.[80] Given this fact, it is almost certain that Plácido was consciously speaking to and of an audience of color as well as White Creoles. The poem illustrates the way Plácido's racial ideology resides within his expressions of national connectedness. In addition, though, the poem illustrates that the linking of racial and national affinities on the part of Cuban people of color during the revolutionary period of 1868– 98, identified and analyzed by Ada Ferrer and Fernando Maríinez Heredia, among others, also had a strong presence well before the Grito de Yara. Also present was the kinship between the political ideology of Plácido and the exiled poet Heredia (among other anti-Spanish Cuban Creoles).

The presence of both connections raises questions about the applicability of Du Bois's notion of double consciousness to Plácido in particular, if not Cubans of African descent in general. As stated earlier, the notion is based on a divorcing of racial and national affinities, and the feeling of being "torn asunder" by the simultaneous pull of both. By extension, the two presences also suggest that Plácido was not speaking to, of, or from the type of Black identity of which William Wells Brown, Martin Delany, or other African American abolitionists spoke. His identity, as represented in his nation poems, was composed of both national and racial affinities. The relative irrelevance of his Cubanness to Brown and Delany contrasts with the importance of his Cubanness to him. The poems suggest that Plácido was as committed to ousting Spain (and by extension to Cuban self-determination) as he was to abolition. Clearly, the historical contexts that produced Plácido's and Brown and Delany's identities and/or approaches to conceptualizing the relationship between racial and national identities differed greatly. Plácido had an access to Cubanness that Brown and Delany never had to Americanness, and he chose to embrace it. Cuban independence ideology was in development as Plácido was writing, and he had the opportunity to participate in it.[81] U.S. independence, on the other hand, happened long before either

Delany or Brown began to write, so they had little access to it or opportunity to participate in its growth. That the battles for independence and
abolition took place at the same time distinguishes Cuba from the U.S., and
by extension, as we shall see, distinguishes the identity ideology of Cubans
of color, such as Plácido, from their contemporaries in the United States.

Poems to Monarchs

The poems Plácido wrote in honor of the Spanish monarchs also lend
insight into Plácido's racial ideology because they illustrate his ability to dis-
semble through his poetry. He is able to write praise poems that the monarchs could read and be content with, while also including subtle criticisms
of their tyranny. He was particularly fond of writing poems about the Spanish Queen Isabel II.[82] One of these, "A Dona Isabel II, en Su Dia" (To Lady
Isabel II, on her Day) reads

Tu reinarás en paz; con pena estrana
Pondré del Orco en la mansion profunda,
Al traidor que con alma furibunda
Mi ley ofende y a su patria engaña:

Libre por ti respirará la España
En talentos y en héroes tan fecunda,
Y el viva solo de Isabel segunda,
Valdrá por un ejército en campana.
Dijo el Eterno; el templo de Memoria
Resonó con mil ecos de alegría:
Brillante sol de libertad y gloria

La parte iluminó de Mediodia,
Rejía gala ostento la hispana corte,
Y temblaron los despotas del Norte.[83]

(You will reign in peace: with difficulty being foreign
I will put in the huge mansion in Hell
The traitor who with an enraged soul
Offends my sense of loyalty and deceives your nation

Free for you Spain will breathe
So fecund in talents and heroes
And the only life of Isabel II,
Will be equal to a whole army on a mission

The Eternal One says: the temple of Memory
Resonated with a thousand echoes of happiness:
The brilliant sun of liberty and glory

The brightest part of Midday
The ruling prodigy of the Hispanic court,
And the despots of the North trembled in fear.)

Plácido praises Isabel II, the new monarch who will oversee the continuing oppression of himself and his countrymen. He uses hyperbole to
criticize the former queen even as he seems to be praising her. The irony in
his reference to her ruling in peace is unmistakable and powerful. His use
of liberty in relation to Spain is similarly ironic, given that Spain was, as
Plácido suggests in his other poems, withholding liberty from the people
of Cuba. In addition, the poem is replete with images of abundance ("so
fecund," "a thousand echoes of happiness," "brightest part of Midday), illustrating Plácido's use of hyperbole to launch a subtle critique of the excesses
of the crown. The last line points to Spain's new role as despot and its new
battles with the U.S. (despotic from Spain's perspective) over Cuba.[84] This
poem shows how well Plácido can use literary techniques to speak on two
levels at once, and more specifically to launch a critique that is evident only
to those who read or listen carefully. In this ability, he parallels other
Romantic writers from Cuba as well as England. A recognition of this talent
and propensity in Plácido's case is particularly significant, though, because
it suggests that he may use that skill in other poems, particularly with respect to race. This poem to the monarch, therefore, provides guidelines for
reading race in Plácido's other poems, and encourages a deeper analysis of
the appearances or apparent absences of racial terminology in his poems.

The poem "La rosa inglesa" (The English Rose) similarly demonstrates
Plácido's skill. The poem uses the Romantic trope of nature in general, and
the rose in particular, to celebrate the success of English abolitionism, to
note the fact that it has not blossomed in Cuba, and to shame those who
support slavery in Cuba.[85] The fable portion of the poem begins

Hay una especie de rosa	There's a type of rose
Que acá llamamos inglesa,	That here we call English,
Tan fértil, que todo el ano	So fertile that all year
Esta de verdor cubierta.	It is covered with freshness
Infinidad de botones	An infinity of buds
En cada renuevo echa;	In every shoot;

Pero no llegan a flores,	But they don't become flowers
Porque en botones se quedan	Because they remain buds

Plácido uses the metaphor of buds and flowers brilliantly to speak of the failure of abolitionism in Cuba. He ends this part of the poem asking for freedom from the anti-abolitionists, saying

Personas hay en el mundo	There are people in the world
Que solo a palos son buenas,	Who are only good with stalks
Como el rosal antedicho;	Like the aforementioned rose
¡Pero Dios nos libre de ellas![86]	But God free us from them!

He wants to be free from those who would prevent the flowers of abolition from blooming. He reiterates this idea even more powerfully, but by beginning with a typical animal-centered fable line, in the decima part of the poem. This section reads

Persigue el gato al ratón	The cat chases the rat
No por servir a su dueño,	Not to serve its master
Mas por natural empeno	But out of natural earnest desire
De maligna oposición.	For perverse opposition.
¡Cuantos hay que tales son	There are so many like that
Viendose en alta privanza,	Seeing themselves in high favor at court
Pues con rastrera asechanza	Because with abject ensnaring
Y depravada malicia,	and depraved malice,
Finjen amar la justicia	They pretend to love justice
Por ejercer la venganza.[87]	To exercise vengeance.

Again, Plácido does not speak specifically about the enslavement of Blacks, or about England itself, or about Richard Madden, the English abolitionist who was traveling in Cuba and publishing his "The Island of Cuba" detailing the conditions of slaves there. He protects himself from persecution by the authorities by not including specifics, and by writing the poem in such a way that it could apply to the struggle of the Creoles against the *peninsulares* as much as it could to the fight of enslaved Blacks for freedom. This poem illuminates Plácido's skill, one shared by so many New World Blacks, at saying but not saying, talking back while seeming to be in agreement. This poem reflects Plácido's sense of racial solidarity without his explicitly naming it. It bolsters the idea that he could have and would have participated in a broad conspiracy like the Conspiración de la Escalera.

The poem "La rosa inglesa" also illustrates that the foreign was a key trope used by Plácido to craft his incisive yet not readily evident political commentaries. In a fashion similar to the way in which he used the English rose in the poem discussed above, Plácido uses Poland in "A Polonia" (To Poland) to comment on the political situation in Cuba. He cleverly uses the unsuccessful Polish revolution against Russia in 1830 to speak to the contemporary situation in Cuba. The poem, in part, reads

Calma, nación heróica, tu agonía
Y contempla olvidando tus horrores
Que mil pueblos se hicieron opresores
Y sufrieron despues la tiranía.
. . .
Si andando el tiempo con la Europa embiste

Horda inmensa de bárbaros armada,
Y ves al Czar doblar la frente triste
Exclamarás a su enemiga aliada;
—Esas son las cadenas que me diste
Tuyas son, te las vuelvo, estoy vengada.[88]

Calm your agony, heroic nation,
And try to forget your horrors
That a thousand people became oppressors
And suffered tyranny afterwards
. . .
If in time you charge with Europe

As an immense horde armed with barbs
And you see the Czar's face becoming saddened,
You will exclaim to your allied enemy;
Those are the chains that you gave me
They are yours, I return them to you, I have gotten my revenge.

The reference at the beginning of the poem to the oppressors themselves suffering tyranny speaks directly, through the metaphor of Poland, to the political unrest in Spain. As mentioned previously, internal tensions surfaced during the rule of Ferdinand VII and increased after his death, ultimately leading to the exile of his daughter Queen Isabella II. Plácido uses the Polish revolution to suggest a future threat to the weakened Spanish monarchy, while his use of the word "chains" links Polish/Cuban oppression to the specific details of Cuban slavery. It works on the level of the foreign—he is actually speaking to and of Poland and uses specific Russian and Polish terms and references within the poem to reflect that. It also operates on the level of the particularly Cuban—as illustrated by the reference to

Spain implicit in his indexing of oppressors suffering tyranny. The criticism on the level of race is present but is, significantly, the best hidden. Given Plácido's demonstrated skill at couching political criticisms, and particularly ones related to race, in a range of metaphors, scholars would be wise to read through the simple presence or absence of Blackness in his poetry and his genes.

The foregoing discussion raises the question of whether it even matters that Plácido rarely used explicit racial terminology or references or that he rarely explicitly spoke of his connection to his (racial) people. A corollary of that question is to whom did/does it matter that he did or did not do so? His relationship to race clearly mattered to the colonial government officials who wrote the Escalera sentence as well as to the White and African American abolitionists who wrote about him. As discussed in the previous chapter, they all went to great lengths to represent and emphasize his belief in racial solidarity. Plácido was clearly a political radical, who suffered and died at the hands of the government in Cuba for both having and circulating his beliefs. That radicalism, however, was clearly not enough for those who wrote about and represented Plácido in the nineteenth century (and beyond). For them, his radicalism had to have a racial basis. The notion that he was a Cuban nationalist, an anticolonial radical, or a radical who was equally committed to racial and national (and perhaps also global) liberation was not as compelling for them.[89] His commitment to Cuba in particular, and to the world in general, was rendered virtually nonexistent by these race-focused representations. This inability to acknowledge the complexity of his politics illustrates the ways in which a focus on race functioned to effectively negate the possibility of other affinities. Plácido's poetry reveals a nuanced approach to identity and affinity, one that differs significantly from the one-dimensional representations of him. The role that race was made to play in these representations, and more specifically in the process of making him into that one-dimensional figure, yields insight into the ways in which racialization takes place as well as into the politics that drive the racialization process. As delineated here, those processes may be significantly different from those taken by the individual determining and/or representing his own relationship to racial identity.

Plácido's poetry shows that some of his biographers were correct in assuming that he had a broad notion of racial solidarity. His conception of racial solidarity is far from simplistic and his path to expressing it far from easy. While there is clear evidence that he sees color, and recognizes the racial classification system in Cuba, as the love poems show, his connection to

romanticism and his literary relationship to the Cuban fight for independence from Spain complicate what he can and does think about Black racial
solidarity. He never explicitly mentions anything about Africa, the African
race, or the Black race, even though some who write about him attribute this
narrowly racial perspective to him. The readings of his poetry undertaken
above show that such attributions should be approached with caution, even
in the case of this individual thought of as the ultimate Black Cuban antislavery martyr, this Gabriel de la Concepción Valdés, a.k.a. Plácido. Renowned
Afro-Hispanicist Edward J. Mullen speaks of the gaps that led to Plácido
being mis-placed or dis-placed in Afro-Hispanic literary studies.[90] I submit
that individuals like Plácido can best be included in broader discussions of
Caribbean, New World, and African Diaspora ideology through sustained
analysis of their approaches to identity and the disparate issues that they
confront on their path to self-definition and self-representation.

The scholarly treatment of Frederick Douglass stands in contrast to that
of Plácido, in that Douglass has most often been conceptualized as one of
the major figures in the development of U.S., and, more broadly, African
Diaspora writing and intellectual thought. (As the foregoing discussion has
shown, Plácido is frequently positioned as a pivotal figure in Cuban and
Afro-Latin American thought, but not of African Diasporan writing more
broadly.) Scholars have explored, among other issues, Douglass's complex
relationship to the African American community and to the United States.
What has not been examined, however, is the way in which both of those
aspects of his thought were implicated in and constituted by his envisioning of and interactions with people of African descent in other parts of the
Americas. Plácido and Douglass are generally studied in separate academic
spheres, with Plácido being read by Latin Americanists and Douglass being
analyzed by U.S.-focused scholars. My juxtaposition of readings of Plácido's
and Douglass's approaches to identity is intended to illustrate the productive possibilities inherent in having these spheres intersect.

"We Intend to Stay Here": The International Shadows in Frederick Douglass's Representations of African American Community

Frederick Douglass, over the course of his life, went from being a slave on U.S. soil to being U.S. consul in Haiti. That is to say, he went from being one not even considered fully human according to U.S. law, to being a representative of the U.S. government in a foreign country. The contours of his journey have been the subject of a plethora of scholarly and popular works, including Philip Foner's seminal biography, first published in 1948, and Deborah McDowell's important essays (1989, 1993), questioning Douglass's place at the head of the genealogy of African American literature. Douglass had a close-up view of the depths of slavery, the Civil War, Reconstruction, and Manifest Destiny. He is often thought of as the consummate exemplar of W. E. B. Du Bois's notion of "double consciousness."[1] Douglass strives, throughout his life, to reconcile his affinity for the U.S. nation with the pain of being rejected by that nation because of his race. In his descriptions of the African American condition, Du Bois, in fact, echoed Douglass's language. Douglass characterized African Americans as "a nation, in the midst of a nation which disowns them."[2] African Americans, Douglass said, are in a position that is "anomalous, unequal, and extraordinary." As illustrated by his description of African Americans as "aliens . . . in our native land,"[3] he often spoke from both within and outside America, simultaneously insisting on African Americans' rights as Americans and speaking of Americans as "them." The contradictions that permeate Douglass's thought are certainly due, in part, to his own ambivalence about his own biracial heritage.[4] As he notes, he was often singled out for punishment at particular moments and for rewards at others because he was of mixed parentage.[5] His internal conflicts show up first in his represented relationships with his fellow African Americans, and later and even more strikingly in his engagements with the world beyond the United States.

Significantly, Douglass for much of his public life was staunchly opposed to the idea of African American emigration.[6] As he explained to Harriet Beecher Stowe in a letter, "we are here and here we are likely to remain. Individuals emigrate—nations never . . . we have grown up with this republic."[7] Chris Dixon rightly notes that Douglass was "the most prominent advocate of the stay and fight ideology."[8] Although he understood why his fellow African Americans might want to leave, he insisted that staying and fighting for his people's claims to Americanness and American soil was the most desirable path. He stated clearly in an 1853 speech on "The Present Condition and Future Prospects of the Negro People" that "I am not for going any where. I am for staying precisely where I am, in the land of my birth."[9] Based on his commitment to this idea, he was as opposed to African American-led emigration schemes as he was to the White-led American Colonization Society program. He was particularly opposed to schemes that would take (free) African Americans to Africa, far away from the American continent, arguing that the strong White support for such movements came out of a desire to ensure the strengthening and perpetuation of the slave system. The goal of the proponents of colonization, Douglass argued, was to purge the U.S. of free African Americans and to get them to leave their enslaved kin in the hands of the slaveowners. He countered, "the free colored people generally mean to live in America, and not in Africa. . . . We do not mean to go to Liberia. . . . While our brethren are in bondage on these shores; it is idle to think of inducing any considerable number of free colored people to quit this for a foreign land."[10] Douglass wanted his fellow African Americans, and those who would deny them, to know that "a home, a country, a nationality are all attainable this side of Liberia."[11]

In the process of making his arguments against the colonization and emigration of African Americans in an 1848 speech, Douglass links African Americans to other people of African descent on the American continent: "Americans should remember that there are already on this continent, and in the adjacent islands, all of 12,370,000 Negroes, who only wait for the life-giving and organizing power of intelligence to mould them into one body, and into a powerful nation."[12] He goes on to detail the sizes of the African-descended populations of Brazil, the Spanish colonies, British, French, Dutch, and Danish colonies, the South American republics, Haiti, Mexico, and Canada. The language and content of his anti-emigration and anticolonization arguments illustrate that for Frederick Douglass, his position on emigration was profoundly tied to his commitment to African American rights to American soil and American citizenship. Furthermore, they illustrate that

for Douglass African Americans' relationship to the international was a battleground upon which the battle over African Americans' identity was to be
fought. For Douglass, the question of whether articulating a cosmopolitan
subjectivity would hinder African Americans' progress toward U.S. citizenship was a crucial one.

I am suggesting here that Douglass's "double consciousness" complicates and is complicated by another difficult dialectic—the tension between
being (or more accurately trying to be accepted as) a U.S. American and
embracing a racially based connection to people of African descent in other
parts of the world. The result is what might usefully be termed a "twice-
doubled consciousness."[13] Douglass's material and ideological relationships
with "foreign" people of African descent, I contend, are a crucial part of his
conceptualization, articulation, and representation of identity. His decisions
about how to respond to the charge of being more a Haitian than an American, for example (discussed in further detail in Chapter 5), yield insight
into not only his ideas about the relationship between African Americans
and Haitians in particular, but also the underpinnings of his conceptualization of African American identity. Consequently, a full understanding of his
arguments about African American identity in general, and African Americans' relationship to the United States more specifically, cannot be gleaned
without a consideration of the ways those arguments are created, bolstered,
or undercut by his engagements with the Black world beyond the U.S.[14] This
chapter centers on the elements of his textual relationship with other members of the African American community that I am arguing foreshadow his
often troubled and troubling engagements with the Black world beyond the
U.S. In particular, Douglass's desire (for himself and the Black community)
to be recognized as part of the U.S. citizenry shaped both his ambiguous
representations of his fellow African Americans and his similarly ambiguous later engagements with people of African descent in other American
sites. That desire appears in his autobiographies in his alternating embrace
and rejection of U.S. individualism, his ambivalent relationship to African
American community, and his apparent unwillingness to address intraracial
differences publicly.

The complexities implicit in his representations of his own relationship with the African American community are both the roots and the
results of his perceptions of the place of the Black other in his identity, life,
and work. Through his autobiographies—*The Narrative of the Life of Frederick
Douglass, an American Slave* (1845),[15] *My Bondage and My Freedom* (1855),
and *Life and Times of Frederick Douglass* (1881)—Douglass writes not only

himself, but also a notion of Black community (more specifically a Creole, meaning New World-born, Black community) into being. As Houston Baker has noted, Douglass's *Narrative* is an exemplar of the southern slave's use of autobiographical writing in his "quest for being," and a counterpoint to perception of the slave as a brute.[16] William Andrews similarly points out that autobiography allowed the free man to "declare himself a new man, a freeman, an American."[17] As autobiographies, Douglass's texts exhibit the crafting, silences, and conventions identified by numerous scholars in texts so defined.[18] At the same time, Douglass's texts also raise many of the same questions long asked by scholars of autobiography in general, as well as of African American autobiography in particular. Included among these are the issue of the relationship between the individual's voice and that of the community. Baker has argued that through the *Narrative* "Douglass wrests significance" "from what appears to be a blank and awesome backdrop."[19] He wrests significance for himself, for his self-hood, certainly, but I ask, what is the place of others and other selves in that significance?

I contend that in the 1845 *Narrative*, his first public, published autobiography/slave narrative, as well as in the other autobiographies, Douglass has to figure out more than one type of self-definition. As a U.S.-born individual he must determine whether and how he wants to imagine himself as part of the U.S. national whole. As a U.S. Black he must work through his ambivalence toward this nation that has locked him out, the nation's negation of him. Importantly, though, he must also consider the nature of, grounds of, and means of realizing his connection (or disconnection) with others who share his circumstances, specifically other Blacks, in the U.S. In other words, he must think about whether there is, can be, or should be such a thing as a U.S. Black collectivism. What may not be readily obvious is that in grappling with these possible identities, he is also articulating a relationship to the world beyond the U.S.,[20] and particularly the Black world beyond the U.S. The way he imagines community (whether U.S. Black or U.S. in general) to be defined, actualized, and articulated when he is not explicitly focusing on the Black international, mirrors the conceptual model he uses when he does engage the Black Other.

Autobiography and Audience

In the case of the *Narrative*, all these decisions are taking place in the context of trying to please a White audience that wants slave narratives to be primarily purveyors of facts about slavery, rather than the delineation of any individual's philosophy of life, commentary on the political system, or politics of identity.[21] As William Andrews notes, the commentaries by White abolitionists William Lloyd Garrison and Wendell Phillips that frame the narrative deemphasize the peculiarities of Douglass's experience in favor of the ways the text advances the abolitionist cause.[22] Phillips comments that the horrors Douglass recalls "are no incidental aggravations, no individual ills, but such as must mingle always and necessarily in the lot of every slave. They are the essential ingredients, not the occasional results, of the system."[23] Although by the time Douglass writes his second autobiography, *My Bondage and My Freedom* (1855), he has become a well-known spokesman for abolition and an international lecturer, he is still constrained by the fact that slavery has not yet ended. As he says himself in the text, he withholds facts to protect those who are still enslaved. He says "we owe something to the slaves, south of Mason and Dixon's line, as well as to those north of it," so "we should be careful to do nothing which would be likely to hinder the former, in making their escape from slavery."[24] His third and final autobiography, *Life and Times of Frederick Douglass* (1881), published virtually at the end of his public career (and life), is by far the lengthiest and most detailed, written and published two decades after the abolition of slavery in the United States. He even published a revised edition several years after the initial one that included an Appendix with extensive information on his tenure as consul to Haiti. That autobiography, however, also exhibits significant recalcitrance in terms of certain details and emotions, due in large part, I would argue, to his aspirations for fully recognized and actuated U.S. citizenship for himself and for African Americans in general.[25]

Douglass certainly did not develop or articulate his worldview in a vacuum. His public statements, including his methods of representing and defining self, community, and other, were influenced by his cognizance of the composition of his audience and of their expectations. His demarcation of the territorial or ideological grounds of "wes," "theys," and "Is" speaks not only to his *weltanschauung*, but also, and perhaps even more clearly, to the ways that worldview was the result of a negotiation between his own views and those he knew that his audience expected of him.[26]

That his constructions and representations of self, community, and other arose out of a consciousness of audience does not, however, undercut their significance as indicators of a specific worldview. In fact, I would argue that it is precisely the fact that they developed out of a negotiation of the audience's gaze that makes them of special importance. The role of the White

American gaze in African Americans' self-consciousness and self-definition is also highlighted by W. E. B. Du Bois in the delineation of his concept of "double consciousness."[27] William Andrews has rightly noted that Black autobiography in general, and Douglass's autobiographies in particular, "tried to move the white reader from an alien to a consubstantial relationship with the text and the Black self presumably represented by the text."[28] A key aspect of that goal, particularly in Douglass's texts, was to move the White reader to seeing that Black self as American. In the process of pursuing the goal of exposing the fissures and hypocrisies within popular notions of Americanness, Douglass constructs and deconstructs a range of visions of self and community, including ones based on race, geographical location, and condition.

Douglass and U.S. Individualism

Douglass's autobiographies evince a definite tension between the individual ("I") and the community ("they").[29] David Van Leer identifies a tension between representative (they or us) and exceptional (I) characteristics in the *Narrative*. He argues that "the personal story validates the politician by establishing the existence of a self from which, by definition, he has 'escaped.'"[30] The tension between individual and community in the *Narrative* is, therefore, inherently troubled. His centering of the "I" in the narrative, then, is usefully understood as being born of his desire to claim Americanness.

The similarities between Frederick Douglass and Benjamin Franklin, for example, are evident in the tone as well as in the content of their autobiographies.[31] Both are clearly the stories of their growth into "literary gentlemanhood," to echo Belinda Edmondson with a difference. The "I" Douglass constructs, models, and engages and, therefore, the Americanness he seeks are gendered male. Consequently, the racial community Douglass invokes, particularly in the *Narrative* when the battle for the I's humanity is most evident, is also generally gendered male. For instance, in his recounting of the moment he decided to physically fight the slave breaker Covey in *My Bondage and My Freedom*, he mentions that a slave woman's refusal to aid Covey helped him to his ultimate victory over Covey: "Covey attempted to rally her to his aid. Strangely—and, I may add, fortunately—Caroline was in no humor to take a hand in any such sport. We were all in open rebellion that morning."[32] Douglass does not mention Caroline when he recalls that fight in the *Narrative*, even though he does reference Bill, another slave who ignored Covey's orders. He only discusses Caroline's "miserable" life as a "breeder" for Mr. Covey.[33]

Zafar notes that both Douglass and Franklin "exhibit a peculiar, perhaps American, form of short-sightedness; some might call . . . egomania."[34] I am arguing that for the African American Douglass the approach to self-definition he shares with Franklin, whether consciously or unconsciously, complicates his relationship to non-U.S. Blacks. The ways he shows himself to be (and is) American, such as the viewpoints he shares with Franklin, correspond to the ways he differentiates himself from other national Black Americans.

The tension between the assertion of the Black individual and the slave community in African American slave narratives is a microcosmic reflection of the difficulties concomitant with embracing one's particular American Blackness as one is engaging transnational hemispheric Blackness. In asserting himself and his experience the writer of the slave narrative, on one level, prioritizes the particular Self over the larger community. Unlike Franklin, however, whose autobiography need only be about himself, Douglass feels an obligation to speak for his community as well. Douglass's fellow community members are enslaved, and his narrative has an aim that is not just about telling the story of his development as an individual but about calling for the abolition of this horrible and peculiar institution. For Douglass, the resolution of this tension between the desire to tell one's own story and to speak for one's community is not the wholesale erasure of the community from the entire story of the Self, but rather the alternation between focusing on the person and the community at different points in the text. So, despite the approaches that Douglass has in common with Franklin, his position as a Black (ex)slave in U.S. society and sense of obligation to community results in a narrative that tells his story as well as that of his people.[35]

The commonalities with Franklin's identify his narrative as sharing in nascent U.S. American ideologies, and the differences mark it as articulating a particularly African American viewpoint. The DuBoisian double consciousness raises its head here in profound fashion.

The connection between Douglass's narrative and broader American ideology, specifically the notion that the American individual will eventually triumph over any and all obstacles, is evident at the end of the third chapter of Douglass's *Narrative*. This instance of individualism comes after Douglass is chosen, from among all the slaves owned by Colonel Lloyd, to be the one to move to Baltimore and presumably have a better life. He is convinced that he has been specially chosen by God: "I was chosen from among them all, and was the first, last, and only choice. I may be deemed superstitious, and even egotistical, in regarding this event as a special interposition of divine Providence in my favor" (47). His is a narrative of the individual, but also of a consciousness of the need to embrace and protect the Black community. That he gives credit for his selection to "divine Providence" rather than to himself speaks to this individualism-with-a-difference. His consciousness that such a statement could seem egotistical indicates also his consciousness of Whites possibly reading him as presumptuous. This move on Douglass's part is also a gesture towards community, in that he does not sacrifice the community's interest to make himself a hero. He turns again to indicating that he is unique: "From my earliest recollection, I date the entertainment of a deep conviction that slavery would not always be able to hold me within its foul embrace" (47). The sense here is that he, the individual, is battling slavery's hold on him. His belief in his own exceptionalism underlies this statement.

African Americans as "They"

At several points in his autobiographies Douglass refers to other African Americans as "they," creating a distance between the speaking self and the spoken of other. The crucial question here is, when he speaks of a "they," who is he implicitly saying that he is?[36] Robert Reid Pharr implicitly asks and answers this question by turning it into a statement—Douglass "is" because he constructs a "they." He contends that Douglass "gains his 'self' through the 'corporealization,' some might say bestialization of his Aunt Hester."[37] Douglass's representation of the trauma of knowledge, specifically of knowledge about the system of slavery that he gained from the *Columbian Orator*, also exemplifies the tension between the "they" and the "I." He bemoans his situation, saying, "In moments of agony, I envied my fellow slaves for their stupidity."[38] That he "envied" his "fellow slaves for their stupidity" further illustrates his individual narrative pulling against his sense of U.S. Black community. He claims them as his "fellow slaves," but differentiates himself from them using his encounter with the agony of literacy. Although Douglass refrains from explicitly situating himself above them because he has become literate, as is evident in his use of the verb "envy," he effects a distinction by marking their "stupidity." His saying "I envied" implies that the other slaves had a positive attribute that he desired. Naming that attribute as "stupidity," generally understood as negative, brings the collectivism he expressed earlier into question.

In this statement, Douglass is presenting himself as a member of the community who has been detached and differentiated from the community. Although he seems to be speaking about a specific situation, he is also speaking more broadly to his own complicated position as a "representative man," a representative ex-slave who is supposed to be writing a representative text, but who is, as Zafar puts it, an "unrepresentative African American."[39] This alternation between positioning himself as a member of the community and distancing himself from that same community illustrates Douglass's ambivalence, at this stage of his life, about his relationship as an individual to such a thing as a Black community. Despite the fundamental commitment to the slave community and to abolition in the *Narrative*, it also evinces an ambiguity about and ambivalence towards a notion of African American community. That Douglass is dealing with this issue in his narrative is significant for this study because it illustrates the tentativeness with which publicly articulated African American nationalism, as such, came about. It further complicates Du Bois's notion of double consciousness by demonstrating that the struggle lies not only in being both Negro and American, but also in defining what that Negroness is. Douglass's difficulty here is a precursor to the even greater struggles (his own and those of African American public intellectuals in general) that come about once the issue of the position of the non-U.S. Black world vis-à-vis this American Negroness come to the fore in public, published African American discourse.

African Americans as "We"

The question of just who constitutes Douglass's "we" is a complicated but important one. At various moments in his autobiographies, his references to "we" refer to "we" slaves, "we" Americans, and "we" Black Americans. The grounds of his notions vary from geographical to experiential to national to ideological. Tension between all of these "wes" as well as between the "wes" and the "I" permeates all the autobiographies.

At points in Douglass's *Narrative*, for example, there is little sense of any kind of Black community beyond the immediate places where he is enslaved. The community members he imagines are bound to each other by their common slave condition, by their shared experiences. The "we" he invokes is grounded in the experience of being enslaved on specific plantations and farms rather than in any sense of Blackness per se. Soon after these points, though, he often moves outward toward talking about the experience and/or community as reflective of the experience of a broader "we." For instance, he writes of his time at Covey's (his most violent master),

My term of actual service to Mr. Edward Covey ended on Christmas day, 1833. The days between Christmas and New Year's day are allowed as holidays; and, accordingly, we were not required to perform any labor, more than to feed and take care of the stock. This time we regarded as our own, by the grace of our masters; and we therefore used or abused it nearly as we pleased. . . . From what I know of the effect of these holidays upon the slave, I believe them to be among the most effective means in the hands of the slaveholder in keeping down the spirit of insurrection. Were the slaveholders at once to abandon this practice, I have not the slightest doubt it would lead to an immediate insurrection among the slaves. (44)

The paragraph begins by locating the "we" on a particular plantation, indicating the work schedule for Covey's slaves. At the same time, though, there is an ambiguity about the "we" arising from the absence of an explicit naming of the "we" as Covey's slaves that suggests that the "we" is both a worksite-specific and a trans-worksite community. The tentative articulation of a pan-slave community moves beyond the particular plantation surface in the last five lines of the quotation. Douglass abandons any notion of speaking only to the issues of the "we" on the specific plantation, and moves definitively toward speaking of the slave situation in general, of "the" slaves and "the" slaveholders. Here is a firmly claimed worksite-specific "we" coupled with a broader, more detached notion of "the slaves." What is not evident at this point, though, is a comfortable balancing of the deep connectedness that comes from sharing a plantation and the cross-plantation collectivism. The feeling of intimacy in the first half of this quotation is absent from the second. The tone of the second half recalls that of an observer, albeit an empathetic one, simply describing what the observer sees or can deduce from what is before him or her. There is little difference between the tone of the second part and the letters of the White abolitionists that precede Douglass's narrative. Douglass's switching between the sense of community rooted in the sharing of specific locations and a broader translocational sense of collective reveals the inherent difficulty in self and group definition fostered by the attempt to balance the global and the local in self-definition I have identified is quite clear here.

Douglass is endeavoring to find a way to speak simultaneously from the inside and the outside, as a slave telling his own story and an abolitionist chronicler. His shift to the objective voice after an expression of connectedness likely speaks of a desire to infuse his commentary with more authority. The phrase "from what I know of" exemplifies the balancing act he is undertaking, in that it simultaneously implies both a scientific distance and an insider's knowledge. Douglass also attempts to speak from/of the local and the global in the moment from the narrative above—local in this case being a particular farm, global being that beyond a specific farm and including all the farms and plantations. The challenges encountered by Douglass in defining his community, even within the territorial bounds of the U.S., portends similar, if not greater, challenges in locating himself in relation to a transnational collective.

A conception of community based on common condition and/or experience appears in Douglass's descriptions of the escape plot that he hatched along with his fellow slaves at the Freelands'. Evident in his discussion are a tension between the voices of the individual and the community, a notion of the grounds of community, and a specific approach to representing tensions or differences within the community. In all his autobiographies Douglass frames the description of the plot and the attempted enactment of it both as an act born of an individual's desire for freedom and as a collective action born of a profound group bond. In the *Narrative*, for instance, he describes the slave community with great passion, saying,

We were linked and interlinked with each other. I loved them with a love stronger than any thing I have experienced since. It is sometimes said that we slaves do not love and confide in each other. In answer to this assertion, I can say, I never loved any or confided in any people more than my fellow- slaves, and especially those with whom I lived at Mr. Freeland's. I believe we would have died for each other. We never undertook to do any thing, of any importance, without a mutual consultation. We never moved separately. We were one; and as much so by our tempers and dispositions, as by the mutual hardships to which we were necessarily subjected by our condition as slaves. (49)

The intensity of the sense of community felt by Douglass and the other slaves comes across clearly in his use of superlatives ("a love stronger than any thing I have experienced since), emotion-packed phrases ("we would have died for each other"), and powerful images ("we never moved separately"). Douglass's connection to the slave "we" is unmistakable here. The grounds of that community, as he presents it, are both spiritual and material—that is to say, based on the bond between their "tempers and dispositions," as well as on their common condition.

Just after this emotion-filled description, though, Douglass first speaks of his awakening, and his decision to seek freedom at all costs: "I was no longer content, therefore, to live with him or any other slaveholder. I began, with the commencement of the year, to prepare myself for a final struggle, which should decide my fate one way or another . . . I therefore resolved that 1835 should not pass without witnessing an attempt, on my part, to secure my liberty."[40] Through these words he constructs this moment as the birth of an individual's true knowledge of self. After describing his own awakening, Douglass returns to his emphasis on this plot as not only a collective action, but an illustration of his strong connection to his fellow slaves. He indicates that he could not and did not wish to "cherish this determination alone," and that he desired that his fellow slaves "participate with [him] in this, [his] life-giving determination." In this formulation, Douglass positions himself as the originator of the determination to take freedom, and his beloved fellow slaves as beneficiaries of and participants in the actuation of this drive. He goes one step further by describing the ways in which he sought to educate them on the "gross fraud and inhumanity of slavery."[41]

The continuing tension between the individual and the community in Douglass's description shows the incomplete nature of the "self-effacement" for the good of the community and the message identified by Wilson Jeremiah Moses. Moses argues that, early on, Douglass had to constrain himself, to be a racialized self in a literary box in which the message was more important that the individual. This was especially true of the slave narrative, given the purpose behind the genre—to represent slavery for White readers. That the tension remains in the description of this moment in all three autobiographies, however, suggests that even as he escaped the constraints of the slave narrative, he chose to maintain this approach to representing the relationship between the individual's coming into himself and the community's being persuaded to participate. Kenneth Warren, in his critical analysis of *Life and Times*, argues rather convincingly that Douglass refers to the real political needs of his disenfranchised group to silence criticisms of himself.[42] At the very least, Douglass's emphasis on the "I" even when speaking to the needs of or connection with the "we," suggests a complexity or tension in his conceptualization of and relationship with his own racial community.

Douglass and Intraracial Difference

Douglass's discussion of the source of the betrayal of the plot, and the fact that the name of the traitor is present only in *My Bondage and My Freedom* and *Life and Times*, lend insight into Douglass's reactions to tensions or differences within the community, as well as into his decisions about how and when those tensions can or should be revealed to those outside.[43] As Douglass tells the story in his second and third autobiographies, he and most of his fellow conspirators firmly believed that the traitor was Sandy, a fellow slave and "root man" with whom Douglass had become extremely close. According to Douglass, they "suspected, and suspected *one* person *only.*"[44] Despite this focused suspicion, Douglass, again emphasizing the depth of the bonds between the members of the slave community, tells his reader "we could not suspect him. We all loved him too well to think it possible that he could have betrayed us" (297). They decide not to focus on this "tension," but rather to downplay it and move forward.

The issue of how Douglass handles and represents tensions within the community arises again in Douglass's discussion of the (free) Black community in New Bedford, Massachusetts. The New Bedford sections also reveal Douglass's embrace of a racially based notion of community, one that includes free Blacks as well as slaves. In all three autobiographies Douglass's representation of the community of color in New Bedford is overwhelmingly positive. He lauds the refinement and "cheerful earnestness" of the people of New Bedford (67). The people of color there "better understood the moral, religious, and political character of the nation,—than nine tenths of the slaveholders in Talbot county, Maryland" (68). He is particularly positive about the "determination" he "found among them . . . to protect each other from the blood-thirsty kidnapper, at all hazards" (67). In all three narratives, he, with what can be described as joy (albeit measured), narrates the story he was told of the New Bedford Black community's punishment of one who threatened to betray another member of the community. A free Black threatened to turn a fugitive slave, with whom he had gotten into a fight, in to the slave catchers. Upon hearing this, the community organized a special meeting, made sure that the betrayer-to-be attended, and had several members set upon him and attempt to kill him. In the 1845 *Narrative*, Douglass comments, he "has not been seen in New Bedford since. I believe there have been no more such threats, and should there be hereafter, I doubt not that death would be the consequence" (68). The response to this intracommunity tension and that evident in the escape plot are parallel in that they manifest a determination to preserve community wholeness at whatever cost. That Douglass decided to include these moments in his autobiographies suggests a commitment to (representing) this vision of community in general, and of the African American community in particular.

The slight differences in the details of the conspiracy and New Bedford episodes in the autobiographies indicate the importance to Douglass of how he represents the state of the African American community. As mentioned earlier, Douglass does not include the name of the suspected traitor in the *Narrative*, but does include it in his other two autobiographies. This decision speaks to a hesitance on Douglass's part to admit any fissures within the slave community. That reluctance is borne out by the fact that he still chooses to frame the naming of the traitor in *My Bondage and My Freedom* and *Life and Times* with the statement that they "all loved him too well" to even "think it possible that he could have betrayed us."[45] With regard to the certain members of the community of (free) people of color of New Bedford, Douglass's approach is conspicuously different. Although his representation of the people of color there is wholly positive in the *Narrative*, in *My Bondage and My Freedom* he speaks quite negatively of the acquiescence of the "colored members" of the Methodist church he joins to segregated communion (353).[46] He describes their behavior as "most humiliating," and them as the White pastor's penned "Black sheep" and "poor slavish souls" (353). Douglass goes on to note that he found a "small body of colored Methodists" that initially brought him "peace and joy," but that he ultimately left because he "found that it consented to the same spirit which held my brethren in chains (353–54). Contained within his characterization is a rather strident, but subtle, critique of free northern Blacks who are less committed to true freedom than they should be, and even, as Douglass represents them, less committed than Garrison and the other White abolitionists of the *Liberator* (355–56). It is the White abolitionists, according to Douglass, who "increased [his] hope for the ultimate freedom of [his] race" (356).

In contrast, in *Life and Times*, the only autobiography that Douglass published after the end of slavery, he spends significantly more space discussing the behavior of Whites—both criticizing the practices of racist New Bedford Whites (and the racist New Bedford social infrastructure) and praising the generous actions of antislavery Whites. In fact, the issue of the Methodist churches in New Bedford, and by extension the critique of sycophantic free Blacks, does not even appear in *Life and Times*. His focus is not on disparities and shortcomings within the African American community, but rather on the crucial need for affirmative actions by progressive Whites. He notes that, although the schools were integrated, the city did not "till several years after [his] residence allow any colored person to attend the lectures delivered in its hall. Not until such men as Hon. Chas. Sumner, Theodore Parker, Ralph W. Emerson, and Horace Mann refused to lecture . . . while there was such a restriction was it abandoned."[47] In addition, the joy evident in Douglass's earlier descriptions of the punishment of the man who threatened to turn in a fugitive slave is not present in *Life and Times*. Whereas in the *Narrative* and *My Bondage and My Freedom* he almost seems to exult in the closeness of the community as illustrated by the punishment, in *Life and Times* he tells the story in a matter of fact fashion. In the earlier autobiographies he speaks of this moment as illustrative of their "spirit."[48] He sees it as evidence that "the colored people in that city are educated up to the point of fighting for their freedom, as well as speaking for it."[49] This shift can usefully be read as illustrative of the increasing disillusionment with the idea of racial community on Douglass's part described by Wilson Jeremiah Moses. Significantly, it is at this point in his career that Douglass explicitly engages the Black world beyond the U.S. in his autobiographical writings.

"More a Haitian Than an American": Frederick Douglass and the Black World Beyond the United States

Reading (Through) Absence

Before the Appendix to *The Life and Times of Frederick Douglass*, his final autobiography, Douglass virtually never mentions the other Black Americas in his autobiographies. The silence on the other Black American world can certainly be explained in part by recalling the historical context. The fear of national or transnational Black uprisings provoked by the Haitian Revolution decades earlier was still quite present in U.S. society, as were individuals who had fled Haiti with their slaves to escape sure death.[1] The silence also arises out of the fact that the control of African Americans' movement, both physical and ideological, had always been and continued to be fundamental to the maintenance of the slave society. As Douglass's *Narrative* illustrates, slaves had to be prevented not only from running North, but even from moving freely between counties or plantations. I would go so far as to argue for the conception of the control of movement as an element of the "social death" identified by Orlando Patterson. In addition to the specific fears prompted by the Revolution, there was the more general fear that African Americans would begin to determine their own movements, and by extension would begin to understand themselves as part of a broader national or even transnational community, one that made them the brothers and sisters of the Haitian revolutionaries. Douglass was certainly cognizant of this element of the social control those in power sought to exert over slaves. He took the approach that was least likely to ignite White fear of the loss of this control of slave identity and ideology. He provides a glimpse of the underpinnings of his strategy when he notes in *Life and Times*,

Slaveholders are known to have sent spies among their slaves to ascertain, if possible, their views and feelings in regard to their condition; hence the maxim established among them, that "a still tongue makes a wise head." They would suppress the truth rather than take the consequences of telling it, and in so doing they prove themselves a part of the human family.[2]

The "still tongue" protects slaves' claim to humanity, and by extension, to freedom. Douglass's stated goal in writing the *Narrative*, in particular, is to plead the case for freedom for U.S. Blacks. He indicates as much in the last paragraph of the text summing up his reason for writing the narrative: "Sincerely and earnestly hoping that this little book may do something toward throwing light on the American slave system, and hastening the glad day of deliverance to the millions of my brethren in bonds—and solemnly pledging myself anew to the sacred cause."[3]

The silences in the *Narrative* surrounding knowledge about other American places suggest that Douglass chooses to leave out his knowledge of the international scene to advance his cause.[4] Douglass signals several times that he is leaving out the names of individuals or particular details in the service of "prudence," but factual inconsistencies indicate a more subtle crafting process. As he narrates the development of the escape plot he hatched with his fellow slaves, he insists that they "knew nothing about Canada" and "could see no spot, this side of the ocean where we could be free."[5] Even the idea that a group of U.S. slaves did not know about Canada seems questionable, especially when juxtaposed with his indication they knew about England. The strategic nature of Douglass's represented ignorance of Canada becomes clearer when he undermines his own assertion. He recalls that after he has successfully run away and found an abolitionist friend in the North, his friend (Ruggles) "wished to know of [me] where I wanted to go; . . . I thought of going to Canada" (65). Nowhere in this conversation does Douglass indicate that Ruggles told him about Canada, so the logical conclusion is that Douglass, the slave, likely already knew of Canada's existence and that freedom could be found there.

If this inconsistency is considered along with the fact that he resolves to try to secure his liberty and that of his fellow slaves in 1834—the year the Emancipation of West Indian slaves took effect—and makes absolutely no mention of the coincidence, it becomes clear that much more is happening behind the scenes of this narrative, particularly in terms of the mentioning or nonmentioning of the other Black Americas, than Douglass is willing to say.[6] The strangeness of this silence is even more apparent if we compare his saying "in the early part of the year 1838, I became quite restless" in the text

of the narrative, with a letter referring to the final ending of the apprenticeship system (1834–1838) of gradual emancipation put in place to "ease"
slaves' transition to freedom written to Douglass by abolitionist Wendell
Phillips and published as an introduction to the narrative along with that of
William Lloyd Garrison. Phillips writes

> I remember that, in 1838, many were waiting for the results of the West India exper-
> iment, before they could come into our ranks. Those "results" have come long ago;
> but, alas! few of that number have come with them, as converts. A man must be dis-
> posed to judge of emancipation by other tests than whether it has increased the pro-
> duce of sugar . . . before he is ready to lay the first stone of his anti-slavery life.[7]

This letter paves the way for Douglass to mention West Indian emancipation in the context of his narrative, and to parallel or connect either his
foiled escape or his restlessness in 1838 to the happenings in the West Indies.
At the same time, it indicates why Douglass may not have taken that path—
emancipation had greatly reduced the profits of British landowners and
merchants, and was not likely to be persuasive to those who were not already abolitionists. Douglass's express goal of speeding abolition in the U.S.
was better served, then, by his not mentioning West Indian emancipation.

The West Indies

Douglass does mention West Indian emancipation in his final autobiography, *Life and Times of Frederick Douglass.* He does so in the reproduction of
a speech he gave at a West Indian Emancipation day celebration in 1880.[8] In
that speech he indicates that West Indian Emancipation Day was considered
a day for major celebration by him and his fellow slaves, and is so considered by free and newly emancipated African Americans. Here Douglass explicitly articulates and celebrates the political, ideological, and identificatory
links between people of African descent in the U.S. and the Caribbean. He
speaks of West Indian Emancipation Day as "preeminently the colored man's
day" and of Black West Indians as "our brothers in the West Indies" (494).
"Emancipation in the West Indies," he pronounces, was "the first tangible
fact demonstrating the possibility of a peaceable transition from slavery to
freedom, of the Negro race."

He goes on, though, to emphasize the particularities of the American situation and, by extension, to name and claim the Americanness of the African Americans who are celebrating this day: "Let no American, especially

no colored American, withhold a generous recognition of this stupendous achievement" (497). His relationship to the Black world beyond the U.S. shapes and is shaped by his relationship with Americanness, and his drive for full citizenship for African Americans. He spends half the speech speaking directly to the recent political history of the United States in general (the Civil War) and the condition and history of the African American in particular. He argues stridently that, although emancipation has taken place, conditions for the African American have changed little: "The citizenship granted in the fourteenth amendment is practically a mockery, and the right to vote, provided for in the fifteenth amendment, is literally stamped out in the face of government" (503). In an implicitly comparative statement, he notes, "history does not furnish an example of emancipation under conditions less friendly to the emancipated class than this American example." His discussion of the West Indies serves as a point of departure for his discussion of the condition of African Americans, rather than as a focal point in itself.

At the same time, Douglass highlights that the situations and responses of both African Americans and West Indians are reflective of the human condition, and that both groups are part of the human brotherhood, along with the Whites who enslaved them and those who fought for their emancipation. He says, "The emancipation of our brothers in the West Indies comes home to us and stirs our hearts and fills our souls with those grateful sentiments which link mankind in a common brotherhood" (494). He continues to interweave the idea of a racial connection between Blacks in the U.S. and the West Indies with African Americans' claims to Americanness with the common humanity they share with the Whites, saying "Human liberty excludes all idea of home and abroad. It is universal and spurns localization . . . it is bounded by no geographical lines and knows no national limitations (496).

In the absence of mention of the other Black Americas, Douglass's *Narrative* actually parallels all extant nineteenth-century U.S. and Caribbean slave narratives discovered to date. This trend, particularly when contrasted with the presence of the Black world in fiction and political essays of the same period, including those of Douglass, suggests that the writers were of the opinion that articulating the story of the individual or community from a specific geographic site in a slave narrative was incompatible with referencing or discussing individuals or communities from another site. I want to suggest the term "binaristic blackness" to describe this idea that only one group of Blacks can or should be the focus of a text, particularly a text concerned with uplift or amelioration of conditions. The concept is based on the image of a see-saw, in which if one is to be above, the other must be below.

William Andrews rightly notes that "tensions, disjunctions, and silences can serve as an index to a struggle going on in a narrative."[9] The point implicit in Douglass's nonrepresentation of the other Black Americas in *Narrative* and the bulk of the other autobiographies is that the furthering of the African American agenda within the U.S., particularly while slavery continued, necessitated a textual distancing from the other Black Americas. The point rests on the presumption that the battle for rights or citizenship in the particular national context must necessarily exclude the articulation of a transnational notion of community.

Both the limited geographical scope of American slave narratives and binaristic blackness are outgrowths of the slave system's obsession with controlling the movement of slaves in particular, and people of African descent more broadly. (This continent-wide issue was discussed in detail in the first chapter, through a specific case study of Cuba.) The control of slaves' movement resulted in controlled movement within slave narratives for two reasons. (Ex)slave narrators, like Douglass, were aware of the fear of people of African descent's transnational movements and, controlled the geographical (and identificatory) scope of their narratives in the service of their broader goals (U.S. citizenship for Blacks in Douglass's case). The simultaneously very local and very global nature of slavery itself also determined the geographical scope of slave narratives.

In his second autobiography, Douglass himself provides an excellent and enlightening theory of a reason for his silences on the world beyond the United States. He suggests that slaves are inherently resistant to thinking about "removal" or migration because of their history of forced placement and displacement. He opines "free people generally, . . . have less attachment to the places where they are born and brought up, than have the slaves. Their freedom to go and come, to be here and there, as they list, prevents any extravagant attachment to any one particular place."[10] He states further that "the slave is a fixture; he has no choice, no goal, no destination; but is pegged down to a single spot, and must take root here, or nowhere." The slave cannot move anywhere, and must therefore become bonded to the location in which he finds himself. Furthermore he notes,

the idea of removal elsewhere, comes, generally, in the shape of a threat, and in punishment of crime. It is, therefore attended with fear and dread. A slave seldom thinks of bettering his condition by being sold, and hence he looks upon separation from his native place, with none of the enthusiasm which animates the bosoms of young freemen, when they contemplate a life in the far west, or in some distant country where they intend to rise to wealth and distinction. (176–77)

Slaves are forced to stay and forced to move, the latter generally as punishment. The result of this treatment is that slaves have a negative perception of any suggestion that they or anyone they love should move. As Douglass says, "Nor can those from whom they separate, give them up with that cheerfulness with which friends and relations yield each other up, when they feel that it is for the good of the departing one that he is removed from his native place" (177). He also locates slaves' contempt for movement in the absence of the possibility of reunion with those who leave. For free people who move, "there is, at least, the hope of reunion, because reunion is *possible*," but "with the slave . . . There is no improvement in his condition *probable*, —no correspondence possible,—no reunion attainable." He actually equates a slave's "going out into the world" with "a living man going into the tomb." His silence on the other Black Americas can therefore usefully be read as reflecting his desire to represent both the lack of knowledge of the world beyond on the part of the slave and his own apprehensions (as a former slave) about going out into the world (physically or conceptually). Douglass's theory lays bare the relationship to place that drove his own relationship with the world, and also the ways slavery encouraged, produced, and fed on the provincialism/parochialism of slaves. It stands to reason, then, that the ideology of slavery also discouraged, sought to destroy, and was weakened by the cosmopolitanism of slaves and others of African descent.

Africa

Douglass does return to African Americans' African past at a few moments. His treatment of the significance of Africa for African American identity illustrates the extent to which the grounds of African American identity were not settled in Douglass's mind.[11] Africa appears in Douglass's 1845 *Narrative* both as a place to which he is completely unconnected and as his and his fellow slaves' ancestral home.[12] This ambiguity arises because he is simultaneously trying to articulate African Americans' claims to American citizenship (albeit subtly) and to emphasize his own commitment (and that of his fellow slaves) to the emancipation of all the enslaved. He is trying to link African Americans to the broader U.S. nation while also illustrating the profound bonds they share with each other. On one hand, he speaks of the "different looking class of people . . . from those originally brought to this country from Africa," who are "now held in slavery" (3). Douglass's literal reference to racial mixture serves as a metaphor for cultural mixture. He is implicitly arguing that the African American is a profoundly American product with virtually nothing in common with the original African one. On the other hand, though, he bemoans the fact that his enslavers had "gone to Africa, and stolen us from our homes, and in a strange land reduced us to slavery" (24). Here, he represents African Americans as children of Africa, who have been taken from their home (Africa) and brought to a place wholly foreign to them (America).[13] The phrase "a strange land" links the plight of African Americans with the story of the children of Israel in the Bible common in nineteenth-century African American discourse.[14] This statement suggests an ongoing level of unsettledness in African American identity as he understands or chooses to represent it. It also bolsters my earlier readings of the absence of the other Americas in the rest of the *Narrative* as reflective of the conventions of the slave narrative (including presumed geographical scope), twice-doubled consciousness, and binaristic blackness.

Douglass begins to articulate a resolution to this unsettledness, particularly as it relates to Africa, in *My Bondage and My Freedom* (1855), a revised and expanded version of his *Narrative*, when he clearly identifies African Americans as descendants of Africans, descendants who must work toward liberty and progress in "this country":

I have felt it to be a part of my mission . . . to impress my sable brothers in this country with the conviction that, notwithstanding . . . the blood-written history of Africa, and her children, from whom we have descended . . . progress is yet possible . . . and that "Ethiopia shall yet reach forth her hand to God."[15]

He puts forward a notion of identity that is based on African Americans' common membership in the "sable race," common African descent, and common location in "this country." His use of the phrase "Ethiopia shall yet reach forth her hand to God," a phrase fundamental to the Ethiopianist discourse of the period, speaks to a decision on his part about how he can usefully link African Americans' claims to the U.S. to notions of community not explicitly linked to the U.S. without undercutting those claims. Waldo Martin has explicated Douglass's connections to Ethiopianism, noting "Douglass and his black colleagues, including Delany, William Wells Brown, Edward W. Blyden, and [Henry Highland] Garnet, argued that the ancient Egyptians were primarily a Negroid people."[16] He "believed that it was futile, moreover, to try to separate Negroes from 'Ethiopians, Abyssinians, Nubians, Carthaginians, Egyptians,' because all Africans were fundamentally one people."[17]

Douglass also indexes Africa's presence in the language of his fellow slaves at Colonel Lloyd's plantation: "There is not, probably, in the whole south, a plantation where the English language is more imperfectly spoken than on Colonel Lloyd's. It is a mixture of Guinea and everything else you please."[18] He explains the specific character of their speech, including which aspects of correct (English) grammar their speech lacked: "They never used the 's' in indication of the possessive case" (76). He makes a point of noting that "there were slaves there who had been brought from the coast of Africa." These statements further illustrate Douglass's ambiguous and ambivalent relationship not only to Africa, but also to Africa's presence in African American culture and life. He complains, "I could scarcely understand them when I first went among them, so broken was their speech; and I am persuaded that I could not have been dropped anywhere on the globe, where I could reap less, in the way of knowledge, from my immediate associates, than on this plantation" (77). His disdainful attitude toward his fellow slaves' speech and toward them because of their speech reveals his desire to distinguish himself from them, and I would argue, by extension from perceptions of all Blacks as uncivilized, ignorant, and worthy of dehumanization. His discarding of racial affinity here serves the purpose of elevating him above the masses.

Significantly, Douglass simultaneously distances himself from this dialect, brought by those uncivilized "slaves who had been brought from the coast of Africa" (not the Creole slaves who are, of course, civilized and worthy of freedom and citizenship) and proves himself exceptional (and worthy of citizenship) by elevating himself above the plantation owner's son, who "by his association with his father's slaves, had measurably adopted their dialect and their ideas, so far as they had ideas to be adopted" (77). He goes on to state that "Mas' Daniel could not associate with ignorance without sharing its shade." Douglass suggests that if he had known that Mas' Daniel was tainted in this way, he would not have spent as much time with him as he did.

Later in *My Bondage and My Freedom*, though, Douglass details his close relationship with Sandy, "a genuine African," who "had inherited some of the so called magical powers, said to be possessed by African and eastern nations" (238). Although he hints that he did not fully embrace Sandy's religion, noting that at first he found it "absurd and ridiculous, if not positively sinful," he did carry the roots Sandy gave him "in [his] right hand pocket" (239). This discussion, while reflecting a measure of ambivalence, does not reflect the level of disdain evident in the earlier statements, and, in fact, suggest a modicum of affinity. (This positive vision and relationship is later undercut, though, by his suggestion that Sandy was the one who betrayed the escape plot he hatched with his fellow slaves: "we suspected, and suspected one person only" (297), further illustrating the ambivalence and ambiguity I have been discussing.)

The revised and expanded final autobiography, *Life and Times of Frederick Douglass* (1892), reveals visions of Africa and African Americans' relationships to it not evident in the earlier autobiographies. At one point, for instance, Douglass mentions Africa in order to decry emigration and to emphasize the need for African Americans to focus on elevating the race rather than moving to this place or that:

> Let us then, wherever we are, whether at the North or at the South resolutely struggle on in the belief that . . . we, by patience, industry, uprightness and economy may hasten that better day . . . Put us in Kansas or in Africa, and until we learn to save more than we spend, we are sure to sink and perish.[19]

From Douglass's perspective, geographical location should be less of a concern for African Americans than should improving their moral and economic character. It does not matter, for Douglass, whether Africa is African Americans' ancestral home or an utterly foreign place, nor does it matter whether Kansas is in the free North or the slave South.

Later in *Life and Times* Douglass casts off questions about his racial heritages and affinities in a similar fashion. He argues that whether he has been a moral man matters more than whether he has more of affinity for his African or European blood. He uses the obsession with his color rather than his morality to decry the state of the American character, saying, "When an unknown man is spoken of in their presence, the first question that arises in the average American mind . . . is Of what color is he? . . . It is not whether his is a good man or a bad man" (512). Along with this question he lists myriad other short-sighted race- or color-related questions that have been posed to him, including "whether [he] considered [himself] more African than Caucasian, or the reverse?" and "will the Negro go back to Africa or remain here?" (513). He concludes this discussion by reemphasizing how this race focus reflects negatively on the American character:

> under this shower of purely American questions . . . I have endeavored to possess my soul in patience and to get as much good out of life as was possible with so much to occupy my time. . . . I have like all honest men . . . answered to the best of my knowledge and belief, and I hope I have never answered in such wise as to increase the hardships on any human being of whatever race or color. (513)

In this statement, he posits himself as the standard-bearer for morality in general and American morality in particular. He has found a rather crafty way of claiming Americanness while also negating racial stereotypes and decrying the complete displacement of discourse on racism by the relocation of blacks themselves to either Africa or Kansas.[20] In contrast to his earlier statements, here he does not display a concern with even noting historical or present day linkages with Africa. Neither Africa nor the character of African Americans' relationship to Africa is of particular concern to Douglass here. Norman Dean Haskett goes so far as to say that "in the pages of Douglass's autobiography, Africa comes off second best," and further that "for him the image of Africa was all but irrelevant."[21] I argue that is, in significant part, because his primary concern is claiming Americanness. Twice-doubled consciousness is clearly exemplified by the tension between his apparent belief in the connection between African Americans and Africa and the desire to claim Americanness.

This persistent conflict between Douglass's ambivalent and ambiguous representational relationship to Africa and his profound desire to be recognized as a U.S. citizen comes across even more clearly when he speaks as an "American tourist" (to use his phrasing) of the parallels to African culture he observes in Italian and French phenotypes and culture: "I saw in France and Italy evidences of a common identity with the African."[22] He notes, "as the traveler moves between [Paris and Rome] he will observe an increase of black hair, black eyes, full lips, and dark complexions" (562). In addition he speaks of the prevalence of the "habit of carrying the burdens on the head" often alleged in America to be "a mark of inferiority peculiar to the Negro." He does not completely negate his and other African Americans' relationships to Africa. He approaches it subtly and without making any explicit links between the two. Instead he represents himself as an American speaking to Americans about the similarities between these foreign cultures: "American ideas, however, would be . . . shocked by the part borne by the women in the labors of the field" (563). The effect of explicitly linking "them" is to make himself part of the American "we," and distinguish himself (along with White Americans) from the Old World "them." He is suggesting that "we" are more civilized than "they" are because we do not treat our women this way. Given the continuing reliance on manual labor by Black women in the U.S. at the time, the factual ground of his statement was clearly shaky. His goal here, though, is not to state facts, but rather to try to push America to a higher moral ground, one that would allow Americans to differentiate themselves from the barbaric nations.

At the same time that he is linking himself and by extension African Americans to the American "we" and differentiating them along with other

Americans from the "them," he is also implicitly referencing the profound connections and parallels between "them" and "us," in addition to playing with the meanings of "them" and "us." He uses his observations of traits "alleged" to be the "mark of the inferiority of the Negro" to prove racist American racial discourse wrong. Douglass illustrates that these qualities are not particular to the Negro. In doing so, he shifts the meaning of "we," making African Americans part of a "we" with Africans (as well as the Italians and the French), and by extension making White Americans part of a "them." Russ Castronovo, in his essay "'As to Nation, I Belong to None': Ambivalence, Diaspora, and Frederick Douglass," delineates the processes through which Douglass defamiliarizes the United States in his writing. Illustrating the way Douglass's relationship to the Black world beyond is bound up with his relationship to the United States, he argues that Douglass refers to the Caribbean in general and Haiti in particular in order to defamiliarize the United States, and make it as "unheimlich" for his readers as it feels to him.[23] Despite his rejection of the U.S., though, he does work to prove himself part of it. As he does that, he runs the risk of replicating conventional U.S. approaches to engaging the other Americas in his relationships with the other Black Americas.

Haiti

Frederick Douglass served as U.S. consul to Haiti and chargé d'affaires of Santo Domingo from 1889 to 1891. Annexationist sentiment in the United States was extremely high during this period. Rayford Logan's seminal text *The Diplomatic Relations of the United States with Haiti, 1776–1891* (1941) explicates the methods by which the U.S. government engaged Haiti in the service of its Manifest Destiny objectives. Douglass found himself caught between the imperialist desires of his country and his desire to help maintain the independence of these countries replete with large numbers of his racial kin. Consequently, his speeches and correspondence during and surrounding this appointment provide special insight into choices about how to represent and engage the other Black Americas. The tensions, ambivalences, and incongruities evident in his articulation of African-American community, his relationship to the U.S., and his nonmentioning of the other Black Americas in the other two autobiographies and the main body of his final one, are magnified in his representations of his tenure as consul to Haiti. In Douglass's going from a solely U.S. context to one that is not only foreign,

but also Black and laden with significance for the pan-Black collective because of its status as the first Black nation in the Americas and as the location
of the most successful Black slave revolution, the twice-doubled consciousness I am identifying comes to the fore. Not only does he have to struggle to
be both American and Negro, but also to be a "good" U.S. citizen, and a
good "brother" to the Haitians.

This twice-doubled consciousness becomes especially evident in Douglass's discussions of one particular issue that arises while he is Consul—
the issue of the Môle St. Nicholas. During this period, the U.S. government
was endeavoring to expand its imperial power by building a military base
on Haitian soil, specifically on the island of Môle St. Nicholas.[24] As consul,
Douglass's job was to ensure the furthering of U.S. interests in Haiti, in this
case to procure the island and get the Haitian government's agreement to
U.S. intentions. This duty placed him squarely between national and pan-Black
affinities, between double consciousnesses. His discussion of the negotiations over the Môle in his final autobiography, *Life and Times*, highlights not
only his uncomfortable position but also the tension between his engagement with the subjectivity of the Haitian government in his struggle to
articulate his own subjectivity from this cramped between space.

President Harrison appointed Douglass to the post in 1889, and from
the moment it was announced his appointment met with resistance, particularly from powerful White U.S. statesmen and businessmen who were
opposed to Douglass on purely racial grounds.[25] They feared that a Black
man would not strongly support or advance U.S. interests but would instead
advocate for Haiti and plot with the Haitians against the U.S. The way Douglass negotiates this negativity while also trying to express his sense of connectedness to Haiti is absolutely fascinating. I therefore quote at length from
several parts of his discussion in *Life and Times*. Douglass writes:

This clamor for a white minister for Haiti is based upon the idea that a white man
is held in higher esteem by her than is a black man, and that he could get more out
of her than can one of her own color. It is not so, and the whole free history of Haiti
proves it not to be so. Even if it were true that a white man could, by reason of his
alleged superiority, gain something extra from the servility of Haiti, it would be the
height of meanness for a great nation like the United States to take advantage of
such servility on the part of a weak nation. (601–3)

At the same time that Douglass is asserting his connectedness to Haiti,
implying that a Black man can "get more out" of Haiti than a White man, he
is adopting the language of U.S. imperial/supremist discourse, calling Haiti

a "weak nation" and the U.S. a "great nation." At the same time that he is attacking the "alleged superiority" of the White man, he is positioning Haiti as an infant that the all-powerful U.S. should pity and protect rather than take advantage of. So we clearly see how the double consciousness of race and nation, being both American and Negro, leads to a twice-doubled consciousness (a struggle to balance affinities), and a hierarchy that subordinates the non-U.S. Black to the U.S. His representation of his handling of this position recalls those moments in the *Narrative* and the other autobiographies in which he refers to his fellow African Americans as "they." The hierarchy evident in this statement about Haiti also positions the non-U.S. Black as a child in relation to the African American, through its simultaneously paternal and patronizing tone. This approach recalls his statement that he "envied" his fellow slaves' "stupidity," once he learned to read and began understanding the nuances of slavery. The implication is that Haiti is to be protected from U.S. meanness, and the African American is the protector. On the one hand, Douglass is squeezed, almost crushed in the middle, between national and pan-Black affinity, but on the other he situates himself above the non-U.S. Black. So while he is being crushed, he is engaging in creating some destructive torque of his own, just as he did at times in his representation of his own countrymen. Binaristic Blackness as it appears in his troubled engagements with Haiti is an unintended consequence of his striving for a recognition of his humanity, equality, and U.S. citizenship. Similarly, his desire to be recognized as human and as an individual (one equal to American individuals like Benjamin Franklin) led him periodically to distance himself from other African Americans.

The pressure of having an affinity for both his own nation and his racial kin, in particular the desire to be recognized as American/U.S., comes to bear in a most profound way on Douglass. The way he chooses to defend himself speaks volumes about the evolution of the worldview initially foreshadowed in the *Narrative*. The twice-doubled consciousness hinted at by the absence of the Caribbean from the narrative, now appears full-blown in Douglass's final autobiography. In his own defense he states:

I am charged with sympathy for Haiti. I am not ashamed of that charge, but no man can say with truth that my sympathy with Haiti stood between me and my honorable duty that I owed to the United States or to any citizen of the United States. . . . The attempt has been made to prove me indifferent to the acquisition of a naval station in Haiti, and unable to grasp the importance to American commerce and to American influence of such a station in the Caribbean Sea. I said then that it was a shame to American statesmanship that, while almost every other great nation in the world had secured a foothold and had power in the Caribbean Sea, where it could anchor in its own bays and moor in its own harbors, we, who stood at the very gate of that sea, had there no anchoring ground anywhere. I was for the acquisition of Samana, and of Santo Domingo herself, if she wished to come to us. While slavery existed I was opposed to all schemes for the extension of American power and influence. But since its abolition, I have gone with him who goes farthest for such extension. (602)

Here we see Douglass even more explicitly trying to walk the fine line between asserting his right to U.S.-ness, his loyalty to the U.S., without wholly disregarding his racial bond with the Haitians. He is fighting against the presumption that U.S. Blacks are not really U.S. Americans and so incapable of understanding or concurring with the capitalist, Manifest Destiny ideology that drives the U.S. coveting of the Môle. He evinces not only a general concern with the U.S. nation's place vis-à-vis the other nations of the world, but a specific desire that the U.S. should use its power to secure a solid relative position. He speaks of other nations and the U.S. needing to have "power in the Caribbean Sea." He almost explicitly embraces the Manifest Destiny ideology in his invocation of the same geographical language of that discourse, of the U.S. being at the "gate of the (Caribbean) Sea" and therefore needing to have some anchor for military power there. He positions the Caribbean as a site where the U.S. and other nations can achieve or lose power.

This vision comes across even more clearly toward the end of the quotation, where he specifically ties his support or lack of support of Manifest Destiny to the abolition or continuation of slavery. Since the U.S. nation has now freed African Americans, he is fully supportive of U.S. attempts to take over the land of others. At the same time, though, his statements also suggest a concern for his Caribbean brethren. He does not want his brothers to be reenslaved, particularly by way of U.S. imperialism. For this reason, he opposed U.S. expansion while slavery was still legal in the U.S. He makes a point of referring to Santo Domingo's part in the determination of whether the U.S. would acquire "her." He "was for the acquisition" only "if she wished to come to us." In his concern for his brothers in the Caribbean, Douglass reiterates the embrace of condition and race as grounds for "we-ness" evident in the previous autobiographies, while adding a transnational dimension to that conception. He is willing to see the people of the Caribbean as part of his community. This expansive notion of community, however, coexists in Douglass's mind with a notion of expanding community—Manifest Destiny, as the presence of both in the abovementioned statement shows. The coexistence is clearly an uneasy one.

In the process of defending himself against the charge of allowing his

loyalty to the Haitians to overtake his loyalty to the U.S., Douglass makes a
point of calling attention to Haitian agency in the negotiations over the
Môle St. Nicholas. He notes,

One fundamental element in our non-success was found, not in any aversion to the
United States, or in any indifference on my part, as has often been charged, but in
the Government of Haiti itself. . . . Nothing is more repugnant to the thoughts and
feelings of the masses of that country than the alienation of a single rood of their
territory to a foreign power. (612–13)

The U.S., Douglass is arguing, is not the only player in the game of expansion. Douglass's emphasis on Haitian agency is not untroubled, however. He
notes that the Haitian government "was evidently timid," recalling his characterization of Haiti as a "weak nation," earlier in this section. He does
historicize the Haitian fear of foreign occupation, noting that it was a natural result of "the circumstances in which Haiti began her national existence,"
when "the whole Christian world was," in his words, "against her." He goes
on to remind his fellow Americans that another cause of the Haitian rejection of their offer for the Môle was that "our peculiar and intense prejudice
against the colored race," that had "not been forgotten" (613). Here, Douglass is claiming his Americanness and speaking as an American ("our"),
defending his Haitian brethren and othering them at the same time, certainly recalling his earlier treatment of his fellow African Americans.

His approach to representing the Haitians here parallels his representation of African Americans in the main body of *Life and Times* and in the
other autobiographies in terms of positioning of himself as a between figure. He presents his position as both positive and negative. This position, as
he describes it, allows him to speak up for his oppressed fellowmen in the
halls of power. At the same time, though, it forces him to suffer the consequences of racism directed at him both because he has presumed to differentiate himself from the others in his community and because he is visibly part
of that community. The tension between the individual's exceptionalism
and the community's story (as well as the story of the individuals' association with the community) evident in the previous autobiographies reap-
pears here in his engagement with the Black world. Both here and in the
earlier texts he is markedly protective of his community despite his similarly evident othering and/or marginalizing of its other members. He goes
so far as to say to Mr. Clyde, "as they will not allow you to put a hot poker
down their backs, you mean to make them pay for heating it" (617). Although
he himself is ambivalent, at times, about whether they are a "we" of which

he is a part or a "they" of which he is not, he is sure to defend them against the attacks of others.

In his thinking, as he represents it in this text, Douglass perceives the grounds of the kinship between himself and the Haitians to be primarily racial. Although he clearly resents the presumption that he could not serve the interests of the U.S. properly because of his race, he does not disavow the significance of his race for his relationships with the Haitian leadership. He argues, in fact, that his racial connection to the Haitians makes him a more appropriate minister: "This clamor for a white minister for Haiti is based on the idea that a white man is held in higher esteem by her than is a black man. . . . It is not so, and the whole free history of Haiti proves it not to be so" (601). Douglass goes so far as to use his kinship with the Haitians to raise questions about a White man's suitability for the job of gaining concessions from Haiti. Douglass argues that, although the focus has been on his race, and incorrectly so, the historical realities demand that the race and the racism of a White man trying to get those concessions should disqualify him from being chosen as the negotiator. He says, for example, of the White U.S. businessman William Clyde who wanted the Môle so that he could "ply a line of steamers between New York and Haiti," that for Clyde "it was impossible . . . to conceal his contempt for the people whose good will it was his duty to seek" (615). He contends that the real concern of those who wanted the U.S. to get the Môle, then, should not have been the negotiator's race or Americanness, but rather his attitude towards the Haitians, that is, the people with whom they were attempting to negotiate.

Frederick Douglass's textual treatment of differences between himself and Haitians in this part of *Life and Times* echoes at points his approach to dealing with differences within the African American community. As he did in his discussion of the betrayal of the escape plot he hatched with his fellow slaves, he exhibits a hesitance about calling attention to intracommunity tensions. Douglass speaks abstractly about the government's timidity (a sentiment he goes on to represent as logical) and notes that he "thought that it would be in many ways a good thing for Haiti to have the proposed line of steamers." He never indexes any fissures in the relationship between himself and the Haitian leadership (618). In fact, he discloses that he refused his superior's demand that he inveigle the Haitian foreign minister into granting him the desired concessions (616).

His approach to engaging the Haitians textually differs from his method of presenting differences between himself and other members of the African

American community in one significant way—whereas he allows readers of the autobiographies to get to know the "characters" in his life, he does not do so with the Haitians. He focuses on the Haitian leaders' actions rather than their personalities, political views, or culture, and generally does not have them speak. William Andrews argues, "dialogue in slave narratives tells us something about the negotiation of power that goes on in discourse, whether between a master and slave or a black autobiographer and a reader."[26] In *Life and Times* Douglass includes no dialogue between himself and the Haitians or between the Haitians and anyone else. The result is that his voice is the only Black voice in the text. By omitting dialogue, he locates the key battle as that between himself and his White accusers in the U.S. This, I argue, is reflective of his desire to be recognized as human and as an individual.

Fundamentally, Douglass's relationship to the Black world beyond the U.S., as he represents it in his autobiographies, is the result of his conception of the way in which he needs to represent himself in order to answer his critics, to stake his claim to Americanness, and to improve the conditions of African Americans. Two approaches to conceptualizing the Black Caribbean result from the intertwining of these struggles to define a self and a collective. The first is an implicit othering of the non-U.S. Black that, in Douglass's case, is manifested in the silence on/of the non-U.S. black in the bulk of the autobiographies and in his characterizations of Haiti as a nation that needs the help of the great and mighty nation that is the United States. The goal of the autobiographies, in addition to presenting Douglass himself, is to improve the situation of African Americans. No wonder, then, that James McCune Smith emphasizes the Americanness of *My Bondage and My Freedom* rather than its linkage to the revolutionary genealogy begun by Toussaint L'Ouverture: Douglass "is a Representative American man . . . and bears upon his person and upon his soul every thing that is American. And he has . . . full sympathy with every thing American."[27]

Another element of this implicit othering inheres in Douglass's complex embrace and rejection of the underpinnings of Manifest Destiny ideology. He accepts the premise that the United States is the mightier nation, but argues that the U.S. must aim to use that power to help weaker nations rather than to hurt them. His statement that he supported annexation only after slavery was abolished in the United States evinces this belief in a benevolent Manifest Destiny. The point here is not that Douglass differs from his fellow African American leaders or from other progressives in this belief—

even African American leaders like Martin Delany who were politically at odds with Douglass embraced Black versions of the civilizing mission, but rather how it is a factor in the relationship between this African American and the Black world beyond the U.S.[28] His embrace of this notion necessarily determines the conditions of possibility for his simultaneous claiming of Americanness and his envisioning of a connection to the non-U.S. members of his race.

Douglass's second approach, primarily evident in his discussion of West Indian emancipation, is the incorporation of the non-U.S. Black into a broad Black collectivism, while also using the non-U.S. Black as a jumping off point for addressing the condition of African Americans, and for talking back to the dominant forces within the U.S. context. In this, Douglass recalls David Walker, who in his *Appeal* invoked the Haitian Revolution to remind African Americans to have faith that God will ultimately deliver them from their "wretched condition."[29]

Douglass's autobiographies make clear that double consciousness (of being Black and trying to be recognized as American) and the "twice doubled consciousness" (of being African American and trying to articulate a sense of connection to non-U.S. Blacks) are difficult, if not impossible for him to escape. They always already determine relationships between people of African descent across national boundaries.[30] Twice doubled consciousness and binaristic blackness are two of the most enduring legacies of slavery's denial of people of African descent's citizenship and humanity— legacies that make the overturning of the transnational and national conditions of oppression that created and fed them especially challenging. The persistence of these pitfalls, however, makes one wonder whether perhaps there is no greater illustration of people of African descent's humanity than the prevalence of this tendency to oscillate between acknowledging multiplicity and negating it in the service of articulating a singular identity. As Edouard Glissant notes, "The principles of creoleness regress toward negritudes, ideas of Frenchness, of Latinness, all generalizing concepts—more or less innocently.[31]

The extent to which these approaches to engaging the Black world beyond the U.S. are a result of the demands of the genre of autobiography is less evident in the autobiographies themselves, however. An analysis of Douglass's approach in his other writings allow for a more complete and nuanced understanding of his thinking on the Black world and for a testing out of Glissant's theory.

The Black World in Douglass's Fiction, Essays, Speeches, and Newspapers

In his fiction, essays, speeches, and newspapers, Douglass engages the Black world more frequently. In these texts he replicates the emphasis on African Americans' rights to Americanness evident in the *Narrative, My Bondage and My Freedom*, and the bulk of *Life and Times*. For example, when he is asked by one of the readers of his newspaper, *Douglass's Monthly*, to publish his views on emigration to Haiti, he likens telling African Americans to emigrate to telling an Englishman or an Irishman to leave England or Ireland, again implicitly naming African Americans' ties to the U.S.: "but as we should not be in favor of saying to all the people of these countries, be off, so we are not in favor of saying to all the colored people here, *move off*."[32] In these texts not explicitly marked as autobiographies, he also exhibits openness to transnational notions of community not evident in the autobiographies. His engagement with the Black world beyond the U.S. is qualitatively different in these texts, in part, because he not required, by either genre or publisher, to focus on his own voice/story, to provide a narrative that is presumed to be purely a reflection of an experience, or to defend himself against specific personal accusations. That is not to say that this writing is wholly unfettered, but rather to say that the limitations and expectations differ significantly from those with which he had to contend as he wrote the autobiographies.

One particularly instructive instance is a series of speeches Douglass made as Haiti's representative at the World's Columbian Exposition in 1893. He gave these speeches merely a year after publishing this part of *Life and Times* on his tenure in Haiti discussed earlier in this chapter. In the speech "Haiti and the Haitian People," Douglass celebrates the significance of Haiti not just for African Americans (although he does detail that), but for Americans and the world more broadly. Haiti, like Greece, Rome, England, Germany, and the U.S. had a mission in the world. Haiti's was to teach "the world the danger of slavery and the value of liberty." It has been, he argues, "the greatest of all our modern teachers."[33] In fact, in many ways, Haiti was ahead of the rest of the world. He points out, "until Haiti struck for freedom, the conscience of the Christian world slept profoundly over slavery" (528). He defends Haiti against charges that it is a barbarous, backward country that is incapable of having any impact on the world. He reminds Whites that Haiti has already had a major impact: "while slavery

existed amongst us, her example was a sharp thorn in our side and source
of alarm and terror . . . her very name was pronounced with a shudder"
(520). He criticizes the U.S. for giving Haiti, a country so close and with so
much potential, the cold shoulder. He defends Haiti's right to refuse to grant
the U.S. the coveted Môle St. Nicholas. He speaks positively of Haiti's future,
noting that "with peace firmly established within her borders . . . Haiti might
easily lead all the other islands of the Caribbean Sea in the race of civilization" (518). All these comments are important because they show that Douglass
sees the importance of articulating a positive vision of Haiti, particularly
because, as he says "it reflects upon the colored race everywhere." They also
provide a much more detailed representation of Haiti than that contained
in the final section of *Life and Times*.

More striking, though, are his discussions of the call to make Haiti a
U.S. protectorate and of the prevalent stereotypes of Haitians as superstitious, lazy, snake-worshipping people who allowed their children to run the
streets naked. With regard to the protectorate, he states simply that Haiti, as
a proud nation, one no less proud than the U.S., will never allow the U.S. to
take over any part of its soil: "Haiti has no repugnance so deep-seated and
unconquerable as the repugnance to losing control over a single inch of her
territory" (518). Here he cleverly reinforces his celebration of Haiti while
also decrying the assumption implicit in arrogant Manifest Destiny that the
U.S. is capable of wresting anything it wants from any country. He reminds
his listeners that Haiti has the resources to become "the richest country in
the world" (514). He treats the presumably less savory aspects of "Haiti and
the Haitian People" in a no less savvy fashion. He provides an "ethnography" of Haiti (a term to be discussed in further detail in the next chapter),
in which he details the typical appearance, occupations, and ideologies of
the Haitian people in the process of defending them. He agrees that Haiti
continues to be torn by revolutions sparked in part by the Haitians themselves. He is sure to note, however, that quite often the unrest is aided by co-
conspirators in the U.S. He notes with contempt that many of the leaders of
these uprisings are given the right of asylum and end up living a good life
in places like Kingston, Jamaica (516–18). He concedes that "there is much
ignorance and much superstition in Haiti," but only after detailing the
atrocities committed by the Spanish in the name of Christianity and just
before emphasizing the present superstition in several countries of Europe
and parts of the U.S., including specifically New England (524). He agrees that
there is snake worship in Haiti, but argues that the Haitians got it from the
overwhelming prevalence of the snake in Christianity, recalling in particular

the Garden of Eden (526). He counters the idea that Haitians are lazy, arguing, "a revenue of millions does not come to a country where no work is
done" (527).

One of the most curious defenses he mounts of Haiti is to answer the
charge that nude children run rampant throughout the streets of Haiti. He
begins the defense by agreeing that there are "more of them [nude children]
than we . . . would easily tolerate," but notes that for every "one hundred
decently dressed children" there is only "one that is nude" (526). The curious aspect of the defense is his statement that "It should be remembered
also, than in a warm climate like that of Haiti, the people consider more the
comfort of their children in this respect than any fear of improper exposure
of their little innocent bodies." Although at other points, there are paren-
thetical notes marking where the audience applauded, there are none here.
If the statement was meant in jest or as a joke among Haitians, it seems that
the audience (a group of "fifteen hundred of the best citizens of Chicago,"
509) was unable to grasp the humor.

The statement does, therefore, raise the question of audience, and by
extension authorial identity—that is, what audience did Douglass anticipate
or envision for his public representations of the Black world, and who was
he aiming to be as he spoke to them?[34] In this case Douglass is speaking to
fifteen hundred Americans, and appears to be positioning himself as connected to both the audience ("more of them than *we* would easily tolerate")
and to the Haitians whom he goes out of his way to defend. As phrased and
framed, his statement marks him as one who is so connected to the Haitian
community that he views himself as having the right to make jokes about
Haitian conditions without fear of being read as playing into the stereotypes
he aims to disprove.

At the same time as the statement suggests that he is attempting to
position himself as an insider with respect to Haiti, it also hints at the
possible presence of a casual hyperbole in his characterizations of Haiti
and Haitians, one that reflects a level of discomfort in attempting to engage
these less savory aspects of Haiti. His use of words "improper exposure" and
"little innocent bodies" in his defense of the Haitians also index his discomfort. Underlying his defense is the implied statement that the parents should
view this exposure as improper and seek to cover their children's "little
innocent bodies." Even if his statement is a joke, it seems a rather strange
joke to be making in front of non-Haitians, given the prevailing views of
Haitians as barbaric. If the statement is matter-of-fact, it is undercut by
the terms used, which imply disagreement with the Haitian parents' decisions.

Douglass's approach, in fact, recalls that which he took in the discussion (or more appropriately nondiscussion) of Sandy's likely betrayal of the conspiracy plot Douglass planned along with his fellow slaves, as well as his treatment of his fellow slaves' "stupidity," as he characterized it in the autobiographies. The tensions and differences within the communities he attempts to construct or celebrate are present, and he is clearly uncomfortable with representing or engaging them in a public arena.

His statements in this speech, "Haiti and the Haitian People," are more overtly pro-Haiti and pro-Black world than the autobiographies. In his novella *The Heroic Slave* (1853) he also reveals a pro-Black world stance. In rewriting the true story of the mutiny undertaken by Madison Washington and the other slaves on the *Creole* ship near the Bahamas, Douglass makes a point of noting in the presence of Bahamians on the shore cheering the rebels' accomplishments and welcoming them to their islands. By including the Bahamians, Douglass situates the rebels, whom he has set up as descendants of the patriots of the American Revolution, as also part of a Black world. The rebels are both heirs to the American Revolution and brethren to these Black Bahamians.[35]

Douglass's fundamental focus is the recognition of the facts that African Americans are U.S. citizens who should be accorded all the corresponding rights, and that they too are heirs to the legacy of the founding fathers of the American Revolution. At the same time as he is making this argument, though, Douglass does address transnational concerns, both historical and contemporary. Beyond his autobiographies, he does engage both the impact of the Haitian Revolution and West Indian emancipation on African Americans and the potential impact of U.S. Manifest Destiny on Blacks outside of the United States. Significantly, there are moments in which Douglass articulates a broader transnational notion of Americanness that encompasses the whole continent, not just the United States. In a speech on Santo Domingo in 1873, for instance, he argues that Santo Domingo was American before the Puritans' America even existed. He describes the island as "that part of American soil where Columbus first stood."[36] In these moments, Douglass illustrates a worldview much broader than that which he articulates in his *Narrative*, when he entreats the mighty ocean to take him away . . . to Pennsylvania. In the *Narrative*, he yearns for the freedom symbolized by ships: "I have often, in the deep stillness of a summer's Sabbath, stood all alone upon the lofty banks of that noble bay, and traced, with saddened heart and tearful eye, the countless number of sails moving off to the mighty ocean.[37] Here he sounds as if he dreams of going beyond the shores of the United States to freedom. He does, however, only indicate a general destination—"the mighty ocean," and not specifically England, Canada, the by now emancipated British Caribbean, or even Africa. When he does specify a destination in his subsequent apostrophe to the ships it is the U.S. north. He dreams

I will take to the water. This very bay shall yet bear me into freedom. The steamboats steered in a north-east course from North Point. I will do the same; and when I get to the head of the bay, I will turn my canoe adrift, and walk straight through Delaware into Pennsylvania. When I get there, I shall not be required to have a pass. (38–39)

The world of Douglass the slave, the world symbolized by his use of the image of "the mighty ocean," does not extend beyond the United States. So, even though he never mentions the United States explicitly, it structures his definition of the world and his (and by extension U.S. Blacks') place in it.

The differences between the approaches he takes to engaging the Black world in general and Haiti in particular are not attributable simply to chronology. That is to say, they cannot be read just as a result of a change in his ideology over time, although that may have contributed to the differences. *The Heroic Slave* was published two years before *My Bondage and My Freedom*, the text described by James McCune Smith as being so essentially American. The difference cannot be explained by simply saying that he did not know about the Black world when he wrote the *Narrative* (and was therefore silent on the Black World), and that he did know about it in his final autobiography and therefore mentioned it. This fact is reinforced by his references, in *Life and Times*, to his celebration of West Indian emancipation when a slave, a celebration not mentioned in either of the autobiographies published before the end of slavery in the U.S., and the publication of the Appendix with its simultaneous defense and othering of Haiti a year before his speeches at the Exposition.

Throughout his career, Douglass continued to fight for full recognition of African Americans' U.S. citizenship. He employed a multitude of strategies in order to make his argument more convincing. Among those was textual engagement with the Black world beyond the U.S. That is not to say that Douglass only engaged the Black world beyond the U.S. in the service of this goal, but rather to say that his engagements were shaped by his fundamental goal, whether he decided to be silent on the Black world as in the *Narrative, My Bondage and My Freedom,* and the bulk of the *Life and Times* or to speak directly of or from the Black world as in his speeches at the Columbian Exposition. In Douglass's case, the connection to the nation, or the desire for that connection, overwhelms all other linkages, including racial ones. The next chapter explores the impact that the negation of the nation can have on the creation and articulation of racial bonds.

PART THREE

Negating Nation, Rejecting Race

*The desire (even the need) to migrate is at the heart of West Indian
sensibility—whether that migration is in fact or by metaphor.*
—*Edward Kamau Brathwaite,* Roots

I was in a word, a mulatto among blacks.
—*Juan Francisco Manzano, "The Life of the Negro Poet"*

A s Part Two has illustrated, in the wake of the Haitian Revolution, people
of African descent's juggling of racial consciousness and national identity, a challenge born of both their need to defend themselves in the face of
others' notions of their identities and their internal struggle with self-definition
in the context of the denial of their humanity and subjectivity, frequently
led them to contradict themselves as they articulated visions of the bases of
their individual identities and conceptions of community. Part Three centers
on the ways in which the historical moment produced not only the aforementioned juggling, but also decisions to ignore one or the other (racial or
national) affinity in the public representation of one's subjectivity.

The individuals under study here are British West Indian (ex-)slave
Mary Prince and Cuban (ex-)slave and poet Juan Francisco Manzano. Prince,
for whom access to national (or colonial in this case) identity is impossible
because of both her status and her race, negates national identity in favor
of a "cosmopolitan consciousness" that emphasizes her racial affinity as well
as her epistemological and emotional connection to the broader Atlantic
world. Juan Francisco Manzano uses the indeterminacy of Cuban racial categories (particularly the fungibility of terms such as *pardo* and *mulato* that
were simultaneously used to index people's mixed ancestry and to mark class
distinctions within the community of color) in order to escape being dehumanized and equated with the masses of those classified as negro and, by
extension, to assert his own exceptionality, humanity, and subjectivity.

Prince and Manzano are the focus of this section not only because of
their negation of nation and rejection of ascribed racial categories, respectively, but also because by identifying and articulating themselves in these

ways both subvert conventions of the nineteenth-century slave narrative. Prince's "cosmopolitan consciousness," evident in both her "community auto-ethnography" and her "cosmopolitan cartography," stands out in a genre dominated by geographically limited visions. Manzano's distancing of himself from *los negros*, particularly given the lack of evidence to support his claim to mixed ancestry, contrasts with the presumption (widely held both then and now) that a slave narrator speaks from and for the good (the emancipation) of the Black community.

Chapter 6
A Slave's Cosmopolitanism:
Mary Prince, a West Indian Slave,
and the Geography of Identity

Mary Prince, the orator of the first slave narrative by a woman in the Americas, was born into slavery in 1788, just three years before the foundations of the Caribbean and the Atlantic world more broadly were to be profoundly shaken by the revolution in Haiti. She was born in Bermuda, an island chain 988 miles from Haiti, and even spent several years working on Turks Island, a site through which many British slaves escaped to Haiti.[1] Her narrative, *The History of Mary Prince, a West Indian Slave*, was published in 1831, three years before the official abolition of slavery in the British colonies. Prince's representations of the grounds of connection or disconnection between enslaved Blacks throughout the region, and her approach to finding and articulating her own sense of regional, colonial, and racial identity intervene in debates about the meanings and limits of West Indianness, Englishness, subjectivity, and humanity swirling throughout the Anglophone Atlantic world during her lifetime.

Her status as a pivotal pioneer in the public and published articulation of Black West Indian identity is highlighted by the fact that her concerns and her approaches to conceptualizing and articulating identity are echoed frequently in both later nineteenth-century and twentieth-century Caribbean texts. Afro-Trinidadian John Jacob Thomas, author of *Froudacity*, the famous 1889 rejoinder to English writer J. A. Froude's questioning of Blacks' capacity for civilization, is a descendant of Prince in terms of his public back-answering of colonial ideas about West Indian Blacks.[2] The 1980s and 1990s witnessed a relative explosion in critical attention to nineteenth-century Black women writers, Afro-Caribbean writers in general, and Afro-Caribbean women writers in particular. Cheryl Fish, for example, keys in on the "mobile subjectivity" of free Black women traveler-writers African

American Nancy Prince and Jamaican-born Mary Seacole, both free black women.[3] From Jean D'Costa and Barbara Lalla's *Voices in Exile* published in 1989, a pathbreaking collection of eighteenth- and nineteenth-century Jamaican texts, to Moira Ferguson's edited work *Nine Black Women,* a compilation of nineteenth-century Black women writers of the Americas published in 1998, early Caribbean writing has been resituated in the discourse on Caribbean Literature, and on early Black Americas writing. Key critical works by Sandra Pouchet Paquet and Amy Robinson have affirmed early Afro-Caribbean women's writing as an especially vital and fruitful locus of inquiry. In two major articles published in *African-American Review* Paquet holds up Mary Prince and Mary Seacole as presenting two distinct models for West Indian identity.[4] Amy Robinson adds to this discourse by reading Mary Seacole's crafting of her public image in order to garner authority, to establish her reputation as an "exceptional British subject."[5] In the introduction to *Out of the Kumbla,* a collection of critical essays on twentieth-century Caribbean women's writing edited by Carole Boyce Davies and Elaine Savory Fido, the editors point to the longstanding silencing of Caribbean women writers, specifically "the absence of critical discussion of existing works by Caribbean women writers."[6]

A major concern of this growing critical discourse can be aptly characterized as the exploration of roots and routes—of articulations of West Indian subjectivities and of the impact of travel/displacement/movement on relationships to and definitions of West Indian subjectivity.[7] Slaves and self-determined movement or relationships to place are, however, often presumed to be mutually exclusive, both in this discourse and beyond. I am arguing that this is not so, and that Prince's approaches to defining self and other and her relationships to home, region, and world certainly identify her as a foremother of this discourse. She should be a crucial part of the burgeoning discourse on Black transnationalism, a discourse that has focused primarily on men and primarily on twentieth-century texts. Slave narratives, whether as cosmopolitan as Prince's or as geographically limited as Douglass's, must be understood as part of the background of discourses on/ of Black transnationalism. If these texts are key indicators of the processes by which Black identities developed (as work by scholars like Houston Baker, William Andrews, and Frances Smith Foster highlights), they are also key indicators of the processes by which the conceptual groundwork was laid for writers/thinkers like W. E. B. Du Bois, Langston Hughes, and Gayl Jones.

Prince in Context

Prince, the slave, begins life in Bermuda as the "little n____r" (pet) of "Miss Betsey." As she herself notes, as a child she was blissfully unaware of the horrors of slavery: "This was the happiest period of my life; for I was too young to understand rightly my condition as a slave."[8] When her mistress dies, her life and perspective are changed forever. In addition to suffering through slavery on the island of Bermuda, Prince is forced to endure two of the most brutal situations for slaves in the British Caribbean—the salt mines of Turks Island and the plantations of Antigua. Toward the end of her life she goes to England with her enslavers with the hope that she will be able to secure her freedom there—after all, slavery on English soil had been declared illegal in 1772.[9] While in England, Prince narrated *The History of Mary Prince* to Susanna Strickland, guest of Anti-Slavery Society secretary Thomas Pringle. (Prince disappeared from the public record in 1833.)

The British West Indies of Mary Prince's era was a physical and ideological battleground. Apart from the numerous and ongoing battles with rebellious slaves in Jamaica and Antigua in particular, British West Indian planters also had to deal with the significant dips in prices and in the availability of markets and suppliers brought about by the American Revolution, the Haitian Revolution, and the British Crown's determination to protect its own financial interests, even if doing so came at the expense of the West Indian planters.[10] In addition, the already formidable abolitionist movement in England was gaining steam. Organizations such as the Anti-Slavery Society, of which Prince's editor was the secretary, were mounting successful challenges to the White West Indians' way of life, challenges that forced the White West Indians to begin to talk about reform and/or gradual emancipation to maintain a semblance of financial security. At the same time insecurity about the meaning of Englishness and English national identity was rampant both in England and throughout the colonies. In particular, as historian Kathleen Wilson details, there was an ongoing debate throughout the eighteenth and nineteenth centuries about whether Englishness was an inborn essence (as Burke suggests when he describes nation as "a moral essence, not a geographical arrangement"), or a contingency based on "proximity and shared language, laws, government and social organization."[11] White West Indian planters' anxieties about whether the right to Englishness ended on the shores of England come across clearly throughout the eighteenth and nineteenth centuries in their complaints about royal policy that are framed as pleas for assistance and/or protection. The records of the Jamaica Assembly from the early to mid-eighteenth century, for example, reveal that the members felt the need constantly to emphasize their position as English subjects, and by extension as individuals entitled to royal protection. The Assembly, for example, writes in 1740:

We, your majesty's most dutiful and loyal subjects, the council and assembly of the island of Jamaica, being conscious to ourselves, of your gracious, constant, and paternal care of your subjects in general, and of this your colony of Jamaica in particular, should be highly wanting in our duty, did we not faithfully represent unto your majesty, our grievances and apprehensions. We beg leave, with the greatest humility, to lay before your majesty how much we are alarmed at the endeavours of designing men to import foreign rum, without paying of the duty, contrary to the known and confirmed laws of this island; and it is a matter of the greatest concern to us, when we reflect, that this importation is supported by an order of your majesty's council.[12]

The members emphasize their position as English subjects, and by extension as individuals entitled to royal protection, repeatedly. Also evident in the comments, though, is a nascent sense of themselves as West Indian subjects, as subjects who, while linked to England, also have separate interests and affinities.

This burgeoning sense of West Indian particularity is evident even earlier in the eighteenth century when the members of the assembly in 1714 write a letter to the Queen expressing their displeasure with a Crown appointee:

We most humbly beseech your majesty that William Brodrick, esquire, your majesty's late attorney general here . . . may never for the future be admitted into any office or employment of honour, profit, or trust *in this island*. The assembly of this, *your majesty's island*, on the eighteenth day of December last, taking into consideration the behaviour and evil practices of the said William Brodrick, did resolve, that he was a forger of lies, . . . and a common disturber of the peace of *this island*; and that your majesty's subjects of this *your majesty's island* could never expect to be at ease or in safety, while he continued in any office or place of honour, profit, or *trust in this island*.[13]

The assembly members, while making sure to seem appropriately humble ("humbly beseech," "your majesty's island"), strongly speak for and from their island and demand that the Queen go along with a decision they have already made on their own. The rhetorical parrying, specifically the balancing of humility and assertiveness, in this letter is striking. They alternate between attributing the island to her majesty, and speaking as if their knowledge of what is best for the island should supersede hers. The assembly members go on to go so far as to feel they need to appoint "an agent in

Great-Britain, to solicit the passing of laws, and other the public affairs of this island," the implication being that neither the Crown-appointed governor nor the English foreign affairs officials could really understand or represent the particular issues confronted by West Indians.[14]

The *History of Mary Prince, a West Indian Slave* was published during a period when the battle over slave emancipation was at its height. (Emancipation in the British West Indies was officially pronounced in 1834, but did not take effect until four years later after the slaves had gone through an "apprenticeship system," by which they learned how to live as free people.) As the abolitionist movement became stronger, tensions between the West Indian planters' growing sense of West Indian rights to self-determination and the crown's imposition of royal laws and pursuit of its own imperial interests were also heightened. The White West Indian planters had already been pushed into the position of advocating reform, and the British Parliament was clearly leaning heavily towards emancipation.[15] *The History of Mary Prince*, as readers are told in the preface that precedes the narrative, was recorded and published at the request of Prince, who was in England at the time, and apparently cognizant of the special potential of this moment.

The debate over whether Blacks were civilized enough to handle being set free was profoundly implicated in the battle over emancipation. The idea that Blacks were not adequately prepared for life as free people was persistent in both proslavery and abolitionist discourse of the time. For example, in a moving antislavery treatise that powerfully details and decries the inhumanity and ungodliness that is slavery in the British West Indies, the Revered Mr. Richard Bickell still notes that he is "no friend to immediate emancipation" because it would be "a great and incalculable injury to the Slaves themselves." He argues for amelioration rather than immediate emancipation because the slaves "are generally speaking in so barbarous and unenlightened a state, so devoid of education and religion, that anarchy confusion, warfare, and blood, would be the dreadful effects of the too hasty and mistaken boon."[16] Furthermore, as Belinda Edmondson details, Englishness was "predicated on a notion of manhood," that demanded that Blacks had to prove that they could become English gentlemen in order to have any possibility at all of becoming Englishmen.[17] Inherent in that formulation was the denigration or displacement of Black West Indian women, who could certainly never become English gentlemen: "Female subjectivity lies outside of the paradigm."[18] Prince as a slave woman has access to neither (gentle)manhood nor, by extension, Britishness. Nevertheless, Prince pushes her way into the debates.

Prince vociferously avows the importance of her Black, female, West Indian voice, and that of her fellow slaves, in these debates over the present and future of the West Indies. The method by which she does so distinguishes her from other nineteenth-century slave narrators. She makes her point by emphasizing her cognizance of and connection to the world beyond Bermuda, by exhibiting what I am terming "cosmopolitan consciousness." This term describes the coexistence of an interest in, knowledge of, and engagement with the world at large with the embrace of a racially based notion of community. My use of the term cosmopolitan in describing Prince is intended both to echo the characterization of cosmopolitanism as a drive to define oneself in relation to the world beyond one's own that undergirds conventional definitions and to interrogate the hierarchy and othering that they often also imply.

Cosmopolitanism was certainly a value in the British world in which Prince lived.[19] Orientalism was one of the many forms it took in English discourse. It was a form that, despite the interest in and engagement with aspects of the Other implicit in it, also reified and reiterated notions of European superiority. Orientalists certainly exhibited an interest in the Other, but also, significantly, invented the Other with which they were engaging. As Edward Said says of Orientalism, it "puts the Westerner in a whole series of possible relationships with the Orient without ever losing him the relative upper hand."[20] He notes further that "it *is*, rather than expresses, a certain *will* or *intention* to understand, in some cases to control, manipulate, even to incorporate, what is a manifestly different (or alternative and novel) world."[21] (In this, Said anticipates the analyses of Mary Louise Pratt, who undertakes detailed analyses of the impact of encounters with the newly discovered, imaged, and imagined others on colonial European ideology, self-concepts, and worldviews.)

I would argue further that imperialism and colonialism themselves are forms of cosmopolitanism. Responses and resistance to these forms, then, are often also cosmopolitan. Pheng Cheah, for example, critiques Immanuel Kant's utopian vision of international commerce and cosmopolitanism. Kant had a vision of cosmopolitical culture as the "promise of humanity's freedom from, or control over . . . human finitude."[22] Karl Marx also posited a utopian cosmopolitanism, through which the proletariat would cast off loyalty to the nation and its economy in favor of the creation of "a universal class transcending boundaries."[23] In using this term to describe a nineteenth-century person of African descent, I aim to suggest that this, along with the other manifestations of cosmopolitanism during the period (and slavery, of course), helped to shape the terms of people of African descents' public articulations of self and representations of each other.

In my use of the term, I am also engaging more recent denotations, such as those put forward by Ulf Hannerz that define cosmopolitanism as "an intellectual and esthetic openness toward divergent cultural experiences," "a competence of both a generalized and a more specialized kind," "a personal ability to make one's way into other cultures."[24] I am arguing that Prince is not just an object, but is responding to a cosmopolitanism from above that is often violent, oppressive, White, and male, and positing an alternative vision of the meaning of cosmopolitan.[25] The specific ways in which Prince, as a slave woman, presents herself as a cosmopolitan subject while speaking to context-specific (to the British Empire and Bermuda) demands are my focus here.

Prince's approach to representing and conceptualizing home is also part of her philosophy of identity, her cosmopolitan consciousness. Cosmopolitanism as traditionally defined also implies a particular relationship to home—specifically a detachment from a singular local place in favor of an embrace of all places, of the world. As Timothy Brennan puts it, the cosmopolite is "at home in the world."[26] Cosmopolitan consciousness does not, however, necessarily depend on a detachment from home. It recalls Anthony Appiah's notion of the "cosmopolitan patriot" in that sense. He characterizes the cosmopolitan patriot as one who "can entertain the possibility of a world in which everyone is a rooted cosmopolitan, attached to a home of one's own, with its own cultural particularities, but taking pleasure from the presence of other, different places that are home to other, different people."[27] I distinguish my concept by its emphasis on positing oneself not only as a citizen of the world more broadly, but also of a Black world more specifically, while also acknowledging and maintaining a connection to one's "native place," as Prince terms Bermuda.

Connection to the "native place," however, can become the "binaristic Blackness' described in the previous chapter. Cosmopolitan consciousness and binaristic blackness can, therefore, coexist in the same mind. As Ulf Hannerz notes, "cosmopolitanism also has a narcissistic streak."[28] I have chosen to introduce the idea of the relationship between cosmopolitanism and parochialism, between cosmopolitan consciousness and binaristic Blackness, through Prince, rather than through Douglass, though, because Prince's cosmopolitan consciousness appears in a nineteenth-century slave narrative, a genre traditionally limited in its geographical scope. Douglass's more substantive engagements with the world beyond the U.S. take place in texts published after his narrative. Prince's narrative is distinctive because *The History of Mary Prince, a West Indian Slave, Related by Herself* simultaneously brings into focus and raises questions about the identificatory, geographical, and spatial conventions of the slave narrative.

Prince's Racial Consciousness

As is evident in the content, context, and language of the references to those to whom she feels connected in the narrative, Mary Prince clearly values a conception of group identity based on race and condition. She unambiguously embraces the idea of Black and slave collectivism. She presents herself as fully invested and involved in the community. She speaks often of herself and her fellow slaves as a collective whose members share the same emotions, experiences, and dreams. In her recollection of the impact of the death of her first mistress, for example, she remembers, "all the slaves cried."[29] The effect of this highlighting of the collective is to make her narrative a text from which the voice of the collective, rather than that of an individual, emanates. Throughout the narrative she emphasizes the extent to which she is invested in telling the collective story of Black slaves in the West Indies.[30] In reporting the atmosphere surrounding the sale of her and her siblings away from her mother, Prince calls attention to the collective voice of the story she tells in two ways. She speaks of her mother's sense of common destiny with a fellow slave mother named Moll who watches the separation. Mary notes, " 'Ay,' said my mother seeing her turn away and look at her child with the tears in her eyes, 'your turn will come next" (4). Prince also highlights the collective by referencing the empathy felt by the broader slave community for her family, acknowledging sadly that "The slaves could say nothing to comfort us; they could only weep and lament with us." She uses the opportunity to situate this collective story within an even broader context, using it as an example of the damage that slavery in general does to all involved: "slavery hardens white people's hearts towards the blacks." The former statements illustrate Prince's view of social condition as a bond; the latter shows her explicit embrace of race as a basis for connection. Prince links them. She expresses a profound sense of connection to her fellow slaves, and repeatedly notes their demonstration of their connection to her. When she is sold away for the first time, she speaks warmly of the two slave women who welcomed her, and warned her of the harshness of the life she was beginning: "'Poor child, poor child!' they both said; 'you must keep a good heart, if you are to live here'" (5).

Significantly, neither geographical origin nor linguistic background matters to Prince in her conceptualization of her (racial) community. She shows as much empathy and love for "Hetty, a French Black," as she does for "a mulatto called Cyrus, who had been bought while an infant in his mother's arms," Jack, "an African from the coast of Guinea," and all the slaves she meets and works with in Turks Island and in Antigua (6). In these moments of empathy, the grounds of her cosmopolitan consciousness surface. She is willing and able to acknowledge the varied geographical and cultural origins of individuals, while also recognizing and embracing them as members of her community. In Prince's eyes, the fact that Hetty is (or speaks) French presents no obstacle to her sentiments for Hetty. (Her bond with Jack, "an African who my master had brought from Guinea" similarly illustrates this fact.) It is significant that she feels this bond even before she has any personal contact with Hetty, further reiterating the racial aspect of her collectivism. Prince's attitude toward Hetty suggests that she sees Hetty as kin because they are both black, both slaves, and both women.

The only person of African descent with whom she does not express kinship is Martha Wilcox, a free mulatto woman. She describes Martha as "a saucy woman, very saucy," who "went and complained of me" to the mistress. Prince says of her relationship with Martha that "I thought it very hard for a coloured woman to have rule over me because I was slave and she was free" (14). Although this tension seems to suggest that Prince felt less connected to those who did not share her slave condition, the fact that she later married a free Black man suggests otherwise. What it does index is her disgust with an individual who seems not to share her ideas about the significance of racially based community. Martha Wilcox angers her not simply because she is free, but rather because she believes that her freedom makes her superior to slaves like Mary.

Mary Prince's "we" also extends to slaves on Turks Island and Antigua. Prince was sent to Turk's Island as punishment for her supposed incorrigibility. She makes a point of noting the connection between herself and the other Blacks on the ship, saying that she would "almost have been starved had it not been for the kindness of a black man, Anthony, and his wife, who had brought their own victuals, and shared them with me" (9). Significantly, the bulk of this extensive Turks Island section is primarily told in the first person plural. Prince details at length how "we" worked, what "we" did, what "we" were given to eat, and all that "we" experienced. For example, she says,

When we were ill, let our complaint be what it might, the only medicine given to us was a great bowl of hot salt water, with salt mixed with it which made us very sick. If we could not keep up with the rest of the gang of slaves, we were put into the stocks, and severely flogged . . . Yet, not the less, our master expected, after we had thus been kept from the rest, and our limbs rendered stiff and sore with ill usage, that we should still go through the ordinary tasks . . . then we had no sleep—no rest—but were forced to work as fast as we could, and go on again all next day the same as usual. (11)

In addition, Prince tells the stories of individual slaves on Turks Island, showing her own and her fellow slaves' empathy for their colleagues and providing deeper insight into the horrors of slavery through these particular instances. She tells her readers of old Daniel, who was "lame in the hip" and whom the master would have beaten until "his skin was quite red and raw" and then have a bucket of salt thrown upon his never-healing wounds, which were often filled with maggots. She explains "he was an object of pity and terror to the whole gang of slaves, and in his wretched case we say, each of us, our own lot, if we should live to be as old" (11). She also tells the stories of Ben, strung up by his wrists for a crime actually committed by the master's son, and of the infirm old woman Sarah, beaten mercilessly by the overseer for not moving the wheelbarrow fast enough. Her sense of kinship with the slaves there is further illustrated by her attribution of the flood that "came down soon after and washed away many houses" to the Whites' wickedness.

In her discussion of her time in Antigua, Prince speaks warmly of an old slave woman who saved her life when she was sick with rheumatism. She tells her audience, "the old slave got the bark of some bush that was good for the pains, which she boiled in the hot water, and every night she came and put me into the bath . . . I don't know what I should have done, or what would have become of me, had it not been for her" (14). She also tells the emotional story of Henry, the black driver, who is wracked with pain over the atrocities he has been forced to commit against his people. In powerful and poignant language she tells of seeing him at a Methodist prayer meeting praying that both God and his fellow men would forgive him. She continues her argument that slavery strips the humanity of everyone involved by recalling, "he said it was a horrid thing for a ranger to have sometimes to beat his own wife or sister; but he must do so if ordered by his master" (16).

Mary Prince, as she presents herself in the narrative, clearly embraces both the idea of a black community and the need for the members consciously to manifest and act on that notion of community. In addition, her inclusion of Turk's Island and Antigua Blacks suggests that her conception of that community is not limited by geographical boundaries. It indexes a willingness to conceive of herself as linked to a world broader than her own "native place."

Prince's Ethnography

Mary Prince's detailed discussion of slave life in Turks Island and Antigua is more than an expression of racial kinship and identificatory breadth. It is also more than a useful detailing of specific instances that illustrate the horror that is life in slavery. It is the autoethnography of a community. Community autoethnography is another method by which cosmopolitan consciousness becomes manifest in Prince's text. Mary Louise Pratt defines ethnographic texts as "a means by which Europeans represent to themselves their (usually subjugated) others." Autoethnographic texts, then, are texts "the others construct in response to or in dialogue with those metropolitan representations."[31]

Prince directly challenges the widespread notion that slaves are happy:

I am often much vexed, and I feel great sorrow when I hear some people in this country [England] say, that the slaves do not need better usage, and do not want to be free. They believe the foreign people [the West Indians], who deceive them, and say slaves are happy. I say, Not so. How can slaves be happy when they have the halter round their neck and the whip upon their back? And are disgraced and thought no more of than beasts. (22–23)

She directly attacks the notion that slaves are incapable of forming or being part of civil society, by going into great detail in her descriptions of their values, social structures, and relationships with each other. In the process of introducing her fellow slaves' humanity, emotional life, family life, and civil society to the people of England, she makes the White West Indians into foreigners, "the foreign people" who deceive the English "and say slaves are happy" (22).

Community autoethnography is a text produced by the "othered" both to tell the story of the community and to talk back to the dominant discourse on the group. The ethnographic element of such a text resides not only in the references to the social structures or values of the community, but also in the way that detailing takes place. The use of the objective voice, in particular, highlights the ethnographic aspect of these discussions of other Blacks. Through her discussions of slave life in Turks Island and Antigua, that is, her community autoethnography, Prince tells the story of her broad community (one based on both race and condition) both as an objective outsider providing information to an uninformed public and as an invested insider experiencing the treatment described. She provides information in a way that suggests an expectation that the subject under discussion is foreign to her audience.

Prince's discussions of Turks Island and Antigua are clearly intended to provide information about the conditions under which these slaves must work. One quotation about Antigua in particular bears out this informational purpose in her outlining of the specific sequence of Sunday tasks: "On Sunday morning, each slave has to go out and gather a large bundle of grass; and, when they bring it home, they have all to sit at the manager's door and wait till he come out: often they have to wait there till past eleven o'clock, without any breakfast" (16). Her approach here reiterates her valuation of telling the story of her community. The almost objective tone decenters her, the individual, and spotlights others. I say almost objective because she does not completely distance herself from those about whom she speaks. Her insertion of the phrase "have to" in the phrase "they have to wait there till past eleven o'clock" communicates her, as the narrative voice's, sympathy/empathy for those who wait. The clause "without any breakfast" has a similar effect, magnifying the harshness of having to wait. This balancing of the objective/informational and the empathetic tone marks this section as illustrative of community autoethnography.[32]

The mere fact that she even mentions Turks Island and Antigua distinguishes her narrative and the philosophy of Black identity contained therein from that of other nineteenth-century slave narrators. Mentioning other slave colonies, particularly one so closely linked to Haiti, and by extension her demonstrated determination to broaden her attack on slavery to include its functioning in multiple sites in the British empire, is simply not done in other nineteenth-century narratives, whether from the U.S. or from the other Americas. Autoethnographic tendencies are clearly evident in fiction and nonfiction texts of the nineteenth century, including African American intellectual Martin Delany's novel *Blake; Or, the Huts of America* (1859–1862) and Black Bostonian missionary Nancy Prince's pamphlet *The West Indies* (1844), both published after Prince's narrative.[33] For example, wherever he goes, Delany's revolutionary protagonist, Henry Blake, always collects information on the opinions and experiences of those with whom he comes into contact. When he arrives in Cuba he asks the young slave woman he meets "how are the slaves used here in Cuba? I understand they are well treated." In addition, he says to her, "what is your age? You look like a young woman, but you're quite gray and careworn," an approach that allows her to answer with information that iterates the point Delany wishes to make about brutality of slavery in Cuba.[34] Through Henry's questions and her answers he contradicts the idea that slavery was less harsh in Cuba than in the U.S. Delany's decision to construct his text in this way, that is, through an individual who presents himself as a foreigner and objectively gains/tells information about the communities, reveals a tendency towards community autoethnography. He chooses to communicate contextual information through an ethnographer-subject situation. Henry, like Mary Prince, goes back and forth between the objective and subjective voice in his requesting and articulating of information.

Black Bostonian missionary Nancy Prince provides a multitude of details about the people, culture, and history of Jamaica in a voice that is, while empathetic, fundamentally informational. She explicitly acknowledges the ethnographic (getting information to introduce someone to a people foreign to them) and the autoethnographic (seeking to engage with or disprove dominant beliefs about people) elements of her project when she tells one of her subjects "We have heard in America that you are lazy, and that emancipation has been no benefit to you. I wish to inform myself of the truth respecting you and give a true representation of you on my return."[35] Carla Peterson astutely analyzes Nancy Prince's movement between the "depersonalized ethnographic" voice and that of the "participant-observer" in both her pamphlet on the West Indies and her own autobiography. Through the ethnographic text, Peterson argues, Prince authorizes herself "to scrutinize the Other" while "refusing to be gazed at."[36] Ethnography functions as a way for Nancy Prince to control perceptions and readings of her subjectivity and authority.

Eighteenth-century slave narratives, in particular that of Olaudah Equiano, also include autoethnographic representations of people from disparate Atlantic sites.[37] In the section containing the most explicit and strident critique of slavery, Equiano uses an autoethnographic detailing of experiences of individual slaves and references to the experiences of the group to mount his critique. He notes, "I have often seen slaves, particularly those who were meager, in different islands, put into scales and weighed, and then sold from three pence to six pence or nine pence a pound."[38] He tells of the separation of families caused by these sales, and the slaves' concomitant emotions. After that relatively objective description, he confesses "oftentimes my heart has bled at these partings," expressing empathy for (connection to) the subjects. He then tells the particular story of "a poor Creole Negro," who "after having been often thus transported from island to island at last resided in Montserrat." He tells of the slave's love of fishing and the master's theft of his catch. He then sweeps back out to the general condition of slaves everywhere: "Nor was such usage as this confined to particular places or individuals, for in all the different islands in which I have been (and I have visited no less than fifteen) the treatment of the slaves was nearly the same" (98). Equiano moves back and forth between the voice of the objective observer, the interested observer, and the potential subject, noting that he empathized with the man because he would "some time after suffer . . . in the same manner" (99).

What distinguishes Prince's community autoethnography, however, is that hers is ethnography from the perspective of an insider who aims to speak unequivocally in the voice of the community being described. Mary Prince's text features a person who is simultaneously a racial insider and a geographical or national or cultural outsider representing a community to which she feels profoundly connected. Martin Delany is a free Black from the Northern U.S. who seeks to describe southern Black slaves and Cubans of color. Nancy Prince writes of the Jamaicans, a group she views as less than civilized. Equiano, on the whole, maintains a significant psychological and descriptive distance from the Blacks he encounters in the Americas. All these individuals use details to construct an image of a community that has already been constructed negatively by the dominant racist and proslavery discourses. Their ethnographies have work to do, and are not simply catalogs of interesting tidbits of information about an exotic foreign culture. The character of that work differs in each text, but all have the task of counteracting the dominant negative construction, if only because should it be allowed to remain, the author, as one linked to that group, runs the risk of being tainted. The key point here is that community autoethnography is always subversive, in that the author, the presumed other, is speaking, but it is not always an expression of community and/or kinship. Prince's narrative is both, and as such is an important exemplar of the methods by which the two arms of cosmopolitan consciousness—the cosmopolitanism and the (racial) consciousness—are linked.

Prince's Cartography

Mary Prince's narrative is distinctive because it simultaneously brings into focus and raises questions about the conventional geographical boundaries and frameworks for self-definition of the slave narrative. In addition, she reveals herself to be in almost constant motion during the course of her narrative, moving between houses within Brackish Pond (the town of her birth), between houses and parishes in Bermuda (her country of birth), between and within other islands in the Caribbean, and between sites in

England. As she moves among all these places, she asserts a profound Ber-
mudian/West Indian groundedness that is evident not only in her way of
speaking (as discussed by Sandra Pouchet Paquet) and the titling of her narrative (*The History of Mary Prince, A West Indian Slave*), but also in the way
she talks about space (home, "foreign," or epistemological). Her concept of her
self (regional, national, and racial) is influenced by her actual movements and
evident in the very way in which she frames her narration of her movements.

As she speaks, Mary Prince also paints herself into the geographical,
epistemological, and identificatory worlds about her, creating her own cartography. Cartography here signifies the making of a conceptual map of
places—whether of sites of knowledge, places in social hierarchies, the place
of one region vis-à-vis another, or one's "native place." As an object moved
from place to place and positioned wherever best suits the mapmaker,
Prince's cartography is inherently radical in its persistent mapping of the
specific island of Bermuda, as well as of the world beyond Bermuda, including the West Indian region, as hers. It undercuts the plotting of her physical
and (cross)cultural movements by slaveowner cartographers who presume
their maps to be the absolute. In this sense, she refuses to be dislocated.
I term Prince's mapping "cosmopolitan slave cartography" to reflect the
outward looking concern, the anticolonial rebellion, and the geographical
concern that inhere in her published articulation of selfhood. Hers is an implicitly resistant cartography, that "back-answers" discourses that position
her a slave—as an object of slaveowners' political, economic, geographical,
or legal mapmaking. Henri Lefebvre has noted that "the producers of space
have always acted in accordance with a representation, while the 'users' passively experienced whatever was imposed upon them."[39] Prince unsettles this
presumed hierarchy.

Her "cosmopolitan cartography" asserts definitions of Bermudianness,
West Indianness, and Blackness, in addition to suggesting how those definitions relate to the world beyond these islands. Prince's map has elements in
common with the European/Eurocentric maps produced by European colonial cartographers throughout the exploration and the colonial period. She
has basic references to America and the West Indies that recall basic territory-
only maps. She also has more detailed ethnographic descriptions that mirror
Occidental maps such as Emanuel Bowen's *An Accurate Map of the West Indies*
(1747), Guiljelmo Blaeu's *Americae Nova Tabula* (1630) and Martin Walseemuller's *Tabula Terre Nove* (1513), which include drawings of Amerindian
individuals, families, and cultural referents.[40] Prince's mentions of the particular colonial masters of her fellow slaves (her reference to Hetty as a

French Black, for example) echo Joseph Speer's 1796 *Chart of the West Indies*, which included a listing and color coding of the Caribbean islands based on specific colonial power.[41] Prince's cartography operates on a parallel conceptual plane. Maps, for colonial powers, as Walter Mignolo has detailed, were a way to further document and illustrate their control over and claim to the mapped terrain. Mary Prince elbows her way into this discourse.

The very first line of her narrative illustrates this approach and the concomitant knowledge. She says, "I was born in Brackish Pond, Bermuda, on a farm belonging to Charles Myners" (1). James Olney has keyed in on the "I was born" beginning typical of African American slave narratives, because of its affirmation of Black slave humanity and its spotlighting of the unavailability to slaves of the anticipated concomitant details about birthdate and parentage.[42] Her specifically locating and naming the town, the island, and the very specific type of place it is immediately calls attention to the significance of place/geography in her story. The rhetorical value of the geographical origin of the slave in slave narratives has been productively analyzed by scholars such as Melvin Dixon.[43] Prince's specificity, however, is unusual among slave narratives, particularly among the ones that have received the most critical attention. For example, spatial referents are wholly absent from the early pages of the narrative of Cuban slave Juan Francisco Manzano. The beginning of African American Linda Brent's narrative is similarly devoid of such specific referents. Frederick Douglass, while very specific about the location of his birth in the town of Tuckahoe, does not specify his country as Prince does. This suggests that geography matters to Prince in a way that it does not appear to matter for these other slave narrators.

Prince's reference to Bermuda demonstrates a consciousness of a world beyond Bermuda. If she imagined herself as only speaking to Bermudians, she would not need to name the island. Prince's mention of her island illustrates not only her cognizance of the broader world, but further her desire to demonstrate that awareness in her public statement. That desire is borne out by the persistence of such spatial referencing and detailing throughout the narrative. For example, Prince's hemispherist concern comes across in her statement that "Mr. Darrel's son-in-law, was master of a vessel which traded to several places in America and the West Indies, and he was seldom at home long together," clearly illustrating the hemispheric understanding implicit in Prince's first sentence, that situates her geographically (1). Here she demonstrates her knowledge of the other entities that compose the broader region and continent in which her Bermuda is located, and of a major entity in the wider hemisphere.

Creole slaves born in the Caribbean, in the British West Indies in particular, would likely, because of the inter-island trade, the wars, the smallness of the islands, and, of course, the Haitian Revolution, have a cognizance of other islands besides their own.[44] Whether they came to know of these other places through other slaves who had been there, or, as in Prince's case, through knowing where the master was when he was gone so often, this broad knowledge was part of these slaves' conceptual lives. Prince's demonstrated regional knowledge suggests a cross-island cognizance that would seem to have arisen out of the West Indian islands' common tense relationship to the British crown, the constant trade between islands, and the overwhelming fear of being attacked by other colonial powers during wars.

This reference to America and places in the West Indies is more than evidence of historical fact. Prince continues her cosmopolitan cartography through her verbal marking of America and the West Indies. By mentioning them she adds two more points to her map. In addition, the matter-of-fact tone, specificity, and placement of this description of Mr. Darrel's son's trip suggest that Prince meant for this statement to perform a significant function in her narrative. The first paragraph begins with the key "Brackish Pond, Bermuda, farm" sentence and ends with the sentence referring to America and the West Indies. That she chooses to make these specific statements instead of speaking more generally, saying I was born in Bermuda, and that Mr. Darrel was always gone, somewhere, doing something, affirms not only her human (ontological) subjectivity, but also her intellectual (epistemological) subjectivity. Mary Prince, then, uses both specific geographical-local place and hemispheric-global place to pronounce her-self into public/published being.

This alternation of locational referent, between the local and the global, permeates the remainder of the narrative, reiterating her perception of it as integral to the telling and to the understanding of her story: *The History of Mary Prince, a West Indian Slave.* Her gaze is both inward, at the local (Bermuda, Brackish Pond, the farm) and outward, toward the hemispheric/regional. At times Prince articulates both perspectives in the same sentence. In discussing Mr. Darrel's infidelity, she says: "He often left her, in the most distressed circumstances, to reside in other female society, at some place in the West Indies of which I have forgot the name" (1). Her valuation of place, whether global or local, is further illuminated here by her continuing use of spatial language—"reside" and "place." Furthermore, in this statement she highlights not only her involvement in the affairs of the farm, thereby wresting conceptual ownership from the White men, but also her knowledge of

West Indian (regional) geographies. She could have simply said "some place in the West Indies," but she goes farther by indicating that she knew the name, that she had conceptual possession of the place in her use of the word "forgot."

Her mention of America and the West Indies in itself has great significance, especially given that similar mention (that is, of other sites in the region not physically connected to the narrator's home country) is not made in U.S. narratives. The fact that the U.S. narratives do include mentions of other states demands attentiveness to the possible impact of the size of these African Diasporan subjects' country on their approach to articulating a cosmopolitan consciousness. One could argue, based on the ideological distance between the free and slave states during this period, that Pennsylvania is as foreign to Douglass as America and the rest of the West Indies are to Prince. Seen in that context, Prince's reference to America is equivalent to Frederick Douglass's reference to Pennsylvania (and his references to Canada).

The qualitative difference in the references seems to indicate a relationship more complex than equivalence. Douglass refers to Canada in terms of its status as a place where African Americans could be free from the shackles of slavery. He mentions Pennsylvania in the same way. He mentions Canada within the context of recalling the escape plot hatched by him and his fellow slaves. At that time, he notes, they were not even aware of Canada. Prince, in the sentence under discussion here, does not mention America and the West Indies as sites where she might find freedom. She names them in a rather nonchalant fashion, without explicitly imbuing them with significance for herself. They are simply, as she presents them, part of her world. The difference in size between the U.S. and Bermuda would seem almost to mandate differing approaches to conceptualizing and engaging the world beyond, though. The total area of Bermuda is only 21 square miles. The United States, although still growing, was already hundreds of times larger when Douglass published his narrative (Florida was added as a state that very year).[45] The smallness of her island (and by extension the lack of a solid infrastructure) made it impossible for her to imagine an audience consisting only of Bermudians, for her to limit her conception of the world to just Bermuda.

Cosmopolitanism had to be part of Prince's worldview. Karen Fog Olwig explicates the global vision that seems to inhere in Afro-Caribbean island culture, specifically the culture and identity of the Caribbean island of Nevis.[46] Her point is not that such a global vision is always present in the Caribbean, or always absent in larger countries, but rather that there is a remarkable prevalence of it in the island region. Kathleen Wilson, in a similar vein, argues that England's islandness has long been pivotal to the English sense of self. She refers to Churchill's and later Thatcher's use of the phrase "the island race" as descendants of "a conception of national identity that eighteenth-century Britons would have recognized."[47] Prince's island origins undoubtedly had an effect on her relationship to other places, as did her historical and political context. There were debates still circulating about whether White West Indians were British, so, to be sure, arguing for Black West Indians' Britishness would have been an exercise in futility.[48] Wilson encapsulates this reality well in her discussion of English expansion into Africa and the South Seas, when she notes, "If white, Protestant English people living abroad were not able to claim the same liberties as English people at home, what hope was there for the other, proliferating ranks of people under British rule."[49] Prince's focus on geography highlights the inaccessibility of national identity for her, a colonial subject.

The geography argument does not completely explain the differences between the narratives of Prince and Douglass in references to the world beyond their own.[50] The differences between their relationships to their place of origin, their definitions of home (the place to which they belong), and by extension their visions of the most effective path to freedom within their contexts also play a part. Frederick Douglass, as is especially evident in his later writings, was in pursuit of the recognition of his and other African Americans' claim to U.S. citizenship, and by extension equality. Prince, however, does not express any interest in being or becoming British, or in defining herself solely through Bermuda. She focuses on geography, race, and culture as bases for identity and community.

The power differential between the U.S. and the smaller western Atlantic places must also be considered. The Bermudians, as residents of a geographically as well as economically and politically small place, had to be conscious of their much more imposing neighbor. Among other reasons, they needed the U.S. for trade, to bolster their economic status.[51] The U.S., and by extension, U.S. Blacks, by virtue of the country's relative power, did not need to think about Bermuda at all. So although, as the narratives of both Douglass and Prince show, geography, in particular the envisioning of places other than the one where one finds him/herself, has import for African Diasporan self and group definition and self-representation during this period, the differences between the places they choose to mention and their approaches to those references show that the relative power of their country of residence is also a factor.

Prince's Agency

In her emphasis on spatial language, Prince powerfully asserts her own agency, her own right to determine where and why she moves. The difference in title between her narrative and the other extant West Indian narrative from this period further highlights the emphasis on agency in Prince's narrative. Whereas the aforementioned Jamaican apprentice James Williams's narrative centers the (ostensible) slaveowner in the title: "Narrative of the Cruel Treatment of James Williams, a Negro Apprentice in Jamaica . . . till the Purchase of His Freedom in 1837 by Joseph Sturge, Esq. of Birmingham, by Whom He Was Brought to England," Prince's narrative centers her voice, providing "The History of Mary Prince, a West Indian Slave, Related By Herself."[52] (The uniqueness of Prince's move may be even clearer if we think of her as countering the obscuring of agency in the discourse Pratt describes as "anti-conquest"—"imperial eyes [that] passively look out and possess."[53]) Her taking ownership of her own movements, of the world about her, in the face of being owned by others, comes across in her characterization of her move to Turks Island. She names it as a displacement forced by her master, but then reclaims it as serving her own purposes: "At length he [her master] put me on board a sloop, and to my great joy sent me away to Turk's Island" (9). Here Prince refuses to surrender the whole sentence—to yield all the subjectivity surrounding trip to the master. She resists erasing her opinion and emotion from the narration of this movement. There are two subjects here—the master who puts her on board the sloop, and Prince herself, who feels great joy. In structuring the description this way, Prince recenters herself by refusing to present her master as the only one whose opinions and emotions matter.

    In addition to positioning herself as an emoting agent, Prince also presents movement (displacement in particular) as a cause of estrangement. Prince's approach here, I would argue, subverts/undercuts traditional notions of cosmopolitanism as a leisure activity born of and/or producing joy. Although Prince is certainly a cosmopolite, she is a cosmopolite who is subject to and subjected by others. Her "great joy" about going to Turks Island is tempered by the fact that she "was not permitted to see [her] mother or father, or poor sisters and brothers, to say good by, though going away to a strange land, and might never see them again" (9). She engages in what might be labeled "rhetorical resistance" when she identifies herself as an agent of the move to Turks Island in the earlier portion of the sentence, thus shifting the locus of spatial power to herself. Once again, though, she balances that assertion of power with a cognizance of the underlying mitigating factors. In this case, that factor is the material and emotional detachment from family the move to Turks island forces. Prince, therefore, both employs movement as a locus for her subversion of the dominant order and presents it as a cause of estrangement. Through her presentation of this move we can read not only her refusal to represent herself as purely a victim, and her demand to speak from/of her knowledge as a traveler, but also the more sobering side of her expansive cosmopolitanism—her recognition that movement/displacement creates alienation.

Prince continually alternates between asserting her own agency and calling attention to the impositions of slave owners. In doing so, she discourages the perception of her self, life and narrative as exceptional, and, simultaneously and conversely, as an example of the fact that slaves' lives were not so bad.[54] In fact, as she ends the narrative she complains that the English believe the White West Indians

who deceive them, and say slaves are happy. I say, Not so. How can slaves be happy when they have the halter round their neck and the whip upon their back? and are disgraced and thought no more of than beasts?—and are separated from their mothers, and husbands, and children, and sisters, just as cattle are sold and separated? (22–23)

Her anger here is clear. This statement also reads like a delayed table of contents for the narrative, with each phrase referring to an event she detailed in her history, from the beating of her friend Hetty (whip upon their back) to her own displacements (separated from their mothers, and husbands, and children, and sisters). She reiterates that she is both a speaking subject and an oppressed object. Through her presentation of space we can read not only her refusal to represent herself as purely a victim, and her demand to speak from/of her knowledge as a traveler, but also her sense that migration to a place she deigns unfamiliar and/or foreign creates alienation.

In commenting on her experience on Turk's Island, Prince plays to English readers' moral consciousness: "Work—work—work— Oh that Turk's Island was a horrible place! The people in England, I am sure, have never found out what is carried on there. Cruel, horrible place" (11). Here she exhibits a level of cosmopolitanism, a level of knowledge about England, a place that is at once outside the West Indies (geographically) and profoundly part of the region (culturally, economically). Although the purposeful provoking of the guilt and shame of the "good whites" (English in this case, U.S. northerners in others) is a common trope of slave narratives, Prince's use of specific spatial language—Turks Island, horrible place, distinguishes her employment of the trope.[55] Prince's play on English guilt, shame, and self-image is skillfully furthered by her siting of the horror in the place/the geography/land itself—it is Turks Island that was a horrible place. Her use of geography/place works to minimize any reflex defensiveness on the part of English or West Indian abolitionists that her criticism of slavery in the West Indies might provoke. What is also evident here is Prince's familiarity with the "mother country," a particularly figured cosmopolitan consciousness. She toys with English pride in a fashion reminiscent of post-1843 *Narrative* Frederick Douglass and William Wells Brown. She subtly urges the English to live up to their own moral and national ideals, while also soothing their moral conscience by pleading their ignorance.

Prince's knowledge of and interest in the world beyond Bermuda is again evident in her response to hearing that one of the slaveowners was going to Antigua: "I felt a great wish to go there, and I went to Mr. D—— and asked him to let me go in Mr. Wood's service" (14). This sentence indicates not only her knowledge of places outside those she has traveled to physically, but also her determination to chart her own paths despite her owner. She also demonstrates this determination in her discussion of how she came to be in England: "About this time my master and mistress were going to England . . . and they took me with them. . . . I was willing to come to England; I thought that by going there I should probably get cured of my rheumatism" (18). Here again we see Prince's inversion of displacement and insertion of herself as an agent in her movement. She says she was willing to go to England, insisting on the unquestionable significance of her own volition in the move, and goes even farther by specifying why she was willing to go. In doing so she reiterates the import of her will in determining the map she makes with her body as she moves from place to place. That she anticipates being relieved of her rheumatism seems to indicate a cognizance of either the English climate or medical advancements. A knowledge of either "back-answers" the belief in slave ignorance with slave cosmopolitanism.

Juxtaposed with this determined cosmopolitanism, though, is a sense of ambivalence about foreign or unfamiliar places. When Prince is kicked out of the house by her master and mistress, she expresses her feeling of utter isolation in this foreign country: "I was a stranger, and did not know one door in the street from another, and was unwilling to go away" (19). Significantly, even in this expression of despair, her resistant cartography surfaces. It is revealing that she chooses to use spatial language instead of saying "I did not know anyone." What we see here is Prince's spatial orientation, her affinity for spatial language that distinguishes her from some of the best-known slave narrators. Her refusal to leave is also significant because it again emphasizes the role of her will in determining the course of events. Also evident, though, are the limits of her cosmopolitanism, her desire to cling to familiar places.

Prince's "Native Place(s)" and Strange Places

Bermuda

Prince never embraces any site other than Bermuda as home. She maintains a psychological connection to Bermuda throughout the narrative. Although she was happy to go to Turks Island because it was an opportunity to escape from her harsh master, in retrospect, she expresses her anger at "going away to a strange land" without being permitted to say goodbye to her family (9).[56] Her definition of home appears early in the narrative to be very locationally specific. When Prince is hired out by her first mistress, Mrs. Williams, to a lady who lives five miles away, she characterizes the new place as utterly strange: "a strange house" where she finds herself among "strange people." She is displaced a second time when Mrs. Williams dies and she returns (to the Williamses') home to be sold. It is at this point that her love of this particular home place becomes especially clear: "When I left my dear little brothers and the house in which I had been brought up, I thought my heart would burst" (4). For Prince, home is the place where her family is. This conceptualization in and of itself is not particularly strange or different. What is important here is how she defines home as she moves, her attitude toward balancing here and home, the place she is and her "native place," while also adjusting her notion of collective.

Prince calls the place she is taken to her "new home," but implies a distinction between this place where she must live and the place she feels connected to. When she arrives at her "new home" two slave women ask her whom she belongs to and she replies "I am come to live here" (5). Because she has been clear in previous episodes about her sense of home, and particular in her use of the words, this answer implies that she does not consider this place home. Her response also, once again, situates Prince at the pivotal center of any discourse about her movement. The agency is in this way wrested away from her owners.

At several points in the narrative Prince speaks of yearning to return to her "native place." After working on Turks Island for ten years she is able to return to Bermuda because her master decides to retire to his house there. She is overjoyed: "I was joyful, for I was sick, sick of Turk's Island, and my heart yearned to see my native place again, my mother, and my kindred." She clings to Bermuda as her home despite moving from place to place. Again, it is clear that her definition of home is intimately tied to where her family is. Unlike Olaudah Equiano, who comes to claim England as home—as the place that he longs for while he is in the West Indies—Mary Prince's definition of home is not reconfigured by her movements.[57]

Despite living in Antigua for at least ten years, Prince never explicitly calls Antigua her home. She lives there, builds relationships with the Blacks there, including the man who became her husband, but never asserts a particular affinity for it. It is not her home place. In two particular instances, while she is in England, she illustrates this apparently lukewarm attitude toward Antigua. While Prince is suffering from rheumatism, her mistress continues to treat her especially horribly, and she laments "I was sorry that I had come from Antigua" (19). She is sorry not because she misses Antigua, but because of the mistreatment she suffers after she leaves. This treatment persists and Prince gets into an argument with her master in which he threatens to take her back to Antigua. She responds, "I would willingly go back, if he [you] would let me purchase my own freedom" (19). She is not interested in going to Antigua because she has a particular love for it. She ties her willingness to go there to a demand for her own freedom. Here we have verbal back-answering layered on top of spatial-cartographic back-answering. She expresses not a particular affinity for Antigua, the territorial site, but rather a special concern for her own health and freedom.

This prioritization is markedly different from that she displays upon leaving the "cruel, horrible" Turk's Island, where she expresses both a displeasure with the place she is leaving and a bond with the "place" and her people there (12). At that stage in her displacement she still fixates on the specific territorial place that is Bermuda. Her non-claiming of Antigua, even while in England, suggests a change in her relationship to slavery, displacement, and home in the years between her leaving Turk's Island and her living in England. She does not mention Bermuda either, at this stage. Although she still implicitly posits the West Indies as home while she is in England, she avoids reifying the specific place. Here she focuses less on claiming a particular territorial location as home, than on finding a home in freedom.

The West Indies

The idea that Prince's cartography is distinctively West Indian, perhaps distinctively West Indian woman, becomes particularly viable when it is considered alongside Mrs. Mary Seacole's preoccupation with traveling and becoming deeply involved in the affairs/wars of both American and European countries, the Crimean war being the most significant example.[58] Although their social statuses are vastly different, and although Seacole's travel narrative was published in 1857, twenty-six years after Prince's text, both Prince and Seacole exhibit a keen sense of and interest in the world outside their islands of origin, not only because of but also undergirding their travels (the root of their routes). Their works evince a concern with other places, other people, and other societies. Seacole writes "It is not my intention to dwell at any length upon the recollection of my childhood. . . . As I grew into womanhood I began to indulge that longing to travel which will never leave me while I have health and vigor" (2, 4). Although Prince is not able to chart her own journeys materially, she does so conceptually, demonstrating the "longing to travel" felt by Seacole. After Prince leaves Turks Island to return to Bermuda, she continues to be interested in news from that place, and clearly voices her interest in her published oral history, as her description quoted earlier about the Whites pulling down the place the slaves built for prayers (13). Similarly, when she describes her time in Antigua she does not simply say, I was there, I did this, and then I was taken elsewhere. Instead, she details her substantial knowledge about slave life in Antigua, gained first from observing and later from interacting with Antiguan slaves. That she watches intently enough to provide the considerable detail that she does, further illustrates her interest in knowing about other people and other places, her outwardly reaching concern.

These statements mark a notion of the Caribbean region, a sense that Antigua and Turks Island are part of her world—the world she views herself as intimately inscribed in—not just part of the wide world beyond Bermuda. She maps the Caribbean sites into her cartography of identity not just by speaking of her fellow slaves there, but by speaking of them with empathetic tone. These sites become more than just parts of her cosmopolitan cartography, of her general knowledge of the world about her, but part of the way she views her own place in the world.

The tension between Prince's marking of other Caribbean places as not-home and her detailed signaling of a connection to those same places raises the issue of the relationship between experience and cosmopolitan-ism. It begs the question—is her cosmopolitan consciousness simply a re-sult of her physical travel to these sites? Did she have to physically travel to Antigua and Turk's Island to conceptualize them as part of her identificatory world? This question can be thought through in a variety of ways, includ-ing migration/borderlands theory (how migrants create imagined homes when they are detached from their physical home), "travel-in-dwelling" anthro-pology, and critical geography (the relationship between place and identity). Carole Boyce Davies's concept of "migratory subjectivities" encourages us to read across as well as outside national boundaries and argues that spatially bounded readings of Black women's literature miss the crux of the writing: "Black women's writing, I am proposing, should be read as a series of bound-ary crossings and not as a fixed, geographical, ethnically, or nationally bound category of writing."[59]

This approach is helpful for thinking about Prince and about the rela-tionship between cosmopolitan consciousness and experience because it calls for attentiveness to modes of conceptualizing identity that are not tied to living in a particular place. In fact, Davies's methodology suggests a dis-juncture between experience and cosmopolitanism. One can envision a place as part of one's identity without physically being there, regardless whether one has one's own memories of a place. Similarly, one can feel absolutely no connection to a place in which one lives or has visited. Davies speaks speci-fically about Caribbean women writers' rewritings of home, of their con-nection to the Caribbean, in the face of "racial discrimination and foreign bias, Caribbean male phallicism, and American imperialism."[60] Their con-nection to Caribbean identity is mediated by these factors, as their connec-tion to Caribbean geography is mediated by their geographical detachment from the islands. Their rewritings of home/identity are grounded in dis-placement, in detachment from home.

James Clifford's demand for anthropological analyses that take the sub-jects' cosmopolitan engagements into account also encourages a de-reification of place, of spatial location in readings of cultures and identities, suffers from an incongruous fetishization of the physical site. He cites Christina Turner's critique of his work's insistence on literal travel: "'It's a mistake', she told me, to 'insist on literal travel.'" She argues, he tells us, that doing so "begs too many questions and overly restricts the important issue of how subjects are culturally 'located'."[61] Anthropological fieldwork is still based on going to a particular site where the subjects are, even if the subjects are conceptualized as having contacts beyond that site. Being situated in the physical place is understood as central to identity. Both Boyce Davies and Clifford push for a disaggregationof place and identity, but, significantly, not for a complete disaggregation. The physical site remains a fundamental part of their conceptualizations of identities and cultures.

England: The Ultimate Strange Land

Prince's narrative reflects the same ambiguity evident in Davies's and Clifford's arguments. Despite the fact that she is legally free in England, she expresses no affinity for it and has no desire to remain there. She makes several statements reflecting this feeling: "I knew that I was free in England, but I did not know where to go, or how to get my living; and, therefore, I did not like to leave the house," and "I am a stranger in this country" (20). Her attitude of distance toward England, even while she is there, suggests that experience, simply living in a place, is not enough to make her feel intimately connected to a place and its people. This fact returns us to the idea that the notion of Caribbean region is especially compelling for her, and by extension that her articulation of Caribbean region is more profound than simply a chronicling of where she has been, but rather a detailing of her coming into her identity. She lives in England, but does not feel connected to it, whereas she felt connected to Antigua when she lived there, and to Turks Island when she was there, and even afterward. It is significant, though, that her expressions of distance from England relate primarily to her feeling as if she had no community there. She says forlornly that the Moravian Missionaries were "the only persons I knew in England" (20). Prince feels detached from this place (England) because she has no "people" there—no people related to her kin, blood, race, or culture. Community rather than experience, simply being somewhere, is central to her cosmopolitan consciousness. This valuation is clear in the fact that her discussions of life in Antigua and Turks Island focus on the experiences of other slaves, rather than on the experience of the individual confronting a foreign place. Her discussion of her time in England reflects the converse attitude—it is a foreign place, and she focuses on herself and her own experiences in this foreign place.

Prince verbally marks her cultural defamiliarization in England, specifically to the cultural differences between England and the West Indies and their negative effect on her. She complains

My mistress sent me into the wash-house to learn to wash in the English way. In the West Indies we wash with cold water—in England with hot. I told my mistress I was afraid that putting my hands first into the hot water and then into the cold, would increase the pain in my limbs. The doctor had told my mistress long before I came from the West Indies, that I was a sickly body and the washing did not agree with me. But Mrs. Wood would not release me from the tub, so I was forced to do as I could. (18–19)

She is put off both physically and psychologically by the cultural disparities. I can hear echoes here of Paule Marshall's "poets in the kitchen" speaking of their defamiliarization in "this man country," as these Caribbean emigrant women called the U.S.[62]

Despite the fact that she also never fully embraces Antigua as her home, she conceptualizes it as part of the generic West Indian region that she identifies herself with. As her detailing of her time in England progresses she uses "West Indies" more and more, and specific national (island) references less and less. She would prefer to return to any place in the West Indies, even Antigua, rather than stay in England (19). Her horrible experiences in those two sites do not prevent her from identifying them as part of her home region, but do stop her from desiring to return to them. So, for Prince, it seems that physical travel, physically residing in a place, is unnecessary for cosmopolitan consciousness. She does not have to live in either Antigua or Turks Island to consider them part of her conceptual map. She is able to separate imagining them as part of her identificatory world, and actually being there. This reading of her recollection of her time in England bolsters my earlier readings of the cosmopolitanism evident in her locating herself using a national marker indicating a consciousness of the world beyond Bermuda, her references to America and Guinea, her description and embrace of Hetty, the French Black, as well as her detailing of slave life in Antigua and Turks Island. All of this evidence illustrates that Prince's cosmopolitan consciousness and cartography are not immutably linked to experience, to the experience of visiting a place. Conceptual travel is as constitutive of her map as is physical travel.

As her attitude toward England also shows, Prince's cosmopolitanism has its limits, limits that might usefully be read as parochial, but are, perhaps, more appropriately read as a fundamental element of her cosmopolitanism. As both the earlier quotations from Said and Hannerz index, White Western cosmopolitanism, the example through which cosmopolitanism has long been defined, has always been self-centered, and often ethnocentric. Prince's cosmopolitanism, in this way, meshes with that of her context. In addition, Prince's clear demarcation of what is "my native place" implies a cognizance of what is "not my native place." Her specific references to the strangeness of English culture, such as the washing technique, highlight her disdain for this truly strange and foreign place.[63] Her narrative is the textual representation of her continuing effort to demarcate the lines between home and foreign places and people.

Her representation of that effort also, however, reflects a cognizance of the danger inherent in articulating a notion of Black community that is too broad—one that might be seen as not just "uppity" but downright threatening in this moment. Prince's narrative, like all extant American narratives of the period, does not mention Haiti or the Haitian Revolution. This non-mentioning is especially strange given her demonstrated cosmopolitan consciousness. It is not strange, though, given the context.

Through asserting her cosmopolitanism—knowledge of other places, then embracing more regionally and conceptually oriented definitions of home—Mary Prince takes epistemological and rhetorical ownership of the world about her. She claims the worlds of the farm, Brackish Pond, Bermuda, Antigua, America, the West Indies, and England as hers not simply to know, but to evaluate and to critique. Her cosmopolitan cartography is more than a mapping of sites. Through this map, she draws these locations into her epistemological world, claiming them as part of that world. Her map inheres not simply in her mention of places she has been to, but also in her articulation of views about the politics, people, history, or culture of those sites. While she is reaching out and claiming these worlds, she also asserts a clear regional rootedness and refuses to see the two as contradictory.

Her text argues that, although one can stand in and claim several places at the same time, geographical or regional rootedness and cross/transnational mobility do not coexist in a tension-free fashion, whether in an individual's material life or her psyche. It is this complexity in Prince's understanding and presentation of place that anticipates the concerns of Paule Marshall, Louise Bennett, and generations of "Caribbean" women writers. Marshall's work delves further into the tensions inherent in trying to balance both roots and routes, and creates as well as posits possible recuperative cartographies. Bennett's work emphatically asserts Jamaican roots, while not wholly discarding or escaping the way those roots are shaped and troubled by colonially imposed geographies or more "voluntary" routes. As the precursor of this twentieth-century work, Prince's narrative resists a reading of it as simply a cataloging or reflection of the life of a slave who is bounced around from place to place, demanding instead a reading of it as a crafted, complex, but troubled text evincing the clear, fiercely assertive voice of Mary Prince, a West Indian slave. More important for this project, though, her maintained bond to Bermuda even with her cosmopolitan perspective suggests a hierarchy that elevates her region or "native place" above others—a black binaristic worldview. It is this underlying viewpoint that anticipates many of the less discussed tensions within the abovementioned texts, as well as between individuals, texts, and ideologies of the Black Americas.

Disidentification as Identity: Juan Francisco Manzano and the Flight from Blackness

Juan Francisco Manzano was born in Cuba in 1797 to the slaves Maria Pilar Manzano and Toribio Castro. For the first twelve years of his life, Manzano lived a life of relative privilege, doted upon by his mistress as "the child of her old age."[1] When this mistress died, he and his family ended up in the service of a mistress who was as cruel to him as his previous mistress was doting. Manzano then became truly acquainted with the horrors of slave life, including the stocks, the beatings, and the range of tortures that the sadistic slaveowner's mind devised. He eventually escaped to Havana, where he was able to begin to build a life for himself as an urban slave.[2] While working in the home of Nicolás de Cardenás y Manzano in Havana, he went out of his way to learn to write. He had memorized many sermons at an early age, but made a special effort during this period to turn that interest in words into a finely honed poetic skill. As he was building this life, he married a mulatta named Delia and sharpened his poetic skill by both writing his own poems and copying those of canonical poets. He eventually became very well known in Cuban literary circles, one of the very few people of color to do so. He published three books of poetry while still enslaved, *Cantos à Lesbia* (1821), *Poesías liricas* (1830), and *Flores pasajeros*. His poems were published in many of the most important Cuban newspapers and literary magazines of the day, including *El aguinaldo habanero*, *La moda o recreo de las bellas damas*, and *El album*. His poetry led Domingo Delmonte, the organizer of the chief literary workshop and one of the most prominent advocates for slavery reform, to bring Manzano into his circle and become his patron. It was at Delmonte's urging that Manzano wrote his autobiography.[3] It was, in significant part, through Delmonte that Manzano was able to buy his freedom in 1836. In 1844, Manzano was accused of participating in the Conspiración de la Escalera, the alleged uprising for which Plácido was executed, but managed to escape execution. He was ultimately released, but not before being jailed for several months. Manzano discusses this experience himself in a letter written to a friend in 1844. He referred to the unimaginable "calamities and bitternesses" that he has suffered as a result of the accusations, and notes that they only served to expose the accusers' "misguided imaginations."[4] After being acquitted, he virtually disappears from the records.[5]

    The autobiography of Juan Francisco Manzano is the only extant Spanish American slave narrative discovered to date. It was first published in 1840, in English, by British abolitionist Richard R. Madden, who had been working to hasten abolition in Cuba. Madden included it in a collection he entitled *Poems by a Slave in the Island of Cuba, Recently Liberated Translated from the Spanish by R. R. Madden, M.D. with the History of the Early Life of the Negro Poet, Written by Himself*.[6] It was not published in Spanish until 1937, when scholar José Franco uncovered an original Spanish text in the José Martí National Library in Cuba.[7] Before Franco's Spanish language text appeared, biographical sketches of Manzano and his best-known poems were often included in Spanish language collections such as Francisco Calcagano's *Poetas de color* (1878) and Antonio López Prieto's *Parnaso cubano* (1881).[8] Domingo Delmonte also wrote a comparative sketch on Manzano and Plácido for the magazine *Liceo de la Habana* (1859).[9] As Calcagano himself notes, although Manzano's name was well known in Cuba decades after his death because he had been one of few poets of color, and one of the few poets to come out of slavery, little was known about his actual life.[10] The publication of Franco's text led, although not immediately, to an increased intellectual interest in Manzano both within and outside Cuba. Franco's text, although now beginning to be criticized for the way it "corrected" Manzano's "errors," spawned several editions of the autobiography, including a modernized Spanish version published by Ivan Schulman in 1975 and an English translation published by Lloyd King circa 1990.[11] These multiple versions have led to a plethora of critical and theoretical works that analyze a range of aspects of Manzano's life and context. Especially noteworthy is the work of Richard Jackson, who notes, "the search for Black identity in Hispanic literature began with Juan Francisco Manzano."[12] Other scholars, such as William Luis and Antonio Vera-León, have analyzed other "textual multiplicities," including the "internal struggle between the slave he was and the educated writer he became."[13] Less work has been done on Manzano's textual and/or ideological relationships to non-Latin American writers and discourses and/or the implications of his work for such writers and discourses. Two essays exploring the striking similarities between Manzano's 1840 autobiography and Frederick Douglass's 1845 narrative, one by Martha Cobb and the other by Luis Jiménez, have sought to counter this trend.[14] Susan Willis's essay, "Crushed Geraniums: Juan Francisco Manzano and the Language of Slavery," reads Manzano in relation to contemporaneous and post-colonial Caribbean discourses.[15] This chapter explores Manzano's approach to representing his relationship with Blacks in the autobiography and, by extension, the commentary that approach makes on the modes of identification available to people of African descent in the nineteenth century.

Throughout most of his autobiography, Manzano distances himself from *los negros*, representing them primarily as purveyors of pain. *Los negros* are the ones who beat and torture him for the slaveowners. I argue through this case that not-Blackness and disidentification with the "Black" community were key modalities of African Diasporan identity in the wake of the Haitian Revolution. Such a reading is vital to the development of fuller and more nuanced conceptions of African Diasporan literary and ideological genealogies. People of African descent who do not explicitly identify as "Black" have long been implicitly incorporated into genealogies of "Black" thought. When William Wells Brown included the Cuban poet of color Plácido (who, as Chapter 2 shows, exhibited an ambiguous racial identity) in *The Black Man, His Antecedents, and His Genius*, he is implicitly engaging Plácido's not-Black racial identity. Brown's engagement, however, is ultimately a subsuming of Plácido into Blackness and a negation of his not-Blackness. The analyses above of Martin Delany and Frederick Douglass in particular have lent insight into the possible rationales behind such a treatment of other-locational people of African descent. Here, I am suggesting that not-Blackness needs to be engaged directly and explicitly in both scholarship and in the construction of genealogies of thought.

By disidentification I mean an individual's explicit distancing of himself from Blacks.[16] In the case of Manzano, scholars such as Jerome Branche have surmised, correctly, that Manzano's distancing of himself from *los negros* likely has its roots in his keen understanding of anti-Black racism among his potential readers, and by extension the negative reaction they would have to his lumping himself in the same category as their Black slaves. As Branche suggests, "his own interests could be served in pointing to the distance between himself and the purported baseness of the *negros*."[17] Manzano purposely shaped his representation of his relationship to others of African descent.

I have chosen to employ the term disidentification in my analysis because, as distinct from passing, it emphasizes movement away from an identity group rather than a movement toward one. José Muñoz, in his analysis of performances of identity by queers of color, makes a similar point about the importance of disidentification as an approach, noting that it "would always foreground that lost object of identification."[18] Racial passing has frequently been the subject of scholarly writing, particularly writing focused on African-Americans. Recent years have witnessed a profound and recurring interest in the complication of the meaning of African-Americanness evident in texts like Nella Larsen's 1929 novel, *Passing*, James Weldon Johnson's *Autobiography of an Ex-Colored Man*, that feature African American characters that "cross the line," to echo Gayle Wald's use of the phrase.[19] In recent years, substantial attention has been accorded to the ways in which the possibility and reality of passing illustrate the always already present fissures in "racial reasoning," as Cornel West terms racialist thinking. Wald takes this approach a step further by characterizing passing as "a practice that emerges from subjects' desires to control the terms of their racial definition, rather than be subject to the definitions of white supremacy."[20] Passing, she suggests, is a fight "for control over racial representation." The passing individual has refused to acquiesce to imposed conceptions of his or her identity, and has instead crossed the line.

The clouding of the racial line has also been the subject of much Latin Americanist scholarship. In particular, representations of the mulatta figure in Spanish American literature have been of great interest to scholars. The recurring presence of the mulatta figure in Cuban literature from the nineteenth century forward, in particular, has received significant attention. Vera Kutzinski's *Sugar's Secrets* (1993) and Claudette Williams's *Charcoal and Cinnamon* (2000) stand out in their persistent attentiveness to the gendered and sexualized dimension of these representations.[21] Kutzinski argues that Cuba "encodes its national identity in the iconic figure of a mulatta."[22] Williams contends, for example, that in the Spanish Caribbean "writing about mulatto women in the colonial period was a sign of the birth of local consciousness. . . Literary interest in the *mulata* illustrates how the unfixing of the racial poles in this period served to mitigate the racial disparagement of nonwhites popularized in the preceding European artistic tradition."[23] The underside of this celebration of the *mulata*, however, she continues, was the "exclusion or disparagement of black women."

Scholars and intellectuals throughout the late nineteenth and twentieth centuries also delineated the central role *mestizaje* has played in the construction of nationalist discourses in Latin America in general, and in Cuba in particular.[24] José Martí's famous characterization of Nuestra America in general and Cuba in particular as essentially *mestizo* is an even earlier example of this link.[25] José Vasconcelos' idea of the cosmic race similarly celebrates racial and cultural mixture as the quality that makes the Americas unique and divine.[26] The scholarly discourses on passing, *mestizaje*, and the mulatta/o, particularly in the poststructuralist era, share a special concern with the ways in which these ideas represent the crossing, and often the undercutting, of racial boundaries.

As suggested in the reference to the work of Branche among others, significant attention has been paid to the meaning of Manzano's representation of himself as a mulatto in particular. His constructed mulattoness is important to note, as it speaks, as the work of both the Latin Americanists and the African Americanists mentioned above do, to the presence of a certain malleability or shakiness in the founding presumptions of American racial infrastructures. I am less interested, however, in analyzing what Manzano defines himself as, than in what he defines himself as not. My study centers on the ideological, material, and representational relationships between people of African descent, and as such is logically more concerned with the implications of Manzano's self-definition for his relationship to others of African descent. Disidentification, as I am employing it, implies a racial border crossing, but is intended to emphasize the disidentifying individual's relationship to the community from which he is distinguishing himself, rather than the one with which he is aligning himself. I aim to determine how and whether an individual who disidentifies can be included in the ideological genealogies of the community with which he disidentifies.[27]

The Mechanics of Manzano's Disidentification

Manzano's ambiguous relationship to *los negros* on the estate with him is explicitly in evidence as he tells of the death of his first mistress. He notes "all night long all the negroes of the estate made great lamentation, repeated the rosary, and I wept with them" (82). In this statement Manzano simultaneously identifies with and differentiates himself from *los negros*. He does not completely identify with them, which he could have done by saying that "we" made great lamentation. Instead, he maintains a distinction between "I" and "them" throughout the statement. At the same time, though, the fact that he is weeping with them suggests a commonality, in this case a shared emotion. Significantly, he decides to express (and to indicate that he expressed) that shared emotion "with" them rather than in his own space away from them. After the death of his mistress he goes to her daughter's house where he was treated "like a white child," and not allowed "to pray with the other negro children at church" (83). Here he calls attention to the way that his separation from the *negros* was influenced and enforced by his White owners.

As mentioned earlier, *los negros* are represented throughout the autobiography in large part as those who carry out the sadistic orders of the masters.[28] He recalls: "frequently I would receive from a stout Negro lashes in abundance" and that his mother was "stripped by the negroes and thrown down to be scourged" (84, 87). At another point he states that "a negro came in followed by the overseer wrapt in his cloak; they took me out and put me on a board fixed on a kind of fork" (88–89).

He returns to subtly indicating a connection between himself and *los negros* just after this most recently discussed scene of torture. He was working with the "negro Andres Criollo" when the roof "gave way, burying" his coworker. The injury proves fatal. In a statement emphasizing the profundity of his mourning, he says "my heart was so oppressed, that neither . . . kindness nor eating, nor drinking could comfort me" (91). He goes on, however, to mention "I was known at this time under the name of . . . the little mulatto of the Marquesa," again indexing a distance between himself and the other slaves (100). He ends the autobiography by hinting again, in his narration of his final escape, at a connection to *los negros*. He reflects, "I thought that nobody saw me, but as I knew afterwards, I was seen by several of the Negroes, but nobody offered any impediment to my flight" (106). Tellingly, the escape itself, as he writes of it, was prompted by someone chiding him for allowing himself to be "treated worse than the meanest slave" (105).[29]

The scenes analyzed above appear in all editions of the autobiography. Versions of the autobiography that surfaced or were published in the twentieth century include a moment in which Manzano refers to himself as a "mulatto among Blacks."[30] Although the statement does not appear in the initial published version (Madden),[31] it does appear in the first version published in Spanish (Franco) and therefore in all subsequent versions, the overwhelming majority of which are explicitly identified by their editors as modernizations or translations of Franco's text. Racial references are certainly less evident in the Madden version than in the Franco version. The latter version is replete with references to the race of individuals absent from the Madden version or sans racial references. These include "la parda [mixed race woman] libre Catalina Monzón" and "la parda Rosario Brindis."[32]

The appearance and disappearance of these references suggest that the various editors of the autobiography saw them as either contributing to or undercutting their goals for their edition. Roberto Friol emphasizes in *Suite para Juan Francisco Manzano* (1977), after critiquing both Madden and Calcagano, that "Como el de Madden, el libro de Calcagano sirvio para dar a concocer, aunque parcialmente, la autobiografía, y aun hoy, descartados sus errors, resulta obra de utilidad" (like that of Madden, Calcagano's book serves to bring to light, even if in part, the autobiography and even today with its errors is still a useful work).[33] Gregg Courtad similarly notes that the reduced racial references are intended to "suit a specific political end."[34] Although one could certainly undertake an analysis of sources of the multiple versions and the subtle differences in the treatment of Manzano's racial identity, my goal here is to analyze a theme common to all the versions—Manzano's disidentification with Blacks. I am less interested in the goals of the disparate editors than in the implications of Manzano's distancing of himself from *los negros*. This attitude is present in all versions, indicating, definitively, that it was present in the original and/or source texts used by both nineteenth and twentieth-century editors.

The presence of this attitude makes placing Manzano within a literary genealogy based on race a challenge, and as such poses a special challenge for editors of anthologies, those who plan English and/or Modern Language department curricula, and African-Americanist as well as Latin Americanist scholars.[35] Afro-Hispanic writers in general rarely appear in U.S. anthologies. Edward J. Mullen noted in 1995 that "out of a literary production spanning some 500 years in Spanish-America exactly four writers of African descent have been included in major teaching anthologies in the United States during the last 145 years."[36] Scholars in Latin American studies have largely been responsible for the reproduction and critical analysis of Manzano's work. Scholars with specific interests in Afro-Latin American and Cuban Studies have analyzed him in relation to literary descendants such as Nicolas Guillén and Nancy Morejón. as well as contemporaries such as Domingo Delmonte and Anselmo Suárez y Romero.[37] Richard Jackson is correct when he states "Manzano's *Autobiografía* can be viewed in the broader perspective of black American literature as a tradition."[38] The question of how to contextualize, anthologize, teach, or write about an Afro-Hispanic individual who disidentifies with Blackness alongside other writers of African descent with differing (and often more positive) relationships to Blackness is a crucial one.[39] (This question becomes even more pressing as the number and popularity of writers who are both "Black" and "Latino" like West Indian Panamanian African American Veronica Chambers increase.) In African American literature, works like Paul Laurence Dunbar's "We Wear the Mask,"

W. E. B. Du Bois's "The Criteria for Negro Art," Langston Hughes's "The Negro Artist and the Racial Mountain," and Larry Neal's "The Black Aesthetic" have exemplified the large-scale debates that have taken place in African American literature over what makes a writer Black, and whether one wants to be viewed as a Black writer or as a writer who happens to be Black.[40] Within the field of Afro-Hispanic literature scholars have debated the rationale behind and implications of Manzano's racial self-positioning.[41] Manzano's disidentification has been interpreted by a range of scholars in Latin American and Afro-Hispanic literature. Raquel Romeu, for instance, describes his poetry as "ajena de una africanidad, a una sensualidad negra" (detached from an Africanness, a black sensuality).[42] She goes even further, by saying that he had "la mentalidad de blanco aunque negro haya sido su color" (a white mentality, even though he was black in color).[43] She ultimately defends his approach, however, noting that he had no other choice because of the horrific context within which he lived. Netchinsky decries scholars' criticisms of Manzano for not embracing his race more explicitly, contending that "the achievement of the authority that is embedded in the voice of the master necessitates a kind of doubleness for the slave."[44] Netchinsky's comment points to a key way of linking the disparate approaches to Blackness taken by Delany, William Wells Brown, Plácido, Douglass, Mary Prince, and Manzano, a recognition of the fact that their relationships to Blackness, while different, are born of the same relationship to power—disempowerment. Teaching or analyzing Manzano alongside such writers, without regard for the original language, allows both the fundamental commonality and the diverse methods of coping to surface. In the case of writers of African descent, in particular, teaching or anthologizing based on language or nationality would obscure one or the other. Manzano does disidentify. About that there can be no doubt. That does not mean, however, that he should be cast off and understood as wholly separate from other writers of African descent of the era who claimed their Blackness more explicitly. It is important that we pay closer attention to the rationale behind and nuances of that disidentification.[45] To unpack the complexities of his disidentification, though, we must first understand his relationship to his own exceptionality.

Manzano's Exceptionality

Slave narratives are always already sites where exceptionality crosses paths with commonality. The slave writing the narrative is already distinctive in that he has access to the public/published sphere. In many cases, the slave is already distinctive because he can write. In the case of Douglass and Manzano, they are already distinctive because they are already public figures by the time their narratives are published. Manzano, treated "like a white child" during his early years, is especially exceptional (83). The qualities and experiences that made him an exceptional individual, slave, and person of color are clearly in evidence from the very beginning of the autobiography. Instead of starting with his geographical origin or birthdate, it begins with a description of Manzano's mistress and the special treatment she accorded special slaves, "the finest Creole children" (80). From the very beginning Manzano appears to be born into exceptionality. His mother was one of "the finest Creole children." She was "a favourite young slave," "who was greately esteemed for her intelligence." Within this context he was "ushered into the world." In addition his "master took a fancy to" him. He was "more in his arms than in those of my mother." He was "called by this lady, 'the child of her old age.'" He was "brought up by the side of my mistress without separating from her." Everyone, including his parents, was prohibited from flogging him. The circumstances of his birth and the structure of his enslavement as described in the autobiography clearly distinguish him from other slaves.

Manzano also shows himself to be differentiated from the others by his relationship to knowledge and the speed with which he learned new skills. He notes "at ten years of age, I learned by heart some of the longest sermons of Father Louis, of Granada, and the visitors who came to the house on Sundays, used to hear me repeat them when I came from the chapel" (81). He takes his master's "book of rhetoric" and "learnt by heart a lesson every day," which he "used to recite like a parrot" (96). He tires of simple memorization and makes the decision "give myself up to study" and "to learn to write." He purchases his own supplies and begins to trace characters so well that "at the end of the month I could write almost the same hand as my master's" (96–97). The text continues by providing significant detail on his love of writing. He "employed the hours from five to ten every evening, exercising my hand to write," until he could "imitate the best hand-writing" (96). His master forbade him from writing "in vain," as he puts it. He waited until everyone went to bed and used a candle to continue writing, "thinking that if I could imitate these [verses], I would be come a poet." He notes that even at this early stage it was evident to Doctor Coronado that he would be a "great poet." Sonia Labrador rightly characterizes the autobiography as a manifestation of the desire for liberty and his struggle to be able to express his subjectivity. The author, she suggests, is intimidated by his reader, as reflected in the structuring of the text. He aims to create a subject that is less slave and more human, enabling the reader to engage with him. His emphasis on his exceptionality bears out Labrador's point.[46]

Manzano walks a fine line between highlighting his own exceptionality and speaking to the horrors of slavery more broadly. His difficulty with this line becomes clearest in his descriptions of his moments of rebellion. He wishes to emphasize his exceptionality (i.e. his rebelliousness) while also referencing the ways in which slavery denigrated slaves and quashed individuals' instinctive rebelliousness. At one point, for example, he writes that he "ventured to ask [his mistress for] paper and ink, in order to advertise for a new master" (98). He notes that she was "astonished" by his "boldness" and reported it to her sister. He then had an audience with her sister, who "tried to persuade me to desist from my intention" (99). He recalls "I plainly told them, that I was afraid of my mistress's fiery temper; this conversation ended by the Countess advising me to stop with my mistress till she thought proper to give me liberty." These sentences index that a discussion of his intentions took place, marking his exceptional situation. In most circumstances slaveowners would not have discussions with slaves and attempt to "persuade" them to "desist." In these sentences he calls attention not simply to his humanity, but also to the Whites' recognition of that humanity. At the same time, he does listen to the Countess, for that time being, and does not persist in writing the advertisement.[47]

The Special Slave

Manzano's racial disidentification and emphasis on exceptionality are profoundly interwoven. He often disidentifies in his recollections of abuse and torture. It is easy to read these moments as his expression of resentment towards the blacks who participated in his degradation. Other critics have read his representations of blacks as reflective of mutual resentment, born of the special treatment received by Manzano and his family.[48] His matter-of-fact tone ("six Negroes surrounded me, and at the word 'upon him' they threw me down; two of them held my hands, two my legs, and the other sat upon my back" 90), however, suggests otherwise. An alternative reading is also encouraged by the fact that he does not use negative adjectives (such as passive, hateful, and so on) in his identification of the blacks who torture him. The presence of moments in which he hints at a bond between himself and the blacks (such as the moment discussed above in which he shows himself crying with the blacks) also implies a relationship other than resentment. The disidentification in his reconstructions of scenes of torture is, I contend, often actually an expression of affinity. He shows, through these scenes, the subjection and subjugation suffered by himself as well as by *los negros*.

Although he appears to represent the blacks as passive, mindless robots who simply do the bidding of the masters, his representations of their emotions and by extension their humanity in other instances reveal a more sympathetic sentiment. He shows them weeping when the mistress dies. He tells of them moving immediately to rescue his co-worker Andres Criollo from beneath the rubble of the roof. One instance in which a cook, Simona, lies in order protects him from more punishment also shows the blacks as emotional beings (91). In commenting on his final escape, he notes that they refrained from offering "any impediment to my flight" (106). This more sympathetic sentiment is also apparent in Manzano's poetry, indexing its persistent presence in his psyche. For example, the poem "To Cuba" reads, in part,

Cuba, of what avail that thou art fair!
Pearl of the seas, the pride of the Antilles!
If thy poor sons, have still to see thee share
The pangs of bondage, and its thousand ills;
. . .
Oh, if the name of Cuban! Makes my breast
Thrill with a moment's pride, that is soon o'er,
Or to throb with joy to dream that thou art blest!
Thy sons were free—thy soil unstained with gore.
Reproach awakes me, to assail once more,
And taint that name, as if the loathsome pest
That spreads from slavery had seized the core
Polluting both th'oppressor and the oppressed:—
. . .
To think unmoved of millions of our race,
Swept from thy soil by cruelties prolonged,
Another clime then ravaged to replace
The wretched Indians; Africa then wronged
To fill the void where myriads lately thronged,
And add new guilt to that long list of crimes,
That cries aloud, in accents trumpet-tongued,
And shakes the cloud that gathers o'er these climes,
Portending evil and disastrous times. (125–27)[49]

In his reference to the abuses suffered by "our race" he clearly links himself with the other children of Africa. Here they are even more obviously the objects of "cruelties prolonged." As in the autobiography, they are those who are forced to suffer in bondage, further illustrating that his intention in the autobiography was not to represent the blacks as willing actors. The connectedness he displays in this poem parallels the sentiment he exhibits in the autobiography. The difference between the two lies in his way of communicating his feelings. Whereas in the poem he speaks directly to the larger context, in the autobiography he uses his own particular experiences as a medium for commenting on the larger picture.

The tension between Manzano's exceptionality and his affinity for those of his race does, however, persist throughout the autobiography, despite his expressions of a bond with them. He has a desire to be special and/or different, a desire revealed by his emphasis on his racial difference, the special treatment he received early in his life, and his special intellectual attributes. He repeatedly references the ways the Whites viewed Blacks as an undifferentiated mass while, at times, simultaneously elevating him above that mass. After his early childhood with the doting mistress, "fortune's bitterest enmity was turned on me," and he was forced to suffer being continuously and alternatively unceremoniously grouped with and elevated above the undifferentiated mass. His life with his subsequent evil mistress was marked by this alternation. At times he would escort his mistress to the theater or parties with the elite of Havana (with "the most distinguished persons of the town") but at others he would be "put for a night in the stocks" for falling asleep while at those events (86). He was special enough to attend with her, to stay in her room, and to sew with her, but could also be physically punished at her word like all the other slaves. Significantly, one of her favorite punishments for him was sending him to the sugar mill to undertake the hard labor of working sugar with the other blacks. His writing reflects his ambiguous existence. He is both irritated by the generalizations about blacks and appreciative of being marked as different.

Manzano refers to those generalizations when he emphasizes the uniqueness of the privileges he is accorded. When he says he was "treated . . . like a white child," he implicitly indexes the other side—being treated like a black child. An image of this other side is even more specifically evoked when he goes on to provide particulars about the meaning of being treated like a White child—having someone make sure that he "was properly clothed," and combing his hair herself. As if to even more clearly highlight the contrast between the treatment of White and Black children, he includes in the list of specifics the fact that he was not allowed "to pray with the other negro children" (83). He was simultaneously grouped with the "other" Black children and distinguished from them by being prevented from praying with them. Also included is the detail that "at mealtime [his] plate was given to [him] to eat at the feet of the Señora." He was not truly "a white child," so he had to eat at her feet, but because he was unlike the other Black children, he got to eat in her presence.

Manzano's emphasis on his love of literacy and learning similarly invokes racist generalizations about Blacks as a group. In particular, it counters the notion that people of African descent have no interest in or are not capable of learning. He details how he developed and practiced his drawing, puppet making, writing, and recitation. These descriptions serve not only to illuminate Manzano's exceptionality, but also to contradict stereotypes about the group. Importantly, he points to a *mulata* as a key figure in his growth as a poet: "I had already at the age of twelve years composed some verses in memory, because my godfather did not wish me to learn to write, but I dictated my verses by stealth to a young mulatto girl, of the name of Serafina" (83). By including this reference, he notes that he was not the only member of his race to have that interest, thereby more directly taking on the generalization.

Manzano holds firmly to his exceptionality, however, being sure that no other person of color in the text is perceived as equaling him in intelligence, poetic skill, or privileges. He communicates his dislike of the racist generalizations by subtly referencing the treatment Blacks received and its impact on them as well as by insistently showing other people of color as having emotions and as not being the stereotype. As he works to distance himself from these generalizations, however, he, at times, also uses terms that group Blacks as an undifferentiated mass. At times he does not use the names of individuals, and instead uses general terms. Although statements such as "all the Negroes of the estate made great lamentation," or "I would receive from a stout negro lashes in abundance" index the common condition he shares with his fellow slaves, the general terms he employs also mark Blacks as a generalizable whole in which the "stout negros" and the "negros of the estate" are interchangeable and indistinguishable from each other.

These general terms, however, appear within the context of his own discomfort with and appreciation of the ways in which those in power distinguish him in racial terms from *los negros*. Significantly, only once in the text does he refer to himself as either a *mulato* or a *negro*. (In that case one could argue that he is speaking to class more than to race or color. He describes himself as a "mulato entre negros" when he is at el Molino—the place his mistress sends him when she wishes to remind him that he is not different from the other members of the undifferentiated mass of Blacks.) Although he speaks of his first mistress's practice of making choice of "the finest Creole children" and refers to himself as the "little Creole" that his mother gave to the mistress, he describes himself primarily through the racial terms and descriptions given by others. When he speaks of not being permitted to pray with the other *negro* children, he is implicitly referring to his classification as one of the *negro* children. When he notes that he "was known at this time under the name of the Chinito, or the little Mulatto of the Marquesa," he indexes another way in which he was classified racially (100).

Based on the text, it is difficult to determine how Manzano classified himself.[50] What is clear is that he simultaneously saw himself as grouped with Blacks (whether he chose/embraced that grouping or not) and as exceptional. His emphasis on the non-race/color related qualities that made him exceptional suggests that he did not view his exceptionality in racial terms. (In any case, that would have been difficult for him to do since both his parents were Black enough to be slaves.)

Humanity and Difference: A Slave's Deepest Desire

Manzano's disidentification, ambiguous expressions of a bond to Blacks, and emphasis on his exceptionality reflect a fundamental desire to be recognized as human, and by extension as an individual. Houston Baker indexes this desire in broad terms in an analysis of Frederick Douglass's narrative, noting that the Black slave autobiographer's quest is necessarily a quest for being. It was a quest undertaken in a context that "explicitly denied the slaves grounds of being." Consequently, "the slave's task was primarily one of creating a human and liberated self."[51] I am suggesting that this quest for being results not only in the creation of a (readable) self, but also of a particularly complex relationship to the other (de)human(ized) (non)beings. Manzano, on one hand, is aware of the common condition that he shares with others of his race, and, at times, embraces that connection. On the other hand, though, he wants desperately to escape the prison-house of the undifferentiated mass of which all Blacks are assumed to be a part. He cares about Andres Criollo, Simona, and the Blacks with whom he lamented his mistress' death, but he also wishes to be viewed as a unique human being. His repeated references to his own emotions and specifically the love he shared with his mother and brother, also illustrate his deeply held wish. For example, in one instance the *mayoral* (overseer) whips his mother for trying to prevent him from punishing young Juan. Manzano responds by becoming "all at once like a raging lion" and "fell on [the mayoral] with teeth and hands" (87). His highlighting of moments in which Whites treat him as a human being and an individual provides a model for his readers of how to perceive him. He speaks fondly of one gentleman for whom he worked, noting that he "was always very kind to me, I used to sleep in his room, and whenever he was afflicted with headache, I gave him warm water" (96).[52] Manzano presents this relationship as a mutually beneficial one, rather than as a one sided one in which the slave simply serves his master. He says of the gentleman's son (for whom he eventually worked), he "esteemed me not as a slave, but as a son, notwithstanding his youth. In his company the sadness of my soul began to disappear" (96). His statement here (that he was treated as a "son" rather than a "slave") parallels his earlier statement that his mistress treated him "like a white child." Both statements reinforce the same point—he wishes to be seen as a human being rather than a slave, that is, as part of an undifferentiated mass. Significantly, he makes a point of noting that this instance, this recognition of his humanity, made the sadness of his soul begin to disappear. In another illustration of his deepest desire, he expresses, in a letter to Delmonte dated June 25, 1835, his fear that Delmonte will come to think him unworthy of esteem when he reads Manzano's story of his life as a slave and remembers that "el esclavo es un ser muerto ante su señor" (the slave is a dead being in front of his master).[53]

Manzano appreciates kindness shown to him by Whites not simply because it comes from Whites, but rather because it comes from those defined as human. Manzano, for example, recalls the kindness of Don Saturnino, a mayoral at the Molino who shielded him from the manual labor at the mill despite the fact that his mistress had sent him there to be punished. Don Saturnino went so far as to pretend that Manzano had worked, saying "'as your mistress is coming tomorrow . . . to save appearances, I will put on you the fetters, and send you to work; but if she inquires whether you have been whipped you must say yes'" (102). Through these moments, Manzano indicates to the reader how he wishes to be seen. It is with special glee that Manzano recalls the first member of Havana's elite who foretold that he would "be a great poet, notwithstanding all opposition," and encouraged young Juan when he heard that he had taught himself to write, "saying, that many of the great poets began in the same way" (97).

Similarly, his disidentification with and othering of Blacks is not born simply of self-hatred or a superiority complex from "mulattoness." The moments of connection with Blacks and his representation of the condition he shares with them illustrate this fact. His disidentification is an outgrowth of his profound desire to be recognized as a human being and as an individual, rather than to be grouped with the undifferentiated mass. In a poem entitled "La esclava ausente," his speaker, the absent slave, verbalizes her (and his) sentiments: "El agravio que sufro, la injusticia / la opresión, el dolor, cierto con males / que al noble corazón jamás arredran / más padezco, que soy mujer al cabo / Y como humana, es justo me resienta" (The aggravation that I suffer, the injustice / the oppression, the pain, certainly with horrors / that no longer daunt the noble heart / I will suffer more, I am a woman in the end / and as a human, its only logical that I'll show the effects).[54] That is to say, not that he did not have a superiority complex or that he did not harbor negative feelings toward Blacks, but rather that the desire to be recognized by the larger society as human and an individual played a crucial role in shaping his relationships with and representations of Blacks. Although Manzano already had a reputation as a poet by the time his autobiography was published, the speed with which he was arrested and jailed for suspicion of participating in the Escalera conspiracy shows that he was still in the same precarious position he occupied with his evil mistress—accorded privileges but subject to being lumped in with the Blacks at any time.

Manzano's desire to be recognized as a human being is also manifested in his connection to the nascent Cuban nation. Although he does not explicitly reference this nation in the autobiography, the passion with which he does so in his poetry and personal correspondence suggest that his affinity for Cuba also undergirded the autobiography. The poem "To Cuba" illustrates his love for his country, while also emphasizing the ways slavery makes both the oppressed and the oppressors inhuman. He makes a point of linking the plight of the Blacks in Cuba to that of "men," those who are defined as human: "tis not alone the wretched negro's fate / that calls for pity, sad as it may be / there's more to weep for in that hapless state / of men who proudly boast that they are free / whose moral sense is warped to that degree / that self-debasement seems to them unknown / and life's sole object, is for means to play / to roll a carriage, or to seek renown / in all the futile follies of the town" (126). They are called men, but their moral sense is warped and their behavior is inhumane. He represents the nascent Cuban nation as the utopia where men can be most human. The evil that foists inhumanity upon Cuba's sons, however, prevents Cuba from becoming that place. He asks "Cuba, of what avail that thou art fair! / pearl of the seas, the pride of the Antilles / if thy poor sons, have still to see thee share / the pangs of bondage, and its thousand ills" (125). The dehumanization of slavery keeps Cuba a site of barbarism. He invokes that history of barbarism, and the lost opportunity to supercede it in the present when he writes "To think unmoved of millions of our race / swept from thy soil by cruelties prolonged / another clime then ravaged to replace / the wretched Indians; Africa then wronged / to fill the void where myriads lately thronged /and add new guilt to that long list of crimes" (127).

In a letter to Domingo Delmonte dated June 5, 1835 Manzano voices his desire to "write a truly Cuban novel."[55] One could, following Manzano's train of thought as illustrated in the poem above, add the phrase "and that novel would certainly not be a narrative of slavery."[56] In the Cuba of Manzano's dreams/imagination slavery would not exist, and all would be free to be not only Cubans, but also fully moral, fully civilized people. This point is bolstered by his presentation of himself as a model for human morality and as a Cuban who loves his fair country: "Of, if the name of Cuban! makes my breast/thrill with a moment's pride, that soon is o'er . . . / reproach awakes me, to assail once more / and taint that name, as if the loathsome pest/that spreads from slavery had seized the core / polluting both th'oppressor and the oppressed / yet God be thanked, it has not reached my breast" (126). He continues to emphasize that slavery is alien to the essential nature of Cuba, and at the same time to define humanness as the core of the nation.

Significantly, it is in only in this poem about Cuba that Manzano exhibits an unambivalent, unambiguous connection to other people of African descent. As discussed earlier, the ambivalence is clear throughout the autobiography. Others of African descent are rarely if ever mentioned in his other poems, save for "La esclava ausente," and even there he does not explicitly signal a connection to Africa. This fact suggests that his affinity for the nascent nation in some way frees him from the fear of being lumped with the undifferentiated mass of Blacks. His connection to the nascent nation, in his eyes, makes him not only more human, but also more exceptional. This is certainly not so because the others do not have access to the nation. He calls them Cuba's children. Being truly Cuban, being part of the utopian Cuba of which he dreams, humanizes all and banishes the dehumanized, undifferentiated mass.

To Be (Hu)man and Different: The Dreams of Delany, Plácido, and Douglass

Manzano was not alone in this desire or in his responses. This desire has had significant implications for relations between people of African descent within and across national borders. The place of this desire in the writing of the others studied in this book is beyond the scope of the present project, as the goal has been to identify the range of approaches to identity taken by people of African descent during this period, but is provocative to consider even if briefly. The tension between individual and community so persistent in Douglass's narrative (Chapter 3), as well as between his Americanness and his Blackness in his engagements with Haiti, are a reflection of this desire. A similar tension is present in Martin Delany's *Blake* (Chapter 1) in the person of the protagonist, Henry, who is both the universal human and the blackest possible Black man. He is also both an exceptional man and a man who speaks with and from the broader Black community and a man who is both tied to a nation and completely transnational. Through *Blake*, Delany attempts to articulate a connection based on (racial or national) commonality while also celebrating (racial or national) exceptionality. Plácido clings to the nascent Cuban nation as Manzano does, but, I would suggest, was spared the label of "blanco aunque negro haya sido su color" (white although black in color) by his martyrdom—his execution for allegedly being a race man.[57]

That Mary Prince does not seem to exhibit these drives to disidentify or to focus on her exceptionality (national or individual), raises the question whether these drives have gendered underpinnings. This is also a question best tackled in another study, but suffice it to say here that something about Prince's experience led her to take a very different path from the others. Her desire to be human was certainly no less fervent than theirs, nor was her experience in slavery any less harsh. In fact, one could easily argue that hers was especially harsh, given the fact that she never had any period when she was treated well by her masters or celebrated by abolitionists or anyone else. The goal of this chapter, however, has been to explicate the connection between disidentification, the desire to be human and individual, and national identity in the writing of Juan Francisco Manzano, and to suggest that this link is also present in the writing and thought of others public and published people of African descent during this period. The conclusion of the study will index the implications of this and other approaches to identity developed in the wake of the Haitian Revolution.

Conclusion

We should be international. Not just provincial. We shouldn't just be a provincial people. That's what they want, just to keep us thinking we're a provincial people, and they're the universalists. That their perspective is the universal perspective. They claim for their provincial perspective universality. We're a universal people. We're more universal. 'Cause we don't think everybody's supposed to be like us.

—*Mosquito, from Gayl Jones*, Mosquito

Acknowledging differences does not compel one to be involved in the dialectics of their totality. One could get away with: "I can acknowledge your difference and continue to think it is harmful to you."

—*Edouard Glissant*, Poetics of Relation

This book has traced the underpinnings of people of African descent's frequently troubled and, too often, troubling representations of and engagements with each other to the Atlantic power structures' denial of their humanity. My argument has been that, in the wake of the Haitian Revolution, people of African descent's desire to be recognized as human and equal drove them variously to embrace and reject cosmopolitanism as a framework for defining self and community. Their dehumanization, as the Cuban government documents analyzed in the first chapter illustrate, was constituted not only by the material conditions of slavery, but also by a denial of access to both cosmopolitan and national subjectivity and a construction of them only and always through race. People of African descent sought to break free of these limitations by claiming the identities forbidden them, reconfiguring those imposed on them, and discarding those they viewed as chaff. Their methods included constructing their own nation based on race, complete with its own intellectual genealogy, historical identity, and political framework, as Martin Delany and William Wells Brown did (Chapter 2); stubbornly claiming national identity and expressing a connection to the world of oppressed people as Plácido did (Chapter 3); historicizing and therefore proving their citizenship in their nation of residence as Frederick Douglass did (Chapters 4 and 5); and displaying a clear and clearly transnational racial consciousness while indexing knowledge of the world at large as Mary Prince (Chapter 6) did.

That freedom to define oneself and one's community, however, often comes at the expense of treating people of African descent both at home and from other sites as equals. The writings of Delany and Brown reflect their struggle to acknowledge differences between people of African descent while constructing this necessarily essentialist national history and genealogy. Similarly, Frederick Douglass found himself advocating U.S. imperialism, as long as it was benevolent. The rigid limits of Mary Prince's racial consciousness and cosmopolitanism are evident in her hatred for the mulatto woman Martha Wilcox, the absence of Black Britons from her text, and her refusal to consider anywhere outside the West Indies as her "native place."[1] The simultaneity of Juan Francisco Manzano's disidentification with *los negros* and his emphasis on his own intellectual exceptionality (Chapter 7) exemplifies and profoundly encapsulates my point about the impact of the desire to be seen as human and equal on relations between people of African descent. All of these methods are evidence of the confrontation between African Americans (in the continental sense) and the Atlantic power structures' attempt to keep them in their place(s).

Identifying the desire to be recognized as fully human and equal as the root of these troubled engagements enables us to gain a deeper understanding of a number of issues evident in people of African descent's interactions and public representations of each other, both during the nineteenth century and beyond. Not the least of these is the extent to which the equality sought by people of African descent is always already gendered male. If it is thus gendered, the question whether and how public women of African descent, particularly during the nineteenth century but also subsequently, choose to represent people of African descent in or from other sites becomes especially significant. Do they employ the same strategies and speak from the same bases as their male counterparts, or must they develop an alternative mode of defining their community?

The analysis of Mary Prince's cosmopolitan consciousness begins to shed light on this question and provide a framework for uniquely enlightening readings of the public and published works of Maria Stewart, for example. In one of her texts, Stewart at once indexes an at the very least rhetorically transnational Black women's community, the "daughters of

Africa"; reminds the "great and mighty men of America" that "charity begins at home, and that those that provide not for their own are worse than infidels"; and calls for the recognition of the equality of the children of Africa in terms that are gendered male, in accordance with the discourses of African American equality at the time and with humanistic discourse more broadly: "Then why should man any longer deprive his fellow-man of equal rights and privilege?"[2] Stewart's text simultaneously acknowledges that both the discourse of equal rights into which she intervenes and her specific demands for equality for African Americans respectively are and must be gendered male first and foremost. Significantly, she does so by defining African Americans in terms that point to the broader (beyond the U.S.) dimension to their identity and history.

This emphasis on the cosmopolitan functions, then, as a way to strengthen her argument to those in power—those whom she, crucially, defines as American throughout the text. At the same time, she insists on carving out a space for African American women's equal rights by also speaking of and to them in those broader terms. In so doing, she elbows her own and African American women's way out of the domestic sphere (in both sense of the term) and into the discourses on the rights of man and on African American's rights to a history and a cosmopolitan identity. Comprehending the multiple dimensions (and locations) of Stewart's (and other public women's) thinking demands that we understand that the object of investigation should not just be whether or how African American women in particular, or women of African descent more generally, engage the Black world or the world at large, but also why they do so—what motivates them and the specific character of the goal(s) they pursue.

Viewing interactions between people of African descent through the lens of the fight for equality provides a framework for interpreting approaches to self-representation that do not obviously demand recognition of people of African descent's equality, alongside other texts that do. In so doing, it provides a basis for expanding our conception of "Black" intellectual thought, particularly but not only in the nineteenth century, because it reveals that people of African descent in the Americas were confronting the same basic demon but employed divergent strategies for doing so. It is less useful, then, to read the form and content of people of African descent's texts (especially but not only in the nineteenth century), as reflective of an a priori mastery or brilliance than as a representation of their attempt to use the master's tools or any other tools available to them to destroy or to get into the master's house.

Reading through the search for equality enables us to grasp the unstated relationship to other people of African descent within a particular text, as exemplified in my earlier explication of the absence of the Caribbean in African American slave narratives. From this vantage point, we come to understand, for example, that Frederick Douglass's ambivalent and ambiguous representations of African Americans in his 1845 *Narrative*, especially when read alongside both the more explicit embraces of African American community in his own contemporaneous speeches, and the racial disidentification exhibited by Juan Francisco Manzano in his autobiography, are disparate but profoundly linked textual manifestations of a fundamentally common Atlantic experience of being perceived and treated as a nonhuman who does not have the right to determine the basis of his or her own identity. The equality framework allows us to acknowledge and engage differences between people of African descent while also speaking of and from the histories that connect them. It facilitates the recognition of variance and serves as an alternative to subsuming all people of African descent into the category "Black" in order to index the common horrific history that they share. topics, then, is no longer a litmus test by which the worthiness of a text that could be read as part of the African Diasporan literary discourse is judged. The implicit and explicit responses to dehumanization within a text becomes the focus, allowing us to see how a text fits in with others by people of African descent without demanding that the author or the text explicitly be Black.

Victor Séjour's short story "Le mulâtre" (1837), set in St. Domingue, features a mulatto man (Georges), who kills his master/father (Alfred) for killing his wife (Zelia). Such a text could be read primarily through its racial markers—the self-hating/white-hating/confused/angry mulatto murders the white man who is the personification of his struggle with identity.[3] A more nuanced reading, however, could call attention to Séjour's choosing to have the master's killing of the mulatto's wife (who is also mulatto) be the catalyst for Georges' violence, emphasizing the fact of Georges' humanity (his love of his wife), the assault on his humanity (in the form of his right to protect his wife), and the fact that his actions are a response to that attack. As Séjour constructs the tale, it is Georges' anger about the treatment of his wife, rather than his specific racial makeup or confusion about it, that drives the climax of the story. Race is undoubtedly the basis of the context (as evident in both the title and the fact that the text begins with Georges' mother being bought), but it is the dehumanization fed by this racialist and racist framework that prompts violent action. Georges pauses in the middle of his vengeance because Alfred has hinted that he knows the name of Georges' father: "My father . . . my father,' . . . Do you know him . . . oh! Tell me his name . . . What's his name . . . oh! Tell me, tell me his name . . . I'll pardon you . . . I'll bless you."[4] He desperately wants to know his father. Séjour presents this desire in terms that could be used by any fatherless child, not just a mulatto one. Georges is not a racially lost soul, and Séjour illustrates that by portraying him as having positive relationships with a number of communities and individuals of African descent, including the Maroons. For Séjour, Georges' mulattoness reflects a reality of slave society, but he ultimately seems to be more interested in illustrating the impact of the multiple challenges to Georges' humanity.[5]

At the beginning of this book, I tied the development of this project to the questions about relations between African Americans, West Indians, Latinos (and Latin Americans) raised by my personal and academic experiences. Fundamentally, I wanted to better understand the histories of and impetuses behind material and representational tensions between the groups as they function in the United States today. Terms I have developed through this study, such as binaristic blackness, twice-doubled consciousness, and collective autoethnography, provide a language for marking the past and present manifestations of these tensions. In addition, my exploration of the contrasting mechanics of the construction of a "Black" intellectual genealogy (that implicitly downplays disparities) and of racial disidentification (that highlights differences) flags and suggests analytical entry points for discussing contemporary relations. This book reveals that the nineteenth-century roots of these tensions are quite deep and lie in a range of areas, including some that are more readily apparent, such as the demands of particular historical contexts, genre considerations, and choices about the relationship between political vision and literary technique, and some that are less obvious, such as disparate valuations of national and racial identity and the concomitant varying perceptions of the grounds of community, the subsuming of differences that was inherent in the construction of "Black" intellectual and political genealogies, and differences in worldview influenced by the geographies of sites of origin. I have identified nineteenth-century approaches to identity that are foundational to contemporary notions of self and community among people of African descent in the Americas.

What remains is perhaps the more difficult task—formulating ways to minimize the material and representational tensions in the service of political advancement without negating differences. My positioning of the chapter on disidentification as the final chapter indexes the ongoing presence of this

challenge. Disidentification is the ultimate difference, and therefore the ultimate challenge to the conception of a transnational Black community. It
exemplifies the range of disparities that characterize the African Diaspora,
as well as the inherent tension between the very real presence of those diver-
gences in approach to self-definition and the common experience (of enslavement) that produced both them and the very notion of a transnational
Black community. The understanding of and earnest engagement with that
tension is absolutely crucial to political coalition building between African
Americans, Latinos, and West Indians in the present day United States. Building such bridges, as well as bridges with poor whites, whose equality and
humanity have also been negated, demands that we are attentive not only to
those texts, people, or communities that define themselves as Black, but that
we develop a more expansive framework that can recognize the multiple forms
of marginalization and the multiply configured responses they prompt, while
not losing sight of the unique experiences, histories, exigencies, and expectations with which each group has had to contend. *Black Cosmopolitanism* has
been my contribution to that greater good.

Notes

Introduction

1. At first glance, Lauryn Hill's cross-cultural ease may not seem strange to those who are familiar with contemporary discourse on the multi-locationality and multi-culturality of Caribbean diasporan identities. Juan Flores's work on Newyorican identity, Paule Marshall's novels on West Indian/African American life, and Stuart Hall's work on hybrid Black British subjectivities all elucidate the multiple cultural and identificatory sites negotiated by Caribbean diasporan people. Lauryn Hill's work would seem to fit perfectly into this paradigm, except that she is not Caribbean diasporan. Juan Flores, *Divided Borders: Essays on Puerto Rican Identity* (Houston: Arte Publico Press, 1993); Paule Marshall, *Soul Clap Hands and Sing* (New York: Atheneum, 1961); Marshall, *The Chosen Place, the Timeless People* (New York: Harcourt, Brace, 1969); Marshall, *Brown Girl, Brownstones*, with an afterward by Mary Helen Washington (Chatham, N.J.: Chatham Bookseller, 1972); Marshall, *Praisesong for the Widow* (New York: Putman's, 1983); Marshall, *Daughters* (New York: Atheneum 1991); Stuart Hall, "New Ethnicities," in *The Post-Colonial Studies Reader*, ed. Bill Ashcroft, Gareth Griffiths, and Helen Tiffin (London: Routledge, 1995); Hall, "Cultural Identity and Cinematic Representation," in *Black British Cultural Studies: A Reader*, ed. Houston A. Baker, Jr., Manthia Diawara, and Ruth H. Lindeborg (Chicago: University of Chicago Press, 1996); Hall, "Cultural Identity and Diaspora," in *Contemporary Postcolonial Theory: A Reader*, ed. Padmini Mongia (London: Arnold, 1996); and Hall, ed., *Representation: Cultural Representations and Signifying Practices* (London: Sage, 1997).

2. In addition, Melvin B. Rahming, for example, has detailed the prevalence of stereotypical images of West Indians in earlier African American literature including Ellison's *Invisible Man* and Du Bois's *Dark Princess*.

3. Although it addresses a more immediately violent history, see also Michel-Rolph Trouillot, *Silencing the Past: Power and the Production of History* (Boston: Beacon Press, 1995).

4. Carole Boyce Davies among others has pointed out the difficulty with descriptive terminologies for Blacks in the Americas. Carole Boyce Davies, *Black Women, Writing and Identity: Migrations of the Subject* (New York: Routledge, 1994), 5. This difficulty exemplifies why the transnational heading toward supranational conceptual framework I suggest here is necessary. There has been so much migration and movement within the Americas that defining an individual or group through a specific site, or tying a specific site only to a specific group, is virtually impossible, not to mention inaccurate. As a result I vary the terms that I use throughout the

book, highlighting the tension associated with the use of those terms. I use the terms U.S. Black, U.S. descended Black, and African American (albeit reluctantly) to describe Blacks who are born, raised, and have multigenerational roots in the U.S. I use the terms Caribbean and Caribbean descended Blacks to describe people who have roots in the Caribbean (which is difficult to do since so many "African Americans" have eighteenth-, nineteenth-, or twentieth-century Caribbean roots). By including Hispanophone Caribbean writers in this project, I call them Black by implication. I want to point out here that this is simply a heuristic, and that part of the project of this book is to interrogate the expectation that all people with African blood must define themselves racially, and that if they do not they are "sell outs." The other side of this interrogation is the questioning of the significance of disassociating from Black racial identification for inter-American relations. Most frequently, I use the term people of African descent in the Americas. I believe that African American is the more appropriate term, but at present, it connotes a specific (U.S.) national site in many minds. Like Davies, I am dissatisfied with the available terms, but cognizant of the fact that neologisms can impede reader comprehension. In the service of achieving the larger ends my project identifies, I dare to tread on the quicksand that is the field of descriptive racial/ethnic/national terminology in the Americas.

5. Aimé Césaire, *Notebook of a Return to the Native Land*, 1947, trans. and ed. Clayton Eshleman and Annette Smith (Middletown, Conn.: Wesleyan University Press, 2001), 15.

6. James Theodore Holly, "A Vindication of the Capacity of the Negro Race for Self-Government and Civilized Progress as Demonstrated by Historical Events of the Haytian Revolution; and the Subsequent Acts of That People Since Their National Independence" in James Theodore Holly and J. Dennis Harris, *Black Separatism and the Caribbean, 1860*, ed. Howard H. Bell (Ann Arbor: University of Michigan Press, 1970), 23.

7. Holly, "A Vindication," 65.

8. David Walker, *David Walker's Appeal to the Coloured Citizens of the World* (1829; University Park: Pennsylvania State University Press, 2000), 23.

9. William Wells Brown, *St. Domingo: Its Revolutions and Its Patriots* (Boston: Bela Marsh, 1855), 8.

10. Julius S. Scott, "The Common Wind: Currents of Afro-American Communication in the Era of the Haitian Revolution," Ph.D. dissertation, Duke University, 1986; W. Jeffrey Bolster, *Black Jacks: African American Seamen in the Age of Sail* (Cambridge, Mass: Harvard University Press, 1997); Peter Linebaugh and Marcus Rediker, *The Many-Headed Hydra: Sailors, Slaves, Commoners, and the Hidden History of the Revolutionary Atlantic* (Boston: Beacon Press, 2000); Maggie Montesinos Sale, *The Slumbering Volcano: American Slave Ship Revolts and the Production of Rebellious Masculinity* (Durham, N.C.: Duke University Press, 1997); Cheryl J. Fish, *Black and White Women's Travel Narratives: Antebellum Explorations* (Gainesville: University Press of Florida, 2004); William Andrews, *To Tell a Free Story: The First Century of Afro-American Autobiography, 1760–1865* (Urbana: University of Illinois Press, 1986).

11. U.S. Constitution, Article I, Section 2, Clause 3.

12. Walter Mignolo makes a similar point when he writes of the intrinsic link between cosmopolitanism and coloniality, and more specifically of colonialism's "global designs." Walter Mignolo, "The Many Faces of Cosmo-polis: Border Thinking and Critical Cosmopolitanism," *Public Culture* 12, 3 (2000): 721–48.

13. Edward Said, *Orientalism* (New York: Vintage, 1979), 12. Said anticipates the analyses of Mary Louise Pratt, who delineates the impact of encounters with the newly discovered, imaged, and imagined others on European and creole American ideology, self-concepts, and worldviews. Pratt's reading of creole intellectual Domingo Faustino Sarmiento's travel book on Europe is particularly instructive. Sarmiento, author of *Civilization and Barbarism* (1847), a text that both established and analyzed racial hierarchies in Spanish America, is forced to reflect on his own discursive and identificatory position as he travels through Europe. As Pratt puts it, "he takes up the question before him . . . how does the creole citizen and man of letters position himself with respect to Europe?" Mary Louise Pratt, *Imperial Eyes: Travel Writing and Transculturation*, 1992 (New York: Routledge, 1998), 190.

14. Pheng Cheah, "Given Culture: Rethinking Cosmopolitical Freedom in Transnationalism," *Boundary 2* (Summer 1997): 176, 175.

15. Cheah, "Given Culture," 176.

16. I employ the term cosmopolitanism to emphasize that the Haitian Revolution brings about and/or creates the assumption of a certain global sophistication (the most common definition of cosmopolitanism) on the part of people of African descent in the Americas. White fear was based on the notion that people of African descent everywhere had knowledge of the revolution and felt connected to the revolutionaries. At the same time, people of African descent were endeavoring to conceptualize and articulate the grounds of a globally oriented notion of community. My use of the term builds on definitions of the term that emphasize interest in global knowledge and engagement, and runs counter to definitions that ascribe cosmopolitanism only to White Europeans and/or members of the elite. Thomas Schlereth, for example, provides a useful history of the term, characterizing it as an attempt to overcome provincial national affinities and associating it with the elite. He identifies the cosmopolite as one who values knowledge of a range of people and places of the world. Thomas Schlereth, *The Cosmopolitan Ideal in Enlightenment Thought: Its Form and Function in the Ideas of Franklin, Hume, and Voltaire, 1694–1790* (Notre Dame, Ind.: University of Notre Dame Press, 1976). Several scholars have recently pondered the role of cosmopolitanism in the intellectual's work, most particularly in the intellectual's work as a radical. See Paul A. Bove, "Afterword: Global/Local Memory and Thought," in *Global/Local: Cultural Production and the Transnational Imaginary*, ed. Rob Wilson and Wimal Dissanayake (Durham, N.C.: Duke University Press, 1996); David A. Hollinger, "Ethnic Diversity, Cosmopolitanism, and the Emergence of the American Liberal Intelligentsia," *American Quarterly*, 27, 2 (May 1975): 133–51.; Tim Brennan, "Cosmopolitans and Celebrities," *Race and Class: A Journal for Black and Third World Liberation* 31, 1 (July–September 1989): 1–19; Robin D. G. Kelley, *Freedom Dreams: The Black Radical Imagination* (Boston: Beacon Press, 2002).

17. Elisa Tamarkin revisits, for example, African Americans' relationships to and representations of England. Elisa Tamarkin, "Black Anglophilia; or the Sociability of Antislavery," *American Literary History* 14, 3 (2002): 444–78.

18. For a more detailed historicization of Pan-Africanism, see Ronald W. Walters, *Pan-Africanism in the African Diaspora: An Analysis of Modern Afrocentric Political Movements* (Detroit: Wayne State University Press, 1993).

19. Sankar Muthu's *Enlightenment Against Empire* (2004) shows clearly the extent to which even the idea that European identity should be constituted by the type of cosmopolitanism that Empire represented was a subject of substantial debate. Sankar Muthu, *Enlightenment Against Empire* (Princeton, NJ: Princeton University Press, 2004).

20. In this, my project's approach to cosmopolitanism differs significantly from that of Paul Gilroy, especially as it appears in Gilroy, *Against Race: Imagining Political Culture Beyond the Color Line* (Cambridge, Mass: Belknap Press of Harvard University, 2000); he posits such engagements as a means for achieving the "liberation from 'race'" which he argues "is an especially urgent matter for those peoples who, like modern blacks in the period after transatlantic slavery, were assigned an inferior position in the enduring hierarchies that raciology creates" (15). Especially troubling are his equation, throughout the work, of the embrace of racial community with backwardness and history and the embrace of universality with progress and the future and his decrying the fact that "nobody ever speaks of a human identity," suggesting that there is an inherent contradiction between being attentive to a community's humanity and defining that community as a culturally or historically identifiable community. I am arguing that it was precisely the negation of people of African descent's humanity that led them to claim or reject Blackness and/or cosmopolitanism as bases of identity. As the remainder of my study shows, I concur fully in taking a critical view of Blackness and specifically of the ways particular notions of Blackness have been used to exclude, subsume, and marginalize a range of individuals and populations, but the answer is not to negate either the forces that led to its production or the extent to which it has served a range of individuals and communities well, and provided the basis for casting off various oppressive millstones. Carole Boyce Davies in a review of *Against Race* makes a similar point, noting that the book "challenges the philosophy of 'race' as a formation but it leaves intact the . . . hierarchy of racial oppression and racial structuring." Carole Boyce Davies, "*Against Race* or the Politics of Self-Ethnography," *Jenda: A Journal of Culture and African Women Studies* 2 (2002): 1

Black Cosmopolitanism recalls Joan Dayan's characterization of her difference from Gilroy: "I am less interested in how the enlightenment and philosophers of modernity, whether called Habermas or Du Bois, Hegel or Douglass crafted their analyses . . . than in how slaves and their descendants interpreted and revealed what white enlightenment was really about." In Gilroy's pursuit of an anchor for "black modernism," "slavery. . . becomes nothing more than a metaphor." Joan Dayan, "Paul Gilroy's Slaves, Ships, and Routes: The Middle Passage as Metaphor," *Research in African Literatures* 27, 4 (Winter 1996): 7; see also Simon Gikandi, "Race and Cosmopolitanism," *American Literary History* 14, 3 (Fall 2002): 600, 602, 610.

21. Mihai Grunfeld's article, for example, uses this description as a conceptual basis. Mihai Grunfeld, "Cosmopolitismo modernista y vanguardista," *Revista Iberoamericana* 55, 146–47 (January–June 1989): 33.

22. See, for example, Bruce Robbins's analysis of Martha Nussbaum's *For Love*

of Country. Bruce Robbins, *Feeling Global: Internationalism in Distress* (New York: New York University Press, 1999), 147–68.

23. I use this phrase instead of "vernacular cosmopolitanism" to index the dialogical relationship between "cosmopolitanism from below" and cosmopolitanism as more typically understood—a cosmopolitanism that is really a "cosmopolitanism from above." Both are, in significant part, constituted by their interaction. Identifying a cosmopolitanism as being "from below" necessarily calls attention to not only the cosmopolitanism from above in and of itself, but also the power that it has vis a vis any other cosmopolitanism—its always already hegemonic position. The term vernacular cosmopolitanism is used most often to complicate the binary between native and foreign. For an explication of a vernacular cosmopolitanism, see, for example, Mamadou Diouf, "The Senegalese Murid Trade Diaspora and the Making of a Vernacular Cosmopolitanism," *Public Culture* 12, 3 (2000): 679–702.

24. Here, I refer to the alternating cooperation and conflict between the dominant powers in the slaveocracies of the Americas over the appropriate approaches to preventing another Haiti. The ambivalent relationship between the colonial government in Cuba and the British as well as that between the creole elites in Cuba and the United States (discussed in greater detail in Chapter 1) exemplify this vacillation.

25. My point is not that historical discourse on the early Black Americas has been wholly transnational, because it certainly has not been. The fixation with national borders has certainly been a significant presence in the field. Insightful yet nationally bounded works such as Philip Curtin, *Two Jamaicas: The Role of Ideas in a Tropical Colony, 1830–1865* (Cambridge, Mass.: Harvard University Press, 1955) pepper the historiographical landscape. My point is that transnational and/or comparative methodologies have been valued in historical scholarship.

26. Works considered foundational include Melville J. Herskovits, *Myth of a Negro Past,* with a foreword by Sidney W. Mintz (1941; Boston: Beacon Press, 1990); Sidney Mintz and Richard Price, *Birth of African American Culture* (1976; Boston: Beacon Press, 1992); Richard Price, *Maroon Societies: Rebel Slave Communities in the Americas,* 2nd ed. (Baltimore: Johns Hopkins University Press, 1979); Laura Foner and Eugene D. Genovese, eds., *Slavery in the New World: A Reader in Comparative History* (Englewood Cliffs, N.J.: Prentice-Hall, 1969); Charles H. Wesley, ed., *The Negro in the Americas* (Washington, D.C.: Graduate School, Howard University, 1940); Melvin Marvin Tumin, comp., *Comparative Perspectives on Race Relations* (Boston: Little, Brown, 1969); Roslyn Terborg-Penn and Andrea Benton Rushing, eds., *Women in Africa and the African Diaspora* (Washington, D.C.: Howard University Press, 1996).

27. Herskovits, *The Myth of the Negro Past,* xxvii.

28. These works, however, do not posit Blacks as agents in the creation of their own cultures—a concept presented as an organically occurring process, or of their own identities—identity is not even mentioned as part of the Black experience in the Americas. See for example, Eugene D. Genovese, *The World the Slaveholders Made: Two Essays in Interpretation* (Middletown, Conn.: Wesleyan University Press, 1988). Other works such as Lawrence W. Levine, *Black Culture and Black Consciousness* (New York: Oxford University Press, 1977) and Eugene Genovese *Roll, Jordan, Roll: The World the Slaves Made* (New York: Vintage, 1974) begin to refute the assumption that history "happened" to Blacks in the Americas, and detail ways Blacks crafted their

own American cultures. I engage in a similar project by viewing ex-slave and free Black writers, who Ira Berlin names as "slaves without masters," as participants in African American nation building and as agents to choose to embrace or not embrace non-U.S. Blacks as part of that nation. Ira Berlin, *Slaves Without Masters: The Free Negro in the Antebellum South* (New York: New Press, 1974).

29. Paul Gilroy, *The Black Atlantic: Modernity and Double Consciousness* (Cambridge, Mass.: Harvard University Press, 1993). Positive reviews appeared in several major literary journals; see Peter Erickson, *African American Review* 31, 3 (1997): 506–8; Louis Chude-Sokei, "The Black Atlantic Paradigm: Paul Gilroy and the Fractured Landscape of 'Race,'" *American Quarterly* 48, 4 (1996): 740–45; Alasdair Pettinger, "Enduring Fortresses," *Research in African Literatures* 29, 4 (1998): 142–47; Dwight McBride, *Modern Fiction Studies* 41, 2 (1995): 388–91. A significantly less positive review, one that centers on the lack of depth and concern with the material in Gilroy's work, is Joan Dayan, "Paul Gilroy's Slaves, Ships, and Routes: The Middle Passage as Metaphor," *Research in African Literatures* 27, 4 (1996): 7–14.

30. See, for example, Price, *Maroon Societies*; Herbert S. Klein, *Slavery in the Americas: A Comparative Study of Virginia and Cuba* (Chicago: University of Chicago Press, 1967); Klein, *African Slavery in Latin America and the Caribbean* (New York: Oxford University Press, 1986); Klein, *The Atlantic Slave Trade* (New York: Cambridge University Press, 1999); Klein, *The Middle Passage: Comparative Studies in the Atlantic Slave Trade* (Princeton, N.J.: Princeton University Press, 1978); Alfred N. Hunt, *Haiti's Influence on Antebellum America* (Baton Rouge: Louisiana State University Press, 1988); David Barry Gaspar and Darlene Clark Hine, eds., *More Than Chattel: Black Women and Slavery in the Americas* (Bloomington: Indiana University Press, 1996); and John Thornton, *Africa and Africans in the Making of the Atlantic World, 1400–1680* (Cambridge: Cambridge University Press, 1998).

31. Morrison tracks the persistence of what she calls "American Africanism"— White American writers' use of the African in their construction of Americanness— and criticizes critical approaches that have ignored this presence for impoverishing the literature, for robbing it of its ideas. Toni Morrison, *Playing in the Dark* (New York: Vintage, 1993). Sundquist rereads the American Renaissance in particular and American identity in general as being foundationally about Black revolution, about the right to freedom. He calls into question the imagining of American literature and culture as purely "Anglo-European" and of African American literature as a marginal stepchild. Sundquist's text stands out in its positioning of Delany and Melville's Americas/New World interest as also constitutive of American literature. In suggesting a completely new paradigm upon which American literary genealogies should be based, this work posits one way in which the Americas can be read within the U.S. critical discourse and paves the way for work like mine. Eric Sundquist, *To Wake the Nations: Race in the Making of American Literature* (Cambridge, Mass.: Belknap Press of Harvard University Press, 1993). Nelson explores the functioning of the concept of "race" in colonial and early American literary texts. She is specifically concerned with the ways in which the strategies for dealing with race shaped both texts and society. She delineates the intervention of racial (and often racist) ideology in texts that purport to be supporting the racial other as well as highlighting how both the racially othered and the self-critical (de)racialized self have talked back. My

approach to reading inter-American engagements in both outward reaching and locally fixated Black Americas writing mirrors Nelson's in terms of going beyond simply noting the appearance of the othernational Black (the racialized other in Nelson's work), and into what these modes of engagement say about developing social ideology. Dana D. Nelson, *The Word in Black and White: Reading "Race" in American Literature, 1638–1867* (New York: Oxford University Press, 1993).

32. Chambers speaks to the ways in which the "return of the native," that is the migration of Blacks to England, forces the White English "us" to reconsider who we think we are, to recognize that the stranger is also within us, exposing "the fiction of identity." He extrapolates what is happening in the English context, arguing that migrancy itself puts the presumed identificatory determinism of modernity into question. Caribbean American writers such as Paule Marshall and Edwidge Danticat, if accorded sufficient critical attention, as well as "celebrities" like Colin Powell and Busta Rhymes, will have a similar impact on African American conception of "we." Iain Chambers, *Migrancy, Culture, Identity* (London: Routledge, 1994). In "The Local and the Global," and "Old Identities, New Ethnicities," for example, Hall argues that the old logic of English identity has been put into question by the presence of the Black British and the loss of English world power due to globalization. The approach to English identity that he terms the Thatcherite notion of Englishness has become even more narrow and reactionary in response to this perceived threat. I suggest that a similar turtle response is part of what has ensured continuing tensions between African Americans and Caribbean people. Stuart Hall, "The Local and the Global," in *Culture, Globalization, and the World-System: Contemporary Conditions for the Representation of Identity*, ed. Anthony D. King (Minneapolis: University of Minnesota Press, 1997).

33. Baker calls attention to the (de)formation of modernism and mastery imbricated in seminal texts of the Black intellectual tradition. Through readings of a wide variety of literary, political, and artistic texts including works by W. E. B. Du Bois, Booker T. Washington, Paul Laurence Dunbar, and Charles Chesnutt, Baker posits a theory of Black Modernism based on the revision of (White) forms and the invocation of uniquely Black figures and figurations. He avows not only that Black Modernism exists, but also that it is American. Henry Louis Gates's argument in *Signifying Monkey* recalls Baker's in its emphasis on the intertextual talking back of Black writers and texts. My project is more interested, however, in relations between Black texts across national borders than in how texts within one nation talk either to the dominant discourses in that one nation or to each other. Houston A. Baker, *Modernism and the Harlem Renaissance* (Chicago: University of Chicago Press, 1987).

34. Spillers's introduction to *Comparative American Identities*, "Who Cuts the Border," argues that the analyses of the calibanesque attributes of the U.S. should be included in the discourse interrogating the "made up" European construction called America. She puts this into action through a reading of Our Americanness (to use Marti's term) of Faulkner's *Absalom, Absalom*. Hortense Spillers, ed., *Comparative American Identities: Race, Sex, and Nationality in the Modern Text* (New York: Routledge, 1991), 1–25. Clark argues for the development of Diaspora literacy—the wherewithal to read texts from various diasporan points from an "indigenous" perspective and "marasa consciousness"—going beyond privileging the binaries in critical analysis

and reading intertextual dialogues. Significantly, she locates the beginning of both Diaspora literacy and marasa consciousness in the rise of what she terms the "new letters," in the Americas of the 1920s and 1930s, also known as the Harlem Renaissance, Negrismo, the Trinidad Awakening, and Negritude. Vévé Clark, "Developing Diaspora Literacy and Marasa Consciousness," in Spillers, *Comparative American Identities*, 40–61. Saldivar calls for and enacts a "trans-geographical" American literary analysis that highlights cross currents rather than fixating on national ideologies. Contained within this collection on various texts that would traditionally be classified as Latin American or Latino is his reading of the magical realism of Ntozake Shange's *Sassafrass, Cypress, & Indigo*. He calls attention to the implicit and explicit links Shange has and makes to Afro-Caribbean and Latin American literary models, and criticizes the critical reduction of her work to one national site. José David Saldivar, *The Dialectics of Our America: Genealogy, Cultural Critique, and Literary History* (Durham, N.C.: Duke University Press, 1991).

35. Griffin provides a marvelous, detailed, integrated analysis of the literary, musical, and photographic representations and reflections of African American migration to the North. She delineates the negotiations of space and identity, past and present that shape the migrant's experiences in these migration narratives. Farah Jasmine Griffin, *"Who Set You Flowin'": The African American Migration Narrative* (New York: Oxford University Press, 1995).

36. Gilroy analyzes Du Bois's and Wright's creation of an African American theory of modernity by using and reworking European theoretical models such as those created by Marx and Nietzsche. He argues that narrow readings have ignored the European dimensions of these African American men's thought and writing. He criticizes Cornel West's all-American centered reading of Du Bois and specifically what he sees as West's downplaying of Du Bois's European influences and encounters. He also similarly decries the intellectually impoverishing pigeonholing of Wright that negates his resistance to African American essentialism.

37. Brent Edwards, *The Practice of Diaspora: Literature, Translation, and the Rise of Black Internationalism* (Cambridge, Mass.: Harvard University Press, 2003); James DeJongh, *Vicious Modernism: Black Harlem and the Literary Imagination* (New York: Cambridge University Press, 1990).

38. George Handley, *Postslavery Literatures in the Americas: Family Portraits in Black and White* (Charlottesville: University Press of Virginia, 2000).

39. J. Martin Favor, *Authentic Blackness: The Folk in the New Negro Renaissance* (Durham, N.C.: Duke University Press, 1999), 3; Hazel V. Carby, *Race Men* (Cambridge, Mass.: Harvard University Press, 1998), 5.

40. Hall, "Cultural Identity and Diaspora"; Davies, *Black Women, Writing and Identity*; Myriam Chancy, *Searching for Safe Spaces: Afro-Caribbean Women in Exile* (Philadelphia: Temple University Press, 1997).

41. Franklin Knight, *Slave Society in Cuba During the Nineteenth Century* (Madison: University of Wisconsin Press, 1970); Richard Jackson, *The Black Image in Latin American Literature* (Albuquerque: University of New Mexico Press, 1976); Marvin Lewis, *Afro-American Discourse: Another Dimension of the Black Diaspora* (Columbia: University of Missouri Press, 1995); Caroll Mills Young, "The Unmasking of Virginia Brindis de Salas: Minority Discourse of Afro-Uruguay," in *Daughters*

of the Diaspora: Afra-Hispanic Writers, ed. Miriam DeCosta Willis (Kingston: Ian Randle, 2003), 11–24; Laurence Prescott, *Without Hatreds or Fears: Jorge Artel and the Struggle for Black Literary Expression in Colombia* (Detroit: Wayne State University Press, 2000).

42. Edouard Glissant, *Poetics of Relation*, trans. Betsy Wing (Ann Arbor: University of Michigan Press, 1997), 17.

43. Edwards, *Practice of Diaspora*, 14.

44. Houston Baker's discussion of Douglass's realization of his humanity through the writing of his narrative suggests this, but does not reach the point of explicitly characterizing the slave narrative as an encounter with modernity. The link is evident both in the language of Baker's reading of Douglass (extracting "being from existence," "the slave narrator must accomplish the almost unthinkable . . . task of transmuting an authentic, unwritten self—a self that exists outside the conventional literary discourse structures of a White reading public—into a literary representation") and in Baker's contextualization of his reading of Douglass with the engagement with self undertaken by other American writers of the period. Baker does not, however, discuss the relevance of Douglass's encounters with the world beyond the U.S. to that process of finding and articulating a self. Houston Baker, *The Journey Back: Issues in Black Literature and Criticism* (Chicago: University of Chicago Press, 1980), 39.

45. Frederick Douglass, "Haiti and the Haitian People: An Address Delivered in Chicago, Illinois, on 2 January 1893," in *The Frederick Douglass Papers*, vol. 5, *1881–95*, ed. John W. Blassingame and John R. McKivigan (New Haven, Conn.: Yale University Press, 1992), 523.

46. Kathleen Wilson, *The Island Race: Englishness, Empire, and Gender in the Eighteenth Century* (New York: Routledge, 2003); Eric J. Hobsbawm, *Nations and Nationalism Since 1780: Programme, Myth, Reality* (Cambridge: Cambridge University Press, 1990).

Part One, Introduction

1. Throughout, translations appear in the body of this study either alongside or immediately after the Spanish text.

2. Hazel Carby, *Race Men* (Cambridge, Mass.: Harvard University Press, 1998), 10, 12.

3. I would suggest that the idea of "race man" was created during this period, as a result of the dynamics I explicate throughout the book. The tug-of-war between Frederick Douglass and Martin Delany evidenced in Robert Levine's study of the "politics of representative identity," I would argue, is fundamentally a battle over which was the better "race man." Robert S. Levine, *Martin Delany, Frederick Douglass, and the Politics of Representative Identity* (Chapel Hill: University of North Carolina Press, 1997).

4. Carby, *Race Men*, 25.

5. Scholars have undertaken a wide range of analyses of the (dis)place(ment) of Black women in histories of Black communities. Among these are Jacqueline

Nassy Brown, "Black Liverpool, Black America, and the Gendering of Diasporic Space," *Cultural Anthropology* 13, no. 3 (August 1998): 291–325, and Sandra Gunning, Tera W. Hunter, and Michele Mitchelle, "Introduction: Gender, Sexuality, and African Diasporas," *Gender and History* 15, no. 3 (November 2003): 397–408. The former illuminates the silence on/silencing of Black Liverpudlian women's transatlantic travels in the construction of a Black Liverpudlian history. The latter, the introduction to a special issue on Gender and Sexuality, speaks to the long-standing tendency to address "the experience of black masculinity as a collective identity, without a self-conscious assessment of the continual transformation of gender roles and sexuality within a black diasporic framework" (399).

6. Transcript of appearance on *Newshour with Jim Lehrer*, "Hamilton Holmes Appreciation," November 1, 1995.

7. Zora Neale Hurston, *Tell My Horse* (1938; New York: Harper and Row, 1990), 75.

Chapter 1. The View from Above: Plácido Through the Eyes of the Cuban Colonial Government and White Abolitionists

1. Quoted in Alfred N. Hunt, *Haiti's Influence on Antebellum America: Slumbering Volcano in the Caribbean* (Baton Rouge: Louisiana State University Press, 1988), 2.

2. In his dissertation W. E. B. Du Bois provides a detailed analysis of the failed attempt to suppress the African slave trade to the U.S. that has yet to be superseded by contemporary scholars. W. E. B. Du Bois, *The Suppression of the African Slave Trade to the United States 1638–1870* (1896; Baton Rouge: Louisiana State University Press, 1969).

3. J. G. Wurdemann, *Notes on Cuba* (Boston: James Munroe, 1844), 359.

4. Quoted in Eric Sundquist, *To Wake the Nations: Race in the Making of American Literature* (Cambridge, Mass.: Belknap Press of Harvard University Press, 1993), 183.

5. For a more in-depth discussion on the process and effects of emancipation in Cuba, see Rebecca J. Scott, *Slave Emancipation in Cuba: The Transition to Free Labor, 1860–1899* (Pittsburgh: University of Pittsburgh Press, 2000).

6. Louis A. Pérez, *Cuba and the United States: Ties of Singular Intimacy* (Athens: University of Georgia Press, 1997), 13.

7. The population of free people of color was significant in size because of the "coartado" system by which slaves could purchase their own freedom on an installment basis. Slaves were able to earn money by being hired out or by saving a portion of whatever their master paid them. The slave law (*reglamento de esclavos*) of 1842 also provided for the coartacion of slaves who reported conspiracies or uprisings in the works. Herbert S. Klein, *Slavery in the Americas: A Comparative Study of Virginia and Cuba* (1967; Chicago: Ivan R. Dee, 1989), 196; Phillip Howard, *Changing History: Afro-Cuban Cabildos and Societies of Color in the Nineteenth Century* (Baton Rouge: Louisiana State University Press, 1998), 6–7, 12.

8. As Klein points out, the Roman Catholic church was a fundamental part

of the Spanish crown's plan for consolidating and maintaining its imperial power. Klein, *Slavery in the Americas*, 5.

9. Wurdemann, *Notes on Cuba*, 252.

10. Wurdemann, *Notes on Cuba*, 244.

11. Franklin Knight, *Slave Society in Cuba During the Nineteenth Century* (Madison: University of Wisconsin Press, 1970) 53.

12. Cuban National Archive, Asuntos Políticos, Legajo 99, No. 101.

13. Asuntos Políticos, Legajo 113, No. 58; 117, No. 22.

14. Reales, Cédulas, y Órdenes. Legajo 31, No. 16.

15. Reales, Cédulas, y Órdenes, Legajo 8, No 50.

16. Reales, Cédulas, y Órdenes, Legajo 2, No. 120.

17. Reales, Cédulas, y Órdenes, Legajo 12, No. 18.

18. Reales, Cédulas, y Órdenes, Legajo 31, No. 16.

19. Reales, Cédulas, y Órdenes, Legajo 137. No 13.

20. Reales, Cédulas y Órdenes, Legajo 140, No. 39.

21. Reales, Cédulas, y Órdenes, Legajo 128, No. 78.

22. Reales, Cédulas, y Órdenes. Legajo 74. No 14.

23. Knight, *Slave Society in Cuba*, 81.

24. Howard, *Changing History*, 76. I am indebted to Howard for much of the information on *cabildos* I provide here.

25. Howard, *Changing History*, 75.

26. Miguel Barnet, *Biography of a Runaway Slave*, trans. Nick W. Hill (1968; Willimantic, Conn.: Curbstone Press, 1994), 47. The genesis of this text is extremely controversial as it is Barnet's post-1959 reconstruction of runaway slave Esteban Montejo's story, as told to him by Montejo himself. William Luis, for example, raises questions about the reasons Barnet chose to gather and publish this story when he did, and about the extent to which Barnet's personal and political motives overwhelmed or determined the content, structure, and language of this published version of ex-slave Montejo's story. William Luis, ed., *Literary Bondage: Slavery in Cuban Narrative* (Austin: University of Texas Press, 1990), 199–218.

27. Asuntos Políticos, Legajo 297, No. 102 (on *cimarrones*).

28. Asuntos Políticos, Legajo 12, No. 20.

29. Asuntos Políticos, Legajo 17, No. 22.

30. *Sentencia pronunciada por a Sección de la Comision militar establecida en la ciudad de Matanzas para conocer de la causa de conspiración de la gente de color.* Cuban National Archive. Asuntos Políticos, Legajo 42, No. 15

31. *El Primer censo de población de Cuba colonial,* Lic. Oscar Ramos Piñol, investigator, (Havana: Editorial Estadística, 1990), Appendix , "Censo del Año de 1774."

32. Roxann Wheeler argues convincingly that there were "three main trends in racial ideology in 1790s Britain"—"skin color was more prominent as a public issue than at any time earlier in the century" (19); "an intensified questioning of climate's deterministic effect on national character" (20); and the concern with "the physical body and the skeleton" (20). Roxann Wheeler, "'Betrayed by Some of My Own Complexion': Cuguano, Abolition, and the Contemporary Language of Racialism," in *Genius in Bondage: Literature of the Early Black Atlantic,* ed. Vincent Carreta and Philip Gould (Lexington: University Press of Kentucky, 2001), 17–38.

33. *Pardo* and *mulato* were (and are) terms used to describe people who appear to be or have been classified as being of mixed ancestry. The difference between these terms was not fixed, but was situational and almost wholly dependent on the vicissitudes of those doing the defining/racial marking. The terms also often referred to class position, at times even more than to the actual racial ancestry of an individual. Pedro Deschamps Chapeaux reflects this fact by detailing the place of *pardos* (and *morenos*) *libres* in his work on the place of the Black in the nineteenth-century Cuban economy. Pedro Deschamps Chapeaux, *El Negro en la economia habanera del siglo XIX* (Havana: Unión de Escritores y Artisanas de Cuba, 1971). Contemporary historians of Cuba, including Franklin Knight and Ada Ferrer, generally dispense with the minor, variable, and situational differences between these terms and focus on the fundamentally binary structure of racism and dehumanization (Knight) and the intense sense of connection between politically active people of color (Ferrer). Knight, *Slave Society in Cuba*; Ada Ferrer, *Insurgent Cuba: Race, Nation, and Revolution, 1868–1898* (Chapel Hill: University of North Carolina Press, 1999). Rebecca Scott writing on "The Transition to Free Labor" in Cuba from 1860 to 1899 presents *pardo* and *mulatto* as equivalent terms (*Slave Emancipation in Cuba*, 269–70, 324), but notes that "despite a generally more flexible system of ethnic classification than that prevailing in the U.S. South, the concept of an African 'stain' continued to stigmatize the Cuban descendants of slaves" (9).

34. At the same time, the *Sentencia* also implicitly posits a notion of a unified whiteness, one that obliterates class differences between Whites.

35. Orlando Patterson, *Slavery and Social Death: A Comparative Study* (Cambridge, Mass.: Harvard University Press, 1982), 1.

36. Patterson, *Slavery and Social Death*, 5.

37. Villaverde refers to the 1839 publication date of the first volume in the preface to *Cecilia Valdés, o, la loma del Ángel: novela de costumbres cubanas* (Havana: Editorial Excelsior, 1879). See Cirilo Villaverde, "Prologo del autor," *Cecilia Valdés*, 2 vols., ed. Ana Maria Muñoz (Havana: Editorial Pueblo y Educación, 1990), 1: 49–54.

38. Especially noteworthy among these scholars are William Luis, "Cecilia Valdés: el nacimiento de una novela antiesclavista," *Cuadernos Hispanoamericanos* 451–52 (January–February 1998): 187–93, and Sara Rosell, "Cecilia Valdés de Villaverde a Arenas: la recreación del mito de la mulata," *Afro-Hispanic Review* 18, 2 (Fall 1999): 15–21 and Rosell, "La Novela antiesclavista en Cuba y Brasil, siglo XIX," Ph.D. dissertation, University of Iowa, 1995.

39. Claudette M. Williams, *Charcoal and Cinnamon: The Politics of Color in Spanish Caribbean Literature* (Gainesville: University Press of Florida, 2000), 28.

40. Humberto López Cruz, "Cecilia Valdés: la mulatería como símbolo de identidad nacional en la sociedad colonial cubana," *Hispanofila* 125 (1999 Jan): 56–57.

41. Rodrigo Lazo argues convincingly that the reappearance of such figures and texts reflects "a transnational battle for the control of Cuba." He argues that the 1882 version of Cecilia Valdés is "an attempt to seize the nation at a moment when it appears to Villaverde that the military battle for the island has been lost to Spain." Rodrigo Lazo, "Filibustering Cuba: Cecilia Valdés and a Memory of Nation in the Americas," *American Literature* 74, no. 1 (2002): 1–30.

42. Patterson, *Slavery and Social Death*, 7. Respected historians differ on their

opinion of this concept. David Brion Davis views it in a positive light, noting Patterson's logical conclusion. Michael Craton questions the validity of Patterson's concept of "natal alienation," suggesting that the "vigorous and effective family life" of slaves would not have been possible had they truly been "natally alienated." David Brion Davis, "Of Human Bondage," review of Patterson, *Slavery and Social Death, New York Review of Books,* February 17, 1983, 20; Michael Craton, review of Patterson, *Slavery and Social Death, Journal of American History* 70, no. 4 (March 1984): 863.

43. Patterson, *Slavery and Social Death,* 7.

44. Comunicación dirigida por el Consul de España en la isla de Jamaica al Capitan General de Cuba, fecha Kingston 2 junio 1845, adjuntándole un periódico donde se publica un artículo en el cual se trata de elevar un monumento en dicha Isla al poeta Gabriel de la Concepción Valdés (a) Plácido (Communication directed by the Spanish Consul in Jamaica to the Captain General of Cuba, dated Kingston June 2, 1845, attached a newspaper article on the elevation of a monument in Jamaica to the poet Gabriel de la Concepción Valdés, a.k.a. Plácido), *Boletin del Archivo Nacional de Cuba* 18: 83.

45. Leopoldo O'Donnell was notorious among abolitionists for the level of violence with which he oversaw Cuban slave society. A descendant of the Irish O'Donnell family from Tyrconnel, of the branch that ended up in Spain and South America, he served as governor of Cuba in 1844–1848 after fighting successfully in many campaigns for the Spanish crown. See "Leopoldo O'Donnell," *Columbia Encyclopedia,* 6th ed., <http://bartleby.com/65od/OdonnlL.html>; "O'Donnell, Leopoldo, Duke (duke) De Teutan, *Encyclopedia Britannica* <http://britannica.com/eb/article? eu=58192>; "The Clan O'Donnell," <http://irishclans.com/cgi-bin/iclans.cgi/clandisplay/ site/goti/iclans?alias-e92341059> (May 15, 2004).

46. Soul, as he notes in his letter, got his (mis)information from a well-known English abolitionist who was very active in Cuba, R. R. Madden. He misreads Madden's discussion of Juan Francisco Manzano, a slave poet who is discussed in the final chapter here, as a discussion of Plácido. Ironically, he also misunderstands in whose honor Madden is suggesting a monument be erected. Madden is speaking of Manzano.

47. See also, for example, William G. Allen's essayistic ode "Placido," in *Autographs for Freedom,* ed. Julia Griffiths (Boston: John P. Jewett, 1853), 256–63.

48. William Hurlbert, "The Poetry of Spanish America," *North American Review* 68 (January 1849).

49. Hurlbert, "Poetry of Spanish America," 153, 151. There is certainly also a literary elitism implicit in Hurlbert's treatment of Plácido's poetry. He decides not to display too much of Plácido's "untutored enthusiasm."

50. Hurlbert, "Poetry of Spanish America," 146, 148.

51. Comunicación, 83.

Chapter 2. The View from Next Door: Plácido Through the Eyes of U.S. Black Abolitionists

1. A significantly more detailed discussion of this discourse appears in Chapter 3.

2. William Wells Brown, *The Black Man, His Antecedents, His Genius, and His Achievements,* (1863; electronic edition, University of North Carolina at Chapel Hill Libraries, 1999), *Documenting the American South,* 6. www.docsouth.unc.edu/brownww/menu.html.

3. For a more detailed discussion of Ethiopianism in the nineteenth and twentieth centuries, particularly as it shows up in Du Bois's "poetics of Ethiopianism," see Wilson Jeremiah Moses, *The Golden Age of Black Nationalism, 1850–1925* (New York: Oxford University Press, 1978), 156–69.

4. Brown goes on to delineate how the Anglo-Saxons came to be out of a "rude and barbarous people" who were ultimately amalgamated with the Romans, Saxons, and Normans: "Ancestry is something which the White American should not speak of, unless with his lips to the dust."

5. Edward Wilmot Blyden, *Christianity, Islam, and the Negro Race* (1887; Edinburgh: Edinburgh University Press, 1967), 124.

6. *Comunicación,* 81.

7. Martin Robison Delany, *Official Report of the Niger Valley Exploring Party* (New York: T. Hamilton, 1861), in *Search for a Place: Black Separatism and Africa* (Ann Arbor: University of Michigan Press, 1969).

8. Martin Robison Delany, *Blake; or, The Huts of America,* ed. Floyd Miller (Boston: Beacon Press, 1970). This is the most complexly nuanced of the texts discovered to date.

9. Eric Sundquist, *To Wake the Nations: Race in the Making of American Literature* (Cambridge, Mass.: Belknap Press of Harvard University Press, 1993), 209.

10. Quoted in Louis Pérez, *Cuba and the United States: Ties of Singular Intimacy,* 2nd ed. (Athens: University of Georgia Press, 1997), 36–37 (hereafter *Singular*), from William Shaler to James Monroe, December 6, 1819, Despatches from U.S. Consuls in Havana, 1783–1906, General Records of the Department of State, Record Group 59, National Archives, Washington, D.C.

11. Quoted in Pérez, *Singular,* 39, from Thomas Jefferson to James Monroe, October 24, 1823, U.S. Congress, Senate, Senate Document No. 26, 57th Cong., 1st Sess., Ser. 4220, pp. 3–4.

12. Quoted in Pérez, *Singular,* 42, from Martin Van Buren to Cornelius P. Van Ness, October 2, 1829, House Document No. 121, p. 26.

13. Pérez, *Singular,* 48.

14. For more on Delany's vison, see Maurice Wallace, "'Are We Men?': Prince Hall, Martin Delany, and the Masculine Ideal in Black Freemasonry, 1775–1865," in *National Imaginaries, American Identities: The Cultural Work of American Iconography,* ed. Larry J. Reynolds and Gordon Hutner (Princeton, N.J.: Princeton University Press, 2000), 182–210, and more recently Maurice Wallace, *Constructing the Black Masculine: Identity and Ideality in Black Men's Literature and Culture* (Durham, N.C.: Duke University Press, 2002).

15. Delany, *The Origin of Races and Color* (1879; Baltimore: Black Classic Press, 1991).

16. Paul Gilroy, *The Black Atlantic: Modernity and Double Consciousness* (Cambridge, Mass.: Harvard University Press, 1993), 27.

17. Robert S. Levine, *Martin Delany, Frederick Douglass, and the Politics of Representative Identity* (Chapel Hill: University of North Carolina Press, 1997), 192.

18. That he makes this point here is fascinating because it seems to contradict the staunchly racialist arguments in some of his earlier writing. This novel is a significant departure from his earlier writing because he attempts to empathize with and speak from the perspective of non-U.S. Blacks. Through the novel he seems to become more accepting of disparate ways of being Black and of connecting to the global Black community. His research for the novel seems to have led him on the path to understanding that there are differences between the ways people of African descent define themselves, imagine bases for political action, and relate to Africa. Cf. Delany, *Origin of Races and Color*.

19. Victor Ullman, *Martin R. Delany: The Beginnings of Black Nationalism* (Boston: Beacon Press, 1971), 202.

20. James Theodore Holly, *Facts About the Church's Mission in Haiti: A Concise Statement by Bishop Holly* (New York: Thomas Whittaker, 1897).

21. Frederick Douglass, "Appendix," *Narrative of the Life of Frederick Douglass* (New York: Dover, 1995).

22. Blyden, *Christianity*, 10.

23. His positioning of Plácido in terms of religion was in all likelihood also at least partly based on reading Plácido's most widely translated and circulated poem, "Plegaria a Dios" (Prayer to God), a poem he is said to have written while awaiting execution. The poem shows his high level of faith and religious devotion, especially at this tragic juncture. Since Delany was clearly able to find enough information on the actual Plácido to describe him in detail and write poems that are so reminiscent of Plácido's, it is almost certain that he would have read the "Plegaria." The poem was translated by several North Americans, and appeared in books, newspapers, and magazines including the *North American Review* (Hurlbert).

24. For a more detailed discussion of the verbal and artistic representations of Plácido, see Frederick S. Stimson, *Cuba's Romantic Poet: The Story of Plácido* (Chapel Hill: University of North Carolina Press, 1964), 32–34.

25. Levine, *Martin Delany*, 191, 205.

26. Floyd Miller, "Introduction" to Delany, *Blake*, n. 28.

27. Sundquist, *To Wake the Nations*, 203–4.

28. He speaks standard English, whereas they speak (Delany's version of) African American vernacular. Levine's reading of *Blake* as reflective of Delany's vision of the perfect Black hero as intellectually and culturally above the masses, and more generally his elitism, is instructive for reading this difference. Levine, *Martin Delany*, 193.

29. Ada Ferrer, *Insurgent Cuba: Race, Nation, and Revolution 1868–1898* (Chapel Hill: University of North Carolina Press, 1999).

30. Dana D. Nelson, *National Manhood: Capitalist Citizenship and the Imagined Fraternity of White Men* (Durham, N.C.: Duke University Press, 1998), 179.

31. Nelson, *National Manhood*, 11, 17.

32. Dorothy Sterling, *The Making of an Afro-American: Martin Robison Delany, 1812–1885* (New York: DaCapo Press, 1971); Ullman, *Delany*; Floyd J. Miller, *The*

Search for a Black Nationality: Black Emigration and Colonization, 1787–1863 (Urbana: University of Illinois Press, 1975).

33. Gilroy, *Black Atlantic*, 27.

34. The power of the snake is also exemplified by the phrase "the snake will eat what is in the belly of the frog," used by the West Indian rebel slave Shango in Haile Gerima's film about enslavement, *Sankofa*. Significantly, the slave was played by well-known Jamaican poet-wordsmith Mutabaruka. Haile Gerima, producer, director, writer, *Sankofa*, Negod-Gwad Productions, Ghana National Commission on Culture, Diproci of Burkina Faso, NDR/WDR Television (Washington, D.C. : Mypheduh Films, 1995).

35. *Sentencia pronunciada por a Seccion de la Comision militar establecida en la ciudad de Matanzas para conocer de la causa de conspiracion de la gente de color.* Asuntos Políticos. Legajo 42, No. 15.

Chapter 3. On Being Black and Cuban: Race, Nation, and Romanticism in the Poetry of Plácido

1. A monument to Plácido currently stands proudly in a street corner park in Havana. See also Cintio Vitier, "Dos poetas cubanos: Plácido y Manzano," *Bohemia* 65, 50 (December 1973): 18–21.

2. Jeffrey Belnap and Raúl Fernández, "Introduction: The Architectonics of Jose Martí's 'Our Americanism'," in *José Martí's "Our America": From National to Hemispheric Cultural Studies*, ed. Jeffrey Belnap and Raúl Fernández (Durham, N.C.: Duke University Press, 1998), 3.

3. José Martí, *Our America*, trans. Philip S. Foner (New York: Monthly Review Press, 1977), 313.

4. Three major wars led to Cuban independence from Spain. The first, generally referred to as the Ten Years' War (1868–78), began when white Creole planter Carlos Manuel Céspedes led an uprising of white Creoles and slaves and ended with the signing of the Pact of Zanjon, a treaty that resulted in neither independence nor abolition. Leaders of color, Antonio Maceo in particular, were dissatisfied with the pact because it did not produce changes in either area. The result was the second war of independence, commonly known as the Guerra Chiquita (the Little War) because it lasted a year (1879–80). This was brought to an end by a crime of silence on the part of the Spanish authorities. They had Maceo cornered, and forced him to surrender without knowing that his colleague in arms Calixto García had arrived on the island with reinforcements. For this specific fact, see Philip Howard, *Changing History: Afro-Cuban Cabildos and Societies of Color in the Nineteenth Century* (Baton Rouge: Louisiana State University Press, 1998), 146. The third and final battle lasted from 1895 to 1898, the beginning of the Spanish-American war.

5. Ada Ferrer, *Insurgent Cuba: Race, Nation, and Revolution, 1868–1898* (Chapel Hill: University of North Carolina Press, 1999), 15. Throughout, I employ the term "Creole" to refer to individuals born in the Americas. This usage recalls nineteenth-century usage in Cuba and the Anglophone Americas, evidenced, for instance, in Bostonian J. G. F. Wurdemann's use of the term in his *Notes on Cuba* (Boston: James

Munroe, 1844), e.g., 69, as well as Edward Kamau Brathwaite's use of the term to index the process by which wholly new cultures and identities were developed in the Americas. Edward Kamau Brathwaite, *The Development of Creole Society in Jamaica* (Oxford: Clarendon Press, 1971).

6. Martí, *Our America*, 321.

7. Fernando Martínez Heredia, "Nationalism, Races, and Classes in the Revolution of 1895 and the First Cuban Republic," paper presented at the conference on Open Secrets: Race, Law, and the Nation in the Cuban Republic 1902–1925, University of Michigan, Ann Arbor, November 15, 2001, 10.

8. The term racism here is meant to index both discourses and actions based on the presumption of the inherent inferiority and barbarism of people of African descent and the inherent superiority and civilized nature of people of European descent.

9. Ferrer, *Insurgent Cuba*, 23.

10. Howard, *Changing History*, 5, 38.

11. Ferrer, *Insurgent Cuba*, 23; Howard, *Changing History*, 117.

12. This agreement between the Creoles and Spanish authorities is significant, given that they agreed on virtually nothing else. Much as earlier in the British West Indies, tensions between the Cuban Creoles and the Spanish government ran high. As in the United States, the unfair taxes and tariffs imposed by the Spanish government angered the Creoles, as did what they perceived as government misunderstanding of the particularities of the Cuban/Caribbean context. Agreement between Creole *independentistas* and the Spanish government was rare indeed. Cuba had been a Spanish colony since Spain took control of the island of Cuba in 1511. Although initially just a way station on the way to more important ports (e.g., Cartagena), Cuba became a more productive colony as it took up the slack in the sugar market created by the decimation of Haiti's slave/sugar economy brought about by the Haitian revolution. As Cuba's economy grew, Spain exacted more taxes and tariffs. Needless to say, anti-Spanish sentiments among White Creoles also grew. For further information, see Marta Bizcarrondo, *Cuba-España: el dilema autonomista, 1878–1898* (Madrid: Editorial Colibri, 2001); Louis A. Pérez, *Cuba Between Empires, 1878–1902* (Pittsburgh: University of Pittsburgh Press, 1983) and Robert L. Paquette, *Sugar Is Made with Blood: The Conspiracy of La Escalera and the Conflict Between Empires over Slavery in Cuba* (Middletown, Conn.: Wesleyan University Press, 1988).

13. These back and forth movements resulted in the delayed abolition of slavery in Cuba. Slavery did not officially end in Cuba until 1886, although abolition laws had been put on the books in 1870 and 1880. Several scholars argue further that unofficial slavery continued after 1886 by way of the free labor system put in place afterward. See Eduardo Torres Cuevas, "Partido autonomista—la traicion permanente," *Bohemia* (February 14, 1975), cited in Howard, *Changing History*, 128.

14. Ferrer, *Insurgent Cuba*, 136–37.

15. From very early on, there were tensions between Spanish government officials and settlers and residents over who would control the island (as there were in the English colonies). Although at first the ruling *cabildos*, as they were termed, were elected by the settlers, the crown made a point of intervening to ensure that its candidates were elected and that its control remained as complete as possible. This tension continued throughout the period of Spanish colonialism and ultimately

resulted in the wars of Cuban independence in the late nineteenth century. Herbert S. Klein, *Slavery in the Americas* (Chicago: University of Chicago Press, 1967), 14–15. U.S. observer J. G. F. Wurdemann speaks to the persistence of this tension in the nineteenth century, noting that "the people are taxed beyond any other known community . . . he who has of late mingled among them, will have heard many a bitter complaint against the exactions of the mother country." Wurdemann, *Notes on Cuba,* 251.

16. Cirilo Villaverde, *Cecilia Valdés, o, La loma del ángel: novela de costumbres cubanas* (Havana: Editorial Excelsior, 1879); William Luis, "Cecilia Valdés: el nacimiento de una novela antiesclavista," *Cuadernos Hispanoamericanos: Revista Mensual de Cultura Hispánica* (January–February 1998): 187–93; William Luis, "Cuban Counterpoint, Coffee and Sugar: The Emergency of a National Culture in Fernando Ortiz's *Cuban Counterpoint: Tobacco and Sugar* and Cirilo Villaverde's *Cecilia Valdés." Publication of the Afro-Latin/American Research Association* (*PALARA*) 2 (Fall 1998): 5–16.

17. The actual words are "La pena de muerte fusilado por la espalda: A Gabriel de la Concepción Valdés alias Plácido, acusado por treinta y dos individuos como Presidente de la junta principal, reclutador, instigador y uno de los primeros ajentes para la conspiración, electo, primer director de ella. *Sentencia pronunciada por la comision military establecida el la ciudad de Matanzas para conocer de la causa la conspiración de la gente de color,* Cuban National Archive, Legajo 42, No. 15.

18. Frederick Stimson, *Cuba's Romantic Poet: The Story of Plácido* (Chapel Hill: University of North Carolina Press, 1964). Robert Paquette has produced the most thorough examination of the conspiracy to date. Using the archived documents in the Escoto collection among other documents, he argues quite convincingly that the conspiracy existed as several conspiracies, "each overlapping, if only in some cases at the margin, each dilating and contracting at particular times between 1841 and 1844"(Paquette, "Sugar Is Made with Blood, 263). As I do here, Paquette notes that, regardless of the details of the conspiracy, it is clear that it both reflected and produced a major change in the ideologies of both those who were beginning to consider themselves citizens of a nascent Cuban nation and those, officials in particular, who were agents of the Spanish crown.

19. See, for example, John M. Kirk, *José Martí: Mentor of the Cuban Nation* (Tampa: University Presses of Florida, 1983).

20. Contemporary scholarship on twentieth-century writers also reflects this presumed congruence. In the preface to *Black Writers and the Hispanic Canon,* pioneering Afro-Hispanicist Richard Jackson states that "race (Blackness) in Latin America should be looked at from a Black North American perspective because Black Hispanic writers do it themselves in their literature." He does later point out that "not all Black people have the same perspective," but does not question the term "Black" because certain writers do use it. Richard Jackson, *Black Writers and the Hispanic Canon* (New York: Twayne, 1997), xiii. Cuban scholar Pedro Pérez Sarduy embraces the term Afro-Cuban. In contemporary Cuba, people of color with differing appearances are still clearly distinguished from each other by the terms *mulato* (mulatto) or *negro* (Black). See Pedro Pérez Sarduy's website, www.afrocubaweb.com. We cannot assume that Jackson, Sarduy, and other Cubans of color are defining

Black in the same way. The differences must be noted and incorporated into the discourse.

21. See, for example, the introduction to William Luis, ed., *Voices from Under: Black Narrative in Latin America and the Caribbean* (Westport, Conn.: Greenwood Press, 1984).

22. Miguel Barnet, *Biography of a Runaway Slave*, trans. W. Nick Hill (1968; Willimantic, CT: Curbstone Press, 1994), 37. Although there has been significant debate over the production of this text, including questions about whether Barnet fictionalized part of the narrative, the distinctions made by Montejo have not been questioned. For insight into the debate, see Nina Gerassi-Navarro, "Biografía de un Cimarron: historia de verdades ausentes," *Ciberletras*, August 1, 1999; William Luis, "The Politics of Memory and Miguel Barnet's *The Biography of a Runaway Slave*," *MLN* 104, 2 (March 1989): 475–91, and Elzbieta Sklodowska, "Testimonio mediatizado: ventriloquia o heteroglosia? (Barnet/Montejo; Burgos/Menchu)," *Revista de Critica Literaria Latinoamericana* 38 (1993): 81–90.

23. Howard, *Changing History*, 21–25.

24. *Sentencia*, 1.

25. Wurdemann, *Notes on Cuba*, 250. Historian Herbert S. Klein notes the "tremendous size and importance of the free colored population" of Cuba, describing them as a community fully integrated into the Cuban society and economy. Klein, *Slavery in the Americas*, 194.

26. According to Wurdemann, the number of Whites totaled 418, 291 whereas slaves and free colored totaled 589,333. The Africanness in Cuban culture has been documented and redocumented many times over by scholars such as Fernando Ortiz and Lydia Cabrera and by later writers such as Nicolás Guillén and Nancy Morejón. See, for example, Fernando Ortiz, *Los negros esclavos* (Havana: Editorial de Ciencias Sociales, 1996) and *Poesia y canto de los negros afrocubanos* (Havana: Pubicigraf, 1994); Lydia Cabrera, *El monte: igbo, finda, ewe orisha, vititi nfinda : notas sobre las religiones, la magia, las supersticiones y el folklore de los negros criollos y el pueblo de Cuba* (1983; Miami: Ediciones Universal, 2000); Nicolás Guillén, *Songoro cosongo: poemas mulatos* (1931; Havana: Ediciones Unió, 1999); Nancy Morejón, *Selected Poems, 1954–2000/Mirar adentro: poemas escogidos, 1954–2000* (Detroit : Wayne State University Press, 2002).

27. Howard, *Changing History*, 156 n. 11.

28. For more detail on the political activism of Cubans of African descent during this later period, see Aline Helg, *Our Rightful Share: The Afro-Cuban Struggle for Equality, 1886–1912* (Chapel Hill: University of North Carolina Press, 1995).

29. Olivia Hevia Lanier, *El directorio central de las sociedades negras de Cuba (1886–1894)* (Havana: Editorial de Ciencias Sociales, 1996).

30. Domingo del Monte's literary circle was the source of much of the antislavery literature published in Cuba during the nineteenth century. For more on del Monte, see Jesús Saíz de la Mora, *Domingo del Monte: su influencia en la cultura y literatura cubanas* (Havana: La Propagandista, 1930); Urbano Martínez Carmenate, *Domingo del Monte y su tiempo* (Maracaibo: Dirección de Cultura de la Universidad del Zulia, 1996); William Luis, *Literary Bondage: Slavery in Cuban Narrative* (Austin: University of Texas Press, 1990); and *Diccionario de la literatura cubana* (Havana:

Instituto de Literatura y Linguistica de la Academia de Ciencias de Cuba, 1984), 629–32. The latter also includes a photograph. Richard Madden was an active abolitionist who published a study of Cuba, slavery in particular, that also included Manzano's autobiography. Richard Robert Madden, *The Island of Cuba. Its Resources, Progress, etc., in Relation Especially to the Influence of its Prosperity on the Interests of the British West India Colonies* (London: C. Gilpin, 1849). For the "sell-out" accusation, see Jackson, *Black Writers*, 24.

31. Juan Francisco Manzano, *Zafira: tragedia en cinco actos* (Havana: Consejo Nacional de Cultura, 1962).

32. Nineteenth-century biographies or biographical sketches of Plácido include a substantial and informative entry on Plácido in Francisco Calcagano's *Poetas de color* (Poets of Color)(Havana: Militar de la V. de Soler, 1878), published a year after the official abolition of slavery in Cuba, featuring several nineteenth-century poets of color. Among the collections of Plácido's work published in the nineteenth century is *Poesias completas de Plácido*, ed. Gabriel de la Concepción Valdés (Paris: Libreria Espanola de Mme C. Denne Schmitz e Hijo, 1862).

33. Biographies of Plácido from the first half of the twentieth century include Domingo Figarola-Caneda's critical biography *Plácido (poeta cubano): contribución histórico-literaria* (Havana: El Siglo, 1922), which includes many previously unpublished discussions by his contemporaries; M. García Garófalo Mesa, *Plácido, poeta y martír* (Mexico City: Ediciones Botas, 1938); and Jorge Casals, *Plácido como poeta cubano: ensayo biografico critico* (Havana: Publicaciones del Ministerio de Educacion Direccion de Cultura, 1944). The first biography of Plácido published after the 1959 revolution was Itzhak (Mulstock) Bar-Lewaw, *Plácido: vida y obra* (Mexico City: Botas Impresora Juan Pablos, 1960). Significantly, all these biographies construct Plácido as a symbol of the Cuban nation. What is different is the character of the Cuban nation the biographers imagine him to represent.

Two pathbreaking English-language biographies of Plácido were also published in the twentieth century: Ben Frederic Carruthers's brilliant dissertation, "The Life, Work and Death of Plácido" (University of Illinois, 1941) and Frederick Stimson's extremely well-researched *Cuba's Romantic Poet*. Another important study is Enildo A. García's dissertation, "Cuba en la obra de Placído: análisis y bibliografía comentada" (New York University, 1982) and later book, *Cuba: Plácido, poeta mulato de la emancipación* (New York: Senda Nueva de Ediciones, 1986). In addition to being wonderfully informative on its own, the dissertation includes several significant and useful archival documents as appendices. Among those is Plácido's written defense of himself as a poet, written in response to attacks on his skill published in a Cuban newspaper.

34. Jorge Castellanos, *Plácido, poeta social y politico* (Miami: Ediciones Universal, 1984); Vera M. Kutzinski, "Unseasonal Flowers: Nature and History in Plácido and Jean Toomer," *Yale Journal of Criticism* 3, 2 (1990): 153–79; Kutzinski, *Sugar's Secrets: Race and the Erotics of Cuban Nationalism* (Charlottesville: University of Virginia Press, 1993); García, "Cuba en la obra de Placído."

35. The appearance, modes of operation, and benificiaries of the Casa de Benificencia are described by British traveler James E. Alexander in his informative and detailed travel narrative, *Transatlantic Sketches comprising visits to the most*

interesting scenes in North and South America and the West Indies (London: Richard Bentley, 1833), 341–42.

36. Artisans formed a significant and relatively well-off portion of the population of free people of color on the island; see Howard, *Changing History*, 28.

37. Matanzas was and is the other major city in Western Cuba. Cuba is notorious for the significant cultural and demographic differences between its regions and major cities. Wurdemann's comments on his travels to several cities including Matanzas yield fascinating insight into this Cuban particularity; see Wurdemann, *Notes on Cuba*, 107–19.

38. The poem delves into the profundity of his love for Fela through the repetition of images of light, sunshine, the body, and, as is Plácido's wont, the Spanish monarchy. See *Poesías selectas de Plácido* (Havana: La Moderna Poesia/Libreria Cervantes, 1930), 245–49.

39. *El Pasatiempo* was an important weekly (primarily but not wholly) literary magazine published in Matanzas in 1833–34. Antonio Bachiller y Morales in 1971 lauded the magazine for being the "first to take up the political questions that led to the civil war." The majority of the poems were published under pseudonyms, reflecting the editors' and poets' cognizance of the hostile political climate. The editors expressed on the pages of the first issue their desire to publish a range of materials including business news, political news, poetry, and whatever else would "excite the interest of the readers." Eventually there was also a Havana edition of *El Pasatiempo*. *Diccionario de la literatura cubana*, 715–16.

40. On this point, I concur with Jorge Castellanos and Frederick Stimson. Castellanos's biography includes a well synthesized and detailed analysis of several questions surrounding Plácido's possible relationship to the Escalera. He provides his own analysis of the relevant archival documents as well as critical readings of other scholars' interpretations. Castellanos, *Plácido*, 99–141; Stimson, *Cuba's Romantic Poet*, 79.

41. There are several collections of Plácido's poetry in Spanish, ranging from his complete works to thinner volumes of selected and "most representative" poems. Two that I find particularly useful are *Los poemas mas representativos de Plácido*, ed. Frederick S. Stimson and Humberto E. Robles (Chapel Hill, N.C.: Estudios de Hispanofila, 1976) and *Poesias completas de Plácido*, ed. Valdés. I have chosen to use the versions of the poems reproduced in the greatest number of texts. I will, however, note any disparities between the versions I have chosen and others. The poems most translated into English are his prison poems, including "Plegaria a Dios," and "Despedida a mi madre" ("Farewell to my Mother"). For instance, the excerpt from the *Jamaica Guardian and Patriot* I mention also includes an English translation of "Plegaria a Dios." Stimson in *Cuba's Romantic Poet* (126–38) delves farther into the history of the translation of Plácido's poetry, even discussing arguments between Cuban intellectuals and translators over the translated texts. Francisco Calcagano and Domingo Figarola-Caneda both reference a translation done by Longfellow and published in *North American Review*. Calcagano, "Poetas cubanos," 19; Figarola-Caneda, *Plácido*, 96.

42. "Negra deidad" appears in Antonio López Prieto, *Parnaso cubano: coleccion de poesias selectas de autores cubanos, desde Zequeira á nuestros dias; precedida de una*

introduccion histórico-crítica sobre el desarrollo de la poesía en Cuba (Havana: M. de. Villa, 1881), 143; *Poesias completas*, 4; Bar-Lewaw, *Plácido: vida y obra*; Cintio Vitier, ed., *Los poetas romanticos Cubanos* (Havana: Consejo Nacional de Cultura, 1962), and in a note in Stimson and Robles, *Los poemas mas representativos*, 127. Stimson and Robles print the phrase as "Ciega deidad."

43. López Prieto, *Parnaso cubano*; Bar-Lewaw, *Plácido: vida y obra*; Vitier, *Los poetas románticos cubanos*.

44. That racial discourse included literary texts written by White Creoles, some antislavery and others not, who sought to represent the Cuban person of color in a way that furthered their political goals. Many of the texts were commissioned by Domingo del Monte, and the authors were often members of his literary circle, the best-known of the period. Included among them were Anselmo Suárez y Romero, author of *Francisco* (written in 1839, published in 1880), a novel loosely based on the autobiography of ex-slave and fellow member of the literary circle Juan Francisco Manzano, as were several other of the texts commissioned by del Monte. People of color were portrayed in these texts as tragic and docile figures who, while they did not deserve to be enslaved, needed the White Creole in order to become useful members of civil society. Female slaves in particular are represented primarily as lovers through whom slaveowners work out their own anxieties. William Luis, in *Literary Bondage*, 27–81, identifies these texts as "anti-slavery narratives" that unsettle many of the underpinnings of Cuban society at that time. While I agree that the texts do subvert key understandings of race, these texts, as I see them, also raise the question of whether true anti-slavery ideology can be understood to have coexisted with racist ideology. In terms of English versions of the actual "antislavery narratives," see Cirilo Villaverde, *Cecilia Valdés*; Del Arte e Industria Cinematográficos e Impala S.A. de Madrid, *Cecilia* (New York: Latin American Video Archives International Media Resource Exchange, nd.); Instituto Cubano del Arte e Industria Cinematográficas (Cuban Institute of Art and Film), *El otro Francisco* (New York: Center for Cuban Studies, 1990); Madden, *The Island of Cuba*.

45. Plácido's poetry positions him as an early member of the Cuban school of romantic poetry known as "siboney." Siboney poetry favored the themes popular in European Romantic poetry, including medieval legends, Moorish Spain, the "noble savage," and political freedom. In addition, though, siboney poets endeavored to highlight Cuban particularities in their work. Those particularities included the Cuban landscape (and nature in general) and indigenous Cubans. Stimson, *Cuba's Romantic Poet*, 108–18. Significantly, though, Plácido is markedly different from the other *siboneistas* in that he addresses and decries racial oppression, albeit in a subtle fashion. Others, such as Gertrudis Gómes de Avellaneda in her novel *Sab, novela original* (Madrid : Imprenta Calle del Banco Num. 26, 1841), had texts in which they represented people of color, but for the most part those representations echoed those of the "antislavery narratives." For an analysis of "the hidden racism in *Sab*," see Charlotte Elaine Saulnier Le Moyne, "El racismo escondido de Sab: una perspectiva postcolonial" (M.A. thesis, University of Virginia, 1997).

46. Casals, *Plácido como poeta cubano*, 59.

47. Claudette M. Williams, *Charcoal and Cinnamon: The Politics of Color in Spanish Caribbean Literature* (Gainesville: University Press of Florida, 2000), 25.

48. Casals, *Plácido como poeta cubano*, 87.

49. Kutzinski, *Sugar's Secrets*, 89, 94. Williams's interpretation is similar to Kutzinksi's: "Plácido's subject might easily have been a white woman," Williams, *Charcoal and Cinnamon*, 24. While I agree that he does reference the stereotypical markers of White female beauty, I contend that his emphasis on the woman's brownness marks a subtle attempt to subvert that ideal. His *trigueña* is Cuban and Cubanized. If she were White, he would have no reason to mention her brownness. That mentioning, in and of itself, distinguishes her from her White sister. In addition, he uses the subjunctive, saying "as if the sun . . . burned her," not the indicative,"the sun burned her," suggesting that her color is not from the sun per se, but rather the result of heritage, blood, and genes.

50. His poem "A los ojos de mi amada" (To the Eyes of My Beloved) also illustrates this point. He ends each stanza with "Los negros ojos de me prenda amada" (The black eyes of my dear beloved lady), placing emphasis on her darkness and again, her difference from the alabaster ideal. *Poesias completas de Plácido*, 216–17.

51. Stimson notes that Plácido's birth certificate described him as "al parecer blanco" (white-looking) and references Horrego Estuch's description of Plácido as an "octavón," a person of one-eighth African blood. Stimson, *Cuba's Romantic Poet*, 46. López Prieto in *Parnaso cubano*, 130, quotes Pezuela's description of Plácido as "un mulatto de color claro" (a light-skinned man of color).

52. Casals, *Plácido como poeta cubano*, 92.

53. As my colleague Adela Pinch noted upon reading an earlier draft of this chapter, he significantly represents himself as one who does not labor, marking a class difference in addition to a color difference.

54. Luis, "Cuban Counterpoint, Coffee and Sugar," 10.

55. Luis, "Cuban Counterpoint, Coffee and Sugar,"11.

56. Coffee growers are said to have "preferred white workers or free blacks." Luis, "Cuban Counterpoint, Coffee and Sugar," 9.

57. Stimson, *Cuba's Romantic Poet*, 39. Other scholars insist on describing Fela as a *mulata*. Kutzinksi, for example, does so while also noting that she was a slave. What is clear in all sources is that she was darker and of a different (lower) class from the other loves of his life. Kutzinski herself notes that Plácido's poem "Los ojos de mi morena" (The eyes of my dark woman) was dedicated to Fela, marking her as significantly darker. Kutzinski, *Sugar's Secrets*, 88.

58. Stimson, *Cuba's Romantic Poet*, 39.

59. Casals, *Plácido como poeta cubano*, 169.

60. The material and formal links between British and Spanish Romanticism have been explicated by numerous scholars. See, for example, Diego Saglia, "British Romantic Translations of the 'Romance de Alhama' and 'Moro Alcaide,' 1775–1818," *Bulletin of Hispanic Studies* 76, 1 (January 1999): 35–55; John Curbet, "'Hallelujah to Your Dying Screams of Torture': Representations of Ritual Violence in English and Spanish Romanticism," in *European Gothic: A Spirited Exchange, 1760–1960*, ed. Avril Horner (Manchester: Manchester University Press, 2002), 161–82.

61. John R. Rosenberg, *The Black Butterfly: Concepts of Spanish Romanticism*, Romance Monographs 53 (University, Miss.: Romance Monographs, 1998), 13. On this image in Latin American romantic poetry see Catherina de Vallejo, "La imagen

femenina en la lírica de los poetas del Romanticismo hispanoamericano: inscripción de una hegemonía," *Thesarus: Boletín del Instituto Caro y Cuervo* 48, 2 (May–August 1993): 337–73.

62. José de Espronceda, *José de Espronceda: antologia poética*, ed. Rubén Benítez (Madrid: Clásicos Taurus, 1991), 130.

63. Rosenberg, *The Black Butterfly*, 13.

64. William Blake, "To the Evening Star," in *The Norton Anthology of Poetry*, ed. Alexander W. Allison et al. (New York: W.W. Norton, 1983), 259.

65. See William Blake, "The Little Black Boy," in *The Complete Poems*, ed. Alicia Ostriker (New York: Penguin, 1978), 106. In terms of the scholarship on Romantic poetry, Dwight A. McBride, *Impossible Witnesses: Truth, Abolitionism, and Slave Testimony* (New York: New York University Press, 2001), 17–18, rightly argues that "a deafening silence seems to pervade the scholarship of the period on the contributions of Blacks to and the participation of Blacks in the grand, master narratives of the literary genealogy of Romanticism." He argues that in fact the links between Romanticism and racialized discourse are quite profound. That silence has begun to be countered by scholarship like McBride's as well as that of Debbie Lee and Helen Thomas. See Debbie Lee, *Slavery and the Romantic Imagination* (Philadelphia: University of Pennsylvania Press, 2002); Helen Thomas, *Romanticism and Slave Narratives: Transatlantic Testimonies* (Cambridge: Cambridge University Press, 2000). Mary Persyn's reading of Wordsworth's representation of Haitian revolutionary leader Toussaint L'Ouverture in his sonnet "Lines Composed a Few Miles above Tintern Abbey" is especially relevant to the readings of race in Plácido's poetry proposed here. Persyn argues that Wordsworth's speaking of Toussaint in a "markedly admiring tone" while also counseling him to "submit to Napoleonic tyranny anyway—while taking comfort in the material sublime" exemplifies the fact that "such a contradiction is characteristic of Romantic-era attitudes toward race and the sublime." She notes productively that Wordsworth "organicizes slavery by making it part of a natural process. . . [an] act [that] opens slavery to the consolations of the natural sublime; nature thus ostensibly lessens the pain of slavery by promising its (eventual and naturally evolving) elimination. Mary Persyn, "The Sublime Turn Away from Empire: Wordsworth's Encounter with Colonial Slavery, 1802," *Romanticism on the Net* 26 (May 2002), www.erudit.org/revue/ron/2002/v/n26/005700ar.html, accessed October 5, 2004.

66. Lee, *Slavery and the Romantic Imagination*, 29–43.

67. Like many *siboneistas*, and Latin American Romantic poets in general, Heredia does have poems in which he celebrates, speaks from, or references the indigenous people of the Americas. See for example, José María Heredia, "En el Teocalli de Cholula," in *Los poetas romanticos Cubanos*, ed. Vitier, 12–14. As G. R. Coulthard points out, though, these references, strangely enough, have little relationship to Cuba because there were no indigenous people left in Cuba by the time these poets were writing. He identifies the roots of this "romantic Indianism" in anti-Spanish sentiment, enacted through the construction of "Indian heroes and Spanish villains." G. R. Coulthard, *Race and Colour in Caribbean Literature* (London: Oxford University Press, 1962), 7–9.

68. Heredia and Plácido first met on one of the exiled Heredia's visits to Cuba. He had heard of Plácido's poetry and made a special effort to meet him. One of Plácido's biographers, José Guiteras, describe a close and immediate bonding between the two men, likely because of their shared anticolonial political ideology, and notes that Heredia offered Plácido money to move to Mexico. Plácido, Guiteras says, refused because "he was too much a Cuban ever to leave." Quoted in Stimson, *Cuba's Romantic Poet*, 61–62.

69. José María Heredia, "A mi esposa," in *Los poetas romanticos cubanos*, ed. Vitier, 11.

70. Kutzinski, "Unseasonal Flowers," 154.

71. Jean Toomer, *Cane* (1923; New York: Penguin Books, 1999); Alain Locke, ed., *The New Negro* (1925; New York: Simon and Schuster, 1997).

72. Sibylle Fischer, however, in *Modernity Disavowed: Haiti and the Cultures of Slavery in the Age of Revolution* (Durham, N.C.: Duke University Press, 2004), sounds a cautionary note in her reading of Plácido: "Interpretive approaches that focus on the politics of form are unlikely to be helpful here or at least would have to be radically modified. We cannot assume that artistic forms—the sonnet, the romance—bear political inscriptions the same way they do when used in high-cultural contexts. . . . Instead of assimilating the classical canon under the Law . . . Plácido appeared to submit to no rule at all." Analyzing Plácido's approach to both form and identity (both racial and national) alongside those of Frederick Douglass, Martin Delany, Mary Prince and thinkers of African descent from other American sites during this period leads us to read Plácido's poetry as evidence of the simultaneous "deformation of mastery" and "mastery of form" that Houston Baker, Jr., has argued characterizes much of early African American literature and oral culture. Houston Baker, Jr., *Modernism and the Harlem Renaissance* (Chicago: University of Chicago Press, 1989).

73. It is important to recall that at the time Plácido is writing, Cuba is not only still a Spanish colony, but an economically booming jewel in the Spanish crown. The Grito de Yara that began the Ten Years' War is still decades away. A developing national sensibility is clearly present during this early period, though, due in part to increasingly tyrannical and oppressive Spanish taxation and silencing.

74. Castellanos, *Plácido*, 67.

75. This love of Cuba is also a trope in the poetry of other *siboneistas*, including Heredia. In his poem "Himno del desterrado" (Hymn of the Exile) he gushes, "Cuba, Cuba, que vida me diste / dulce tierra de luz y hermosura" (Cuba, Cuba, what a life you gave me / sweet country of light and beauty). Heredia in *Los poetas romanticos cubanos*, ed. Vitier, 40.

76. Plácido, *Poesias completas*, 6–7.

77. Plácido, *Poesias completas*, 170.

78. *Los poemas mas representativos*, 112–13.

79. In the chapter of his book *Facundo* entitled "Civilización y barbarie," Sarmiento decries the inherent barbarism of the indigenous and black peoples and celebrates the inherent civilized nature of those of European descent. He argues that the barbarous races are contaminating the civilized ones and holding Argentina

back. These races are distinguished, he points out, by their love of laziness and their industrial incompetence. The term "salvaje" (savage) appears throughout the essay as a synonym for barbarous. Domingo Faustino Sarmiento, *Facundo: edición crítica y documentada* (1845; La Plata: Universidad Nacional de La Plata, 1938), 36.

80. Pedro Deschamps Chapeaux, *El negro en la economia habanera del siglo XIX* (Havana : Unión de Escritores y Artistas de Cuba, 1971).

81. Consider, for example, the radical anticolonial and antislavery nature of this excerpt from Heredia's poem, "Himno del desterrado" (41): "¡Dulce Cuba! En tu seno se miran / en el grado mas alto y profundo / las bellezas del fisico mundo / los horrors del mundo moral / Te hizo el cielo la flor de la tierra; / mas to fuerza y destinos ignoras / y de España en el despota adoras al demonio sangriento del mal" (Sweet Cuba! People look at your face/in the highest and most profound ways / the beauties of the physical world/the horrors of the moral world / Heaven made you the flower of the earth / you ignore your strength and your destinies / and adore the despot Spain / the bloody demon of evildoing). He goes on to say that the lush greenness of the island means nothing if only because of the continuing presence of the "clamor of the insolent tyrant" and the "pathetic moan of the slave."

82. Isabel II was actually driven from the Spanish throne and into exile in 1868 by the "Glorious Revolution." Spain had been in deep financial (and consequently political) trouble for some time, in part because of the crown's battles with Cuban Creole elites over tariffs, sugar prices, and other trade issues, leading to unstable sugar prices and major shifts in the revenue Spain received from its colony. Isabel's father Ferdinand VII had been deposed by the Napoleonic invasion. The French were ousted in 1812 and Ferdinand returned; his death in 1833 prompted the civil wars known as the Carlist wars. Ultimately, Isabel II was recognized as the de facto monarch. As she was initially too young to take the throne, her mother Maria Cristina served as regent. Both women appear in Plácido's poems to the monarchs. Knight, *Slave Society in Cuba*, 100–101, 153, 159, 160.

83. *Poesías completas*, 116.

84. For more on the battles between the U.S. and Spain over Cuba between 1878 and 1902, see Pérez, *Cuba Between Empires*.

85. See, for example, William Blake, "The Sick Rose," in *The Complete Poems*, 149, 123; and Robert Burns, "A Red, Red Rose," in *The Poetical Works of Robert Burns* (Boston: Little, Brown, 1863), 182. Although neither poem speaks to national politics (Blake's apparently about a syphilitic woman and Burns's about the girlfriend of a sailor), both illustrate the usefulness of the rose for Romantic poets. Jennifer Rae Krato, "When a Rose Is Not a Rose: Espronceda's Flower Poetics," *Revista de Estudious Hispánicos* 22 (1995): 75–90, for example, analyzes the "flower poetics" of Spanish romantic poet José de Espronceda..

86. *Poesías completas*, 156

87. *Poesías completas*, 157

88. *Los poemas mas representativos*, 110.

89. Twentieth-century Cuban biographies, on the other hand, have emphasized his status as a Cuban radical, more specifically a radical who spoke up for and died for his *patria*. Notably, one of the calls to nationalism created by the 1959 Revolution is "Patria o Muerte."

90. Edward J. Mullen, "The Teaching Anthology and the Hermeneutics of Race: The Case of Plácido," *Indiana Journal of Hispanic Literatures* 6–7 (Spring-Fall 1995): 123–38.

Chapter 4. *"We Intend to Stay Here": The International Shadows in Frederick Douglass's Representations of African American Community*

1. Sundquist states that Douglass constantly fought to overcome "double consciousness." Zafar characterizes Douglass as embodying "double consciousness." Andrews describes Douglass as a classic case of double consciousness. Eric Sundquist, "Introduction" (1) and Rafia Zafar, "Franklinian Douglass" (114), in *Frederick Douglass: New Literary and Historical Essays*, ed. Eric Sundquist (Cambridge: Cambridge University Press, 1990); William L. Andrews, *To Tell a Free Story: The First Century of Afro-American Autobiography, 1760–1865* (Urbana: University of Illinois Press, 1986), 114.

2. Quoted in Chris Dixon, *African Americans and Haiti: Emigration and Black Nationalism in the Nineteenth Century* (Westport, Conn.: Greenwood Press, 2000), 79.

3. Frederick Douglass, "The Present Condition and Future Prospects of the Negro People," speech at annual meeting of the American and Foreign Anti-Slavery Society, New York, May 11, 1853, reprinted in *Frederick Douglass: Selected Speeches and Writings*, ed. Philip S. Foner (Chicago: Lawrence Hill, 1999), 251.

4. Douglass generally downplays the impact of his biracial ancestry on his own identity, focusing primarily on the structural history and implications of biracial slaves: "Men do not love those who remind them of their sins . . . and the mulatto child's face is a standing accusation against him who is master and father to the child" and "if the lineal descendants of Ham are only to be enslaved . . . slavery in this country will soon become an unscriptural institution; for thousands are ushered into the world, annually, who—like myself—owe their existence to white fathers." Frederick Douglass, *My Bondage and My Freedom* (1855; New York: Dover, 1969), 59, 60.

5. Carlos Hiraldo's study of biracial figures in North and Latin American literature provides a useful analysis of the ongoing (but often negated) dialogue between the two traditions on this issue in the nineteenth and twentieth centuries. Carlos Manuel Hiraldo, "Segregated Miscegenations: On the Treatment of Racial Hybridity in the North American and Latin American Literary Traditions" (Ph.D. dissertation, State University of New York, Stony Brook, 1999).

6. The debate over whether African Americans should remain in the U.S. or emigrate to Liberia, Haiti, or elsewhere in the Americas or Africa reached its high point in the early to mid-nineteenth century. Martin R. Delany, along with other emigration advocates, actually undertook a fact-finding journey to the "Niger Valley." Martin Robison Delany, *The Condition, Elevation, Emigration, and Destiny of the Colored People of the United States, Politically Considered* (1852; Baltimore: Black Classic Press, 1993). In addition, significant numbers of African Americans emigrated to Haiti, if only to return because of the harsh conditions and linguistic difficulty. Colonization was a program, supported in significant part by proslavery advocates, to

move free African Americans back to Africa. The organization at the masthead of the program was the American Colonization Society (for more, see Dixon, *African Americans and Haiti*). Douglass briefly supported emigration in 1861 as a result of his anger at "the failure of the Republicans to provide any guarantees of freedom or security to Blacks during the 1860 election" and the Union's inattention to the fate of slaves. He quickly returned to his previous stance, however; see Dixon, 168.

7. Frederick Douglass, *The Life and Times of Frederick Douglass* (1892; New York: Collier, 1962), 286.

8. Dixon, *African Americans and Haiti*, 79.

9. Douglass, "Present Condition," 258.

10. Frederick Douglass, "Colonization," *North Star*, January 26, 1849, reprinted in *Frederick Douglass*, 126.

11. Douglass, "Present Condition," 258.

12. Douglass, "Present Condition," 258.

13. Thanks to Cathy N. Davidson for suggesting this phrasing in her comments on an earlier draft of this project.

14. In this chapter, I employ a range of terms to index non-U.S. people of African descent, including the Black world, the Black world beyond the U.S., the Black International, the other Black Americas (when speaking of this continent), the Black Other, and the Othernational Black. I make no significant distinctions in meaning among these terms; their fundamental goal is to call attention to the reality or possibility of intraracial difference and hierarchy. It is worth noting that I would use the same terms to describe people from the U.S. if I were undertaking a similar analysis from the perspective of a non-U.S. person of African descent.

15. Douglass, *Narrative of the Life of Frederick Douglass, an American Slave* (1845; New York: Dover, 1995).

16. Houston Baker, *The Journey Back: Issues in Black Literature and Criticism* (Chicago: University of Chicago Press, 1980), 34.

17. Andrews, *To Tell a Free Story*, 120.

18. James Olney's edited collection *Studies in Autobiography* (New York: Oxford University Press, 1988) is a useful starting point for surveying this discourse because it juxtaposes analyses of autobiographies from a range of cultural and historical perspectives.

19. Baker, *Journey Back*, 35.

20. The White international appears in two primary ways in Douglass's *Narrative*—as the other half of a comparison to the situation of U.S. Blacks and as a moral standard White America fails to meet. His primary referents are the Irish and the English. For example, on his move to Baltimore he says, "for I had something of the feeling about Baltimore that is expressed in the proverb, that 'being hanged in England is preferable to dying a natural death in Ireland'" (17). Douglass's incorporation of the proverb indicates an awareness of and level of comfort with that which is beyond the boundaries of the U.S. At another point in the *Narrative*, he tells the story of his conversation with two Irishmen with whom he was working on the docks who advise him to run to the North. He does not trust their sentiments because they are White. So, on one level, he seems quite comfortable with the non-U.S., but on the other, he recognizes that what is Irish in a general international conceptual

framework is White in the United States. This distinguishing on Douglass's part suggests that he conceptualizes race as grounds for differentiation within the U.S. context, but not necessarily outside it and that he modifies his U.S. interpretive frameworks when reading "the foreign," an approach that foreshadows the inner conflict discussed in Chapter 5.

21. Despite Douglass's hesitance to focus primarily on himself in the *Narrative*, he was still criticized for committing the great sin of being too self-indulgent. Ephraim Peabody decried his use of "'extravagance and passion and rhetorical flourishes' to make his unsettlingly 'violent' arguments." Andrews, *To Tell a Free Story*, 110.

22. William L. Andrews, *Critical Essays on Frederick Douglass* (Boston: G.K. Hall, 1991), 1.

23. Douglass, *Narrative*, xvi.

24. Douglass, *My Bondage and My Freedom*, 324.

25. Douglass's 1852 address "What to a Slave Is the Fourth of July," directed at a predominantly white audience, sheds light on his definition of and desire for citizenship. The term for him indexes the right to be recognized as human, the right to live the liberty envisioned by the founding fathers, and the right to be perceived as equal by his fellow citizens. In particular, his repeated addressing of the audience as both "citizens" and "fellow citizens," particularly while reiterating the goodness of the values of "your fathers" (the leaders of the American Revolution), simultaneously foregrounds African Americans' claim to American citizenship and highlights the extent to which they are and have been divorced from that heritage. After detailing the wonders of the founding fathers' ideals, he notes "the rich inheritances of justice, liberty, prosperity and independence, bequeathed by your fathers, is shared by you, not by me. . . . Do you mean, citizens, to mock me by asking me to speak to-day?" He soon after again addresses them as fellow citizens, saying "fellow citizens; above your national tumultuous joy, I hear the mournful wail of millions!" and "fellow citizens, this murderous traffic is, to-day, in active operation in this boasted republic." Contemporary scholar Mark S. Weiner notes similarly in his analysis of "citizenship from the beginnings of slavery to the end of caste" that citizenship is most frequently understood in one of two ways—as a marker of a legal status, enjoying "the rights to vote and participate in the process of government . . . as well as the freedom to go about one's life in 'the pursuit of happiness,' and as a status that is fully achieved when "the civic majority recognize[s] that the group 'belongs,' that it shares certain basic characteristics with the community" (8). Frederick Douglass, "What to a Slave Is the Fourth of July," in *The Oxford Frederick Douglass Reader*, ed. William L. Andrews (New York: Oxford University Press, 1996), 108–30; Mark S. Weiner, *Black Trials: Citizenship from the Beginnings of Slavery to the End of Caste* (New York: Knopf, 2004).

26. Wilson Jeremiah Moses has argued that Douglass, particularly early in his public career, saw himself as constrained by the demands of racialized writing and the need to prioritize the message that would serve the best interests of the community over the story and wishes of the individual. Douglass, especially in the *Narrative*, effaced himself in the service of the larger goal of encouraging abolition. Moses puts it well when he says that Douglass's life as a literary creation was "a market

commodity." Wilson Jeremiah Moses, "Writing Freely? Frederick Douglass and the Constraints of Racialized Writing," in *Frederick Douglass: New Literary and Historical Essays*, ed. Sundquist, 71. Kenneth Warren suggests that in his later career Douglass references the real political needs of his disenfranchised group in order to silence criticisms of himself. Kenneth Warren, "Frederick Douglass's *Life and Times*: Progressive Rhetoric and the Problem of Constituency," in *Frederick Douglass: New Literary and Historical Essays*, ed. Sundquist, 256.

27. Andrews calls attention to the ways Douglass actually subverted the audience's expectations about the verisimilitude and representative nature of the text in order to make his own points. Douglass, Andrews argues, "repossesses autobiography as a self expressive, not simply a fact-assertive act," and was a "player of roles, a maker of effects, and a manipulator of readers."Andrews, *To Tell a Free Story*, 134.

28. Andrews, *To Tell a Free Story*, 135.

29. During the 1990s scholars have dedicated several works to the tug-of-war between Douglass's focus on his own story and that of the African American community. Andrews describes Douglass's narrative as a Black jeremiad, using Moses's term, situating it in relation to the American Jeremiad in which "the rebellion of a fractious individual against instituted authority is translated into a heroic act of self-reliance." Both are concerned with the triumph of the individual, the only difference being in the end the authors see for the instituted authority (U.S. society). In the Black jeremiad the U.S. is doomed, whereas in the American jeremiad the future is more hopeful because of the divinity of the nation. Andrews, *To Tell a Free Story*, 124.

30. David Van Leer, "The Anxiety of Ethnicity in Douglass's Narrative," in *Frederick Douglass: New Literary and Historical Essays*, ed. Sundquist, 128.

31. See Rafia Zafar's analysis of the parallels between the narratives. Rafia Zafar, "Franklinian Douglass," in *Frederick Douglass: New Literary and Historical Essays*, ed. Sundquist, 99–117.

32. Douglass, *My Bondage and My Freedom*, 245.

33. Douglass, *Narrative*, 37.

34. Rafia Zafar, *We Wear the Mask: African Americans Write American Literature, 1760–1870* (New York: Columbia University Press, 1997), 107.

35. Houston Baker makes a similar point when he argues "the objective world provided both philosophical and ideological justifications" for the White writer's task. The White writer could "write his autobiography into . . . universality." The Black writer, particularly the Black southern slave writer, on the other hand, was faced with the task of "transmuting an authentic, unwritten self —a self that exists outside the conventional literary discourse structures of a white reading public—into a literary representation." Baker, *Journey Back*, 29, 39.

36. Many thanks to John Wade for posing this vital question in a conversation about this chapter.

37. Robert Reid Pharr, *Conjugal Union: The Body, the House, and the Black American* (New York: Oxford University Press, 1999), 34.

38. Douglass, *Narrative*, 24.

39. Zafar, "Franklinian Douglass," 113.

40. Douglass, *Narrative*, 49. His descriptions of this awakening in his other

autobiographies, particularly in terms of the dialectic of self and community, coincide with those in the *Narrative*. See *My Bondage and My Freedom*, 374 and *Life and Times*, 156.

41. Douglass, *Narrative*, 50.

42. Warren, "Frederick Douglass' *Life and Times*," 254.

43. In *Narrative* (54), Douglass indicates that "we came to a unanimous decision among ourselves as to who their informant was," but he does not mention a name.

44. Douglass, *My Bondage and My Freedom*, 297.

45. Douglass, *My Bondage and My Freedom*, 297; *Life and Times*, 172.

46. Douglass, as one might expect, also strongly criticizes the racist White Christians who promote the segregated communion.

47. Douglass, *Life and Times*, 211.

48. Douglass, *Narrative*, 68; *My Bondage and My Freedom*, 347.

49. Douglass, *My Bondage and My Freedom*, 348.

Chapter 5. "More a Haitian Than an American": Frederick Douglass and the Black World Beyond the United States

1. See Alfred N. Hunt, *Haiti's Influence on Antebellum America: Slumbering Volcano in the Caribbean* (Baton Rouge: Louisiana State University Press, 1988).

2. Douglass, *The Life and Times of Frederick Douglass* (1892; New York: Collier, 1962), 64.

3. Douglass, *Narrative of the Life of Frederick Douglass, an American Slave* (1845; New York: Dover, 1995), 76.

4. Space does not allow me to delve further into it here, but I would argue that Douglass references the White International to advance this cause, particularly in the speeches during and just after his travel to the British Isles. See, for example, Frederick Douglass, "The Cambria Riot, My Slave Experience, and My Irish Mission," in *The Frederick Douglass Papers, Series One—Speeches, Debates, and Interviews*, ed. John W. Blassingame et al. (New Haven, Conn.: Yale University Press), vol. 1, 86.

5. "Cambria Riot," 50.

6. For further information on slavery and emancipation in the British West Indies, see Elsa Goveia, *Slave Society in the British Leeward Islands at the End of the Eighteenth Century* (New Haven, Conn.: Yale University Press, 1965) and David Barry Gaspar, *Bondmen and Rebels* (Baltimore: Johns Hopkins University Press, 1985).

7. Wendell Phillips, Preface to Douglass, *Narrative*, xv.

8. Douglass, *Life and Times*, 494.

9. William Andrews, *To Tell a Free Story*, 105–6.

10. Douglass, *My Bondage and My Freedom*, ed. Philip S. Foner (1855; New York: Dover, 1969), 176.

11. An introductory analysis of the place of Africa in the writings of Douglass and his contemporaries can be found in Norman Dean Haskett, "Afro-American Images of Africa: Four Antebellum Black Authors," *Ufahamu: Journal of the African Activist Association* 3, 1 (1972): 29–40.

12. Sterling Stuckey's essay, "Iron Tenacity: Frederick Douglass's Seizure of the Dialectic," in *Frederick Douglass: New Literary and Historical Essays*, ed. Eric Sundquist (Cambridge: Cambridge University Press, 1990), 23–46, presents a useful analysis of Frederick Douglass's relationship to Africa in general, and to Africanisms in slave culture, in particular. He avows the value of Frederick Douglass's unconscious representation of Africanisms in slave culture, but hints at a preference for a more conscious and political representation.

13. In *My Bondage and My Freedom* (176–77), he argues that, because of this uprooting, African Americans have an ambivalent attitude toward emigration, colonization, or any other mass migration or movement.

14. Melvin Dixon, for example, discusses the ways African Americans used "the Bible as a source of myth and history" and came "to identify with the children of Israel." Melvin Dixon, *Ride Out the Wilderness: Geography and Identity in Afro-American Literature* (Urbana: University of Illinois Press, 1987), 15.

15. Douglass, *My Bondage and My Freedom*, 405.

16. Waldo E. Martin, Jr., *The Mind of Frederick Douglass* (Chapel Hill: University of North Carolina Press, 1984), 203. Martin reconstructs Douglass's relationship to Africa using a range of primary source documents. Although his discussion does not focus on the autobiographies, it provides further proof of my argument about Douglass's ambivalence toward Africa and by extension his unsettledness about the relevance of Africa to African American identity.

17. Martin, *Mind of Frederick Douglas*, 205.

18. Douglass, *My Bondage and My Freedom*, 76.

19. Douglass, *Life and Times*, 504–5.

20. He only claims it for himself here, however. For the tension between individual and community in Douglass writings, see below.

21. Haskett, "Afro-American Images of Africa."

22. Douglass, *Life and Times*, 562.

23. Russ Castronovo, "'As to Nation, I Belong to None: Ambivalence, Diaspora, and Frederick Douglass," *American Transcendental Quarterly* n.s. 9, 3 (September 1995): 250.

24. For a more detailed discussion of the U.S. pursuit of the Môle, see Rayford Logan, *The Diplomatic Relations of the United States with Haiti, 1776–1791* (Chapel Hill: University of North Carolina Press, 1941), 315–96 as well as Myra Himelhoch, "Frederick Douglass and Haiti's Môle St. Nicholas," *Journal of Negro History* 56, 3 (July 1971): 161–80.

25. Merline Pitre's article on this topic, "Frederick Douglass and American Diplomacy in the Caribbean," *Journal of Black Studies* 13, 4 (June 1983): 457–75, provides several fascinating tidbits of information about the relationship between Douglass and Senator Charles Sumner, and the tension in that relationship caused by their opposing views on annexation.

26. William Andrews, "Dialogue in Antebellum Afro-American Autobiography," in *Studies in Autobiography*, ed. James Olney (New York: Oxford University Press, 1988), 91. Although the bulk of Andrews's essay addresses slave narratives, he does suggest that his theory is also applicable to nineteenth-century Black autobiography more generally.

27. James McCune Smith, "Introduction," in Douglass, *My Bondage and My Freedom*, xxv–vi.

28. Martin R. Delany, *Official Report of the Niger Valley Exploring Party* (New York: T. Hamilton, 1861) and *Condition, Elevation, Emigration and Destiny of the Colored People of the United States Politically Considered* (1852; Baltimore: Black Classic Press, 1993) both illustrate this ideology.

29. David Walker, *Appeal to the Coloured Citizens of the World, in Four Articles* (1829; University Park: Pennsylvania State University Press, 2000), 22.

30. Thanks to Cathy N. Davidson for suggesting this phrasing in her comments on an earlier draft of this project.

31. Edouard Glissant, *Poetics of Relation*, trans. Betsy Wing (Ann Arbor: University of Michigan Press, 1997), 17.

32. Douglass, "Haytian Emigration," *Douglass's Monthly*, March 1861, reprinted in *The Life and Writings of Frederick Douglass*, ed. Philip S. Foner, vol. 5, 472.

33. Douglass, "Haiti and the Haitian People: An Address Delivered in Chicago, Illinois on 2 January 1893," in *Frederick Douglass Papers*, vol. 5, 528.

34. The scope of the present study does not allow for a comparative analysis of Douglass's private correspondence and his public writings and later reflections on this topic would likely be exciting and fruitful. Even a comparison of his official letters and speeches and the public/published ones could be interesting. The first speech he gave to the Haitian president upon his appointment, "The Highest Honor Conferred on Me," could usefully be compared, for example, to his later reflections on the moment in *Life and Times*. Frederick Douglass, "The Highest Honor Conferred on Me: An Address Delivered in Port-au-Prince, Haiti on 14 November 1889," in *The Frederick Douglass Papers*, vol. 5, 426–29.

35. *The Heroic Slave* has been analyzed in terms of both the way Douglass' links the rebels to the American revolutionaries and the profoundly gendered notion of Black hero that he puts forward. The analyses I have found particularly useful are those by Maggie Montesinos Sale. See Maggie Montesinos Sale, "To Make the Past Useful: Frederick Douglass's Politics of Solidarity," *Arizona Quarterly* 52, 3 (Autumn 1995): 25–60 and *The Slumbering Volcano: American Slave Ship Revolts and the Production of Rebellious Masculinity* (Durham, N.C.: Duke University Press, 1997).

36. Frederick Douglass, "Santo Domingo: An Address Delivered in St. Louis, Missouri on 13 January 1873," in *The Frederick Douglass Papers*, vol. 4, 346.

37. Douglass, *Narrative*, 38.

Chapter 6. A Slave's Cosmopolitanism: Mary Prince, a West Indian Slave, and the Geography of Identity

1. Moira Ferguson, "Introduction to the Revised Edition," *The History of Mary Prince, A West Indian Slave, Related by Herself*, rev. ed. (Ann Arbor: University of Michigan Press, 1997), 10.

2. Faith Smith, *Creole Recitations: John Jacob Thomas and Colonial Formation in the Late Nineteenth-Century Caribbean* (Charlottesville: University of Virginia Press, 2002) is the first full-length study of Thomas's life, work, and intellectual context. It

is an extremely well documented text that provides much guidance for the scholar interested in his life and/or the intellectual contexts and circuits of the late nineteenth-century Caribbean.

3. Cheryl Fish, "Voices of Restless (Dis)continuity: The Significance of Travel for Free Black Women in the Antebellum Americas," *Women's Studies* 26, 5 (1997): 475–95. Fish's work is particularly useful because of her focus on the resistance inherent in Seacole and Prince's travel writings.

4. Paquet reads Prince's narrative as evincing an "embryonic nationalism" and Seacole's work as reflecting "an enthusiastic acceptance of colonialism." Sandra Pouchet Paquet, "The Enigma of Arrival: The Wonderful Adventures of Mrs. Seacole in Many Lands," *African American Review* 26, 4 (1992): 651. Although the insinuated value judgment, positioning Prince as a rootsy Caribbean person and Seacole as an Anglophile, is troubling, Paquet's work is undoubtedly foundational to the type of inquiry I pursue here. See also Paquet, "The Heartbeat of a West Indian Slave: The History of Mary Prince," *African American Review* 26, 1 (1992): 131–46. Both articles are reproduced in her collection *Caribbean Autobiography: Cultural Identity and Self-Representation* (Madison: University of Wisconsin Press, 2002).

5. Amy Robinson, "Authority and the Public Display of Identity: Wonderful Adventures of Mrs. Seacole in Many Lands," *Feminist Studies* 20, 3 (Fall 1994): 537–57.

6. Their argument about the dearth of critical attention to Caribbean women's literary voices is well substantiated (although, ironically, they implicitly marginalize the early period by not including any essays on nineteenth-century Caribbean women's writing). Carole Boyce Davies and Elaine Savory Fido, eds., *Out of the Kumbla: Caribbean Women and Literature* (Trenton, N.J.: Africa World Press, 1990), 1.

7. Here I distinguish between travel—a term that implies leisure, privilege, and pleasure—and movement—a word that connotes simply going from one location to another, without the baggage that accompanies travel. My distinction recalls that made by Caren Kaplan between travel, exile, and displacement. See Caren Kaplan, *Questions of Travel: Postmodern Discourses of Displacement* (Durham, N.C.: Duke University Press, 1996).

8. Mary Prince, "The History of Mary Prince, a West Indian Slave," in *Six Women's Slave Narratives* (New York: Oxford University Press, 1988), 1. All quotations from the narrative come from this edition.

9. Paquet, *Caribbean Autobiography*, 28.

10. On the battles with Maroons and rebellious slaves in the region, see John Gabriel Stedman, *Narrative of a Five Years Expedition Against the Revolted Negroes of Surinam*, ed. Richard Price and Sally Price (1790; Baltimore: Johns Hopkins University Press, 1988). On slave uprisings in Antigua, see David Barry Gaspar, *Bondmen and Rebels: A Study of Master-Slave Relations in Antigua, with Implications for Colonial British America* (Baltimore: Johns Hopkins University Press, 1985). For a tremendously detailed discussion of the broader picture in the northeastern British West Indies, see Elsa Goveia, *Slave Society in the British Leeward Islands at the End of the Eighteenth Century* (New Haven, Conn.: Yale University Press, 1965).

11. Kathleen Wilson, *The Island Race: Englishness, Empire and Gender in the Eighteenth Century* (New York: Routledge, 2003), 8.

12. *Journal of the Jamaica Assembly*, 548, Thursday, 18 December 1740.

13. *Journal of the Jamaica Assembly*, 125, Friday, 5 February 1714 (my emphasis).

14. *Journal of the Jamaica Assembly*, 347, Saturday, 5 November, 1720. Certainly this developing sense of separateness and/or neglect was not unique to West Indian Whites, as the American Revolution would later illustrate.

15. Goveia, *Slave Society*, 44–49.

16. The Reverend Richard Bickell, *The West Indies as They Are; or A Real Picture of Slavery* (London: Ibotson and Palmer Printers for J. Hatchard and Son, 1825), 5.

17. Belinda Edmondson, *Making Men: Gender, Literary Authority, and Women's Writing in Caribbean Narrative* (Durham, N.C.: Duke University Press, 1999), 29.

18. Edmondson, *Making Men*, 83. See also Simon Gikandi's discussion of Mary Seacole in *Maps of Englishness: Writing Identity in the Culture of Colonialism* (New York: Columbia University Press, 1996), 125–43.

19. For a more in-depth discussion of cosmopolitanism in seventeenth- and eighteenth-century thought, see Thomas Schlereth, *The Cosmopolitan Ideal in Enlightenment Thought: Its Form and Function in the Ideas of Franklin, Hume, and Voltaire, 1694–1790* (Notre Dame, Ind.: University of Notre Dame Press), 1977. He argues convincingly that cosmopolitanism, while crucial to Enlightenment self-concepts, was always already more symbolic and theoretical than actual and practical and delves into the place of cosmopolitanism in the thought of a wide range of figures, including Locke.

20. Edward W. Said, *Orientalism* (New York: Vintage, 1979), 7.

21. Said, *Orientalism*, 12.

22. Pheng Cheah, "Given Culture: Rethinking Cosmopolitical Freedom in Transnationalism," *Boundary 2* 24, 2 (Summer 1997): 10. (accessed via proquest).

23. Cheah, "Given Culture," 10.

24. Ulf Hannerz, *Transnational Connections: Culture, People, Places* (New York: Routledge, 1996), 103.

25. For a description of the cosmopolite as a citizen of the world, see, for example, Mihai Grunfeld, "Cosmopolitismo modernista y vanguardista," *Revista Iberoamericana* 146–47 (June 1989): 33.

26. Timothy Brennan, *At Home in the World: Cosmopolitanism Now* (Cambridge, Mass.: Harvard University Press, 1997).

27. Kwame Anthony Appiah, "Cosmopolitan Patriots," *Critical Inquiry* 23, 3 (Spring 1997): 617.

28. Hannerz, *Transnational Connections*, 103.

29. Prince, *History*, 2.

30. Prince's narrative is less a bildungsroman type text of her own development as an individual, than about the pain of her community. The female gendered exceptionality of Prince's less individualistic approach inheres in her explicit invocation and construction of a community while she is telling her own story. Community is a fundamental part of her articulation of self, evidenced in her frequent references to the bonds she made with a variety of people including her first mistress—Mrs. Williams, a French Black named Hetty, her mother, her sister, as well as many others she happened upon—two slave women at her second worksite, two slave boys, a slave named old Daniel, her fellow slaves in Turks Island and Antigua,

among many others. Karla F. C. Holloway's identification in *Moorings and Metaphors* (New Brunswick, N.J.: Rutgers University Press, 1992) of the connection between community and the word as a fundamental locus of difference between Black men's and Black women's texts is a helpful interpretive tool here. She writes, "The province of the word for black women commands a perspective that does not isolate it from its community source. Black male writers' texts claim the power of creative authorship but do not seem to share the word with the reader, or among the characters, or within narrative structures of the text. Instead, the word is carefully controlled and its power is meagerly shared. Black women writers seem to concentrate on shared ways of saying, black males concentrate on individual ways of behaving" (7).

Prince shares the word with her community, according considerable narrative space to not only the stories but also the voices of her fellow slaves. The search for literacy, that is knowledge and control of the written word, drives both Frederick Douglass's and Juan Francisco Manzano's narratives. Orality, the emphasis on the spoken word (as well as intense verbal expressions of sorrow), characterizes Prince's narrative. Prince's narrative is "oracular," a quality Holloway identifies as characterizing Black women's texts (36–37). My point in this discussion of gender is that cosmopolitan consciousness seems to have a gendered dimension.

31. Mary Louise Pratt, *Imperial Eyes: Travel Writing and Transculturation* (New York: Routledge, 1992), 7.

32. Prince's maintenance of both an objective tone and her connection to the community she describes, as my former colleague Marlon Ross pointed out after reading an earlier draft of this chapter, also highlights a tension between her desire to speak for/from her community (that could be read as reflective of her link with the sentimental and/or feminine writing of the period) and the masculine tradition of the detached ethnographer. Pratt examines primarily the masculine approaches to the colonized other during the colonial period in further detail, while Moira Ferguson delves into the feminine and sentimental approaches. Moira Ferguson, *Subject to Others: British Women Writers and Colonial Slavery 1670–1834* (New York: Routledge, 1992).

33. Martin Robison Delany, *Blake; or, The Huts of America* (Boston: Beacon Press, 1970); Nancy Prince, *The West Indies, Being a Description of the Islands* (Boston: Dow and Jackson Printers, 1841)

34. Delany, *Blake*, 167.

35. Nancy Prince, *The West Indies*, 11.

36. Carla L. Peterson, *Doers of the Word: African American Speakers and Writers in the North (1830–1880)* (New Brunswick, N.J.: Rutgers University Press, 1998), 91, 97.

37. Olaudah Equiano, *The Interesting Narrative of Olaudah Equiano* (1789; Boston: Bedford Books of St. Martin's Press, 1995)

38. Olaudah Equiano, *The Interesting Narrative of Olaudah Equiano* (1789; Boston: Bedford Books of St. Martin's Press, 1995), 98.

39. Henri Lefebvre, *The Production of Space*, trans. Donald Nicholson-Smith (Cambridge: Blackwell, 1991), 43.

40. The Blaeu and Walseemuller maps are reprinted in Walter Mignolo, *The Darker Side of the Renaissance* (Ann Arbor: University of Michigan Press, 1995). The Bowen map is part of the David Rumsey Collection accessible at <http://www.davidrumsey.com> (9 March 2004).

41. Joseph Speer, *Chart of the West Indies*, 1796, Library of Congress American Memory Map Collection.<http://memory.loc.gov/ammem/gmdquery.html>

42. James Olney, " 'I Was Born': Slave Narratives, Their Status as Autobiography and as Literature," in *The Slave's Narrative*, ed. Henry Louis Gates, Jr. and Charles T. Davis (Oxford: Oxford University Press, 1985), 148–75.

43. Melvin Dixon, *Ride Out the Wilderness: Geography and Identity in Afro-American Literature* (Urbana: University of Illinois Press, 1987).

44. Jeremy Black, *Natural and Necessary Enemies: Anglo-French Relations in the Eighteenth Century* (Athens: University of Georgia Press, 1986).

45. "Bermuda," *Encyclopedia Britannica Online* (20 July 1999). The U.S. boasts a total area of 3,679,192 square miles; "United States," *Encyclopedia Britannica Online* (20 July 1999).

46. Karen Fog Olwig, *Global Culture, Island Identity: Community and Change in the Afro-Caribbean Community of Nevis* (Philadelphia: Harwood Academic Publishers, 1993).

47. Wilson, *Island Race*, 54–55. She argues provocatively that England's sense of itself, in particular its sense of Captain Cook's place as the representative Englishman, rested on the islandness of the South Sea Islands.

48. This fact further highlights the crucial impact of the work of J. J. Thomas, who vociferously defended Black West Indians' civilization, and by extension their worthiness to be seen as English. See Faith Smith, *Creole Recitations*. It also calls attention to the work of Edward Wilmot Blyden, mid- to late nineteenth-century West Indian born pan-Africanist pioneer, and the reasons he may have chosen to ground his identity in Africa rather than England or the West Indies. See Edward Wilmot Blyden, *Black Spokesman: Selected Published Writings of Edward Wilmot Blyden*, ed. Hollis Lynch (London: Cass, 1971).

49. Wilson, *Island Race*, 56.

50. Geography is inadequate because, as the case of England illustrates, islandness does not always produce only expansiveness. England's islandness led to parochialism as well.

51. For an extensive history of Bermuda during the seventeenth century, including the relationship between Bermuda and Virginia, see Wesley Frank Craven, *An Introduction to the History of Bermuda*, reprinted from *William and Mary College Quarterly* 2nd ser. 17, 2, 3, 4; 18, 1 (1937–1938). For more historical information on eighteenth-century Bermuda-U.S. relations, see Wilfred Brenton Kerr, *Bermuda and the American Revolution: 1760–1783* (Princeton, N.J.: Princeton University Press, 1936).

52. Like Moira Ferguson (and based on my own research), I read the narrative as Prince's story of herself, rather than the abolitionists' story of her. All the evidence, both within and outside the text, suggests that Prince exerted significant control over it. Ferguson notes, I believe rightly, that "despite the abolitionists' intention to portray her life as a moral fable . . . she radiates as an indomitable self-made heroine" (26). Although Prince herself may not have singlehandedly developed the title, it does index a different approach, in its centering of her as a person with a history, from James Williams's later narrative. Ferguson, "Introduction to the Revised Edition."

53. Pratt, 7.

54. Rosaura Sánchez, *Telling Identities: The California Testimonios* (Minneapolis:

University of Minnesota Press, 1995), identifies a similar twin purpose in testimonios of nineteenth-century Californios. She writes of the testimonios as "mediated
narratives," produced between the Californios' desire to reconstruct their own history and their cognizance they "cannot be as forthright and outspoken as they might
be if they were in positions of dominance" (32). Although there are certainly similarities in approach, purpose, and style between Prince's narrative and the testimonios, I would distinguish them because hers is not an "elicited narrative" (13). She
decided to tell her story and asked Thomas Pringle to transcribe it (1).

55. Free Black missionary traveler historian Nancy Prince and writer Pauline
Hopkins also employ this trope, using the relative goodness of the English to shame
U.S. Whites. See Nancy Prince, *A Narrative of the Life and Travels of Mrs. Nancy Prince*
(Boston: the author, 1853) and Pauline Hopkins, *Contending Forces: A Romance Ilustra-
tive of Negro Life North and South* (1900; Oxford: Oxford University Press, 1988), 17–31.

56. It is important here to distinguish between Prince's rooting of herself,
which I identify as integral to her conception of self, and contemporary critics' rooting of the authors I center on in this study, which I critique as contradictory to the
lives of the authors and the texts themselves. Liisa Malkki interrogates the tenuous
relationship between anthropologists' reification of soil in their readings of Hutu
refugees as nationless and the refugees' view of themselves as a "nation in exile" (66),
one that has become even more powerful through displacement. Liisa Malkki,
"National Geographic: The Rooting of Peoples and the Territorialization of National
Identity Among Scholars and Refugees," in *Culture, Power, Place: Explorations in
Critical Anthropology*, ed. Akhil Gupta and James Ferguson (Durham, N.C.: Duke
University Press, 1997), 52–74.

57. Equiano does, however, spend much of the remainder of his life trying to
find his sister, perhaps paralleling Prince in her association of home with being with
family.

58. Mary Seacole, *Wonderful Adventures of Mrs. Seacole in Many Lands* (1857;
New York: Oxford University Press, 1988).

59. Carole Boyce Davies, *Black Women, Writing and Identity* (New York: Routledge, 1994).

60. Davies, *Black Women*, 116.

61. James Clifford, "Traveling Cultures," in *Routes: Travel and Translation in
the Late Twentieth Century* (Cambridge, Mass.: Harvard University Press, 1997), 28.

62. Paule Marshall, "The Making of a Writer: From the Poets in the Kitchen,"
in *Reena and Other Stories* (New York: Feminist Press, 1983), 6.

63. That she does not mention the Haitian Revolution or Haiti specifically,
though, shows her to be bound by constraints similar to those that prevented Frederick Douglass, among others, from mentioning it. As mentioned earlier in this
chapter, the British West Indian slave economy was in its waning moments by the
time Prince's narrative was published. One of the major concerns in the debate
about how to make the transition from a slave economy to one based on wage labor
was the extent to which blacks were thought to be civilized enough to make that
transition without engaging in either violence or extreme indolence. Given her
understanding of the significance of this moment in British West Indian politics,
Prince would certainly have understood the importance of not raising the specter of

the Haitian Revolution. What she does emphasize is blacks capacity for civilization. She shows repeatedly how Black civil society and values were derailed by the demands of slavery. Her discussion of the black driver who is forced to beat his family as well as of her last master, Mr. Wood's opposition to her marriage exemplify this strategy.

Chapter 7. Disidentification as Identity: Juan Francisco Manzano and the Flight from Blackness

1. Juan Francisco Manzano, "The Life of the Negro Poet," trans. Richard Robert Madden, 1840, in *The Life and Poems of a Cuban Slave*, ed. Edward J. Mullen (Hamden, Conn.: Archon Books, 1981), 80.

2. For more on urban slaves in Havana and their relative freedom, see Pedro Deschamps Chapeaux, *El negro en la economía habanera en el siglo XIX* (Havana: Unión de Escritores y Artistas de Cuba, 1971).

3. Delmonte wanted a narrative of life in Cuban slavery to give to Richard R. Madden, an English abolitionist working in Cuba. In a June 1835 letter to Delmonte, Manzano indicates that Delmonte asked him for the autobiography in February of that year. Manzano to Domingo Delmonte, 25 June 1835, Microfilm from La Academia de la Historía de Cuba, Signatura 679, Caja 203.

4. Juan Francisco Manzano, "Copia de la carta del poeta a Rosa Alfonso de Aldama" (Colección Figarola-Caneda), Legajo 681, Caja 204, 86. He argued, interestingly, that the accusations were mounted to slander Domingo Delmonte.

5. The preface found in the archives at the Academy of History in Havana to the aforementioned letter written by Manzano to Dona Rosa Alfonso de Aldama also indexes this disappearance. The author of the preface notes that Francisco Calcagano, one of the most important collectors of information on and writings by Cuban writers of color in the nineteenth century, does not include any information on Manzano's life beyond 1839. Manzano, "Copia de la carta," 86.

6. Manzano, *Poems by a Slave in the Island of Cuba, Recently Liberated Translated from the Spanish by R. R. Madden, M.D. with the History of the Early Life of the Negro Poet, Written by Himself* (London: T. Ward, 1840). I use the Madden text as my base text because it was the first published version of the autobiography. As Richard L. Jackson correctly notes, "whatever version we read—and there are several . . . we know that Manzano's own words, especially those he misspelled were his own." There are multiple texts that have been identified by scholars as "the original," including one I obtained from the Academy of History in Havana. As far as I can tell, however, definitive proof that any of them is the original is lacking. Richard L. Jackson, *Black Writers and the Hispanic Canon* (New York: Twayne, 1997), 26.

7. Juan Francisco Manzano, *Autobiografía, cartas, y versos*, intro . José L. Franco (Havana: Municipio de la Habana, 1937).

8. Francisco Calcagano, *Poetas de color* (Havana: Militar de la V. de Soler, 1878); Antonio López Prieto, *Parnaso cubano: colección de poesías selectas de autores cubanos, desde Zequeira á nuestros dias; precedida de una introducción histórico-crítica sobre el desarrollo de la poesía en Cuba* (Havana: M de Villa, 1881).

9. Domingo Delmonte, "Plácido y Manzano," *Liceo de la Habana*, viernes 9 de setiembre (sic) de 1859, 84.

10. Francisco Calcagano, "Poetas cubanos," *Revista de Cuba* 4 (1878): 456.

11. Manzano, *Autobiografía de un esclavo* (Madrid: Ediciones Guadarrama, 1975); *Autobiography of a Slave/Autobiografía de un esclavo*, bilingual edition, modernized Spanish by Iván A Schulman, trans. Evelyn Picon Garfield (Detroit: Wayne State University Press, 1996); Manzano, *The Autobiography of a Cuban Slave* (St. Augustine, Trinidad: Lloyd King, 1990–94). José Franco indicated that his version was a reproduction of the original text written in the "puno y letra" of Manzano. Franco, Introduction to Manzano, *Autobiografía, cartas, y versos*, 28. Many scholars, however, including Sonia Labrador-Rodríguez, "La intelectualidad negro en Cuba en el siglo XIX: el caso de Manzano," *Revista Iberoamericana* 62, 174 (January–March 1996): 13–25 and Lorna Williams, *The Representation of Slavery in Cuban Fiction* (Columbia: University of Missouri Press, 1996), have noted that Franco seems to have made many changes to the text, making it also an edition of the autobiography rather than "the original." Several scholars have expressed discomfort with the way the various editions of Manzano's autobiography modify Manzano's content and language. Schulman's text is the object of by far the most criticism because, as one scholar notes, it "imposes a different meaning on Manzano's writing" (L. Williams, *Representation of Slavery*, 32). William Luis, *Literary Bondage: Slavery in Cuban Narrative* (Austin: University of Texas Press, 1990), 84, notes that "the many editions of Manzano's work are not a reproduction of the 'original' but contain enough significant changes, omissions, and distortions to be considered different texts."

12. Jackson, *Black Writers and the Hispanic Canon*, 21.

13. Luis, *Literary Bondage*, 84. See also Antonio Vera-León, "Juan Francisco Manzano: el estilo barbaro de la nación," *Hispamerica* 20, 6 (December 1991): 3–22. Vera-León spotlights the conflict between the "elocuencia 'barbara' del negro" (barbarous eloquence of the black" and the "lengua literaria criolla" (Creole literary language) in Manzano's writing.

14. Martha Cobb, "The Slave Narrative and the Black Literary Tradition," in *The Art of the Slave Narrative*, ed. John Sekora and Darwin T. Turner (Macomb, Ill.: Western Illinois University, 1982), 36–44; Luis A. Jiménez, "Nineteenth-Century Autobiography in the Afro-Americas: Frederick Douglass and Juan Francisco Manzano," *Afro-Hispanic Review* 14, 2 (Fall 1995): 47–52. See also Miriam DeCosta-Willis, "Self and Society in the Afro-Cuban Slave Narrative," *Latin American Literary Review* 16, 32 (July–December 1988): 6–15.

15. Susan Willis, "Crushed Geraniums: Juan Francisco Manzano and the Language of Slavery," in *The Slave's Narrative*, ed. Charles T. Davis and Henry Louis Gates, Jr. (New York: Oxford University Press, 1985), 199–224.

16. Disidentification has been very productively employed as a theoretical departure point by José E. Muñoz in his analysis *Disidentifications: Queers of Color and the Performance of Politics* (Minneapolis: University of Minnesota Press, 1999). He notes that his "thinking on disidentification has been strongly informed by the work of critical race theorists," calling attention to the sense and reality of disempowerment (and by extension, the need to find/construct/perform the means for

self-empowerment, particularly in the realm of identity) shared by queers and people of color (and therefore most certainly by queers of color).

17. Jerome Branche, "'Mulato entre negros' (y blancos): Writing, Race, the Antislavery Question, and Juan Francisco Manzano's Autobiografía," *Bulletin of Latin American Research* 20, 1 (January 2001): 79. Cintio Vitier, Iván Schulman, and Verena Martínez-Alier, for example, also attribute Manzano's distancing to his understanding of or affinity for White Creole Cuban racial ideology. Cintio Vitier, "Dos poetas cubanos: Plácido y Manzano," *Bohemia* 65, 50 (1973): 18–21; Schulman, Introduction to *Autobiography of a Slave*; Verena Martínez-Alier, "El honor de la mujer en Cuba en el siglo XIX," *Revista de la Biblioteca Nacional José Martí* 13 (May–August 1971): 48–49.

18. Muñoz, *Disidentifications*, 30.

19. Nella Larsen, *Passing* (1929; New Brunswick, N.J.: Rutgers University Press, 1986; James Weldon Johnson, *Autobiography of an Ex-Colored Man* (New York: Knopf, 1951); Gayle Wald, *Crossing the Line: Racial Passing in Twentieth-Century U.S. Literature and Culture* (Durham, N.C.: Duke University Press, 2000). On *Passing*, the most recent work includes Zita C. Nunes, "Phantasmatic Brazil: Nella Larsen's *Passing*, American Literary Imagination, and Racial Utopianism," in *Mixing Race, Mixing Culture: Inter-American Literary Dialogues*, ed. Monika Kaup and Deborah Rosenthal (Austin: University of Texas Press, 2002), 50–61, numerous dissertations including Teresa Zackodonick, "Beyond the Pale: Unsettling 'Race' and Womanhood in the Novels of Harper, Hopkins, Fauset, and Larsen" (McMaster University, 1999) and Sachi Nakachi, "Mixed-Race Identity Politics in Nella Larsen and Winnifred Eaton (Otonno Watanna)" (Ohio University, 2002). On Weldon's novel, see Samira Kawash, "*The Autobiography of an Ex-Coloured Man*: (Passing for) Black Passing for White," in *Passing and the Fictions of Identity*, ed. Elaine K. Ginsberg (Durham, N.C.:: Duke University Press, 1996), 59–74; John Sheehy, "The Mirror and the Veil: The Passing Novel and the Quest for American Racial Identity," *African American Review* 33, 3 (Fall 1999): 401–15.

20. Wald, *Crossing the Line*, 6.

21. Vera Kutzinski, *Sugar's Secrets: Race and the Erotics of Cuban Nationalism* (Charlottesville: University Press of Virginia, 1993); Claudette M. Williams, *Charcoal and Cinnamon: The Politics of Color in Spanish Caribbean Literature* (Gainesville: University Press of Florida, 2000).

22. Quoted in Suzanne Bost, *Mulattas and Mestizas: Representing Mixed Identities in the Americas 1850–2000* (Athens: University of Georgia Press, 2000),102.

23. C. Williams, *Charcoal and Cinnamon*, 30.

24. Richard Graham's edited collection, *The Idea of Race in Latin America* (Austin: University of Texas Press, 1990), is one of the pioneering texts in this area, featuring articles on a range of countries including, importantly, Argentina.

25. José Martí, *Our America*, ed. Philip S. Foner (New York: Monthly Review Press, 1977).

26. José Vasconcelos, *La raza cosmica* (Los Angeles: Centro de Publicaciones, Department of Chicano Studies, California State University, 1979). Importantly, though, Vasconcelos's cosmic race rather than symbolizing the nation, is an alternative to the nation.

27. Scholars have certainly explored the autobiographical dimensions of both Johnson's and Larsen's work. See, for example, Donald C. Geoellnicht, "Passing as Autobiography: James Weldon Johnson's *The Autobiography of an Ex-Colored Man*," *African American Review* 30, 1 (Spring 1996): 17–33. I contend, though, that a work that is explicitly autobiographical allows for a distinctive reading of the logic of disidentification.

28. These moments contradict William Luis's statement that "Manzano's disassociation from other black slaves has been suppressed in the English edition." *Literary Bondage*, 94. Luis undertakes a more detailed analysis of the disparities between Madden's translation and Franco's text in "La autobiografía de Juan Francisco Manzano y la traduccion de Richard Madden: un texto con dos interpretaciones sobre la vida del esclavo poeta," *Discurso: Revista de Estudios Iberoamericanos* 11, 1 (1993): 95–111.

29. In other versions of the autobiography this statement has an explicitly racial dimension. Madden's "meanest slave" in these versions is a "negro bozal" or recently arrived African slave, referring to the lowest class in the community of people of color. See Franco version, 68. In addition, the speaker specifically calls Manzano a "mulatto youth." See *Autobiography of a Slave*, 130–31.

30. The earliest version I found that includes this phrase was published in 1852 by Nicolas Azcarate. Juan Francisco Manzano, *Obras completas de Juan Francisco Manzano esclavo de la Isla de Cuba*, ed. Nicolas Azcarate, Primary Source Microfilm by Thomson and Gale, Latin American History and Culture: An Archival Record, Series 1: Yale University Collection of Latin American Manuscripts, Caribbean Collection, Part 5, Unit 1, Reel 1, p. 88. William Luis analyzes the Manzano poems contained in Azcarate's compilation in "Nicolas Azcarate's Antislavery Notebooks and the Unpublished Poems of the Slave Juan Francisco Manzano," *Revista de Estudios Hispanicos* 28 (October 1994): 331–51.

31. The phrase is also absent from the version at the Academia de la Historia in Havana. This version begins with the prefatory paragraph quoted by Franco in his version. *Manzano*, Academia de la Historia de Cuba, Colección Figarola-Caneda, Signatura 679, Caja 203.

32. Manzano by way of Franco, 34, 62.

33. "Roberto Friol, *Suite para Juan Francisco Manzano* (Havana: Editorial Arte y Literature, 1977), 40.

34. Gregg O. Courtad, "The Psychoanalytics of Oppression: The Colonizer and the Colonized in the Antislavery Works of Cuba" (Ph.D. dissertation, University of Cincinnati, 1996), 98.

35. It is worth noting that, although Manzano's narrative was first published in English, it does not appear, for example, in the *Norton Anthology of African American Literature*, although the narrative of West Indian slave Mary Prince does appear. Although one certainly cannot make assumptions about the editor's reasons, which may include simple copyright issues, the absence is worth noting.

36. Mullen provides a very detailed and useful delineation of which anthologies included Afro-Hispanic writers, which writers they included, and the implications of those inclusions. Edward J. Mullen, "The Teaching Anthology and the Hermeneutics of Race: The Case of Plácido," *Indiana Journal of Hispanic Literatures*

6–7 (Spring-Fall 1995): 124. For an even more detailed discussion see also Edward J. Mullen, "The Emergence of Afro-Hispanic Poetry: Some Notes on Canon Formation," *Hispanic Review* 56, 4 (Autumn 1988): 435–53.

37. See Jackson, *Black Writers and the Hispanic Canon* for the comparisons to Guillén and Morejón. For comparisons to other Cuban writers of the day, such as Anselmo Suárez y Romero, see Jill Ann Netchinsky, "Engendering a Cuban Literature: Nineteenth Century Antislavery Narrative" (Ph.D. dissertation, Yale University, 1986).

38. Richard L. Jackson, *Black Writers and Latin America: Cross-Cultural Affinities* (Washington, D.C.: Howard University Press, 1998), 82.

39. Antonio Olliz Boyd addresses this question, in part, by illustrating that Black awareness is a thematic presence in Latin American literature. He positions his argument in opposition to "most critics of Latin American literature" who "refuse to acknowledge non-whiteness as an esthetic concept." Included in his analysis are readings of texts by writers such as Ruben Dario who openly reject Black progenitors or present stereotypical caricatures of Blacks. Antonio Olliz Boyd, "The Concept of Black Awareness as a Thematic Approach in Latin American Literature," in *Blacks in Hispanic Literature: Critical Essays*, ed. Miriam DeCosta (Port Washington, N.Y.: Kennikat Press, 1977), 66.

40. Debates about the constitution of African American canons continue. Michael Awkward argues convincingly that "we need to be expansive in our definitions of an Afro-American 'constitution' so that, unlike the originary Americanist narrative, differences—class, gender, regional, educational, etc.—will not be reduced to a position of mere background. . . . We must not, in other words, be as prescriptive in our definitions of 'blackness' in American contexts as these earlier scholars were in their definitions of Americanness which largely excluded us as significant subjects." Michael Awkward, "'A National Idea': Canons, Power, and (Afro-) American Literary Studies," in *Voix ethniques/Ethnic Voices*, ed. Claudine Raynaud, vol. 2 (Tours: G.R.A.T. avec le concours du Conseil scientifique de l'Universite de Tours, 1996), 60.

41. In his earlier work Jackson took a decidedly unsympathetic approach to Manzano's racial identification, describing him as one of the slave poets in Cuba who were "ignoring their African heritage" and as a "negro bueno." Richard L. Jackson, *The Black Image in Latin American Literature* (Albuquerque: University of New Mexico Press, 1976), 94, 95.

42. Raquel Romeu, *La mujer y el esclavo en la Cuba de 1840* (Uruguay: Asociacion de Literatura Femenina Hispanica, 1987), 2.

43. Romeu, *La mujer*, 2.

44. Netchinsky, "Engendering a Cuban Literature," 103.

45. As Chapter 3 illustrates, there are several moments in Douglass's narrative where he could be accused of disidentifying. He distances himself from the black community frequently. If we were to judge him only by the *Narrative* and the ambivalence about local and foreign black community therein, we would have to question whether he could ever be a "race man." Unfortunately, Manzano did not have the opportunity to demonstrate his ideology more explicitly through a long life as a statesman as Douglass did, so he will continue to be judged, albeit unfairly, based on the ambivalent, ambiguous relationship to Blackness in his autobiography.

46. Labrador-Rodríguez, "La intelectualidad negro."

47. It is important to note that Manzano was writing in a context where the line between slave and free labor was already becoming blurred. Thomas Bremer, "The Slave Who Wrote Poetry: Comments on the Literary Works and the Autobiography of Juan Francisco Manzano," in *Slavery in the Americas*, ed. Wolfgang Binder (Wurzburg: Koningshausen and Neumann, 1993), 487–501.

48. Gregg Courtad described Manzano and his family as an "indigenous petit bourgeosie," "Psychoanalysis of Oppression," 109.

49. The poem is attributed by Madden to Manzano. He places it in a section entitled "Inedited Cuban poems," and indicates that Manzano presented it to him "on his departure from Cuba."

50. Manzano has been classified racially in a range of ways by biographers and critics, but the consensus, particularly among nineteenth-century intellectuals, is/was that he was not mulatto. Delmonte, "Plácido y Manzano," 84, described him as "casi negro," and as "hijo de negra y de mulato, y esclavo de nacimiento." Calcagano, "Poetas cubanos," 457, 458, identifies him as "hombre de color" and his parents as a *negra* and a *mulato*. Antonio López Prieto, *Parnaso cubano*, 251, classifies Manzano as "poeta de raza etiopica." G. R. Coulthard, while not explicitly classifying Manzano as a Negro, does clearly mark his difference from the White Cubans when he asks, "The writers of the antislavery novels were all white Cubans, if we exclude Manzano's autobiographical account of his life as a slave, and we may ask ourselves, how did these non-coloured writers see the Negro, bearing in mind that they were all looking at the Negro from the outside, that is to say, that they did not live with the Negroes, nor lead the same kind of life, and most probably had very little intimate contact with them." G. R. Coulthard, *Race and Colour in Caribbean Literature* (London: Oxford University Press, 1962), 20. Coulthard, as the multiple clauses of the sentence suggests, is clearly struggling to pin down the behaviors or qualities that distinguish noncolored, Negro, and white in nineteenth-century Cuba. Fundamentally, though, it is clear that he sees Manzano as "coloured," albeit not, perhaps, Negro. Iván Schulman, Introduction, categorizes Manzano as a "Cuban Creole mulatto." It is not clear, though, whether he bases the appropriateness of "mulatto" on class, color, Manzano's disidentification, or his singular moment of self-identification as a "mulato entre negros." Friol, *Suite*, 153, writes "tanto fenotipica como genotipicamente este era un mestizo" (he was as phenotypically mestizo as generically); Franco describes Manzano as "negro y esclavo" (9).

51. Houston Baker, *The Journey Back*, 30, 31, 32.

52. Robert R. Ellis's essay suggests the presence of a homoerotic element, one linked to racial solidarity, in such scenes. The homoerotic element in his poetry, Ellis argues, "stands as a counterpoint to the racist and masculinist brutality depicted in the Autobiografía." Robert Richmond Ellis, "Reading Through the Veil of Juan Francisco Manzano: From Homoerotic Violence to the Dream of a Homoracial Bond," *PMLA* 113, 3 (May 1998): 435.

53. Juan Francisco Manzano, letter to Domingo Delmonte, 25 June 1835, reprinted in *Autobiografía, cartas, y versos*, ed. José L. Franco (Havana: Municipio de la Habana, 1937), 84.

54. Manzano, "La esclava ausente," in *Juan Francisco Manzano: esclavo poeta en la Isla de Cuba*, ed. Abdeslam Azougarh (Valencia: Episteme, 2000), 157.

55. Quoted in Jackson, *Black Writers and the Hispanic Canon*, 22.

56. Ironically, the Cuban literary tradition came of age during this period by way of the antislavery novel, as Schulman, Netchinsky, and Yero Pérez detail. Netchinsky, "Engendering a Cuban Literature"; Iván A. Schulman, "The Portrait of the Slave: Ideology and Aesthetics in the Cuban Antislavery Novel," in *Comparative Perspectives on Slavery in New World Plantation Societies*, ed. Vera Rubin and Arthur Tuden (New York: New York Academy of Sciences), 356–67 and "Reflections on Cuba and the Antislavery Literature," *SECOLAS Annals* 7 (March 1976): 59–67; Luis Yero Pérez, "El tema de la esclavitud en la narrativa cubana," *Islas* (September–December 1974): 65–94. For other overviews of the literary scene in Cuba during the nineteenth century, see Manuel Moreno Fraginals, "El problema negro en la poesía cubana," *Cuadernos Hispanoamericanos* (Madrid) (May–June 1948): 519–30, and Salvador Bueno, "La narrativa antiesclavista en Cuba de 1835 a 1839," *Cuadernos Hispanoamericanos* (special issue: *Los negros en América*) (January–February 1988): 169–86.

57. Cintio Vitier praises the Cubanness of Plácido's poetry, saying "Plácido expresa la cubanía de la intranscendencia, de la lisa cotidiana, amargo o dulce, del vaivén en el foundo tan misteriosos de todo lo aparente y efímero." Cintio Vitier, *Lo cubano en la poesía* (Havana: Instituto del Libro, 1970), 96.

Conclusion

1. For more on Blacks in England during this period, see Gretchen Gerzing, *Black London: Life Before Emancipation* (New Brunswick, N.J.,: Rutgers University Press, 1995).

2. Maria Stewart, "Religion and the Pure Principles of Morality the Sure Foundation on Which We Must Build," in *Early Negro Writing*, ed. Dorothy Porter (Baltimore: Black Classic Press, 1994), 462, 469, 469. Interestingly enough, this text was written in the same year Mary Prince's narrative was published.

3. Victor Séjour, "The Mulatto" in *Norton Anthology of African American Literature*, ed. Henry Louis Gates, Jr. and Nellie Y. McKay (New York: W.W. Norton, 1997), 287–99.

4. Séjour, "The Mulatto," 297.

5. Séjour's treatment of Georges' mulattoness further highlights the differences between the approaches to mulattoness taken by Douglass and Manzano—the former embracing both a "Black" identity and an U.S. identity and downplaying his actual biraciality even though it had a significant impact on the ways in which he was treated while a slave, and the latter claiming a mulatto identity in order to distance himself from the utterly dehumanized *negros* and highlight his own individuality and exceptionality. All three cases illustrate the extent to which mulattoness was not just a reality, but also a means by which people sought to construct or imagine particular realities for themselves and their communities.

Bibliography

Alexander, J. E. *Transatlantic Sketches comprising visits to the most interesting scenes in North and South America and the West Indies.* London: Richard Bentley, 1833.

Allen, William G. "Plácido." In *Autographs for Freedom*, ed. Julia Griffiths. Boston: Jewett, 1853. 265–63.

Allison, Alexander W., Mary Jo Salter, Jon Stallworthy, and Margaret Ferguson, eds. *The Norton Anthology of Poetry.* New York: W.W. Norton, 1983.

Andrews, William L.. *Critical Essays on Frederick Douglass.* Boston: G.K. Hall, 1991.

———. " Dialogue in Antebellum Afro-American Autobiography." In *Studies in Autobiography*, ed. James Olney. New York: Oxford University Press, 1988. 89–98.

———. *To Tell a Free Story: The First Century of Afro-American Autobiography, 1760–1865.* Urbana: University of Illinois Press, 1986.

Appiah, Kwame Anthony. "Cosmopolitan Patriots." *Critical Inquiry* 23, 3 (Spring 1997): 617–39.

Awkward, Michael. "'A National Idea': Canons, Power, and (Afro-) American Literary Studies." In *Voix ethniques/Ethnic Voices*, vol. 2, ed. Claudine Raynaud. Tours: G.R.A.T. avec le concours du Conseil scientifique de l'Université de Tours, 1996. 51–61.

Baker, Houston A., Jr. *The Journey Back: Issues in Black Literature and Criticism.* Chicago: University of Chicago Press, 1980.

———. *Modernism and the Harlem Renaissance.* Chicago: University of Chicago Press, 1987.

Bar-Lewaw, Itzhak (Mulstock). *Plácido: vida y obra.* Mexico City: Ediciones Botas/Impresora Juan Pablos, 1960.

Barnet, Miguel. *Biography of a Runaway Slave.* Trans. Nick W. Hill. 1968. Williamantic, Conn.: Curbstone Press, 1994.

Belnap, Jeffrey and Raúl Fernández. "The Architectonics of José Martí's 'Our Americanism.'" In *José Martí's "Our America": From National to Hemispheric Cultural Studies*, ed. Jeffrey Belnap and Raúl Fernández. Durham, N.C.: Duke University Press, 1998.

Bennett, Louise. *Jamaica Labrish.* Kingston, Jamaica: Sangster's Book Stores, 1966.

Berlin, Ira. *Slaves Without Masters: The Free Negro in the Antebellum South.* New York: New Press, 1974.

Bickell, the Reverend Richard. *The West Indies as They Are; or A Real Picture of Slavery.* London: Ibotson and Palmer Printers for J. Hatchard and Son, 1825.

Bizcarrondo, Marta. *Cuba-España: el dilema autonomista, 1878–1898.* Madrid: Editorial Colibrí, 2001.

Black, Jeremy. *Natural and Necessary Enemies: Anglo-French Relations in the Eighteenth Century.* Athens: University of Georgia Press, 1986.

Blake, William. "The Little Black Boy." In *The Complete Poems,* ed. Alicia Ostriker. New York: Penguin, 1978. 106.

Blyden, Edward Wilmot. *Black Spokesman: Selected Published Writings of Edward Wilmot Blyden.* Ed. Hollis Lynch. London: Cass, 1971.

———. *Christianity, Islam, and the Negro Race.* 1888. Edinburgh: Edinburgh University Press, 1967.

Bolster, W. Jeffrey. *Black Jacks: African American Seamen in the Age of Sail.* Cambridge, Mass.: Cambridge University Press, 1999.

Bost, Suzanne. *Mulattas and Mestizas: Representing Mixed Identities in the Americas 1850–2000.* Athens: University of Georgia Press, 2000.

Bove, Paul A. "Afterword: Global/Local Memory and Thought." In *Global/Local: Cultural Production and the Transnational Imaginary,* ed. Rob Wilson and Wimal Dissanayake. Durham, N.C.: Duke University Press, 1996.

Boyd, Antonio Olliz. "The Concept of Black Awareness as a Thematic Approach in Latin American Literature." In *Blacks in Hispanic Literature: Critical Essays,* ed. Miriam DeCosta-Willis. Port Washington, N.Y.: Kennikat Press, 1977. 65–73.

Brathwaite, Edward Kamau. *The Development of Creole Society in Jamaica, 1770–1820.* Oxford: Clarendon Press, 1971.

———. *Roots.* 1986. Ann Arbor, Mich.: Ann Arbor Paperbacks, 1993.

Branche, Jerome. "'Mulato entre negros' (y blancos): Writing, Race, the Antislavery Question, and Juan Francisco Manzano's Autobiografía." *Bulletin of Latin American Research* 20, 1 (January 2001): 63–87.

Bremer, Thomas. "The Slave Who Wrote Poetry: Comments on the Literary Works and the Autobiography of Juan Francisco Manzano." In *Slavery in the Americas,* ed. Wolfgang Binder. Würzburg: Köningshausen and Neumann, 1993. 487–501.

Brennan, Timothy. *At Home in the World: Cosmopolitanism Now.* Cambridge, Mass.: Harvard University Press, 1997.

———. "Cosmopolitans and Celebrities." *Race and Class: A Journal for Black and Third World Liberation* 31, 1 (1989): 1–19.

Brent, Linda. *Incidents in the Life of a Slave Girl.* Intro. Walter Teller. New York: Harcourt Brace, 1973.

Brown, Jacqueline Nassy. "Black Liverpool, Black America, and the Gendering of Diasporic Space." *Cultural Anthropology* 13, 3 (August 1998): 291–325.

Brown, William Wells. *The Black Man, His Antecedents, His Genius, and His Achievements.* New York: Thomas Hamilton; Boston: R.F. Wallcut, 1863. Electronic edition University of North Carolina at Chapel Hill Libraries, *Documenting the American South,* 1999. <http://docsouth.unc.edu/brownww/menu.html>.

———. *St. Domingo: Its Revolutions and Its Patriots.* Boston: Bela Marsh, 1855.

Bueno, Salvador. "La narrativa antiesclavista en Cuba de 1835 a 1839." *Cuadernos Hispanoamericanos: Revista Mensual de Cultura Hispanica* 451–52 (January–February 1988): 169–86.

Burns, Robert. "A Red, Red Rose." In *The Poetical Works of Robert Burns.* Boston: Little, Brown, 1863. 182.

Busta Rhymes. *The Best of Busta Rhymes.* Rhino, 2001.

————. *The Coming*. Elektra, 1996.

————. *E.L.E.* (*Extinction Level Event*). Elektra, 98.

————. *Genesis*. J Records, 2001.

————. *It Ain't Safe No More*. J Records, 2002.

Cabrera, Lydia. *El monte: igbo, finda, ewe orisha, vititi nfinda: notas sobre las religiones, la magia, las supersticiones y el folklore de los negros criollos y el pueblo de Cuba*. 1954. Miami: Ediciones Universal, 2000.

Calcagano, Francisco. "Poetas cubanos." *Revista de Cuba* 4 (1878): 456–76.

————. *Poetas de color*. Havana: Militar de la V. de Soler, 1878.

Carby, Hazel. *Race Men*. Cambridge, Mass.: Harvard University Press, 1988.

Carruthers, Ben Frederic. "The Life, Work, and Death of Plácido." Ph.D. dissertation, University of Illinois, 1941.

Casals, Jorge. *Plácido como poeta cubano: ensayo biográfico critico*. Havana: Publicaciones del Ministerio de Educación Dirección de Cultura, 1944.

Castellanos, Jorge. *Plácido, poeta social y politico*. Miami: Ediciones Universal, 1984.

Castronovo, Russ. "As to Nation, I Belong to None: Ambivalence, Diaspora, and Frederick Douglass." *American Transcendental Quarterly* n.s. 9, 3 (September 1995): 245–60.

Césaire, Aimé. *Notebook of a Return to the Native Land.*. Trans. Clayton Eshleman and Annette Smith. 1947. Middletown, Conn.: Wesleyan University Press, 2001.

Chambers, Iain. *Migrancy, Culture, Identity*. London: Routledge, 1994.

Chambers, Veronica. *Mama's Girl*. New York: Riverhead Books, 1996.

Chancy, Myriam. *Framing Silence: Revolutionary Novels by Haitian Women*. New Brunswick, N.J.: Rutgers University Press, 1997.

————. *Searching for Safe Spaces: Afro-Caribbean Women Writers in Exile*. Philadelphia: Temple University Press, 1997.

Chapeaux, Pedro Deschamps. *El negro en la economía habanera en el siglo XIX*. Havana: Unión de Escritores y Artistas de Cuba, 1971.

Cheah, Pheng. "Given Culture: Rethinking Cosmopolitical Freedom in Transnationalism." *Boundary 2* 24, 2 (Summer 1997): 157–97.

Chude-Sokei, Louis. "The Black Atlantic Paradigm: Paul Gilroy and the Fractured Landscape of 'Race'." Review of Paul Gilroy, *The Black Atlantic: Modernity and Double Consciousness*. *American Quarterly* 48, 4 (1996): 740–45.

Clark, Vévé. "Developing Diaspora Literacy and Marasa Consciousness." In *Comparative American Identities: Race, Sex and Nationality in the Modern Text*, ed. Hortense J. Spillers, 40–61. New York: Routledge, 1991.

Clifford, James. "Traveling Cultures." In Clifford, *Routes: Travel and Translation in the Late Twentieth Century*. Cambridge, Mass.: Harvard University Press, 1997.

Cobb, Martha. "The Slave Narrative and the Black Literary Tradition." In *The Art of the Slave Narrative*, ed. John Sekora and Darwin T. Turner, 36–44. Macomb: Western Illinois University Press, 1982.

Comunicación dirigida por el Consul de España en la isla de Jamaica al Capitán General de Cuba, fecha Kingston 2 junio 1845, adjuntándole un periódico donde se publica un artículo en el cual se trata de elevar un monumento en dicha Isla al poeta Gabriel de la Concepción Valdés (a) Plácido. *Boletin del Archivo Nacional de Cuba* 18.

Cool Runnings. Dir. Jon Turtletaub. Perf. John Candy and Leon. Disney Studios, 1993.

Coulthard, G. R. *Race and Colour in Caribbean Literature.* London: Oxford University Press, 1962.

Courtad, Gregg. "The Psychoanalytics of Oppression: The Colonizer and the Colonized in the Antislavery Works of Cuba." Ph.D. dissertation, University of Cincinnati, 1996.

Craton, Michael. Review of Orlando Patterson, *Slavery and Social Death: A Comparative Study. Journal of American History* 70, 4 (March 1984): 862–63.

Craven, Wesley Frank. *An Introduction to the History of Bermuda.* Williamsbug, Va., 1938. Reprinted in *William and Mary College Quarterly* 2nd ser. 17, 2–4 (April 1937): 175–215.

Asuntos Politicos. Legajos. Cuban National Archive, Havana.

———. *Sentencia pronunciada por a Seccion de la Comision militar establecida en la ciudad de Matanzas para conocer de la causa de conspiracion de la gente de color.* Asuntos Políticos, Legajo 42, No. 15

Curbet, John. "'Hallelujah to Your Dying Screams of Torture': Representations of Ritual Violence in English and Spanish Romanticism." In *European Gothic: A Spirited Exchange, 1760–1960,* ed. Avril Horner. Manchester: Manchester University Press, 2002. 161–82.

Curtin, Philip. *Two Jamaicas: The Role of Ideas in a Tropical Colony, 1830–1865.* Cambridge, Mass.: Harvard University Press, 1955.

Davies, Carole Boyce. "*Against Race* or the Politics of Self-Ethnography." *Jenda: A Journal of Culture and African Women Studies* 2 (2002): 1.

———. *Black Women, Writing, and Identity: Migrations of the Subject.* New York: Routledge, 1994.

Davies, Carole Boyce and Elaine Savory Fido, eds. *Out of the Kumbla: Caribbean Women and Literature.* Trenton, N.J.: Africa World Press, 1990.

Davis, David Brion. "Of Human Bondage." Review of Orlando Patterson, *Slavery and Social Death: A Comparative Study. New York Review of Books,* February 13, 1983, 20.

Dayan, Joan. *Haiti, History, and the Gods.* Berkeley: University of California Press, 1995.

———. "Paul Gilroy's Slaves, Ships, and Routes: The Middle Passage as Metaphor." Review of Paul Gilroy, *The Black Atlantic: Modernity and Double Consciousness. Research in African Literatures* 27, 4 (1996): 7–14.

D'Costa, Jean and Barbara Lalla, eds. *Voices in Exile: Caribbean Women and Literature.* Tuscaloosa: University of Alabama Press, 1989.

DeCosta-Willis, Miriam. "Self and Society in the Afro-Cuban Slave Narrative." *Latin American Literary Review* 16, 32 (July–December 1988): 6–15.

Decker, Jeffrey Louis. *Made in America: Self-Styled Success from Horatio Alger to Oprah Winfrey.* Minneapolis: University of Minnesota Press, 1997.

DeJongh, James. *Vicious Modernism: Black Harlem and the Literary Imagination.* New York: Cambridge University Press, 1990.

Delany, Martin Robison. *Blake; or, The Huts of America.* Ed. Floyd J. Miller. Boston: Beacon Press, 1970.

———. *The Condition, Elevation, Emigration, and Destiny of the Colored People of the United States, Politically Considered.* 1852. Baltimore: Black Classic Press, 1993.

————. *Official Report of the Niger Valley Exploring Party.* New York: T. Hamilton, 1861. Reprinted in *The Search for a Place: Black Separatism and Africa.*

————. *The Origin of Races and Color.* 1879. Baltimore: Black Classic Press, 1991.

Delany, Martin Robison and Robert Campbell. *Search for a Place: Black Separatism and Africa.* 1860. Intro. Howard H. Bell. Ann Arbor, University of Michigan Press, 1969.

Del Arte e Industria Cinematográficos e Impala S.A. de Madrid. *Cecilia.* New York: Latin American Video Archives : International Media Resource Exchange, n.d.

Delmonte, Domingo. "Plácido y Manzano." *Liceo de la Habana* viernes 9 de setiembre (sic) de 1859.

Diouf, Mamadou. "The Senegalese Murid Trade Diaspora and the Making of a Vernacular Cosmopolitanism." *Public Culture* 12, 3 (2000): 679–702.

Dixon, Chris. *African Americans and Haiti: Emigration and Black Nationalism in the Nineteenth Century.* Westport, Conn.: Greenwood Press, 2000.

Dixon, Melvin. *Ride Out the Wilderness: Geography and Identity in Afro-American Literature.* Urbana: University of Illinois Press, 1987.

Douglass, Frederick. "The Cambria Riots, My Slave Experience, and My Irish Mission." In *Frederick Douglass Papers,* vol. 1.

————. "Colonization." *North Star,* January 26, 1849. In *Frederick Douglass: Selected Speeches and Writings,* 126.

————. *The Frederick Douglass Papers: Series One: Speeches, Debates, and Interviews.* Ed. John W. Blassingame et al. 5 vols.. New Haven, Conn.: Yale University Press, 1979–92.

————. *Frederick Douglass: Selected Speeches and Writings.* Ed. Philip S. Foner. Chicago: Lawrence Hill, 1999.

————. "Haiti and the Haitian People: An Address Delivered in Chicago, Illinois on 2 January 1893." In *Frederick Douglass Papers,* vol. 5, 528.

————. "Haytian Emigration." *Douglass' Monthly,* March 1861. In *Life and Writings* vol. 5, 472.

————. *The Heroic Slave.* 1853. In *The Oxford Frederick Douglass Reader,* ed. William L. Andrew. New York: Oxford University Press, 1996.

————. "The Highest Honor Conferred on Me: An Address Delivered in Port-au-Prince, Haiti on 14 November 1889." In *Frederick Douglass Papers,* vol. 5, 426–29.

————. *The Life and Times of Frederick Douglass.* 1892. New York: Collier, 1962.

————. *The Life and Writings of Frederick Douglass.* Ed. Phillip S. Foner. New York: International Publishers, 1950–1975.

————. *My Bondage and My Freedom.* 1855. Ed. Phillip S. Foner. New York: Dover, 1969.

————. *Narrative of the Life of Frederick Douglass, an American Slave.* 1845. New York: Dover, 1995.

————. "The Present Condition and Future Prospects of the Negro People." Speech at the annual meeting of the American and Foreign Anti-Slavery Society, New York, May 11, 1853. In *Frederick Douglass: Selected Speeches and Writings,* 251.

————. "Santo Domingo: An Address Delivered in St. Louis, Missouri on 13 January 1873." In *Frederick Douglass Papers,* vol. 4, 346.

————. "What to a Slave Is the Fourth of July." 1852. In *The Oxford Frederick Douglass Reader,* ed.William L. Andrews. New York: Oxford University Press, 1996. 108–30.

Du Bois, W. E. B. "The Criteria for Negro Art." In *The Norton Anthropology of African American Literature*, ed. Henry Louis Gates, Jr. and Nellie McKay. New York: W.W. Norton, 1997.
———. *Souls of Black Folk.* 1904. New York: Avon Books, 1965.
———. *The Suppression of the African Slave Trade to the United States, 1638–1870.* 1896. Baton Rouge: Louisiana State University Press, 1969.
Dunbar, Paul Laurence. *The Collected Poetry of Paul Laurence Dunbar.* Ed. Joanne M. Braxton. Charlottesville: University Press of Virginia, 1993.
Edmondson, Belinda. *Making Men: Gender, Literary Authority, and Women's Writing in Caribbean Narrative.* Durham, N.C.: Duke University Press, 1999.
Edwards, Brent. *The Practice of Diaspora: Literature, Translation, and the Rise of Black Internationalism.* Cambridge, Mass.: Harvard University Press, 2003.
Ellis, Robert Richmond. "Reading Through the Veil of Juan Francisco Manzano: From Homoerotic Violence to the Dream of a Homoracial Bond." *PMLA* 113, 3 (May 1998): 422–35.
Emerson, Ralph Waldo. *The Collected Works of Ralph Waldo Emerson.* Cambridge, Mass.: Belknap Press of Harvard University Press, 1971.
Equiano, Olaudah. *The Interesting Narrative of Olaudah Equiano.* 1789. Boston: Bedford Books of St. Martin's Press, 1995.
Erickson, Peter. Review of Paul Gilroy, *The Black Atlantic: Modernity and Double Consciousness.* *African American Review* 31, 3 (1997): 506–8.
Espronceda, José de. *José de Espronceda: antologia poética*, ed. Rubén Benítez. Madrid: Clásicos Taurus, 1991.
Favor, J. Martin. *Authentic Blackness: The Folk in the New Negro Renaissance.* Durham, N.C.: Duke University Press, 1999.
Ferguson, Moira. "Introduction to the Revised Edition." In Mary Prince, *The History of Mary Prince, A West Indian Slave, Related by Herself.* Rev. ed. Ann Arbor: University of Michigan Press, 1997.
———. *Nine Black Women: An Anthology of Nineteenth-Century Writers from the United States, Canada, Bermuda, and the Caribbean.* New York: Routledge, 1998.
———. *Subject to Others: British Women Writers and Colonial Slavery, 1670–1834.* New York: Routledge, 1992.
Ferrer, Ada. *Insurgent Cuba: Race, Nation, and Revolution, 1868–1898.* Chapel Hill: University of North Carolina Press, 1999.
Figarola-Caneda, Domingo. *Plácido (poeta cubano): contribución histórico-literaria.* Havana: El Siglo, 1922.
Fischer, Sibylle. *Modernity Disavowed: Haiti and the Cultures of Slavery in the Age of Revolution.* Durham, N.C.: Duke University Press, 2004.
Fish, Cheryl. "Voices of Restless (Dis)continuity: The Significance of Travel for Free Black Women in the Antebellum Americas." *Women's Studies* 26, 5 (1997): 475–95.
Flores, Juan. *Divided Borders: Essays on Puerto Rican Identity.* Houston: Arte Público Press, 1993.
Foner, Laura and Eugene D. Genovese, eds. *Slavery in the New World: A Reader in Comparative History.* Englewood Cliffs, N.J.: Prentice-Hall, 1969.
Foster, Frances Smith. *Witnessing Slavery: The Development of Antebellum Slave Narratives.* 2nd ed. Madison: University of Wisconsin Press, 1994.

————. *Written by Herself: Literary Production by African American Women, 1746–1892.* Blacks in the Diaspora. Bloomington: Indiana University Press, 1993.

Franco, José L. Introduction to Juan Francisco Manzano, *Autobiografía, cartas, y versos.* Havana: Municipio de la Habana, 1937.

Franklin, Benjamin. *The Autobiography.* Parts One and Two. *The Heath Anthology of American Literature.* Lexington, Mass.: D.C Heath, 1990.

Friol, Roberto. *Suite para Juan Francisco Manzano.* Havana: Editorial Arte y Literatura, 1977.

García, Enildo A. "Cuba en la obra de Placído: análisis y bibliografía comentada." Ph.D. dissertation, New York University, 1982.

————. *Cuba: Plácido, poeta mulato de la emancipación.* New York: Senda Nueva de Ediciones, 1986.

García Garofalo Mesa, M. *Plácido, poeta y martir.* México: Ediciones Botas, 1938.

Garnet, Henry Highland. "Speech at an Enthusiastic Meeting of the Colored Citizens of Boston." 1859. In *Early Negro Writing, 1760–1837,* comp. Dorothy Burnett Porter. Boston: Beacon Press, 1971.

————. *Walker's Appeal, in Four Articles, by David Walker. An Address to Slaves of the United States of America, by Henry Highland Garnet.* 1848. New York: Arno Press, 1969.

Gaspar, David Barry. *Bondmen and Rebels: A Study of Master-Slave Relations in Antigua, with Implications for Colonial British America.* Baltimore: Johns Hopkins University Press, 1985.

Gaspar, David Barry and Darlene Clark Hine, eds. *More Than Chattel: Black Women and Slavery in the Americas.* Bloomington: Indiana University Press, 1996.

Gates, Henry Louis, Jr.. *The Signifying Monkey: A Theory of Afro-American Literary Criticism.* New York: Oxford University Press, 1988.

Gates, Henry Louis, Jr. and Charles T. Davis, eds. *The Slave's Narrative.* New York: Oxford University Press, 1985.

Gates, Henry Louis, Jr. and Nellie McKay, eds. *Norton Anthology of African American Literature.* New York: W.W. Norton, 1997.

Genovese, Eugene D. *Roll, Jordan, Roll : The World the Slaves Made.* 1972. New York: Vintage, 1974.

————. *The World the Slaveholders Made: Two Essays in Interpretation.* 1969. Middletown, Conn.: Wesleyan University Press, 1988.

Gerassi-Navarro, Nina. "Biografía de un Cimarron: historia de verdades ausentes." *Ciberletras* (August 1999).

Gerzina, Gretchen. *Black London: Life Before Emancipation.* New Brunswick, N.J.: Rutgers University Press, 1995.

Gibson, Donald. "Faith, Doubt, and Apostasy: Evidence of Things Unseen in Frederick Douglass's Narrative." In *Frederick Douglass: New Literary and Historical Essays,* ed. Eric Sundquist, 84–98. New York: Cambridge University Press, 1990.

Gikandi, Simon. *Maps of Englishness: Writing Identity in the Culture of Colonialism.* New York: Columbia, 1996.

————. "Race and Cosmopolitanism." *American Literary History* 14, 3 (Fall 2002): 593–615.

Gilroy, Paul. *Against Race: Imagining Political Culture Beyond the Color Line.* Cambridge, Mass.: Belknap Press of Harvard University Press, 2000.

————. *The Black Atlantic: Modernity and Double Consciousness.* Cambridge, Mass.: Harvard University Press, 1993.

Glissant, Edouard. *Poetics of Relation.* Trans. Betsy Wing. Ann Arbor: University of Michigan Press, 1997.

Goellnicht, Donald C. "Passing as Autobiography: James Weldon Johnson's *The Autobiography of an Ex-Colored Man.*" *African American Review* 30, 1 (Spring 1996): 17–33.

Gomes de Avellaneda, Gertrudís. *Sab, novela original.* Madrid: Imprenta Calle del Banco Num. 26, 1841.

Goveia, Elsa. *Slave Society in the British Leeward Islands at the End of the Eighteenth Century.* New Haven, Conn.: Yale University Press, 1965.

Graham, Richard, ed. *The Idea of Race in Latin America.* Austin: University of Texas Press, 1990.

Griffin, Farah Jasmine. *'Who Set You Flowin'?' The African-American Migration Narrative.* New York: Oxford University Press, 1995.

Grunfeld, Mihai. "Cosmopolitismo modernista y vanguardista." *Revista Iberoamericana* 55, 146–147 (January–June 1989): 33–41.

Guillén, Nicolas. *Cuba Libre: Poems.* Trans. and ed. Langston Hughes and Ben Frederic Carruthers. Los Angeles: Anderson and Ritchie, 1948.

————. *Songoro Cosongo: poemas mulatos.* 1931. Havana: Ediciones Unió, 1999.

Gunning, Sandra, Tera W. Hunter, and Michele Mitchell. "Introduction: Gender, Sexuality, and African Diasporas." *Gender and History* 15, 3 (November 2003): 397–408.

Hall, Stuart. "Cultural Identity and Cinematic Representation." In *Black British Cultural Studies: A Reader,* ed. Houston A. Baker, Jr., Manthia Diawara, and Ruth H. Lindeborg. Chicago: University of Chicago Press, 1996. 210–22.

————. "Cultural Identity and Diaspora." In *Contemporary Postcolonial Theory: A Reader,* ed. Padmini Mongia. London: Arnold, 1996. 110–21.

————. "The Local and the Global." In *Culture, Globalization, and the World-System: Contemporary Conditions for the Representation of Identity,* ed. Anthony D. King. Minneapolis: University of Minnesota Press, 1997.

————. "New Ethnicities." In *The Post-Colonial Studies Reader,* ed. Bill Ashcroft, Gareth Griffiths, and Helen Tiffin. London: Routledge, 1995. 223–27.

————, ed. *Representation: Cultural Representations and Signifying Practices.* London: Sage, 1997.

Handley, George. *Postslavery Literatures in the Americas: Family Portraits in Black and White.* Charlottesville: University Press of Virginia, 2000.

Hannerz, Ulf. *Transnational Connections: Culture, People, Places.* New York: Routledge, 1996.

Haskett, Norman Dean. "Afro-American Images of Africa: Four Antebellum Black Authors." *Ufahamu: Journal of the African Activist Association* 3, 1 (1972): 29–40.

Helg, Aline. *Our Rightful Share: The Afro-Cuban Struggle for Equality, 1886–1912.* Chapel Hill: University of North Carolina Press, 1995.

Heredia, José María. "A mi esposa"; "En el Teocalli de Cholula"; "Himno del desterrado." In *Los poetas románticos cubanos,* ed. Cintio Vitier. Havana: Consejo Nacional de Cultura, 1962.

Herskovits, Melville J. *Myth of the Negro Past.* 1941. Foreword by Sidney W. Mintz. New York: Harper and Row, 1990.

Hill, Lauryn. "Every Ghetto, Every City." *The Miseducation of Lauryn Hill.* New York: Ruffhouse/Columbia Records. 1998.

Hiraldo, Carlos Manuel. "Segregated Miscegenations: On the Treatment of Racial Hybridity in the North American and Latin American Literary Traditions." Ph.D. dissertation, State University of New York, Stony Brook, 1999.

Himelhoch, Myra. "Frederick Douglass and Haiti's Mole St. Nicholas." *Journal of Negro History* 56, 3 (July 1971): 161–80.

Hobsbawm, Eric J. *Nations and Nationalism Since 1780: Programme, Myth, Reality.* Cambridge: Cambridge University Press, 1990.

Hollinger, David A. "Ethnic Diversity, Cosmopolitanism, and the Emergence of the American Liberal Intelligentsia." *American Quarterly* 27, 2 (1975): 133–51.

Holloway, Karla F. C. *Moorings and Metaphors.* New Brunswick, N.J.: Rutgers University Press, 1992.

Holly, James Theodore. *Facts About the Church's Mission in Haiti: A Concise Statement by Bishop Holly.* New York: Thomas Whittaker, 1897.

———. "A Vindication of the Capacity of the Negro Race for Self-Government and Civilized Progress as Demonstrated by Historical Events of the Haytian Revolution; and the Subsequent Acts of That People Since Their National Independence." In James Theodore Holly and J. Dennis Harris, *Black Separatism and the Caribbean 1860,* ed. Howard H. Bell. Ann Arbor: University of Michigan Press, 1970.

Hopkins, Pauline. *Contending Forces: A Romance Illustrative of Negro Life North and South.* 1900. Oxford: Oxford University Press, 1988.

Howard, Philip. *Changing History: Afro-Cuban Cabildos and Societies of Color in the Nineteenth Century.* Baton Rouge: Louisiana State University Press, 1998.

How Stella Got Her Groove Back. Dir. Kevin Rodney Sullivan. Perf. Angela Bassett and Taye Diggs. Fox, 1998.

Hughes, Langston. "The Negro Artist and the Racial Mountain." In *Within the Circle: An Anthology of African American Literary Criticism from the Harlem Renaissance to the Present,* ed. Angelyn Mitchell, 55–59. Durham, N.C., Duke University Press, 1994.

Hulbert, William. "The Poetry of Spanish America." *North American Review* 68 (January 1849).

Hunt, Alfred N. *Haiti's Influence on Antebellum America: Slumbering Volcano in the Caribbean.* Baton Rouge: Louisiana State University Press, 1988.

Hunter-Gault, Charlayne. "Hamilton Holmes Appreciation." Transcript of appearance on *Newshour with Jim Lehrer,* November 1, 1995.

Hurston, Zora Neale. *Tell My Horse.* 1938. New York: Harper and Row, 1990.

I Like It like That. Dir. Darnell Martin. Perf. Lauren Velez, Jon Seda, Rita Moreno and Griffin Dunne. Columbia Tristar Home Entertainment, 1994.

In Living Color. Created by Keenan Ivory Wayans. Fox, April 1990–1994.

Instituto Cubano del Arte e Industria Cinematográficas (Cuban Institute of Art and Film). *El otro Francisco (The Other Francisco).* New York: Center for Cuban Studies, 1990.

Jackson, Richard L. *The Black Image in Latin American Literature.* Albuquerque: University of New Mexico Press, 1976.

———. *Black Writers and the Hispanic Canon.* New York: Twayne, 1997.

————. *Black Writers and Latin America: Cross-Cultural Affinities.* Washington, D.C.: Howard University Press, 1998.

Jiménez, Luis. "Nineteenth Century Autobiography in the Afro-Americas: Frederick Douglass and Juan Francisco Manzano." *Afro-Hispanic Review* 14, 2 (Fall 1995): 47–52.

Johnson, James Weldon. *Autobiography of an Ex-Colored Man.* New York: Knopf, 1951.

Jones, Gayl. *Mosquito.* Boston: Beacon Press, 1999.

Journal of the Jamaica Assembly. 1714–1740. Housed at the University of North Carolina, Chapel Hill.

Kaplan, Caren. *Questions of Travel: Postmodern Discourses of Displacement.* Durham, N.C.: Duke University Press, 1996.

Kawash, Samira. "*The Autobiography of an Ex-Coloured Man*: (Passing for) Black Passing for White." In *Passing and the Fictions of Identity*, ed. Elaine K. Ginsberg, 59–74. Durham, N.C.: Duke University Press, 1996.

Kelley, Robin D. G. *Freedom Dreams: The Black Radical Imagination.* Boston: Beacon Press, 2002.

Kerr, Wilfred Brenton. *Bermuda and the American Revolution: 1760–1783.* Princeton, N.J.: Princeton University Press, 1936.

Kirk, John M. *José Marti: Mentor of the Cuban Nation.* Tampa: University Presses of Florida, 1983.

Klein, Herbert S. *African Slavery in Latin America and the Caribbean.* New York: Oxford University Press, 1986.

————. *The Atlantic Slave Trade.* New York: Cambridge University Press, 1999.

————. *The Middle Passage: Comparative Studies in the Atlantic Slave Trade.* Princeton, N.J.: Princeton University Press, 1978.

————. *Slavery in the Americas: A Comparative Study of Virginia and Cuba.* Chicago: University of Chicago Press, 1967.

Knight, Franklin. *Slave Society in Cuba During the Nineteenth Century.* Madison: University of Wisconsin Press, 1970.

Krato, Jennifer Rae. "When a Rose Is Not a Rose: Espronceda's Flower Poetics." *Revista de Estudious Hispánicos* 22 (1995): 75–90.

Kristeva, Julia. *Strangers to Ourselves.* New York: Columbia University Press, 1991.

Kutzinski, Vera. *Sugar's Secrets: Race and the Erotics of Cuban Nationalism.* Charlottesville: University Press of Virginia, 1993.

————. "Unseasonal Flowers: Nature and History in Plácido and Jean Toomer." *Yale Journal of Criticism* 3,2 (1990): 153–79.

Labrador-Rodríguez, Sonia. "La intelectualidad negra en Cuba en el siglo XIX: el caso de Manzano." *Revista Iberoamericana*, 62, 174 (January–March 1996): 13–25.

Lamming, George. *In the Castle of My Skin.* Foreword Sandra Pouchet Paquet. Ann Arbor: University of Michigan Press, 1991.

Lanier, Olida Hevia. *El directorio central de las sociedades negras de Cuba (1886–1894).* Havana: Editorial de Ciencias Sociales, 1996.

Larsen, Nella. *Passing.* 1929. New Brunswick, N.J.: Rutgers University Press, 1986.

Lazo, Rodrigo. "Filibustering Cuba: Cecilia Valdés and a Memory of Nation in the Americas." *American Literature* 74, 1 (2002): 1–30.

Lee, Debbie. *Slavery and the Romantic Imagination.* Philadelphia: University of Pennsylvania Press, 2002.

Lefebvre, Henri. *The Production of Space.* Trans. Donald Nicholson-Smith. Cambridge: Blackwell, 1991.

Le Moyne, Charlotte Elaine Saulnier. "El racismo escondido de Sab: una perspectiva postcolonial." M.A. thesis, University of Virginia, 1997.

Levine, Lawrence W. *Black Culture and Black Consciousness: Afro-American Folk Thought from Slavery to Freedom.* New York: Oxford University Press, 1977.

Levine, Robert S. *Martin Delany, Frederick Douglass, and the Politics of Representative Identity.* Chapel Hill: University of North Carolina Press, 1997.

Lewis, Marvin. *Afro-Argentine Discourse: Another Dimension of the Black Diaspora.* Columbia: University of Missouri Press, 1996.

Linebaugh, Peter and Marcus Rediker. *The Many Headed Hydra: Sailors, Slaves, Commoners, and the Hidden History of the Revolutionary Atlantic.* Boston: Beacon Press, 2000.

Locke, Alain, ed. *The New Negro.* 1925. New York: Simon and Schuster, 1997.

Logan, Rayford. *The Diplomatic Relations of the United States with Haiti, 1776–1891.* Chapel Hill: University of North Carolina Press, 1941.

López Cruz, Humberto. "Cecelia Valdés: la mulatería como símbolo de identidad nacional en la sociedad colonial cubana." *Hispanófila* 125 (January 1999): 51–61.

López Prieto, Antonio. *Parnaso cubano: colección de poesías selectas de autores cubanos, desde Zequeira á nuestros días; precedida de una introducción histórico-crítica sobre el desarrollo de la poesía en Cuba.* Havana: M de Villa, 1881.

Luis, William. "La autobiografía de Juan Francisco Manzano y la traducción de Richard Madden: un texto con dos interpretaciones sobre la vida del esclavo poeta." *Discurso: Revista de Estudios Iberoamericanos* 11, 1 (1993): 95–111.

———. "Cecilia Valdés: el nacimiento de una novela antiesclavista." *Cuadernos Hispanoamericanos: Revista Mensual de Cultura Hispanica* 451–52 (January–February 1998): 187–93.

———. "Cuban Counterpoint, Coffee and Sugar: The Emergency of a National Culture in Fernando Ortiz's *Cuban Counterpoint: Tobacco and Sugar* and Cirilo Villaverde's *Cecelia Valdes.*" *Publication of the Afro-Latin/American Research Association (PALARA)* 2 (Fall 1998): 5–16.

———. *Literary Bondage: Slavery in Cuban Narrative.* Austin: University of Texas Press, 1990.

———. "Nicolas Azcarate's Antislavery Notebooks and the Unpublished Poems of the Slave Juan Francisco Manzano." *Revista de Estudios Hispanicos* 28, 3 (October 1994): 331–51.

———. "The Politics of Memory and Miguel Barnet's *The Autobiography of a Runaway Slave.*" *MLN* 104, 2 (March 1989): 475–91.

———, ed. *Voices from Under: Black Narrative in Latin America and the Caribbean.* Westport, Conn.: Greenwood Press, 1984.

Madden, Richard Robert, ed. *The Island of Cuba: Its Resources, Progress, etc., in Relation Especially to the Influence of Its Prosperity on the Interests of the British West India Colonies.* London: C. Gilpin, 1849.

Malkki, Liisa. "National Geographic: The Rooting of Peoples and the Territorialization of National Identity among Scholars and Refugees." In *Culture, Power, Place: Explorations in Critical Anthropology,* ed. Akhil Gupta and James Ferguson, 52–74. Durham, N.C.: Duke University Press, 1997.

Manzano, Juan Francisco. *Autobiografía, cartas, y versos*. Intro. José L. Franco. Havana: Municipio de la Habana, 1937.

———. *Autobiografia de un esclavo*. Modernized Spanish by Iván A Schulman. Madrid: Ediciones Guadarrama, 1975.

———. *The Autobiography of a Cuban Slave*. Trans. Lloyd King. St. Augustine, Trinidad: Lloyd King, 1990–94.

———. *Autobiography of a Slave/Autobiografia de un esclavo*. Bilingual edition. Modernized Spanish by Iván A Schulman, trans. Evelyn Picon Garfield, 5–38. Detroit: Wayne State University Press, 1996.

———. "Copia de la carta del poeta a Rosa Alfonso de Aldama." Colección Figarola-Caneda, Asuntos Políticos, Legajo 681, Caja 204, 86.

———. "La esclava ausente." In *Juan Francisco Manzano: esclavo poeta en la isla de Cuba*. Ed. Abdeslam Azougarh. Valencia: Episteme, 2000.

———. "Juan Francisco Manzano to Domingo Delmonte." June 25, 1835. Microfilm from La Academia de la Historia de Cuba, Signatura 679, Caja 203.

———. "Letter to Domingo Delmonte." June 25, 1835. Reprinted in *Autobiografía, cartas, y versos*, 7.

———. "The Life of the Negro Poet." Trans. Richard Robert Madden. In *The Life and Poems of a Cuban Slave*, ed. Edward J. Mullen. 1840. Hamden, Conn.: Archon Books, 1981.

———. *Manzano*. Academia de la Historia de Cuba, Colección Figarola-Caneda, Signatura 679, Caja 203.

———. *Obras completas de Juan Francisco Manzano esclavo de la isla de Cuba*. Ed. Nicolas Azcarate. Primary Source Microfilm by Thomson and Gale, Latin American History and Culture: An Archival Record, Series 1: Yale University Collection of Latin American Manuscripts, Caribbean Collection, Part 5, Unit 1, Reel 1, 88.

———. *Poems by a Slave in the Island of Cuba, Recently Liberated Translated from the Spanish by R. R. Madden, M.D. with the History of the Early Life of the Negro Poet, Written by Himself*. London: T. Ward, 1840.

———. *Zafira: tragedia en cinco actos*. Havana: Consejo Nacional de Cultura, 1962.

Marshall, Paule. *Brown Girl, Brownstones*. 1959. Afterword Mary Helen Washington. Chatham, N.J.: Chatham Bookseller, 1972.

———. *Chosen Place, Timeless People*. New York: Harcourt, Brace, 1969.

———. *Daughters*. New York: Atheneum, 1991.

———. "The Making of a Writer: From the Poets in the Kitchen." In *Reena and Other Stories*. New York: Feminist Press, 1983.

———. *Praisesong for the Widow*. New York: Putnam's, 1983.

———. *Soul Clap Hands and Sing*. New York: Atheneum, 1961.

Martí, José. *Our America*. Trans. Philip S. Foner. New York: Monthly Review Press, 1977.

Martin, Waldo E., Jr. *The Mind of Frederick Douglass*. Chapel Hill: University of North Carolina Press, 1984.

Martínez-Alier, Verena. "El honor de la mujer en Cuba en el siglo XIX." *Revista de la Biblioteca Nacional José Martí* 13 (May–August 1971): 48–49.

Martínez Carmenate, Urbano. *Domingo Delmonte y su tiempo*. Maracaibo: Dirección de Cultura de la Universidad del Zulia, 1996.

Martínez Heredia, Fernando. "Nationalism, Races, and Classes in the Revolution of 1895 and the First Cuban Republic." Paper presented at a workshop on Open Secrets: Race, Law, and the Nation in the Cuban Republic, 1902–1925, University of Michigan, Ann Arbor, November 15, 2001.

McBride, Dwight A. *Impossible Witnesses: Truth, Abolitionism, and Slave Testimony.* New York: New York University Press, 2001.

———. Review of Paul Gilroy, *The Black Atlantic: Modernity and Double Consciousness. Modern Fiction Studies* 41,2 (1995): 388–91.

McDowell, Deborah. "In the First Place: Making Frederick Douglass and the Afro-American Narrative Tradition." In *African American Autobiography: A Collection of Critical Essays*, ed. William L. Andrews, 36–58. Englewood Cliffs, N.J.: Prentice Hall, 1993.

———. *Slavery and the Literary Imagination.* Baltimore: John Hopkins University Press, 1989.

McKay, Claude. *Banjo: A Story Without a Plot.* New York: Carcourt, 1970.

Melville, Herman. *Benito Cereno.* 1856. Barre, Mass.: Imprint Society, 1972.

Mignolo, Walter. *The Darker Side of the Renaissance.* Ann Arbor: University of Michigan Press, 1995.

———. "The Many Faces of Cosmo-polis: Border Thinking and Critical Cosmopolitanism," *Public Culture* 12, 3 (2000): 721–48.

Miller, Floyd J. *The Search for a Black Nationality: Black Emigration and Colonization, 1787–1863.* Urbana: University of Illinois Press, 1975.

Mills Young, Carol. "Virginia Brindis de Salas vs. Julio Guadalupe: A Question of Authorship." In *Daughters of the Diaspora: Afra-HispanicWriters*, ed. Miriam DeCosta Willis. Kingston: Ian Randle, 2003. 11–24.

Mintz, Sidney and Richard Price. *The Birth of African-American Culture: An Anthropological Perspective.* 1976. Boston: Beacon Press, 1992.

Mohanty, Chandra. *Third World Women and the Politics of Feminism.* Bloomington: Indiana University Press, 1991.

Morejón, Nancy. *Looking Within: Selected Poems, 1954–2000 / Mirar adentro: poemas escogidos, 1954–2000.* Bilingual edition. Detroit: Wayne State University Press, 2002.

Moreno Fraginals, Manuel. "El problema negro en la poesia cubana." *Cuadernos Hispanoamericanos* (May–June 1948): 519–30.

Morrison, Toni. *Playing in the Dark.* New York: Vintage, 1993.

Moses, Wilson Jeremiah. *The Golden Age of Black Nationalism, 1850–1925.* New York: Oxford University Press, 1988.

———. "Writing Freely? Frederick Douglass and the Constraints of Racialized Writing." In *Frederick Douglass: New Literary and Historical Essays*, ed. Eric Sundquist, 68–83. Cambridge: Cambridge University Press, 1990.

Mostern, Kenneth. *Autobiography and Black Identity Politics: Racialization in Twentieth Century America.* Cambridge: Cambridge University Press, 1999.

Mullen, Edward J. "The Emergence of Afro-Hispanic Poetry: Some Notes on Canon Formation." *Hispanic Review* 56, 4 (Autumn 1988): 435–53.

———. "The Teaching Anthology and the Hermeneutics of Race: The Case of Plácido." *Indiana Journal of Hispanic Literatures* 6–7 (Spring-Fall 1995): 123–38.

Muñoz, José E. *Disidentifications: Queers of Color and the Performance of Politics.* Minneapolis: University of Minnesota Press, 1999.

Muthu, Sankar. *Enlightenment Against Empire.* Princeton, N.J.: Princeton University Press, 2004.

Nakachi, Sachi. "Mixed-Race Identity Politics in Nella Larsen and Winnifred Eaton (Onoto Watanna)." Ph.D. dissertation, Ohio University, 2002.

Neal, Larry. "The Black Aesthetic." In *Within the Circle: An Anthology of African American Literary Criticism from the Harlem Renaissance to the Present,* ed. Angelyn Mitchell. Durham, N.C.: Duke University Press, 1994.

Nelson, Dana D. *National Manhood: Capitalist Citizenship and the Imagined Fraternity of White Men.* Durham, N.C.: Duke University Press, 1998.

———. *The Word in Black and White: Reading "Race" in American Literature, 1638–1837.* New York: Oxford University Press, 1993.

Netchinsky, Jill Ann. "Engendering a Cuban Literature: Nineteenth Century Antislavery Narrative." Ph.D. dissertation, Yale University, 1986.

Notorious B.I.G. *Born Again.* Bad Boy Records, 1999.

———. *Life After Death.* Bad Boy Records, 1997.

———. *Ready to Die.* Bad Boy Records, 1994.

Nunes, Zita C. "Phantasmatic Brazil: Nella Larsen's *Passing,* American Literary Imagination, and Racial Utopianism." In *Mixing Race, Mixing Culture: Inter-American Literary Dialogues,* ed. Monika Kaup and Deborah Rosenthal. Austin: University of Texas Press, 2002. 50–61.

Olney, James. "'I Was Born': Slave Narratives, Their Status as Autobiography and as Literature." In *The Slave's Narrative,* ed. Henry Louis Gates, Jr. and Charles T. Davis. New York: Oxford University Press, 1985. 148–75.

———, ed. *Studies in Autobiography.* New York: Oxford University Press, 1988.

Olwig, Karen Fog. *Global Culture, Island Identity: Community and Change in the Afro-Caribbean Community of Nevis.* Philadelphia: Harwood Academic Publishers, 1993.

Ortiz, Fernando. *Cuban Counterpoint: Tobacco and Sugar.* New York: Knopf, 1947.

———. *Los negros esclavos.* Havana: Editorial de Ciencias Sociales, 1996.

———. *Poesia y canto de los negros afrocubanos.* Havana: Pubicigraf, 1994.

Paquet, Sandra Pouchet. *Caribbean Autobiography: Cultural Identity and Self-Representation.* Madison: University of Wisconsin Press, 2002.

———. "The Enigma of Arrival: The Wonderful Adventures of Mrs. Seacole in Many Lands." *African American Review* 26, 4 (1992): 651–63.

———. "The Heartbeat of a West Indian Slave: The History of Mary Prince." *African American Review* 26, 1 (1992): 131–46.

Paquette, Robert. *Sugar Is Made with Blood: The Conspiracy of La Escalera and the Conflict of Empires over Slavery in Cuba.* Middletown, Conn.: Wesleyan University Press, 1988.

Patterson, Orlando. *Slavery and Social Death: A Comparative Study.* Cambridge, Mass.: Harvard University Press, 1982.

Pérez, Louis A.. *Cuba and the United States: Ties of Singular Intimacy.* 2nd ed. Athens: University of Georgia Press, 1997.

———. *Cuba Between Empires, 1878–1902.* Pittsburgh: University of Pittsburgh Press, 1983.

———. "El tema de la esclavitud en la narrativa cubana." *Islas* (September–December 1974): 65–94.

Pérez, Luis Yero. "El tema de la esclavitud en la narrativa cubana." *Islas* (September–December 1974): 65–94.

Persyn, Mary. "The Sublime Turn Away from Empire: Wordsworth's Encounter with Colonial Slavery, 1802." *Romanticism on the Net* 26 (May 2002), <www.erudit.org/revue/ron/2002/v/n26/005700ar.html>, accessed October 5, 2004.

Peterson, Carla L. *Doers of the Word: African American Speakers and Writers in the North (1830–1880)*. New Brunswick, N.J.: Rutgers University Press, 1998.

Pettinger, Alasdair. "Enduring Fortresses." Review of Paul Gilroy, *The Black Atlantic: Modernity and Double Consciousness. Research in African Literatures* 29,4 (1998): 142–47.

Pharr, Robert Reid. *Conjugal Union: The Body, the House and the Black American*. New York: Oxford University Press, 1999.

Phillips, Wendell. "Preface" to Frederick Douglass, *Narrative of the Life of Frederick Douglass, an American Slave*. 1845. New York: Dover, 1995.

Pitre, Merline. "Frederick Douglass and American Diplomacy in the Caribbean." *Journal of Black Studies* 13, 4 (June 1983): 457–75.

Plácido. *Poesias completas de Plácido* (Gabriel de la Concepción Valdés). Paris: Libreria Española de Mme C. Denne Schmitz e Hijo, 1862.

———. *Los poemas mas representativos de Plácido*. Ed. Frederick S. Stimson and Humberto E. Robles. Critical edition. Chapel Hill, N.C.: Estudios de Hispanofila, 1976.

———. *Poesías selectas de Plácido*. Havana: Moderna Poesia/Libreria Cervantes, 1930.

Pratt, Mary Louise. *Imperial Eyes: Travel Writing and Transculturation*. New York: Routledge, 1992.

Prescott, Laurence E.. *Without Hatred or Fears: Jorge Artel and the Struggle for Black Literary Expression in Colombia*. Detroit: Wayne State University Press, 2000.

El primer censo de población de Cuba colonial. Lic. Oscar Ramos Piñol, investigator, Appendix, "Censo del Año de 1774." Havana: Editorial Estadística, 1990.

Price, Richard. *Maroon Societies: Rebel Slave Communities in the Americas*. 1973. Baltimore: Johns Hopkins University Press, 1979.

Prince, Mary. *The History of Mary Prince, A West Indian Slave, Related by Herself*, 1831. rev. ed. Ann Arbor: University of Michigan Press, 1997.

———. "The History of Mary Prince, West Indian Slave." In *Six Women's Slave Narratives*, intro. William L. Andrews. New York: Oxford University Press, 1988.

Prince, Nancy. *A Narrative of the Life and Travels of Mrs. Nancy Prince*. Boston: the author, 1853.

———. *The West Indies, Being a Description of the Islands*. Boston: Dow and Jackson Printers, 1841.

Queen Latifah. "U.N.I.T.Y." *Black Reign*. Motown/Pgd, 1993.

Rahming, Melvin B. *The Evolution of the West Indian's Image in the Afro-American Novel*. Millwood, N.Y.: Associated Faculty Press, 1986.

Robbins, Bruce. *Feeling Global: Internationalism in Distress*. New York: New York University Press, 1999.

Robinson, Amy. "Authority and the Public Display of Identity: Wonderful Adventures of Mrs. Seacole in Many Lands." *Feminist Studies* 20, 3 (Fall 1994): 537–57.

Romeu, Raquel. *La mujer y el esclavo en la Cuba de 1840*. Montevideo: Asociacion de Literatura Femenina Hispánica, 1987.

Rosell, Sara V. "Cecilia Valdés de Villaverde à Arenas: la recreación del mito de la mulata." *Afro-Hispanic Review* 18, 2 (Fall 1999): 15–21.

———. ""Discurso de(r)mografica: la novela antiesclavista en Cuba y Brasil, siglo XIX." Ph.D. dissertation, University of Iowa, 1995.

Rosenberg, John R. *The Black Butterfly: Concepts of Spanish Romanticism.* Romance Monographs 53. University, Miss.: Romance Monographs, 1998.

Saglia, Diego. "British Romantic Translations of the 'Romance de Alhama' and 'Moro Alcaide,' 1775–1818." *Bulletin of Hispanic Studies* 76, 1 (January 1999): 35–55.

Said, Edward W. *Orientalism.* New York: Vintage, 1979.

Saíz de la Mora, Jesús. *Domingo del Monte: su influencia en la cultura y literatura cubanas.* Havana: Impr. y Libr. la Propagandista, 1930.

Saldivar, José David. *The Dialectics of Our America.* Durham, N.C.: Duke University Press, 1991.

Sale, Maggie Montesinos. *The Slumbering Volcano: American Slave Ship Revolts and the Production of Rebellious Masculinity.* Durham, N.C.: Duke University Press, 1997.

———. "To Make the Past Useful: Frederick Douglass' Politics of Solidarity." *Arizona Quarterly* 51, 3 (Autumn 1995): 25–60.

Sánchez, Rosaura. *Telling Identities: The California Testimonios.* Minneapolis: University of Minnesota Press, 1995.

Sankofa. Dir. Haile Gerima. Perf. Kofi Ghanaba and Oyafunmike Ogunlano. Mypheduh Films, 1995.

Sarmiento, Domingo Faustino. *Facundo: edición crítica y documentada.* 1845. La Plata: Universidad Nacional de La Plata, 1938.

Schlereth, Thomas. *The Cosmopolitan Ideal in Enlightenment Thought: Its Form and Function in the Ideas of Franklin, Hume, and Voltaire, 1694–1790.* Notre Dame, Ind.: University of Notre Dame Press, 1976.

Schulman, Iván A. Introduction. In Juan Francisco Manzano, *Autobiography of a Slave/ Autobiografía de un esclavo.* Bilingual edition. Modernized Spanish by Schulman, trans. Evelyn Picon Garfield, 5–38. Detroit: Wayne State University Press, 1996.

———. "The Portrait of the Slave: Ideology and Aesthetics in the Cuban Antislavery Novel." In *Comparative Perspectives on Slavery in New World Plantation Societies,* ed. Vera Rubin and Arthur Tuden, 356–67. New York: New York Academy of Sciences, 1977.

———. "Reflections on Cuba and the Antislavery Literature." *SECOLAS Annals* 7 (March 1976): 59–67.

Scott, Julius S. "The Common Wind: Currents of Afro-American Communication in the Era of the Haitian Revolution." Ph.D. dissertation, Duke University, 1986.

Scott, Rebecca. *Slave Emancipation in Cuba: The Transition to Free Labor, 1860–1899.* Princeton, N.J.: Princeton University Press, 1985.

Seacole, Mary. *Wonderful Adventures of Mrs. Seacole in Many Lands.* 1857. New York: Oxford University Press, 1988.

Séjour, Victor. "The Mulatto." 1837. In *Norton Anthology of African American Literature,* ed. Henry Louis Gates, Jr. and Nellie Y. McKay, 287–99. New York: W.W. Norton, 1997.

Sheehy, John. "The Mirror and the Veil: The Passing Novel and the Quest for American Racial Identity." *African American Review* 33, 3 (Fall 1999): 401–15.

Sklodowska, Elzbieta. "Testimonio mediatizado: ventriloquía o heteroglosía? (Barnet/Montejo; Burgos/Menchú)." *Revista de Crítica Literaria Latinoamericana* 19, 38 (1993): 81–90.

Smith, Faith. *Creole Recitations: John Jacob Thomas and Colonial Formation in the Late Nineteenth-Century Caribbean.* Charlottesville: University of Virginia Press, 2002.

Smith, James McCune. Introduction to Frederick Douglass, *My Bondage and My Freedom*, ed. Phillip S. Foner, xxv-vi. New York: Dover, 1969.

Sommer, Doris. *Foundational Fictions: The National Romances of Latin America.* Berkeley: University of California Press, 1991.

Speer, Joseph. *Chart of the West Indies.* 1796. Library of Congress American Memory Map Collection. <http://memory.loc.gov/ammem/gmdquery.html>

Spillers, Hortense J. "Who Cuts the Border? Some Readings on 'America.'" In *Comparative American Identities: Race, Sex, and Nationality in the Modern Text,* ed. Hortense Spillers, 1–25. New York: Routledge, 1991.

Stedman, John Gabriel. *Narrative of a Five Years Expedition Against the Revolted Negroes of Surinam.* 1790. Ed. Richard Price and Sally Price. Baltimore: Johns Hopkins University Press, 1988.

Sterling, Dorothy. *The Making of an Afro-American: Martin Robison Delany, 1812–1885.* New York: DaCapo Press, 1971.

Stewart, Maria. "Religion and the Pure Principles of Morality the Sure Foundation on Which We Must Build." In *Early Negro Writing*, ed. Dorothy Porter. Baltimore: Black Classic Press, 1994.

Stimson, Frederick S. *Cuba's Romantic Poet: The Story of Plácido.* Chapel Hill: University of North Carolina Press, 1964.

Stowe, Harriet Beecher. *Dred.* Boston: Phillips, Sampson, and Co., 1856.

———. *Uncle Tom's Cabin.* 1878. New York: Chelsea House, 1996.

Stuckey, Sterling. *The Ideological Origins of Black Nationalism.* Boston: Beacon Press, 1972.

———. "Iron Tenacity: Frederick Douglass' Seizure of the Dialectic." In *Frederick Douglass: New Literary and Historical Essays*, ed. Eric Sundquist. Cambridge: Cambridge University Press, 1990. 23–46.

Sundquist, Eric. Introduction to Frederick Douglass, *Frederick Douglass: New Literary and Historical Essays*, ed. Eric Sundquist. Cambridge: Cambridge University Press, 1990. 1–22.

———. *To Wake the Nations: Race in the Making of American Literature.* Cambridge, Mass.: Belknap Press of Harvard University Press, 1993.

Tamarkin, Elisa. ""Black Anglophilia; or the Sociability of Antislavery." *American Literary History* 14, 3 (2002): 444–78.

Terborg-Penn, Roslyn and Andrea Benton Rushing, eds. *Women in Africa and the African Diaspora.* Washington, D.C.: Howard University Press, 1996.

Thomas, Helen. *Romanticism and Slave Narratives: Transatlantic Testimonies.* Cambridge: Cambridge University Press, 2000.

Thornton, John. *Africa and Africans in the Making of the Atlantic World, 1400–1680.* Cambridge: Cambridge University Press, 1998.

Toomer, Jean. *Cane*. 1923. New York: Penguin, 1999.

Trouillot, Michel Rolph. *Silencing the Past: Power and the Production of History*. Boston: Beacon Press, 1995.

Tumin, Melvin Marvin, comp. *Comparative Perspectives on Race Relations*. Boston: Little, Brown, 1969.

Ullman, Victor. *Martin R. Delany: The Beginnings of Black Nationalism*. Boston: Beacon Press, 1971.

Vallejo, Catherina de. "La imagen femenina en la lírica de los poetas del Romanticismo hispanoamericano: inscripción de una hegemonía." *Thesarus: Boletín del Instituto Caro y Cuervo* 48, 2 (May–August 1993): 337–73.

Van Leer, David. "The Anxiety of Ethnicity in Douglass' Narrative." In *Frederick Douglass: New Literary and Historical Essays*, ed. Eric Sundquist, 118–40. Cambridge: Cambridge University Press, 1990.

Vasconcelos, José. *La raza cosmica*. Los Angeles: Centro de Publicaciones, Department of Chicano Studies, California State University, 1979.

Vera-León, Antonio. "Juan Francisco Manzano: el estilo barbaro de la nacion." *Hispamerica* 20,. 60 (December 1991): 3–22.

Villaverde, Cirilo. *Cecilia Valdés, o, la loma del Ángel: novela de costumbres cubanas*. Havana: Editorial Excelsior, 1879.

———. "Prologo del autor." *Cecilia Valdes*. 2 vols. Ed. Ana Maria Muñoz. Havana: Editorial Pueblo y Educación, 1990. 1: 49–54.

Vitier, Cintio, ed. *Lo cubano en la poesía*. Havana: Instituto del Libro, 1970.

———. "Dos poetas cubanos: Plácido y Manzano." *Bohemia* 65, 50 (December 1973): 18–21.

———. *Los poetas romanticos cubanos*. Havana: Consejo Nacional de Cultura, 1962.

Wald, Gayle. *Crossing the Line: Racial Passing in Twentieth-Century U.S. Literature and Culture*. Durham, N.C.: Duke University Press, 2000.

Walker, David. *David Walker's Appeal to the Coloured Citizens of the World, in Four Articles*. 1829. Ed. Peter P. Hinks. University Park: Pennsylvania State University Press, 2000.

Wallace, Maurice. "'Are We Men?': Prince Hall, Martin Delany, and the Masculine Ideal in Black Freemasonry, 1775–1865." In *National Imaginaries, American Identities: The Cultural Work of American Iconography*, ed. Larry J. Reynolds and Gordon Hutner, 182–210. Princeton, N.J.: Princeton University Press, 2000.

———. *Constructing the Black Masculine: Identity and Ideality in Black Men's Literature and Culture*. Durham, N.C.: Duke University Press, 2002.

Walters, Ronald W. *Pan-Africanism in the African Diaspora: An Analysis of Modern Afrocentric Political Movements*. Detroit: Wayne State University Press, 1993.

Warren, Kenneth. "Frederick Douglass' *Life and Times*: Progressive Rhetoric and the Problem of Constituency." In *Frederick Douglass: New Literary and Historical Essays*, ed. Eric Sundquist, 253–70. Cambridge: Cambridge University Press, 1990.

Weiss, Richard. *The American Myth of Success: From Horatio Alger to Norman Vincent Peale*. New York: Basic Books, 1969.

Wesley, Charles H., ed. *The Negro in the Americas*. Washington, D.C.: Graduate School, Howard University, 1940.

Weiner, Mark S. *Black Trials: Citizenship from the Beginnings of Slavery to the End of Caste.* New York: Knopf, 2004.

West, Cornel. *Keeping Faith: Philosophy and Race in America.* New York: Routledge, 1993.

Wheeler, Roxann. "'Betrayed by Some of My Own Complexion': Cuguano, Abolition, and the Contemporary Language of Racialism." In *Genius in Bondage: Literature of the Early Black Atlantic,* ed. Vincent Carreta and Philip Gould, 17–38. Lexington: University Press of Kentucky, 2001.

Williams, Claudette M. *Charcoal and Cinnamon: The Politics of Color in Spanish Caribbean Literature.* Gainesville: University Press of Florida, 2000.

Williams, Lorna. *The Representation of Slavery in Cuban Fiction.* Columbia: University of Missouri Press, 1996.

Willis, Susan. "Crushed Geraniums: Juan Francisco Manzano and the Language of Slavery." In *The Slave's Narrative,* ed. Charles T. Davis and Henry Louis Gates, Jr., 199–224. New York: Oxford University Press, 1985.

Wilson, Kathleen. *The Island Race: Englishness, Empire and Gender in the Eighteenth Century.* New York: Routledge, 2003.

Wurdemann, J. G. *Notes on Cuba.* Boston: James Munroe, 1844.

Zackodnick, Teresa. "Beyond the Pale: Unsettling 'Race' and Womanhood in the Novels of Harper, Hopkins, Fauset, and Larsen." Ph.D. dissertation, McMaster University, 1999.

Zafar, Rafia. "Franklinian Douglass." In *Frederick Douglass: New Literary and Historical Essays,* ed. Eric Sundquist, 99–117. Cambridge: Cambridge University Press, 1990.

———. *We Wear the Mask: African Americans Write American Literature, 1760–1870.* New York: Columbia University Press, 1997.

Index

abolitionists: Black, 25, 48, 49–50, 54, 61–62; English, 42–43; and Plácido's social status, 44–45; White, 25, 48–50

An Accurate Map of the West Indies (Bowen), 171–72

Africa: in Delany's *Blake*, 59; Douglass's relationship to, 136–38, 208, 242nn12, 16; Douglass's references to, 134; language of, 135; *Life and Times* visions of, 137; in *Narrative*, 134–35; in White representations of Placido, 46–47

African Americans, 2, 17–18, 116, 209; and African peoples, 115–16; and Atlantic power structure, 206; citizenship, 151–52; and Cuba 50, 56, 69–71, 74, 76–78; Douglass's characterization of, 114, 116, 135; Douglass's relations to, 121–25, 138–39; emancipation, 131; emigration, 6, 115, 237n6; and Haiti, 6–7, 52–53, 63, 139–45, 147–50; in *Life and Times*, 137; and Latinos, 3–4; narratives of slavery, 120; right to claim Americanness, 114, 147; and West Indians, 4, 130–34, 169. *See also* Blacks; People of African descent

African American literature, 15–17, 190; current scholarship on, 15–21; debates about texts to be defined as, 193–94; multiplicity in, 17; nineteenth century, 19, 207; twentieth century, 18–19

African Diaspora: current scholarship on, 15–21; differences within, 18, 36, 59–60, 63–64, 67–69; literacy (cross-cultural) in, 217n34; methodologies for analysis, 8–9, 207–8; model for genealogies, 193–94, 208

Africanness: as self-definition, 92; White Cuban Creole embrace of, 94–95

Africans in Cuba: and Creoles of color, 93; religious organizations, 92–93; and Haitian Revolution, 29, 33; identities, 92–94; and White fear of Africanization, 29–30, 55–56, 77, 92–93

Afro-Argentinean literature, 17

Afro-Caribbean literature, 158

Afro-Colombian literature, 17

Afro-Latin Americans, literature by and about, 17, 253n39

Afro-Uruguayan literature, 17

Americae Nova Tabula (Blaeu), 172

American Colonization Society, 115

Americanness, 2, 131–32; Douglass claiming, 137–38, 145

Andrews, William, 9, 19, 117, 118, 132–33, 145

Anglophone and Hispanophone world in academia, 4

Antigua: plantations, 159; Prince's experiences, 166, 178, 180, 181; slaves, 159, 168

Aponte, José Antonio, 33, 93; uprising of 1812, 32, 33, 93

Appeal to the Colored Citizens of the World (Walker), 7

Appiah, Anthony, 163

Atlantic power structures, 7, 10, 16; African American confrontation with, 8, 206; control of slave movement, 133–34; and cosmopolitan subjectivity, 10

(Douglass), 116–18, 125–26, 129–30, 151; Africa and African American relationships in, 137; Douglass only Black voice in, 145; excerpts, 130, 137, 140; Môle negotiations, 140; racial heritages, 137–38; West Indian emancipation, 131–32; White behavior in, 127–28
Linebaugh, Peter, 9
Logan, Rayford, 139
Luis, William, 89, 102, 188

Maceo, Antonio, 88
Madden, Richard R., 46–47, 95, 110, 188, 249n6
Manifest Destiny, 142, 148; Douglass's ties to, 142, 145
Manley, Michael, 4
Manzano, Juan Francisco, 8, 21, 155–56, 172, 187, 195, 199; abuse and torture, 196–98; autobiographies, 188, 189, 192–93, 195, 198, 249n6; Black representation, 197; *Cantos à Lesbia*, 187; critical analysis, 193–94; and Cuba, 202–3; disidentification, 189, 191–94, 201–2, 208, 253n45; exceptionality, 194–96, 198; *Flores pasajeros*, 187; individual recognition, 200–203; and Ladder Conspiracy, 187–88; mulatto self-representation, 189, 191, 254n50; Plácido's confused with, 51–52, 95; *Poesías líricas*, 187; relationship with *negros*, 191, 192; "To Cuba," 197–98; "white child" treatment, 195, 198–99
Marshall, Paule, 185
Martí, José, 83, 87–90
Martin, Waldo, 135
Martínez Heredia, Fernando, 88
Marx, Karl, 10, 162
McDowell, Deborah, 114
McKay, Claude, 4, 8
mestizaje, 190–91
Mignolo, Walter, 172
Migrancy, Culture, Identity (Chambers), 16
migration, 16; migration/borderlands

theory, 182; migratory subjectivities theory, 182
Miller, Floyd, 67
Mills-Young, Carol, 17
Mintz, Sidney, 15
mixed race individuals/*mulatos/as*: Douglass's view of own mixed ancestry, 237n4; Manzano's classification as, 191, 254n50; Prince's tense relationship with, 165; Plácido's representation of women, 100–102; Séjour's representation of to counter dehumanization, 208–9
Modernism and the Harlem Renaissance (Baker), 16
modernity, 19–20, 217n33, 218n36
Môle St. Nicholas, U.S. military base, 140, 144, 148
Monte, Domingo del, 95
Montejo, Esteban, 92
Morejón, Nancy, 193
morenos (free Blacks), 36, 94, 222n33; and Ladder Conspiracy, 36–38; *pardos* seduction, 36
Morrison, Toni, 16, 216n31
Moses, Wilson Jeremiah, 125, 128, 239n26
Mosquito (Jones), 205
"Le mulâtre" (Séjour), 208–9
Mullen, Edward J., 113, 193
Muñoz, José, 190, 250n16
My Bondage and My Freedom (Douglass), 116–19, 125–28, 151; Africa represented in, 135; excerpts, 133, 135, 141–42; religion in, 136–37; silence theory in, 133–34
The Myth of the Negro Past (Herskovits), 15

The Narrative Life of Frederick Douglass, an American Slave (Douglass), 20, 116–18, 126–27, 151, 204, 238n20; Africa in, 134–35; binaristic blackness in, 135; definition of Black community in, 122–23; goal of, 130; individual and community tension in,

Acknowledgments

The debt of gratitude I owe to numerous individuals far, near, and in between for providing me with myriad forms of sustenance along the journey represented by *Black Cosmopolitanism* is immeasurable. Although I cannot hope to recall and list everyone by name, I humbly ask that all of you will accept what follows as a token of my appreciation.

Above all, I am eternally grateful to my amazing mother, Margaret, who is my best friend, my confidant, and my valiant soul-guard, ready at a moment's notice to fend off any who would damage my spirit. My heartfelt appreciation to my grandmother, Ethelyn, who both showed me that compassion must be the core of any life worth living, and introduced me the beauty that is literature; and to my grandfather who inspired my own interest in learning about other cultures with his fascinating stories about his encounters with the people, languages, and cultures of Portugal, India, and Cuba, among others.

Eternal thanks to my wonderful, loving, and always supportive friends from Duke—the University Apartments women, Riché, Candice, Evie, Mendi; the University Apartments man, Keith, my brother in our own special version of Nigerianness; Chris Chia and Gary Ashwill, Barbara Shummanfang, Arnetta Girardeau, Donna Daniels, and Lesley Feracho, my closest sister in the struggle, for listening, reading, remaining silent, reminding me to mind my soul, making me laugh, comforting me, or distracting me as necessary. My profound thanks to Karla F. C. Holloway, Cathy N. Davidson, David Barry Gaspar, Walter Mignolo, and Nahum Chandler who continue to serve as founts of support and knowledge.

For the most inspiring and invigorating intellectual dialogues I have ever had, I thank all my colleagues and friends and the University of Michigan. I am especially grateful to Simon Gikandi, Marlon Ross, Mamadou Diouf, and Sandra Gunning for their unbelievable commitment to my journey. I could always count on them to be ready, willing, and able to read or listen and provide detailed constructive feedback. This project also benefited greatly from the invaluable insights of colleagues outside the field of African Diasporan literature, particularly from Adela Pinch, Valerie Traub,

Sara Blair, Jonathan Freedman, Tobin Siebers, and the members of the First Draft Group. The conscious and unconscious mentoring I received from Lincoln Faller, former Chair of the Department of English, and James S. Jackson, Director of the Center for Afroamerican and African Studies, along with their willingness to do all within their power to ensure my success, and their always cheerful greetings, meant and mean more to me than either of them could imagine. Special thanks to the sister-friends whom I met at Michigan and who fed me intellectually and emotionally as I seek and sought to do the same for them. This project absolutely could not have been completed without the dedication, attentiveness to detail, eagerness, and alacrity of the students who assisted me with my research at various points in the writing process—many many thanks Jenny Hobson, Sara Stupak, Shawan Wade, Tamara Walker, Constance Russell, and Ayesha Hardison. I extend a special thank you to Lucia Suarez, my fellow traveler on the path from Duke to Michigan, from graduate student to professor, and beyond.

I am also indebted to a number of other scholars who played crucial roles in advancing this project. Foremost among them are Farah Jasmine Griffin, who heard, saw, and acted almost instantaneously and William Andrews, whose openness, positive feedback, and keen insights came at the perfect time, as did the warmth and encouragement of Nellie McKay. Thanks too to Jerome Branche and Michael Bucknor for conversations that inspired and invigorated me. Audiences at a range of conferences and symposia, among them the Black South conference at the University of Alabama organized by Karla Frye in 1997, the Caribbean Literary Group conference at the University of Miami coordinated by Sandra Pouchet Paquet in 2000, and the Afro-Latin American Research Association conference in Panama City in 2002, also played a significant role in helping me better grasp the multiple implications and dimensions of my work. Also vital to this refined thinking were my editor at the University of Pennsylvania Press, Jerome Singerman, who struck a wonderful balance between keeping me informed and listening to me, the Rethinking the Americas series editors, and the two anonymous readers, whose comments revealed a much appreciated engagement with and investment in the success of this book. I also extend warm thank yous to the staff at the University of Pennsylvania Press, and Theodore Mann in particular, for their evident dedication to ensuring that both the timing and content of the final product were optimal.

Special thanks to the women of the Cuban National Archive, the Institute of Literature and Linguistics, the Academy of History, and Casa de las Americas, whose guidance, encyclopedic knowledge of their collections, and patience made my research trips to Cuba even more productive than I could have ever imagined or wished.

This book also owes its existence to the clearly measurable contributions by a number of fellowship granting institutions and entities including the Ford Foundation and the Jacob Javits Foundation. Without the time and financial means to undertake the multilocational, multinational research required for this project, it would have remained in the realm of thoughts and wishes. In particular, the published text is the fruit of a Career Enhancement Fellowship from the Woodrow Wilson National Fellowship Foundation, along with a number of grants from entities at the University of Michigan, specifically the Office of the Vice-President of Research, the Office of the Dean of the Horace Rackham Graduate School, the Office of the Senior Vice Provost for Academic Affairs, the College of Literature, Sciences, and the Arts, the Center for Afroamerican and African Studies, and the Department of English.

In conclusion, I wish to mirror my dedication of this book to my grandfather by remembering a (much younger) person who came to serve a parallel role in this phase of my life—my late colleague Lemuel Johnson. Thanks Lemuel for "getting" me, for understanding why Miss Lou, Panama, Queen E II, my third form memories, Nicolas Guillén, and Langston Hughes are all so important to me, and for being the touchstone that reiterated for me that working across national and linguistic frames and fields of knowledge is not a strange and curious oddity or an aberration, but rather a natural consequence of the contexts and ongoing dialogues through which many of us have come into being. This book is, I hope, at least close to being all that you thought it would and should be. I trust that it will prove you right.

An earlier version of portions of Chapter 3 appeared as "Commentary," *Cuban Studies* 33 (2002): 129–36. Copyright © 2002 University of Pittsburgh Press; reprinted by permission.

CPSIA information can be obtained at www.ICGtesting.com
Printed in the USA
BVOW01s2043300414

351987BV00001B/23/P